The Medieval City
under Siege

The Medieval City
under Siege

EDITED BY

Ivy A. Corfis and **Michael Wolfe**

THE BOYDELL PRESS

First published 1995
The Boydell Press, Woodbridge
Reprinted in paperback 1999

ISBN 0 85115 561 8 hardback
ISBN 0 85115 756 4 paperback

The Boydell Press is an imprint of Boydell & Brewer Ltd
PO Box 9, Woodbridge, Suffolk IP12 3DF, UK
and of Boydell & Brewer Inc.
PO Box 41026, Rochester, NY 14604–4126, USA
website: http://www.boydell.co.uk

A catalogue record for this title is available from
the British Library

Library of Congress Catalog Card Number: 94–19121

This publication is printed on acid-free paper

Printed in Great Britain by
St Edmundsbury Press Ltd, Bury St Edmunds, Suffolk

Contents

Introduction

Siege Warfare and Cities

Siege Technologies and Urban Fortifications

Siege as Metaphor and Literary Event

Siege Warfare in Transition

Illustrations

The Changing Face of Siege Warfare *Bert S. Hall*

Acknowledgments

The present volume's focus was inspired by the conference "The Medieval City under Siege," held at the University Park Campus of the Pennsylvania State University, 2–4 April 1992, sponsored by the Center for Medieval Studies at Penn State. Some of the articles are amplified, recrafted versions of papers originally read at the 1992 symposium. Others were solicited especially for this publication to round out and diversify the examination of the medieval siege in its various manifestations. We would like to thank the Organizing Committee of the conference, the Penn State Center for Medieval Studies, the College of the Liberal Arts, the Institute for the Arts and Humanistic Studies, the Graduate School, and the Pennsylvania Humanities Council for making "The Medieval City under Siege" possible.

We would also like to thank the following for permission to reproduce illustrations: Special Collections Library, University of Michigan, Ann Arbor; Bodleian Library, Oxford; Bibliothèque Nationale, Paris; Deutsches Archaeologisches Institut – Rom, Rome; and Museé de la Civilisation Gallo-Romaine, Lyon.

Ivy A. Corfis and Michael Wolfe

Introduction

New Perspectives on Medieval Siege Warfare: An Introduction

Michael Wolfe
The Pennsylvania State University, Altoona

The rise of towns in medieval Europe brought profound changes to the nature and practice of war as it had evolved since the demise of the Roman Empire in the West. As economic and population centers, medieval towns held immediate strategic significance in a society where power had long largely resided in the countryside. After the eleventh century, however, from Iberia to eastern Europe, from the Baltic to the Mediterranean, towns began to reassert the political and cultural importance they had previously held in classical antiquity.[1] Once reestablished, this dominance of town over countryside has since remained unbroken in the West. The common interests that bound medieval towns together, though never enough to prevent internal struggles even in the best of times, required elaborate measures of defense against any outside enemies who might try to take them. Walls had to be erected, militias organized, food supplies secured, and armaments industries created to ensure a town's autonomy. The image of the besieged town also took literary and artistic expression, providing a backdrop against which prevailing cultural values and archetypes could be paraded or criticized.[2] As a result, the rising incidence of siege warfare generated new and

---

[1] Among recent general studies on the rise of medieval cities, all with excellent bibliographies, consult Josef W. Konvitz, *The Urban Millennium: The City Building Process from the Early Middle Ages to the Present* (Cardondale & Edwardville: Southern Illinois University Press, 1985); James E. Vance, *The Continuing City: Urban Morphology in Western Civilization* (Baltimore: Johns Hopkins University Press, 1990); and *The Built Form of Western Cities: Essays for M. R. G. Conzen on the Occasion of His Eightieth Birthday*, ed. T. R. Slater (Leicester: Leicester University Press, 1990). An overview of urban military design can be found in Horst de la Croix, *Military Considerations in City Planning: Fortifications* (New York: George Braziller, 1972), pp. 32–38. On ancient cities, see J. B. Ward-Perkins, *Cities of Greece and Italy: Planning in Classical Antiquity* (New York: George Braziller, 1974), and John E. Stambaugh, *The Ancient Roman City* (Baltimore: Johns Hopkins University Press, 1988), pp. 189–91, 246–58, 280–85.

[2] Pierre Lavedan, *Représentation des villes dans l'art du Moyen Âge* (Paris: Vanoest, 1954).

increasingly complex demands on towns and society at large that in time remade the face of medieval Europe.

The essays in this volume examine various features of this new urbanism and the novel forms of warfare it spawned. Part One considers the crucial role played by towns during the long wars between Christians and Muslims in Iberia, rival dynastic claimants in the Holy Roman Empire, and the French and English crowns during the Hundred Years War. Similar patterns of state-building and siege warfare can be discerned despite these markedly different settings. During the Reconquest, as James Powers demonstrates in his piece, the shifting boundary between Christendom and Islam was largely defined by the long, complicated struggle to hold towns. The creeping Christian control of the peninsula, so often colored by images of the Church militant and crusading knight, actually owed its success to the tough, determined settlers who peopled the numerous towns along the Luso-Hispanic frontier.[3] By controlling regional communication and transport networks, these urban strongholds presented formidable logistical obstacles that eventually frustrated the efforts of the Almohad caliphate to win these lands back to Allah. Powers examines how the military needs of these towns, as revealed in early municipal statutes or *fueros*, created "a continual wartime mode of living."[4] The construction and maintenance of walls, militia duty, and a host of related security measures underlay the independence of these frontier towns – an independence prudently ratified by royal charters. By making these frontier towns able to withstand the threat of Muslim siege, the townspeople of medieval Iberia not only ensured the success of the Christian Reconquest, but also established the constitutional framework of provincial liberty so unique to early modern Spain.[5]

This pattern of state formation shaped by fortified towns was not confined to Europe's periphery, as Michael Toch explains in his essay on medieval German towns and siege warfare. He asks how historians should interpret the simple fact that so many sieges were mounted despite the feeble odds of success against even the most modest urban stronghold. Even when a rare victory over a fortified town did occur, as in Cologne in 1206, its defenses were not dismantled but reinforced, thus rendering it even more difficult to retake in the future. Other essays show much the same case in late medieval France and the Crusader

---

[3]   This trend has changed not only with the work by Powers, but also other recent publications, such as Teófilo Ruiz, *The City and the Realm: Burgos and Castile, 1080–1492* (Aldershot: Variorum, 1992), and Elena Lourie, *Crusade and Colonisation: Muslims, Christians and Jews in Medieval Aragon* (Aldershot: Variorum, 1990). The topic of frontiers is closely examined in Maria Teresa Ferrer i Mallol, *Organitzacio i defensa d'un territori fronterer, la governacio d'oriola en el segle XIV* (Barcelona: Consell Superior d'Investigaciones Cientifiques Institucio Mila i Fontanals, 1990), and more generally in *Medieval Frontier Societies*, eds. R. Bartlett and A. MacKay (Oxford: Clarendon Press, 1989).

[4]   Powers, "Life on the Cutting Edge," pp. 21–44. A recent work on these wars is Bernard F. Reilly, *The Contest of Christian and Muslim Spain, 1031–1157* (Cambridge MA: Blackwell, 1992).

[5]   Helen Nader, *Liberty in Absolutist Spain: The Hapsburg Sale of Towns 1516–1750* (Baltimore: Johns Hopkins University Press, 1990).

Kingdom of Jerusalem. Toch argues that a siege served other purposes than those military. The threat of such an attack, for example, could influence the outcome of diplomatic maneuverings. The considerable advantage of defense over attack in medieval siege warfare also added to the import of open field engagements, where mounted knights could reaffirm their traditional martial prowess.[6] In this way, siege warfare spurred the ongoing evolution of chivalry, *faute de mieux* – a theme that recurs in Part Three. The absence of effective attack technologies in the medieval West encouraged the use of ruses and deception to exploit the often festering animosities found in most towns. Thus, centuries before Machiavelli formulated a new ethic of political expediency, such practices – and the moral questions they raised – had long formed an essential part of medieval siege warfare.[7] Meeting the local needs of self-defense required enormous expenditures of funds and labor by medieval German towns, and fueled the expansion of municipal prerogatives and jurisdiction. According to Toch, only in the fourteenth century were territorial lords able to marshal the resources necessary to begin paring down the assertive independence of German towns, though many urban communities tenaciously maintained their freedom on through the period of the Reformation. In fact, some historians have argued that the eclipse of German municipal military and political autonomy only came during the Thirty Years War; others assert it occurred more recently as a result of the Industrial Revolution.[8]

My essay on the *bonnes villes* of France during the Hundred Years War confirms in many regards the findings of Powers and Toch. Again, fractious politics among nobles and town dwellers along with the French crown's patent inability to protect its domains after the disaster at Crécy (1346) made it imperative for towns to look after their own interests. Far from discouraging such municipal independence, the monarchy along with local lords nurtured its development by extending to towns additional privileges and powers of taxation. Most of the funds then raised went directly into local defenses, particularly fortifications. Interestingly, much the same partnership between lordship and town had already arisen in Normandy and Guyenne, thus helping to make

---

[6] On the German nobility, see Benjamin Arnold's *Princes and Territories in Medieval Germany* (Cambridge: Cambridge University Press, 1991), and *Count and Bishop in Medieval Germany: A Study of Regional Power, 110–1350* (Philadelphia: University of Pennsylvania Press, 1991).

[7] James T. Johnson, *Ideology, Reason, and the Limitation of War: Religious and Secular Concept, 1200–1740* (Princeton: Princeton University Press, 1975); Frederick H. Russell, *The Just War in the Middle Ages* (Cambridge: Cambridge University Press, 1975).

[8] See Thomas A. Brady, *Turning Swiss: Cities and Empire, 1450–1550* (Cambridge: Cambridge University Press, 1985); C. R. Friedrichs, *Urban Society in an Age of War: Nördlingen 1580–1720* (Princeton: Princeton University Press, 1979); Heinz Schilling, *Religion, Political Culture, and the Emergence of Early Modern Society: Essays in German and Dutch History* (Leiden: E. J. Brill, 1992); and the seminal study by Mack Walker, *German Home Towns: Community, State, and General Estate, 1648–1871* (Ithaca: Cornell University Press, 1971).

possible England's near realization of its continental aspirations.[9] The advent of
gunpowder artillery, while speeding up France's recovery of lost lands under
Charles VII, did not significantly alter the improved position of the *bonnes
villes*. Indeed, fortified towns often led the way in the development of the new
armament industries associated with gunpowder weaponry, as well as elaborated
new styles of fortification to blunt a cannon's force. These trends, along with the
established habit of townspeople to invest heavily in their own defense, made the
towns indispensable partners – or potent adversaries – of the French monarchy
when it embarked on its own course of expansionism in the next century.[10]

In Part Two, the focus shifts away from medieval state formation to the actual
technologies and tactics of contemporary siege warfare. Drawing on his own
field studies in Palestine, Denys Pringle offers a sweeping survey of urban
fortifications in the Crusader Kingdom of Jerusalem. Using archeological and
documentary evidence, he establishes a typology of municipal defenses based
on the presence or absence of such common features as walls, towers, and
castles.[11] A key difference with European towns at the time was the general lack
of mature municipal institutions in Crusader urban centers; another was that the
prior fortified emplacements of the Muslims largely predetermined how
Crusader rulers approached the defense of newly won towns. An almost imper-
ceptible blending occurred between Islamic fortification techniques and styles
and those brought by European Christians to towns in the eastern
Mediterranean.[12] As will be seen, a similar gradual evolution characterized
urban fortifications in the West during the 150 years that followed the appearance of gunpowder weaponry. Through meticulous investigation, Pringle shows
the complex manner in which these towns developed as a result of the ongoing
cycle of building, demolition, and then rebuilding as towns alternately changed
hands between Christians and Muslims. Further field studies utilizing such
interdisciplinary methods promise to deepen our understanding of the evolving
urban fabric created by fortifications in the Crusader Middle East and Europe.[13]

[9] *La 'France Anglaise' au Moyen Âge* (Paris: Éditions du CTHS, 1988) examines the
influence of English forms on French territories through this period.
[10] Didier Dubant, "Fortifications urbaines en France au XIVe et XVIe siècle. État de la
question," *Sites* 45 (1991), 4–17.
[11] Additional information on some of these sites can be found in T. E. Lawrence, *Crusader
Castles*, ed. Denys Pringle (Oxford: Clarendon Press, 1988), and Pringle's own *The Churches of
the Crusader Kingdom of Jerusalem, a Corpus* (Cambridge: Cambridge University Press, 1993).
This volume covers A-K, excluding Acre and Jerusalem.
[12] On Islamic cities, see *Muslim Cities in the Later Middle Ages*, ed. Ira M. Lapidus (Cambridge: Cambridge University Press, 1984), and Nezar Al Sayyad, *Cities and Caliphs: On the
Genesis of Arab Muslim Urbanism* (New York: Greenwood Press, 1991). After regaining some
port cities, Muslim rulers often purposely dismantled existing fortifications and naval facilities
to interdict future Christian maritime assaults. John Pryor, *Geography, Technology, and War:
Studies in the Maritime History of the Mediterranean, 649–1571* (Cambridge: Cambridge
University Press, 1988), pp. 124–34.
[13] *European Towns: Their Archaeology and Early History*, ed. M. W. Bayley (London & New
York: Academic Press, 1977).

A perennial question in military history is the extent to which theories of war correspond to its practice. The relationship is often a mixed one, as Eric McGeer argues in his essay on siege warfare in the Byzantine Empire during the tenth and eleventh centuries. Unlike the West, which had seen its cities decline after the fifth century, urban life continued to flourish in the Byzantine East, thus keeping alive Greco-Roman traditions of how to attack and defend towns.[14] These classical sources informed Byzantine siege techniques as revealed by contemporary poliorcetic treatises; classical siege technologies also survived judging from these manuals. Such apparent continuities must not be taken at face value, however, according to McGeer. Actual accounts of Byzantine sieges accorded much less place to the intricate war machines used in antiquity, in part because defense technologies had become much more formidable. Even so, this relative absence of advanced technology did not render Byzantine methods of siege warfare any less sophisticated. In theory as well as practice, the emphasis shifted instead to logistics and politics in the struggle to win or hold fortified towns. Control over human variables rather than technological superiority largely determined the success or failure of a siege operation – a finding that has important bearing for both medieval and later Renaissance Europe.[15]

A closer look at the relationship between classical and early medieval military technology is provided in Paul Chevedden's piece on the evolving nature of siege engines, particularly the two-armed torsion catapult. A close reading of Greco-Roman and then later Byzantine sources helps puzzle out apparent textual ambiguities that, when taken together, strongly argue in favor of significant, albeit gradual change in this area of military technology. Archaic descriptions of torsion-powered engines sometimes found their way into medieval manuscripts, although evidence of their actual use in early medieval siege warfare is scanty at best. Indeed, it appears that between the fourth and sixth centuries the use of the older, more technologically complicated two-armed torsion catapult gave way to the cruder, but more easily constructed tension catapult so typical of the Middle Ages. This changeover did not necessarily mean that technological expertise declined across the board.[16] It could reflect, for example, changing tactical priorities, since what the newer catapult lost in accuracy it more than made up

---

[14] These traditions continued to be relevant even later. See Mark Bartusis, *The Late Byzantine Army, Arms and Society, 1204–1453* (Philadelphia: University of Pennsylvania Press, 1992).

[15] There is no focused study of medieval military logistics, though several exist for the early modern period. See the recent study *Feeding Mars: Essays on the History of Logistics*, ed. John Lynn (Boulder CO: Westview Press, 1993); Bernard Kroener, *Les routes et les étapes: die Versorgung der französischen Armeen in Nordostfrankreich (1635–1661): ein Beitrag zur Verwaltungsgeschichte des Ancien Regime* (Munster: Aschendorff, 1980); and the generalized overview by Martin Van Creveld, *Supplying War: Logistics from Wallenstein to Patton* (Cambridge: Cambridge University Press, 1977).

[16] The complex connections between ancient and medieval scientific traditions is the focus of David Lindberg's The *Beginnings of Western Science: The European Scientific Tradition in Philosophical, Religious, and Institutional Context, 600 B.C. to A.D. 1450* (Chicago: University of Chicago Press, 1992). See also J. G. Landels, *Engineering in the Roman World* (Berkeley: University of California Press, 1978).

for in greater rapidity of fire. The improved trigger mechanism of the crossbow, developed well after the sixth century, showed that early medieval society's capacity for progressive technological innovation remained formidable indeed. Evolutionary adaptation of pre-existing military technologies and techniques, out of which new types could develop, seems to have been the rule rather than the exception in the transition from classical antiquity to the early Middle Ages. As will be seen in Part Four, much the same can be said about the consequences brought by the introduction of gunpowder weaponry in Europe after the fourteenth century.

The essays in Part Three move away from a historical consideration of siege warfare and instead look at the besieged city as a literary setting or device. As such, the medieval siege served as a vehicle by which to explore the various cultural values at play in debates about war, love, and social identity.[17] Michael Harney opens with a close analysis of images of the city and sieges in medieval Spanish romances, such as *El Cid* and the *Cantar de Sancho II*. As it developed after the eleventh century, this new genre significantly reworked the established Homeric *topoi* of the besieged city, epitomized by the fate of Troy in the *Iliad*, to reflect the competing interests of feudal and urban society in medieval Spain. Unlike the heroic warriors so typical of epic literature, men whose self-sufficiency rendered them independent of the socially inferior world of the city, chivalric knights like the Cid found that they could not avoid the allure of urban wealth, since it figured so importantly in aristocratic household formation. Yet such entanglements in the world of merchants, where pecuniary profit and loss mattered so much, constantly threatened to undermine chivalric notions of honor. As Harney sees it, literary renderings of the medieval siege in Spain – and probably elsewhere in Europe – reflected the complex pressures facing the nobility as they strove to adjust to a society increasingly dominated by the city.

The siege not only addressed social concerns, but also those of gender, argues Heather Arden in her essay on the famous *Roman de la rose*. The prevalence of military imagery and terminology in the text, she notes, should come as no surprise since its author, Jean de Meun, had previously translated Vegetius' classic treatise on war, the *Epitoma rei militari*. Other ancient war manuals, particularly Frontinius' treatment, circulated in multiple manuscript copies throughout Europe at the time, too.[18] The allegorical siege of the castle sheltering the delicate rose unfolds on a number of different levels, which together reveal the "military-erotic complex" at work in the poem. At one level, the siege is frankly sexual, with the architecture of the castle representing various parts of a woman's body. Under assault by all manner of stratagems and devices, some overtly phallic, the lover's bid to take the rose's stronghold conjured up images

---

[17] *The Study of Chivalry: Resources and Approaches*, eds. Howell Chickering and Thomas H. Seiler (Kalamazoo: Western Michigan University Press, 1988).

[18] On Vegetius, see the new edition of *Epitoma rei militaris*, ed. Leo F. Stelten (New York: Peter Lang, 1990). For Frontius, consult the bibliographical references in the new edition, entitled *Juli Frontini Strategemata*, ed. Robert I. Ireland (Leipzig: Teubner, 1990).

of siege warfare no doubt familiar to contemporary readers in the nobility. It also reflected the threat of aggression that lurked beneath the surface of amorous dalliances between noble lady and knight.[19] Alongside this aspect of the poem existed an equally erotic allegory of individual moral choice, as seen in the combat between mental states or psychomachia. The lengthy siege of the castle thereafter offered Jean de Meun a golden opportunity to satirize the values of courtly culture so elegantly rendered in the first half of the poem. In this way, the siege and eventual conquest of the rose conveyed an ultimately subversive message about the self-delusions and moral compromises made by male suitors to win the object of their desire. And, as we know, similar sorts of ethical misgivings also found expression in commentaries discussing the injustices often perpetrated during sieges.

A similar sort of subversion of chivalric values occurs in English romances during the late Middle Ages, according to Winthrop Wetherbee. Written during the Hundred Years War, works such as *Sir Gawain and the Green Knight* and Chaucer's *Troilus and Criseyde* and *Knight's Tale* chart the growing irrelevance of chivalric values at a time when rulers relied increasingly on paid mercenaries to fight their battles.[20] Hypocrisy and self-aggrandizement, not highminded noble ideals, often animated the knightly pursuit of both love and war, according to Wetherbee. These romances demonstrated the new limits facing knightly heroes, limits imposed by the restrictive discipline of courtly culture and the leveling effects of the longbow and then gunpowder weaponry. Manly prowess in the open field no longer counted as much: witness the lack of decisive resolution following England's stunning victories at Crécy and Poitiers. Instead, the Hundred Years War became a long struggle of attrition and willful devastation typified by endless sieges and the Black Prince's infamous excursions that spread terror in southern France in the 1350s. When coupled with England's ongoing conflict with the Scots, this constant war making created serious social unrest in the country that eventually brought down the ruling house.[21] As a result, Wetherbee argues, the chivalric code and knightly hero became increasingly archaic, epitomized by Sir Gawain's naive self-deception in using the magical green girdle, not his own bravery, to protect himself. While perhaps inevitable, such compromises affirmed the essential ordinariness of the knight – a theme further explored in Chaucer's two tales. Here the siege – in the first of Troy, and the second of the Amazon realm of "Feminye" – created a sort of

---

[19] Aldo D. Scaglione, *Knights at Court: Courtliness, Chivalry and Courtesy from Ottonian Germany to the Italian Renaissance* (Berkeley: University of California Press, 1991).

[20] Gilbert J. Millar, *Tudor Mercenaries and Auxiliaries 1485–1547* (Charlottesville: University of Virginia Press, 1980); Michael E. Mallett, *Mercenaries and Their Masters: Warfare in Renaissance Italy* (Totowa: Rowman and Littlefield, 1974). On the development of scutage, cash payments by vassals in lieu of service – a key first step toward financing a professional standing army, see Thomas K. Keefe, *Feudal Assessments and the Political Community under Henry II and his Sons* (Berkeley: University of California Press, 1983).

[21] M. G. A. Vale, *War and Chivalry: Warfare and Aristocratic Culture in England, France, and Burgundy at the End of the Middle Ages* (Athens: University of Georgia Press, 1981).

theater in which the faltering values of chivalric heroism finally become played out. Troilus' blindness to the duplicity of those around him and Theseus' rage against the Amazons expose the vulnerability of the knight and his doomed attempts to transcend his own violent nature. In response to this failure of chivalry, contemporaries labored to create a new set of rules suitable for the new forms of warfare brought by professional soldiers, gunpowder weaponry, and protracted sieges. In supplanting this earlier code, the new laws of war tended to promote the interests of monarchy over those of the nobility, thereby establishing a trend of development of which the Valois in France and Tudors in England eventually took full advantage.[22]

Renaissance and early modern historians have long argued that the nature of war underwent changes during the sixteenth century so fundamental as to constitute a "Military Revolution."[23] The essays in Part Four dispute this claim. It should already be obvious that medieval siege warfare was far from static and predictable, having for centuries fostered tactical and technological innovations that remained relevant down to Vauban's day.[24] Certainly a large part of the claim put forward for a "Military Revolution" rests on the momentous impact ascribed to gunpowder weaponry, which according to Kelly DeVries first appeared in the West in the early fourteenth century. Its effective use in siege operations did not have to wait for the sixteenth century, however; already in late-fourteenth-century France it could be found in field engagements, like Crécy, and trained against towns. The Burgundians, in particular, demonstrated a remarkable adeptness at developing better methods of founding guns and devising new applications for them, particularly shipboard. Indeed, the specialized skills necessary to cast iron and then bronze cannon grew right out of the medieval artisanal techniques long used to cast church bells.[25] Subsidiary industries, such as saltpeter and gunpowder works, simulanteously sprang up in numerous sites as artillery became integrated into late medieval armies.[26]

Defensive fortifications, so long enjoying the advantage, soon met the peril posed by these new heavy weapons by making incremental modifications that in time refashioned the nature of late medieval siege warfare. As DeVries shows,

[22] M. H. Keen, *The Laws of War in the Late Middle Ages* (London: Routledge & Kegan Paul, 1965).

[23] Michael Roberts, *Essays in Swedish History* (Minneapolis: University of Minnesota Press, 1967), and Geoffrey Parker, *The Military Revolution: Military Innovation and the Rise of the West, 1500–1800* (Cambridge: Cambridge University Press, 1988).

[24] Christopher Duffy, *Siege Warfare: The Fortress in the Early Modern World 1494–1660* (London: Routledge & Kegan Paul, 1979), and *The Fortress in the Age of Vauban and Frederick the Great 1660–1789* (London: Routledge & Kegan Paul, 1985), offer fine introductions to the topic.

[25] *Hommes et travail du métal dans les villes médiévales* (Paris: Picard, 1988).

[26] James R. Partington, *A History of Greek Fire and Gunpowder* (Cambridge: W. Heffer, 1960). A case study on late medieval Germany is Hartwig Neumann, *Das Zeughaus, die Entwicklung eines Bautyps von der spätmittlealterlichen Rustkammer zum Arsenal im deutschsprächigen Bereich vom XV. bis XIX Jahrhundert*, 2 vols. (Koblenz: Bernard & Graefe, 1991–92).

these changes proceeded empirically; a systematic approach to military architecture in the age of gunpowder only began to take shape in the work of Alberti and Martini in the late fifteenth century. Nevertheless, several sites in England and France responded to the new cannonry by building sloping glacis, deeper ditches, and earthen outworks. These alterations foreshadowed many of the defensive techniques associated with the *trace italienne* of the early sixteenth century.[27] Perhaps the most startling adjustment, according to DeVries, was the construction of artillery platforms and gunports to protect towns and castles. Indeed, the defensive potential of cannonry seems to have been realized almost as soon as its offensive capability – a finding not usually emphasized enough, but in line with what we now realize to be the longstanding malleability of medieval military architecture.

In the next essay by Michael Mallett, the focus shifts from the evolving impact of gunpowder weaponry to its actual use in a number of different sieges in fifteenth-century Italy. Well before Charles VIII's celebrated descent into Italy in 1494, he notes, mobile artillery had already been employed in campaigns among the constantly feuding Italian city-states. Yet while openly acclaimed by rulers as essential for making war, it should not therefore be assumed that cannons had the "big bang" so often ascribed to them. Many of the obstacles hindering a successful siege in the Renaissance – the difficulties posed by long range transport, inadequate supplies, and insufficient manpower – remained unchanged from those that had existed in the twelfth century, if not earlier.[28] Even when these were overcome, as at the siege of Volterra by Florence (1472) and the Ottoman attack on Otranto (1480), the ultimate success of the operation lay not in any new offensive superiority provided by gunpowder weapons, but rather in the time-honored stratagems of surprise and deception. Moreover, at the Neapolitan siege of Colle di Val d'Elsa (1479), it was Florence's inability to mount a relief force to aid the town that made it possible for enemy artillery to batter down the town's walls after two months of near constant shelling. Likewise, stout resistance against siege guns did not require radically new fortification design, but rather relied on the morale and organization of the defenders. In both the case of the Turkish defense of Otranto (1481) and Florence's intermittent siege of Pisa (1494–1509), it was the speed by which crumbled fortifications were piled back together, not the style of their construction, that mattered

---

[27] Martha Pollack, *Military Architecture, Cartography and the Representation of the Early Modern European City. A Checklist of Treatises on Fortification in The Newberry Library* (Chicago: The Newberry Library, 1991), pp. xi–xxxvi; Horst de la Croix, "The Literature on Fortification in Renaissance Italy," *Technology and Culture* 6 (1963), 30–50; and J. R. Hale, *Renaissance Fortification: Art or Engineering?* (London: Thames & Hudson, 1977).

[28] An excellent case study is Simon Pepper and Nicholas Adams, *Firearms and Fortification: Military Architecture and Siege Warfare in Sixteenth-Century Siena* (Chicago: University of Chicago Press, 1986), especially pp. xxii–xxiii, which raise doubts about the "crude linkage between . . . the independent city-state of medieval Italy with its imperfect techniques of warfare and . . . the new artillery and the angle bastions of the nascent modern state."

the most in parrying determined attacks. Thus, while large guns could be quite effectively used both in offense and defense in Renaissance Italy, they along with the emerging new bastion-style of fortification design did not drastically alter siege warfare as it had been practiced throughout the Middle Ages. Logistics and *esprit*, not technology, still largely determined which side enjoyed victory or defeat – a point underscored at the time by Machiavelli in his *The Art of War*, yet one for which modern critics have sometimes unfairly chided him.[29]

These continuities between medieval siege warfare and its practice during the Renaissance are further investigated in the volume's last essay by Bert Hall. In it, Hall reevaluates the various arguments advanced in support of a "Military Revolution." Among the criteria for such a change identified by Geoffrey Parker, a prime proponent of this thesis, was the alleged growth in the size of armies over the sixteenth century. According to him, the new technologies of gunpowder weaponry and geometric fortification design acted as catalysts for this expansion, since it became necessary to mount ever larger besieging armies against correspondingly enlarged and more numerous garrison forces as a supposedly new style of siege warfare spread across Europe.[30] Whether war thereby lost its earlier fluidity and mobility is open to question, however, given the prevalence of lengthy sieges throughout the Middle Ages. In fact, evidence assembled by Hall indicates that the average number of days for a siege actually fell during the early modern period. Citing recent work by John Lynn, Hall contends that, at least prior to 1650, army size remained surprisingly stable.[31] When growth did occur, it was probably a function of a rising population and the improved ability of governments to raise funds for war making. The appearance of greater numbers could also simply be a result of better record keeping by early modern governments, interested as they were in making sure that their monies were properly expended. The absence of such documentary validation for comparable armies and garrisons in the Middle Ages could therefore be deceptive. Another point worth exploring regards the shifting composition of such armies. Medieval armies were notoriously motley agglomerations of knightly vassals, hired mercenaries, militia auxiliaries, and all manner of irregular contingents often hastily thrown together for a season's campaigns. This lack of uniformity, along with the usual fragmented chain of command in most medieval armies, reflected the considerable degree of control exercised by local lords and urban communities over their involvement in military matters. Nevertheless, the size of such forces could be quite large, matching at times the more

[29] See J. R. Hale, "To Fortify or Not to Fortify? Machiavelli's Contribution to a Renaissance Debate," in *Essays in Honour of John Humphreys Whitfield*, ed. H. C. Davis (London: Academic Press, 1975), pp. 99–119, and Richard Tuttle, "Against Fortifications: The Defense of Renaissance Bologna," *Journal of the Society of Architectural Historians* 41 (1982), 189–201.

[30] Another recent critic is David Parrott, "The Military Revolution in Early Modern Europe," *History Today* 42 (1992), 36–48.

[31] John Lynn, "The *trace italienne* and the Growth of Armies: The French Case," *Journal of Military History* 55 (1991), 297–330.

uniform and better organized armies assembled by early modern governments.[32] The crucial change, therefore, was perhaps not in scale but rather the greater monopoly over armed violence held by early modern rulers. The logistical limits of maintaining such armies in the field, as Hall graphically demonstrates, only began to be overcome in the seventeenth century. Again, it seems that if a "Military Revolution" did occur, it arose more out of administrative innovations by early modern states than new technologies.

These essays suggest just some of the richness found when studying medieval siege warfare. Other avenues to be explored include how the ongoing military preparedness of towns affected their relationship with the surrounding country-side. While walls could demarcate the urban and rural worlds, their construction and maintenance often depended on funneling local peasant labor and surplus agricultural production into meeting the military needs of the city.[33] Work on medieval building trades, particularly masons and brickmakers, would shed much needed light on the artisanal engineering techniques used to meet the military, not just ecclesiastical, construction needs of urban society in the Middle Ages.[34] The impact of topographical conditions and their progressive alteration by the city also merit investigation for what they might reveal about medieval fortification design and urbanism.[35] How substantially the practice of siege warfare in western Europe had differed prior to the eleventh century represents another important area of future research.[36] Finally, the connections between images of the besieged city and religious culture offer a complement to the allegorical use of the siege found in medieval romance literature and poetry. The idea of the soul as a fortress embattled by sin occurs frequently in medieval sermons, not to mention later in Luther's writings and hymns; siege accounts in the Old Testament also inspired medieval municipal drama. The manipulation of sacred images of the Virgin or patron saints, either in processions circuiting city walls or as symbols incorporated into the very fabric of fortifications, bolstered

---

[32] The changing composition of French armies between the Middle Ages and sixteenth century has been examined respectively in Philippe Contamine, *Guerre, état et société à la fin du moyen âge* (Paris: La Haye, Mouton, 1972), and Ferdinand Lot, *Recherches sur les effectifs des armées françaises des Guerres d'Italie aux Guerres de Religion, 1494–1562* (Paris: Presses Universitaires de France, 1962).

[33] A variety of perspectives on medieval town-country relations can be found in *Villes et campagnes au Moyen Âge. Mélanges Georges Despy*, eds. J.-M. Duvosquel and A. Dierkens (Liege: Édition du Perron, 1991).

[34] Francis B. Andrews, *The Mediaeval Builder and His Methods* (Totowa: Rowman & Littlefield, 1974); Lon Shelby, *John Rogers: Tudor Military Engineer* (Oxford: Clarendon Press, 1967); Alain Erlande-Brandenbourg, "Organisation du conseil d'architecture militaire et du corps des spécialistes sous Philippe Auguste," in *Artistes, artisans et production artistique au Moyen Âge*, ed. Xavier Barral i Altet, Vol. 2 (Paris: Picard, 1987), pp. 221–24.

[35] See Pierre Lavedan, *Histoire de l'urbanisme*, Vol. 1 (Paris: H. Laurens, 1952–66), for an introduction.

[36] Bernard Bachrach, *Merovingian Military Organization, 481–751* (Minneapolis: University of Minnesota Press, 1972), and John Beeler, *Warfare in Feudal Europe, 730–1200* (Ithaca: Cornell University Press, 1971).

in contemporaries' minds at least the decidedly less figurative measures taken to protect a city.[37] The list of possible topics raised by looking at medieval siege warfare is virtually endless. It is hoped that these fine essays will inspire others to mount their own assaults on the medieval city, assaults from which we can all profit.

---

[37] The protective roles played by saints are examined in *Saints and their Cults: Studies in Religious Sociology, Folklore and History*, ed. Stephen Wilson (Cambridge: Cambridge University Press, 1983).

Siege Warfare and Cities

Life on the Cutting Edge: The Besieged Town on the Luso-Hispanic Frontier in the Twelfth Century

James F. Powers
Holy Cross College

There could have been fewer more perilous or exciting places to dwell than in a Luso-Iberian frontier town between the late eleventh through the early thirteenth centuries. Once King Fernando I (1035–65) had established a far-flung frontier from the Cantabrians in the north to the Central Sierras, the ability to control conquered territory and add new lands held the highest priority for the Leonese-Castilian monarchy. The issue also held a paramount place for the rulers of Aragon and Barcelona, as well as for the fledgling monarchy of Portugal which would emerge in the twelfth century. In each of the kingdoms and principalities, the role of towns was destined to be a significant means to this end. A fortified town implanted a population nucleus in exposed terrain as both a unit of economic activity as well as a defensive and offensive outpost. As we know from the current debate over Palestinian lands, the settlement of people is vital to the long-term ability to claim and exploit territory for the sake of the state. The ability of the Christian states to accomplish this task, and the inability of the Muslim states to do so, became the driving force determining the course of the Iberian Reconquest.

If the Christian states captured older towns or established new ones, the Muslims were well aware that they should strive to retake these critical locales. The conquerors possessed the option of resetting such sites or, at the least, destroying them to obviate their use as potential municipal bases. If settled, the inhabitants faced extensive military exposure until the frontier moved far enough away to make them difficult to reach by invading armies. This constituted the chemistry of Reconquest advance, and a normative element in that equation was the reality of frequent raiding into their municipal territory by marauding Muslim armies, often climaxing in a siege. Monastic chroniclers customarily paid scant attention to such activities unless the king was personally involved, and few towns generated city histories to redress the scales (Ávila offering a signal exception). But Islamic writers also composed chronicles, and the municipal documents often specified the extent of urban military responsibilities.

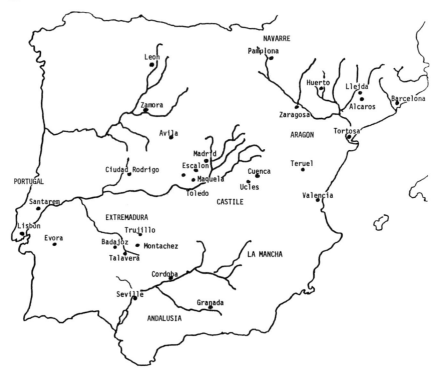

IBERIA *c.* 1250.

Through a careful use of these sources, we can gain a considerable understanding of the role played by sieges in their lives.

Our earliest references are but dimly known, often recounted in the brief chronicles of the early Reconquest and later summarized in compilations such as the thirteenth-century *Primera crónica general*. An example is the nascent town of Zamora, along with its exposed settlers, which occupied the rise overlooking the Duero River, around 120 kilometers south of the newly-established capital at León in the early tenth century. The Roman bridge which still bestrides the Duero made this crossing point a highly strategic location. King Alfonso III of Asturias-León had just occupied the zone north of the Duero, and Zamora was clearly intended as one of the bastions anchoring the southern frontier. The fortifications of the settlement could have consisted of little more than simple wood and stone barricades, but the site's importance was sufficient enough for the Muslims to put it under siege in early July 901, and for Alfonso III to direct its defense in person. After several days the Muslims had endured sufficient losses to abandon the siege. Ibn al-Qitt, the Mahdi of La Mancha and the leader of this audacious attack, died in his attempt to take Zamora, having his head posted on the gateway of the town.[1] Three decades later, in 934, the great Caliph

---

[1] "La crónica de Sampiro," in *Sampiro: su crónica y la monarquía leonesa en el siglo X*, ed.

Abderrahman III brought a larger force to Zamora. Much of the struggle oc-
curred in and around the ditch and palisade which now surrounded the town.
Despite heavy losses sustained in an intense archery exchange, this time the
Muslims prevailed, and Zamora was lost until 959.[2]

The micro-histories of these town bases are little known to us before the
eleventh century, and the settlements were comparatively small in the thinly
populated zone north of the Central Sierras. By the eleventh century under King
Fernando I, however, the settlements in this zone had been permanently secured.
More impressive Muslim towns began to fall victim to Christian expansionist
pressures. Coimbra, for example, succumbed in 1064 and marked the beginning
of a standard siege-and-surrender procedure for future Christian monarchs.
Residents of a town under siege who surrendered promptly could remain with
full freedoms after the conquest. If the Muslims surrendered after having been
under siege for some time, they could leave with only those goods they could
carry. Waiting for the town to fall by force, they faced death or enslavement.[3]
Islamic armies would follow similar procedures. With the siege and capture of
Toledo in 1085 by King Alfonso VI, Christian conquest penetrated the more
densely populated Muslim regions of the central peninsula south of the Central
Sierras in the Tajo Valley. The Reconquest entered its critical central stage.
Toledo's capture provoked an Almoravid counter-attack from North Africa in
1086, and Leonese-Castilian rulers had to be alert to the possibility that their
newly captured towns would face the threat of sieges as the Muslims sought to
drive the Christians from the Tajo Valley.

Since Toledo constituted the key to the possession of the high Meseta plateau
that dominates central Iberia, the Almoravid rulers targeted this town and the
fortresses which controlled its approaches for a steady succession of sieges
through much of the twelfth century. The first strike came in 1090, led by the
Almoravid ruler Yūsuf ibn-Tāshfīn who had defeated King Alfonso VI at
Sagrajas in 1086. Perched on a steep set of escarpments which mark a great
bend in the Rio Tajo, Toledo had a considerable enhancement from nature
sustaining its defense, and a complement of former Muslim walls added to the
task of laying siege to the Leonese-Castilian outpost. While the Almoravid emir
damaged some of the fortifications, King Alfonso, aided by King Sancho
Ramírez of Aragon, held the city and frustrated the Almoravid endeavor to drive

---

Justo Pérez de Urbel, Escuela de Estudios Medievales, Estudios 26 (Madrid: Consejo Superior
de Investigaciones Científicas, 1935), pp. 305–06. *Primera crónica general de España que
mandó componer Alfonso el Sabio y se continuaba bajo Sancho IV en 1289* [Hereafter *PCG*], ed.
Ramón Menéndez Pidal, Vol. 2 (Madrid: Gredos, 1977), p. 389. Cesáreo Fernández Duro,
Memorias históricas de la ciudad de Zamora, su provincia y obispado, Vol. 1 (Madrid, 1882),
pp. 192–93. Armando Cotarelo Valledor, *Historia crítica y documentada de la vida y acciones
de Alfonso III el Magno, último rey de Asturias* (Madrid: V. Suárez, 1933), pp. 448–50. Ursicino
Álvarez Martínez, *Historia general, civil y eclesiástica de la provincia de Zamora* (Madrid:
Editorial Revista de Derecho Privado, 1965), pp. 103–04. Derek W. Lomax, *The Reconquest of
Spain* (London & New York: Longman, 1978), p. 38.

[2] Fernández Duro, pp. 200–04. Álvarez Martínez, pp. 111–12. Lomax, p. 45.

[3] Lomax, pp. 52–54.

the Christians back across the Central Sierras.[4] The combined deaths of Alfonso VI's only son Sancho at Uclés in 1108 and of the king himself in 1109 presented another invitation to strike at Toledo, since León-Castile came under the rule of his apparently defenseless daughter Queen Urraca. Yūsuf's son Emir 'Alī ibn-Yūsuf besieged the city for nine days in 1110 with siege equipment, damaging nearby castles but failing to enter Toledo itself.[5] The governor of Córdoba al-Mazdali made an independent strike against Toledo in 1114, again without success. Three years later the Almoravids led by 'Alī ibn-Yūsuf undertook a twenty-day siege of Coimbra in 1117. This thrust far to the north and west of Toledo also failed to achieve its objective.[6]

While these assaults highlight only some of the strikes at a few major towns on the frontier in the period, defending the major settlements from sieges had become a vital priority. The Almoravids commonly brought siege equipment in their van, including siege crossbows, fire missile hurlers, and torsion catapults which fired stones and spears, along with scaling ladders and tunnelling gear.[7] Aragon's great conquest of the era, the major Muslim town of Zaragoza, experienced little of this pressure, since the advanced position of Toledo posed a far more grievous potential threat to the Islamic heartland of Andalusia. Only Christian offensive pressure could counteract the Islamic assaults and secure the region around Toledo. King Alfonso VII (1126–57), who styled himself *Imperator Hispaniae*, and Count (soon to be King) Afonso I Henriques of Portugal (1128–85) shortly launched these undertakings in the later 1130s. Alfonso VII's attack and siege of the castle town of Oreja in 1139, some sixty kilometers to the northeast of Toledo, provoked one of the most colorful episodes in the history of Western siegecraft.

The Almoravid Emir Tāshfīn ibn-'Alī was campaigning against the rising Almohad dissenters in North Africa and was unavailable for the raising of a large relief force. The governors of Seville and Valencia under the command of al-Zubair ibn 'Umar, the governor of Córdoba and Granada, hastily gathered an army to deal with Emperor Alfonso's onslaught on a key base, critical to the Muslims' ability to threaten Toledo. Unable to prevent Alfonso's attack on Oreja through an ambush, or to break the Emperor's siege there, al-Zubair resorted to the next best tactic, an attack on Toledo. After the customary preliminary devastation of crops, orchards and grapevines in the vicinity (a normal procedure for

4 Bernard F. Reilly, *The Kingdom of León-Castilla under King Alfonso VI, 1065–1109* (Princeton: Princeton University Press, 1988), p. 215. Lomax, p. 71.

5 "Anales Toledanos I," in *España sagrada: Theatro geográfico-histórico de la iglesia de España*, ed. Enrique Flórez, Vol. 23 (Madrid, 1767), p. 387. Bernard F. Reilly, *The Kingdom of León-Castilla under Queen Urraca, 1109–1126* (Princeton: Princeton University Press, 1982), p. 70. Lomax, pp. 76–77.

6 Reilly, *Urraca*, p. 97. Lomax, p. 77. "Chronica Gothorum," in Alfredo Pimenta, ed., *Fontes medievais da história de Portugal. I. Anais e crónicas* (Lisboa: Livraria Sa da Costa, 1948), pp. 26–27. *Cronica Adefonsi Imperatoris* [hereafter *CAI*], ed. Luis Sánchez Belda (Madrid: Consejo Superior de Investigaciones Científicas, 1950), pp. 79–80.

7 *CAI*, pp. 77–78.

both sides in Reconquest campaigning), the commanders drew up their forces around the walls of San Servando castle, a supporting fortress for Toledo on the opposite side of the Rio Tajo. As al-Zubair commenced the task of dismantling its walls, the defending garrison of Toledo mounted the city walls with a great hue and cry, presenting a noisy din to mask their thin numbers. However, the Muslim investment failed to take into account the presence of the resourceful Empress Berengaria within the city.

Berengaria dispatched a message to al-Zubair and his fellow governors. In it, she noted:

> Your Empress, wife of the Emperor, inquires if it is the case that you are aware that it is a woman against whom you wage war, and that it is dishonorable for you [to be attacking me]? If you wish to face combat, go to Oreja and fight with the Emperor, who awaits you with armed and ready battle formations. (*CAI*, pp. 115–17)

As they pondered the communication, the governors noted that Berengaria had seated herself atop the *alcázar*, the highest defensive fortress keep of the city, alone in regal splendor. Adding to the besiegers' consternation, the ladies of the court had mounted the walls with their prayer books. From this lofty position overlooking the Tajo gorge, they sang accompanied by drums, lyres and cymbals. The confrontation of the musical arts with the art of war proved more than al-Zubair and his forces could bear. The Muslims withdrew in apologetic fashion, a tribute both to their chivalry and to the bold initiative of the Empress and her court.[8] It takes no credit away from the bravery of these women to note that the Almoravid forces were probably insufficient in numbers and equipment to undertake a full scale siege of Toledo at that point. The issue of personal honor carried great weight on the Castilian frontier with regard to the relationship of men and women, even leading to capital punishment.[9] This cultural attitude tends to render the account more believable. However, the best contemporary Muslim chronicle makes no reference to this unusual siege or to the loss of Oreja in the following October. Painful encounters or losses are frequently absent from the surviving Islamic accounts.

The next two decades saw a substantial reduction in Toledo's exposure to siege. Along with Oreja, the primary bases used by the Muslims for their

---

[8] *CAI*, pp. 115–17: "Hoc dicit vobis imperatris, uxor imperatoris: nonne videtis quia contra me pugnatis, quae foemina sum, et non est vobis in honorem? Sed si vultis pugnare ite in Aureliam et pugnate cum imperatore, qui cum armatis et paratis aciebus vos expectat." Luis García de Valdeavellano, *Historia de España de los orígenes a la baja Edad Media*, Vol. 1, Part 2, 4th ed. (Madrid: Revista de Occidente, 1968), pp. 441–42. Lomax, p. 89. Heath Dillard, *Daughters of the Reconquest: Women in Castilian Town Society, 1100–1300* (Cambridge: Cambridge University Press, 1984), p. 15. Ibn-'Idhārī al-Marrākushī, "Al-Bayan al-Mugrib," in *Ibn-'Idhārī: Al-Bayan al-Mugrib, Nuevos fragmentos almorávides y almohades*, ed. and trans. Ambrosio Huici Miranda, Textos Medievales 8 (Valencia: Anubar, 1963), p. 225.

[9] James F. Powers, "Frontier Municipal Baths and Social Interaction in Thirteenth-Century Spain," *American Historical Review* 84 (1979), 658–61. Dillard, pp. 92–93, 132–33, 169–79, 190, 203–06.

assaults on the Tajo bastion such as Talavera, Mora, Calatrava la Vieja and Huete were either conquered initially or retaken. While Alfonso VII certainly did not assist the frontier effort by dividing the Leonese-Castilian state between his two sons Fernando II (1157–88) and Sancho III (1157–58), the disintegration of Almoravid Iberia permitted the continued conquest and settlement of the central Tajo region. Berengaria's court ladies had indeed sung a swan song to the future Islamic capability of besieging the capital, at least for a half-century.

King Afonso I's offensive in emerging Portugal had extended his frontier to the lower Tejo, anchored by the conquest of the river towns of Santarém and Lisbon in 1147. Portugal then extended probes beyond the Tejo River into the Ribatejo and Alentejo regions, taking the key outpost town of Évora in 1165. Even when young King Sancho III of Castile died in 1158, an active nobility and the newly-founded domestic military orders continued the pressure on the frontier by seeking lands across the Montes de Toledo south and east into La Mancha and the flanks of the Iberian Cordillera toward adjacent Aragon. The frontier of the Crown of Aragon continued to be located well to the northeast, testing the frontier south of the Ebro River. Its great municipal conquests of Zaragoza, Tortosa and Lleida were not threatened with Muslim sieges after conquest in the manner in which the more advanced Portuguese and Castilian acquisitions soon would be. For a Muslim preacher of fierce orthodoxy, Ibn-Tūmart, had rallied the North Africans to create a new puritanical movement known as the Almohads. This new force soon struck the declining Almoravids in Spain as well, and thereafter confronted the Christian efforts of expansion with a renewed counter-offensive that threatened their bridgehead settlements. Castile and Portugal would thus experience a return to the days of the defensive siege.

Abū Ya'qūb Yūsuf I, the Almohad caliph, crossed over from North Africa in 1171, leading an assault on King Lobo's client state of Murcia in the spring of 1172. Lobo's death placed his dominions located southeast of Castile in Yūsuf's hands. The caliph then invaded the sections of northern La Mancha which Lobo had granted to Castile, capturing the castles of Vilches and Alcaraz. On July 11, they arrived at their next target, Huete, the castle town formerly used by the Almoravids to launch their raids on Toledo. Whether the Muslims intended to destroy Huete as they had other castle towns they were unable to populate, or to resettle it as an assault base, is not known. Either way, the matter was of considerable concern to Alfonso VIII (1158–1214). To that end, the young king had reinforced Huete and its militia early in the campaign season just a few weeks before Yūsuf's arrival. The added numbers may explain why the Muslim force caught the town shy of supplies, particularly water. Moreover, Yūsuf commanded an army sufficient to overwhelm Huete by its sheer size. But the Muslim army's size also constituted a disadvantage. An army this large could not stay in one place for any great length of time in the hot dry La Manchan summer without exhausting nearby water and food supplies.

Huete's defenders dug a supplementary ditch and palisade to slow the Almohad attack, ultimately breeched by the invaders with substantial casualties on both sides. Yūsuf's army had meanwhile cut the Christians off from any neighboring water sources, which the Muslims were overtaxing for their own needs. The Almohads succeeding in penetrating the town, the defenders clinging to a few streets and the *alcázar*. Yūsuf converted a captured church into a mosque, while the attendant religious leaders of both sides besought the heavens for relief or submission, respectively. Forays and surrender negotiations proved unavailing to force the capture or break the siege. Then the arrival of an unusual summer rain storm on Sunday (July 16) refilled the cisterns of Huete and dampened the effectiveness of a July 17 Muslim assault. The Christian defenders, their spirits renewed by waters that were sufficient for them if not for the vast army besieging them, were also invigorated by reports that King Alfonso was raising a relief army in Toledo. Yūsuf sulked in his tent while religious leaders chided his troops for their lackluster fighting, causing Allah to believe that his faithful did not want victory keenly enough. After twelve days on the site, the Almoravid army could no longer hope to secure sufficient food and drink. As a result, on July 23 the frustrated and famished Muslim army withdrew to neighboring Cuenca for resupply. Huete held at the cost of some seventy Christian dead and ten more as prisoners.[10]

The last three decades of the twelfth century witnessed intense give and take along the entire front of the Christian kingdoms. Alfonso II of Aragon (1162–96) captured Teruel in 1171, and Alfonso VIII took Cuenca after an eight-month siege in 1177. The town militias and the military orders launched a series of raids striking at targets in Andalusia. Yūsuf I was continually distracted by North African problems, and the city governors of Seville and Córdoba were often required to make the punishing counter-strokes. Between 1181 and 1184 three accounts of interesting sieges against major Christian frontier towns appear in the Islamic chronicles. Each involve that favorite tactic of the surrounded fortification, a sally of the defending garrison against the besiegers, with varying results. In 1181, a Muslim expedition under Ibn Wānūdīn marched into the Alentejo and laid siege to Évora, the advanced and increasingly isolated Portuguese forward base located there. The chronicler Ibn 'Idhārī describes Ibn Wānūdīn attacking the environs of Évora like a lion on holy war, the residents pinned inside the walls like "howling vixens." One day while the Muslim commander napped and his troops were scattered in assorted forays, the Évoran militia burst from the town and struck his camp. Roused abruptly from his slumbers, Ibn Wānūdīn rallied the available troops and routed the Christian raiders, forcing them into the moat, and capturing many of the Évorans along with their horses. Needless to say, they attempted no additional sallies during the

---

[10] Ibn Sāhib al-Salā, *Al-Mann bil-imama*, ed. and trans. Ambrosio Huici Miranda, Textos medievales 24 (Valencia: Anubar, 1969), pp. 204–17. Abu Muhammad 'Abd al-Wahid al-Marrakusī, "Kitab al-mu'yib fi taljis ajabar al-Magrib," in *Colección de crónicas árabes de la Reconquista*, ed. and trans. Ambrosio Huici Miranda, Vol. 4 (Tetuán: Editora Marroqui, 1955), pp. 203–04. James F. Powers, *A Society Organized for War: The Iberian Municipal Militias in the Central Middle Ages, 1000–1284* (Berkeley: University of California Press, 1988), pp. 47–48. Melchor Martínez Antuña, "Campañas de los Almohades en España," *Religión y Cultura* 8 (1935), 53–67, 327–43, 347–73. Lomax, pp. 114–15.

siege. The entire campaign lasted from May 25 to early June, and Évora held despite battle losses and prisoners taken (400 men and 120 women).[11]

Flush with this transient success against Évora, Ibn Wānūdīn waited late into the campaign season of 1182 for a deep strike into the Castilian Tajo frontier. Advantaged by the short days and cloudy skies of October, the Sevillian army approached Talavera until they routed a mounted patrol of the Talaveran militia. The patrol leader fled and warned the town, stunned by the presence of the Muslim army that arrived on 16 October. The citizens of Talavera had not seen a serious Muslim siege since the court ladies had beaten their drums and crashed their cymbals from the walls of Toledo in 1139. Establishing his army on the high ground above the town overlooking the Tajo River, Ibn Wānūdīn directed the rebuff of all the regional castle garrisons rallied to drive out the invaders. Finally a desperate assault by all of the able-bodied Talaverans led by a priest drove the Muslims from their encampment, although the militia's pursuit proved too reckless, and they were beaten back several miles from the town. Ibn Wānūdīn then withdrew to Seville, the chronicler Ibn ʿIdhārī claiming over ten thousand Christians and Jews killed in the campaign. We have reason to be dubious about the extent of either the triumph or the victims, however. First, the casualties would have considerably exceeded the total population of Talavera at the time, and second, Caliph Yūsuf I subsequently wrote to the governor, chiding the soldiers for their straggling and cowardice.[12] One suspects the Caliph saw in the overstated claims a thin cover for failure. Certainly Ibn Wānūdīn had failed to take Talavera.

Yūsuf I returned to Spain, and launched a major expedition against the Tejo River frontier in Portugal. The Almohad Caliph brought his Andalusian and African force to Badajoz, and combined it there with forces from Extremadura. This time the target was the high-walled town of Santarém, whose militia had been one of the prime Andalusian raiders in the preceding decade. The Almoravids invested the town on June 27, this time well-provisioned and ready for a long siege. Yūsuf pitched his impressive red tent on the high ground near the town, cut the town off from the river, and ordered a series of raids throughout the countryside. The Muslim besiegers devastated the area around Santarém, destroying churches, crops and hamlets and routing the initial sally sent out to deal with the invaders. Then an arrow penetrated the red tent, seriously wounding Yūsuf in the foot. The injured Caliph urgently besought Allah for the gift of Santarém. Allah would ultimately respond by taking the commander's soul to heaven instead. The army assembled its siege ladders and assorted gear, and made its first attack on the walls on June 29.[13]

11 Ibn-ʿIdhārī al-Marrākushī, "Al-Bayan al-Mugrib fi ijtisār Ajbār Mulik al-Andalus wa al-Magrib," in *Colección de crónicas árabes*, ed. and trans. Ambrosio Huici Miranda, Vol. 2, pp. 39–41. "El Anónimo de Madrid y Copenhague, Texto árabe y traducción," ed. and trans. Ambrosio Huici Miranda, *Anales del Instituto General y Técnico de Valencia* 2 (1917), 9–10.

12 Ibn-ʿIdhārī, pp. 49–51. "Anónimo de Madrid," pp. 22–24, contains a very similar account.

13 "Anónimo de Madrid," pp. 32–34. Ibn-ʿIdhārī, Vol. 2, pp. 70–72.

Meanwhile, King Fernando II of León had hastily raised a force and marched to the Portuguese southern frontier, sending messages to aging Portuguese King Afonso I Henriques who initially feared his Leonese neighbor was moving to assist the Almohads. Religion was never a barrier to such alliances during the Reconquest. The relief force caught Yūsuf by surprise, who now found himself in the dangerous position of being caught between the besieged and the relievers. Yūsuf attempted to reposition his forces across the Tejo on July 2, but made a bad job of it with heavy losses. Discouragement piled upon discouragement, including one of the chief Muslim court officials defecting to the Christian side. Rains and a swelling Tejo River finished the project, and the Muslims withdrew, settling for booty-gathering forays on the return trip, during which Yūsuf died of his wound. A large expeditionary army had been repulsed by Santarém's walls and the cooperative actions of allied Christian kingdoms.[14]

Our descriptions of these late twelfth-century Muslim sieges of Christian towns are best accounted in Islamic sources. The royal and ecclesiastical chronicles pay little heed to the difficulties endured by townsmen defending their territory or encased in their towns surrounded by a hostile army. The one good municipal chronicle that covers the period, the *Crónica de la población de Ávila*, while offering much of the flavor of the long-distance raiding of its active militia, has no material on the difficulties of being besieged. Ávila's formidable walls as well as its position in the Trans-Duero north of the Central Sierras placed it well out of the range of Muslim raiding armies in the late twelfth century. However, we can get a sense of the municipal awareness of the threat of siege, and the preparations to live and deal with its realities, if we investigate the growth of municipal law in the age. Three great traditions of extensive law codes, or *fueros*, were forged from the pressures of this conflictive late twelfth century: the Castilian Extremaduran and La Manchan law from the *Fuero de Cuenca* (*c.* 1190), the upland Aragonese law from the *Fuero de Teruel* (*c.* 1177–96), and the Leonese Coria Cima-Coa law from the *fuero* granted to Ciudad Rodrigo toward the end of the century.[15] Each was a summation of regional municipal law intended initially for one town, but to be extended to and copied by other towns in its region. These *fueros* speak to us of the combination of aggression and dread beneath which the municipal residents lived in time of war.

Cuenca offers a striking example of what these towns were like. Its position on the western flanks of the Iberian Cordillera gave it great strategic significance. Muslim Cuenca functioned as a supply base for Andalusian expeditions in La Mancha against Toledo, and controlled a crucial passage through the mountains to Aragon, as well as being adjacent to the road between Toledo to

---

[14] Ibn-'Idhārī, p. 70–73. 'Abd al-Wahid, pp. 210–11. "Anónimo de Madrid," pp. 32–35. Julio González, *Regesta de Fernando II*, Instituto Jerónimo Zurita (Madrid: Consejo Superior de Investigaciones Científicas, 1943), pp. 148–49. Powers, *Society*, pp. 43–44. Lomax, pp. 116–17.

[15] For a full discussion on the emergence of the legal formularies that constitute these traditions, see Powers, pp. 219–29.

Valencia. Ibn Sāhib al-Salā describes the comfort which Yūsuf I, fresh from his failure to take Huete in 1172, derived from seeing this invulnerable Muslim stronghold, crowned by its "lofty citadel, unconquerable, whose height reached heavenward to touch the clouds." The city, sitting astride the Júcar and Huécar river gorges on an extended ridge flanked by precipitous cliffs, had been briefly Christian during Alfonso VI's later reign, but fell to the Almoravids in the wake of the battle of Uclés in 1108. Yūsuf's confidence proved ill-founded, for Cuenca returned to Christian control on 21 September 1177 after a siege of several months.[16] Within thirteen years, Alfonso VIII granted to his conquest the great charter which is one of our best windows into the life of a frontier settlement.

Like the *Fuero of Cuenca*, the charters of Teruel and Coria are rather more like city codes than the simple foundation documents available for the remainder of Western Europe. They extend over two hundred pages in length in a modern printed edition, combine both royal initiatives and local custom, and seek to regulate municipal life with a detail extraordinary for the times. These codes suggest the way in which defensive operations added to the tensions experienced by the municipal frontiersmen, since most of the ordinary advantages sought in combat had to be relinquished. The attacking force usually possessed initiative, planning and surprise. Small raiding forays often evaporated before the town could organize a resistance force, while a large army usually proved beyond the capacity of a single municipality to contain it. On the other hand, the defenders were advantaged by a better knowledge of the terrain, the incentive of defending their own lands, and the hope that the invaders would make a serious mistake. Since the townsmen needed to protect their families, possessions, crops and livestock while maintaining permanent settlement on an exposed frontier, the offensive advantages of the invaders had to be countered. Survival meant a mastery of the techniques of defensive warfare, and this challenge faced the towns from the moment of their establishment or conquest. Moreover, it was a need to be met largely by their own resources. Towns were expected to take care of themselves.

The defensive system of the Peninsula and especially of the municipalities evolved steadily from its first appearance in the eleventh-century charters through the more systematic formulations stated in the Alfonsine codes of the late thirteenth century, the *Espéculo* and the *Siete Partidas*. During its evolution this system displayed both active and passive attributes. The active process of assembling a force to seek out and destroy the invading enemy was covered by the term *apellido*. From its origins as a generic term for warning, *apellido* had by the late eleventh century come to signify the military force mustered by the towns to deal with the danger heralded by that warning. In contrast to musters directed toward military activity initiated by the town, i.e., offensive endeavors,

---

[16] Ibn Sāhib al-salā, pp. 217–18. This is our richest account of Muslim Cuenca. Powers, pp. 48–49. Julio González, *El reino de Castilla en la época de Alfonso VIII*, Vol. 1 (Madrid: Consejo Superior de Investigaciones Científicas, 1960), pp. 924–25.

this situation required rapid assembly under the impending threat of enemy attack. The forces summoned by the *apellido* were expected to meet the enemy expedition in the field, to defeat it if possible, or harry its progress if that force proved too large. The passive side of defense consisted in maintaining an efficient warning procedure and a reliable system of walls and towers. Moreover, townsmen were enjoined to exercise great vigilance and extreme caution while an enemy invading force was in the region. The nature of the frontier induced a continual wartime mode of living which must have exacted a relentless price in stress.

Clearly a need for elaborate precautions existed to protect the territorial boundaries. The *apellido* summons portended the need of hasty preparations and urgent assembly of forces. This warning was sounded in the town and its surrounding countryside by bells, horns, drums or any other instruments which could be heard at a distance, or noted visually by bonfires. The igniters strove to make their signal fires smoke for daytime signaling, and to flame brilliantly for night-time visibility.[17] Once the territory resounded and glowed with the signals of alarm, this warning triggered the defensive muster of the militia; in this way active defense supplanted passive surveillance. The law compelled citizens with militia responsibilities to assemble in the plaza of the town or to seek out the standard of the town council wherever it might be located. The warning call applied to all obligated persons within earshot or who came in contact with another bearing the news. It applied throughout the entire territory under the town's control.

The Cuenca, Teruel and Coria families of charters allow the resident twenty-four hours to arrive at the assembly area, speed being encouraged. The Coria group urged knights to hasten at the gallop and foot soldiers at the run to the standard. Cuenca and Teruel set the distance at that which could be walked in twenty-four hours, while Coria set the limit at twelve.[18] The almost universal

---

[17] While the great *fuero* formularies of Cuenca and Teruel were extended to many towns in Aragon and Castile, I am citing here only the earliest versions identified with the twelfth century: Cuenca's two published Latin manuscripts and Teruel's published Latin manuscript. "Forum Conche, forma sistemática," in *Fuero de Cuenca* [Hereafter *FCfs*], ed. Rafael de Ureña y Smenjaud (Madrid: Tipografía de Archivos, 1935), 31.16. "Forum Conche, Paris Ms.," in "Forum Conche, fuero de Cuenca: The Latin Text of the Municipal Charter and Laws of the City of Cuenca, Spain," ed. George H. Allen, *University Studies Published by the University of Cincinnati*, Series Two 5.4 (Nov–Dec, 1909), 5–92; 6.1 (Jan–Feb 1910), 3–134 [Hereafter *FCmsp*], 31.12. "Forum Turolii," in *El fuero latino de Teruel* [Hereafter *FTL*], ed. Jaime Caruana Gómez de Barreda (Teruel: Instituto de Estudios Turolenses de la Excma. Diputación Provincial de Teruel, 1974), p. 452. "Fuero romanceados de Cáceres," in *Los fueros municipales de Cáceres: Su derecho público*, ed. Pedro Lumbreras Valiente, (Cáceres: Institución Cultural "El Brocense" de la Excma. Diputación Provincial de Cáceres, 1974), p. 253. *Las siete partidas del muy noble rey Don Alfonso el Sabio*, ed. Gregorio López (Madrid, 1843–44), II.xxvi.24. Jaime Oliver Asín, "Origen árabe de 'rebato,' 'arrobda',' y sus homónimos," *Boletín de la Real Academia Española* 15 (1928), 309–10.

[18] "Fuero latino de Sepúlveda, confirmado el 17 de noviembre de 1076 por Alfonso VI," in *Los fueros de Sepúlveda* [Hereafter *LFS*], ed. Emilio Sáez, Publicaciones Históricas de la Excma. Diputación Provincial de Segovia, Ser. 1, Colección de Documentos para la Historia de

requirement that the *peones* respond to the *apellido* distinguishes this service notably from the offensive forms of assembly, where footsoldiers often enjoyed exemption or simply went unmentioned. The implicit philosophy behind such a distinction perceived defense as the ultimate responsibility in the face of the gravest kind of frontier threat, a threat which all citizens must meet, regardless of class.

The town also depended upon its passive surveillance system. If the militia faced an opponent too powerful to be attacked in the field, or if the townsmen encountered defeat in that effort, surveillance remained the chief means of tracking enemies and assessing their intent. Passive defense entailed protection of two basic areas, the town itself, and its surrounding territory, the limits of which were marked by its boundary stones. To provide constant surveillance, the residents kept watches in small fortifications and towers situated at key positions. The kings often granted castles to the towns to assist in the surveillance of their region.[19] Sentries (*velas*, *vigías* and *talaeros*) manned these

---

Segovia 1 (Segovia: Diputación Provincial de Segovia, 1953), p. 48. "Fuero de Oviedo," in *El fuero de Avilés*, ed. Aureliano Fernández-Guerra y Orbe (Madrid, 1865), p. 114, n. 5. For the argument in behalf of a post-1227 date for the Oviedo-Avilés charter, see Ciriaco Miguel Vigil, *Asturias monumental, epigráfica y diplomática: Datos para la historia de la provincia*, Vol. 1 (Oviedo, 1887), pp. 277–82. "Alfonso II, rey de Aragón, confirma los antiguos fueros y costumbres de Jaca, y otorga otros nuevos, 1187," in *Jaca: Documentos municipales, 971–1269*, ed. Antonio Ubieto Arteta (Valencia: Anubar, 1975), p. 72. "Fueros de Medinaceli," in *Colección de fueros municipales y cartas pueblas de los reinos de Castilla, León, Corona de Aragón y Navarra; coordinada y anotada*, ed. Tomás Muñoz y Romero (Madrid, 1847), pp. 440–41. *FCfs*, 31.1. *FCmsp*, 31.1. *FTL*, pp. 447–48. While the great *fuero* formulary of Coria Cima-Coa was extended to many towns in León and Portugal, I am citing only the earliest version identified with the twelfth century: Coria's published Romanceado manuscript. "El fuero de Coria" [Hereafter *FCO*], ed. Emilio Sáez, in *El fuero de Coria*, ed. José Maldonado y Fernández del Torco (Madrid: Instituto de Estudios de Administración Local, 1949), pp. 182, 336. "Fuero de Viguera y Val de Funes, (edición crítica)," ed. José María Ramos y Loscertales, *Acta Salmanticensia* 7 (1956), 50. "Arrendamiento hecho por el concejo de Nora á Nora al de Oviedo de los fueros á que estaba obligado respecto de éste, 1243," in *Documentos para la historia de las instituciones de León y de Castilla*, ed. Eduardo Hinojosa y Naveros (Madrid: Fortanet, 1919), p. 154. "Los fueros de Villadiego, 1254," ed. Amancio Rodríguez López, *Boletín de la Real Academia de la Historia* [Hereafter *BRAH*] 61 (1912), 432. "Privilegio en que el rey (Jaime I) sanciona los estatutos que habían hecho entre sí los aldeanos de Daroca, 1256," in *Documentos históricos de Daroca y su comunidad*, ed. Toribio del Campillo, Biblioteca de Escritores Aragoneses, Sección Histórico-doctrinal, 8 (Zaragoza: Imprenta del Hospicio Provincial, 1915), p. 35. *Siete Partidas*, II.xix.4, II.xxvi.24.

19 "Carta de foral concedida aos habitantes de Mós, Afonso I, 1162," in *Documentos medievais portugueses* [Hereafter *DMP*], Vol. 1: *Documentos régios. Documentos dos condes portugalenses e de D. Afonso Henriques A.D. 1095–1185, Parts 1–2*, ed. Rui Pinto de Azevedo, (Lisboa: n.p., 1948–62), p. 365. "Alfonso VIII da el castello de Olmos al concejo de Segovia, 1166," in González, *Alfonso VIII*, Vol. 2, pp. 141–43. "(Foral de) Rebordãos, Sancho I, 1208," in *Monumento Portugaliae Historica, a saeculo octavo post Christum usque ad quintinm decimum: Leges et consuetudines* [Hereafter *MPH-LC*], eds. Alexandre Herculano & Joaquim J. da Silva Mendes Leal, Vol. 1 (Lisboa, 1856–68), p. 538. "Fuero de Viguera y Val de Funes," pp. 49, 78. Julio González, *Reinado y diplomas de Fernando III*, Vol. 1, Colección Estudios y Documentos, 2 (Córdoba: Monte de Piedad y Caja de Ahorros de Córdoba, 1980), p. 341. "Privilegio rodado de Alfonso X concediendo a Lorca los Castillos y villas de Puentes y Felí, 1265," *Repartimiento de Lorca*, ed. Juan Torres Fontes (Lorca: Ayuntamiento de Lorca, Academia Alfonso X El Sabio,

positions during the day when visibility was good. The night sentries were sometimes called *ascuchas* (listeners) when ears supplemented eyes as detectors of the unusual. Mounted sentinels termed *arrobdas* roamed the town's lands seeking any signs of potential sudden strikes by the Muslims.[20] In all of this watchfulness, protection of the municipality's resources, its population, its livestock and its crops, remained the chief objective. All of these lay open to a sudden foray, but the charters indicated special concern for crops and animals. Since the towns came to base a considerable portion of their economies on the livestock industry, sheep and cattle rustling remained a favorite enterprise for both Christian and Muslim frontiersmen.

All else failing, the municipality relied upon the hard shell of its walls, which were invulnerable to an enemy assault, save for an extended and unrelieved siege or a surprise penetration. The fortifications had the effect of multiplying the number of the defenders by a substantial factor, since fewer individuals were needed to defend a wall effectively than were required to assault it. Much municipal legislation dealt with the town walls, including their construction, maintenance and repair.[21] Such an interest made good sense, given the keenness of both Muslim and Christian armies to destroy walls in order to break resistance or curtail the ability of residents to remain settled in that particular area. Ample indications of walls and their value appear in the charters and the chronicles of the Reconquest. Shortly after their establishment, towns like Ciudad Rodrigo eagerly sought to gird themselves in stone. On occasion, wall-building had to be restricted, as was the case when Bishop Ramiro and King

1977), pp. 57–60. "Alfonso X concedan a los vecinos de Orihuela, para defenderlo contra los moros, 1268," *Cartas de los Reyes de Castilla a Orihuela, 1265–1295*, ed. Vicente Martínez Morellá (Alicante: n.p., 1954), p. 34. "Alfonso X al concejo de Lorca concesión del castillo de Cella, 1277," *Repartimiento de Lorca*, pp. 86–87. Juan Torres Fontes, *Repartimiento de la Huerta y Campo de Murcia en el siglo XIII*, Patronato "José María Quadrado," Academia "Alfonso X" (Murcia: Consejo Superior de Investigaciones Científicas, 1971), pp. 65–84.

20 *FCfs*, 30.1. *FCmsp*, 30.1. *FTL*, p. 426. *FCO*, p. 112. "Fuero de Viguera y Val de Funes," p. 78. Asín, pp. 496–98.

21 Luis Vázquez de Parga, ed., "El fuero de León," *Anuario de Historia del Derecho Español* 15 (1944), 490–91. "Fueros de Villafría, Orbaneja y San Martín, 1039," in *Becerro gótico de Cardeña*, ed. Luciano Serrano, Vol. 3, Fuentes para la Historia de Castilla 3 (Madrid: Librería de Murillo, 1910), p. 379. *Fuero de Miranda de Ebro*, ed. Francisco Cantera Burgos (Madrid: Instituto Francisco Vitoria, 1945), p. 75. "Confirmation de coutumes et concession de privilèges aux habitants de Perpignan, Alphonse I (1176)," in Bernard Alart, *Privilèges et titres relatifs aux franchises, institutions et propriétés communales de Roussillon de Cerdagne, depuis le XIe siècle jusqu'à l'an 1660*, Vol. 1 (Perpignan, 1874), p. 60. "Alfonso VIII concede al concejo de Toledo la renta," in González, *Alfonso VIII*, Vol. 3, pp. 155–57. "El fuero de Llanes," ed. Adolfo Bonilla y San Martín, *Revista de Ciencias Jurídicas y Sociales* 1 (1918), 115. Antonio Ballesteros y Beretta, *Alfonso X el Sabio* (Murcia: n.p., 1963), p. 1064. Ramón Foguet & José Foguet Marsal, eds., *Código de las costumbres escritas de Tortosa, a doble texto, traducido el castellano del más auténtico ejemplar catalán* (Tortosa: Imprenta Querol, 1912), I.1.1, III.11.1–12. "Crónica del Rey Don Alfonso Décimo," in *Crónicas de los Reyes de Castilla*, I, *Biblioteca de Autores Españoles*, 66 (Madrid: Rivandeyra, 1875), p. 21. "Fuero romanceado de Sepúlveda," in *LFS*, p. 63.

Sancho the Strong of Navarre curbed the aggressive construction of internal barriers by the hostile *barrios* of deeply divided Pamplona in 1222.[22]

Towns derived the substantial resources required for wall building and maintenance through taxation, apparently paying residents who performed fortification service a salary drawn from these revenues.[23] When the threat of serious assaults arose, the residents of the countryside could find shelter with some of their livestock within the fortifications, forcing the enemy to mount a siege in order to control the area and tie down the garrison. Should the invader fail to detach some of the strength of his expeditionary force to provide containment, he became liable to a rear assault from the town's militia. Undertaking a formal siege cost time and casualties while detracting from other objectives which the expedition might have been pursuing. Sieges had a high failure rate (witness the numerous Muslim attempts to retake Toledo), and expeditions which squandered their resources of time and energy in these operations stood the risk of returning empty-handed. Thus, every walled town on a line of march presented a dilemma in its balance between opportunity and frustration.

The town walls fulfilled their function only when properly manned. The charters of the Teruel formulary offer particularly detailed accounts of their watch procedures. Sentinels (*velas*) received salaries, carried heavy responsibilities and were policed by an overseer (*sobrevela*). Each tower along the walls required two sentinels, who were fined when they failed to appear. The overseer checked the drowsiness of his charges with periodic challenges, with fining again the penalty for failure to respond within three calls. The sentinels kept their stations from sunset to the matins mass, facing fines for late arrival or premature departure. The custodian of the gate of the town was known as the janitor or *portero*. His tasks included the closing and the opening of the gates at the prescribed times (usually sunset and sunrise). He was fined heavily for procedural violations and awarded a share of booty since he could not serve on campaigns.[24] Towns were especially vulnerable at harvest time and when the militia had departed on campaign. These periods offered the greatest probability of an enemy raid or a surprise siege. The harvest presented an enticing target for

---

[22] *PCG*, Vol. 2, p. 446. *CAI*, pp. 79–80. Lomax, pp. 76–77. Jean Gautier-Dalché, "Islam et Chrétienté en Espagne au XIIe siècle: Contribution à l'étude de la notion de frontière," *Hespéris* 47 (1959), 191. "Historia Compostellana Sive de Rebus Gestis Didaci Gelmirez Primi Compostellani Archiepiscopi," in *España Sagrada*, Vol. 20 (1765), pp. 314–16, 322, 520. *PCG*, Vol. 2, p. 674. "Nueva carta de composición hecha por el Rey don Sancho, el obispo don Remigio y otros consejeros para le pacificación de los habitantes de los barrios de Pamplona," in *Colección diplomática del Rey Don Sancho VIII (El Fuerte) de Navarra*, ed. Carlos Marichalar (Pamplona: Editorial Aramburu, 1934), pp. 181–85.

[23] Only the determination to increase the knightly class for the assault on Andalusia seems to have persuaded the Leonese and Castilian monarchs to exempt that class from the payment of these fortification taxes. *FCfs*, 1.6. *FCmsp*, 1.7. "Fuero latino de Cáceres," *Fueros municipales de Cáceres*, pp. iii–vi.

[24] *FTL*, pp. 129–32. The charter of Molina de Aragón divided the watch service year into two portions, with the first extending from Easter to St. Michael's feast at the end of September, and the second from then to the succeeding Easter. *El fuero de Molina de Aragón*, ed. Miguel Sancho Izquierdo, Estudios de historia de la literatura jurídica español (Madrid: V. Suárez, 1916), p. 153.

raiders, while the campaign season saw the town's military resources fully committed in the field. To diminish this risk many towns never permitted more than a portion of their militia to take to the field at one time, as is especially noteworthy in the Portuguese and Leonese charters. For all of these exposed periods the town had to ready its defenses. With the militia absent, special concern manifested itself regarding night-time security and the movements of strangers in the municipality.

Sunset brought the closing of the gates, marked by cymbal-clashing or bell-ringing which announced to all that night security rules were in effect. At this point strangers unauthorized for overnight stay were expected to depart. In addition to the tower guards, the town placed sentinels in each parish and *barrio*. The *sobrevelas* patrolled the streets, exchanged passwords with the various sentries, and coordinated the surveillance in their area. Anyone moving in the streets of the town after sunset had to carry a light, with the unilluminated facing the risk of immediate arrest and incarceration. Only *barrio* chiefs enjoyed exemption from the need for nocturnal illumination. The overzealous sentry who confined one of these worthies could draw a stiff fine.[25] Non-officeholders apprehended without lights faced the town authorities the following day. A resident was stripped and beaten, then released; a stranger could be executed.[26]

Fire constituted a matter of grave concern. Its outbreak initiated hasty emergency procedures designed to contain and extinguish the blaze before it raged throughout the town. However, while the fire absorbed the complete attention of the residents, a conspirator or his confederates might throw open the gates to an awaiting enemy force. The authorities cast anyone suspected of planning such a scheme out of the town, or imprisoned them until the *concejo* and the militia returned from the campaign. For this reason the charters urged the townsmen to assure themselves that individuals were guarding the town gates before devoting their entire concern to any fire that broke out, whatever the cause. The *Fuero de Plasencia* hints at the reviving classicism of the era by making a very pointed analogy to the fall of Troy in advising this precaution. Indeed, at least one Greek authority of the fourth century B.C. urged similar steps in defense of Greek classical towns.[27]

Important visual evidence exists which illustrates the impact of a siege mentality upon medieval Iberian architecture and art. Town walls and associated defensive structures which offered resistance to the periodic raiding and the

---

[25] *FCfs*, 30.1. *Fcmsp*, 30.1. *FTL*, p. 426. *FCO*, p. 236. *Costumbres de Lérida*, ed. Pilar Loscertales de Valdeavellano (Barcelona: Imp. Escuela Casa Provincial de Caridad, 1946), p. 45. The charter of Castello-Melhor laid a 100 *maravedís* fine on any overseer arresting an *alcalde* under this provision. See "Costumes e foros de Castello-Melhor, 1209," in *MPH-LC*, pp. 897–939, *ley* 368.

[26] *FCfs*, 30.1. *FCmsp*, 30.1. *FTL*, p. 426.

[27] *FCfs*, 30.1. *Fcmsp*, 30.1. *FTL*, p. 426. *Fuero de Plasencia*, ed. Jesús Majada Neila (Salamanca: Librería Cervantes, 1986), p. 491. ". . . por esta manera fue Troya destroída." Aineias the Tactician, *How To Survive Under Siege*, ed. David Whitehead (Oxford: Clarendon Press, 1990), pp. 81–82.

expeditionary forces which threatened their welfare still exist in places such as
Ávila. The Ávilan circuit originally included empty land as emergency pasturage
for sheep during potential attack. In other cases municipal churches took on a
fortified appearance (as with the fortified apse of the Cathedral of Ávila and the
fortified facade of the Cathedral of Sigüenza). Many municipalities had a fortress or *alcázar* as a part of their architectural layout (exemplified by the magni-
ficently preserved *alcázar* of Segovia and the more humble state of the fortress
at Zamora).

Contemporary art gave a primacy to military subjects, both in decorative
sculpture and in manuscript illustrations, and sieges remained a popular theme
from the tenth through the thirteenth centuries. One repeated example can be
seen in the besieged Jerusalem of the Jerome *Commentary on the Book of
Daniel*, as illustrated in the tenth-century Morgan Library Beatus, the eleventh-
century *Beatus* of Fernando and Sancha, and the thirteenth-century Morgan
Beatus, among a number of others in the *Beatus* family of manuscripts. Another
illustration can be found in the Crusader Near Eastern sieges depicted by the
Spanish illustrators of the *Gran conquista de Ultramar*, a thirteenth-century
manuscript. A similar style and theme like the *Ultramar* is evident in the mythi-
cal Islamic siege of Constantinople under Constantine, where the Virgin intervenes decisively by shielding the city walls from the anachronistic trebuchet
with her cloak, depicted in the contemporary *Cantigas de Santa Maria*.[28] In
each case the artist and his audience had ample contemporary models on which
to draw in the real life sieges of their own municipalities, for which such
illustrations may have constituted both an evocative symbol and, at least in the
last instance, a wistfully imagined conclusion to these always imminent threats.

The municipalities thus combined their active and passive measures of
defense to procure the overall protection of their territory and walls. The militia
summoned by the *apellido*, coordinated with the fortifications and augmented
by the vigilance of the residents, proved a combination indispensable to the
protection of the town and its inhabitants. When the varied tasks and duties were
performed efficiently, an enemy expedition could cross the deep frontier zone
only with considerable effort and care. If the Christian towns did not form an
impenetrable wall to Muslim invasion, they at least served as a defense in depth
to entangle, delay and on occasion overcome the enemy expedition. Disciplined
defensive procedures also strengthened municipal resistance to the steady
harassment of frontier raiding, a threat which remained very much alive in the
Alentejo, Extremadura, New Castile and southern Aragon until the thirteenth
century.

---

[28] Beatus of Liebana, *Commentarius super Apocalypsum*, Morgan Library, MS 644, fols.
240v–41r. Beatus of Liebana, *Commentarius super Apocalypsum*, Biblioteca Nacional, Madrid,
MS Vit. 14–2, fols. 266v–67r. Beatus of Liebana, *Commentarius super Apocalypsum*, Morgan
Library, MS 429, fols. 149v–50r. *Gran conquista de Ultramar*, Biblioteca Nacional, Madrid, MS
1.187, fols. 1r–2r. *Cantigas de Santa María*, Library of the Escorial Palace, MS T.I.1, *Cantiga*
28.

This held true because of the military disaster suffered by Alfonso VIII at Alarcos in 1195. The Castilian king endured a serious strategic disaster in that conflict, one that shattered the royal army, the nobility and the military orders for years to come. He lacked a military reserve for over a decade. The Muslims wisely followed up their victory with major expeditions in the summers of 1196 and 1197. The first came up from Seville through Extremadura, capturing the exposed frontier settlements at Montánchez and Trujillo. They then crossed the Tajo and took the newly-founded town of Plasencia as the defenders withdrew from the walls into the keep of the *alcázar* only to capitulate. The Muslims then struck the Castilian Tajo Valley towns, moving in turn against Talavera, Escalona, Maqueda, and devastating the area around Toledo. Discounting the isolated strike against Talavera in 1182, this area had previously been secure for decades. Three newly-conquered towns changed hands. Beyond this, save for a castle or two, this raiding had dented but not broken the frontier shield of towns.

The following year the Andalusians returned to the central Tajo district once more, this time testing the defenses of Maqueda and Toledo, and then swinging north into the Manzanares and Henares valleys to harass Madrid, Alcalá and Guadalajara, finally trying the walls and militias of the municipalities of upper La Mancha at Uclés, Huete, Cuenca, Alcaraz and Alarcón (these last in the process of receiving or soon to receive copies of the *Fuero de Cuenca*). The *Anales Toledanos* likened the two years to a visitation of the "wrath of God." Doubtless the booty was comparatively rich and the disruption of town life substantial, but the Muslims achieved nothing of permanence save three towns and the fortresses of Alarcos and Calatrava.[29] Without any assistance from Alfonso's depleted forces or the military orders, the Tajo Valley and La Manchan towns absorbed the shock of the post-Alarcos assaults and sufficiently discouraged al-Mansūr so as to persuade him to seek a truce with the King of Castile. A more classical example of deep-based defense would be difficult to find. The municipalities constituted a decisive factor in the Christian kings being able to hold their conquered territories even in the aftermath of disasters like Alarcos. To besiege the towns one by one took time and resources, and these were never sufficiently available to the Almohad caliphs. Fifteen years later, the victory of Alfonso at Las Navas de Tolosa in 1212 would end the Islamic threat to these regions for good.

The twelfth century thus provided the ambience in which these tough

---

[29] "Anales Toledanos I," p. 393. *PCG*, p. 682. E. Lévi-Provençal, *La Péninsule Ibérique au Moyen Âge d'après le Kitāb ar-rawd al-Mitār fī habar al-Kitāb d'Ibn ʿAbd al-Muncim al-Ḥīmyarī* (Leiden: E. J. Brill, 1938), pp. 18–19. "Relation de l'expédition de Yaʿqūb al-Mansūr dans la vallé du Tage," ed. E. Lévi-Provençal, in "Un recueil de lettres officielles almohades," *Hesperis* 28 (1941), 66–67. "Anónimo de Madrid," pp. 83–85, 86–89, the only source which adds Guadalajara to the list of towns attacked. Fernando III's concern for the security of Toledo and its defense remained active as late as 1222. "Fernando III concede al Arzobispo Don Rodrigo Jiménez de Rada unas aldeas para seguridad de los habitantes de Toledo (25 Enero 1222)," in *Privilegios reales y viejos documentos de Toledo*, ed. Juan Francisco Rivera Recio, Vol. 1 (Madrid: Joyas Bibliográficas, 1963), p. 7.

municipal dwellers formed their way of life and their outlook. We have no accounts of their difficulties in picking up the pieces after enduring a siege or replacing their damaged crops and vines after a raid. I have noted elsewhere the economic advantages some of them derived from offensive warfare and its periodic bestowal of booty.[30] This study has examined the deficit side of the ledger: defense, sieges, losses. That much of their law is given over to the care and protection of livestock tells us that a fair portion of their wealth was mobile and could be driven out of harm's way or into the perimeter of the walls on some occasions. With their local military forces, they could pursue raiders and sometimes regain some of the goods lost. As with frontier peoples everywhere, the stronger endured the stress, while the weaker probably succumbed. But one conclusion can certainly be drawn. The ability to withstand these dangers over time framed a mentality of taking and holding territory. Formed initially at this point, it persisted as the frontier moved unevenly but relentlessly toward Granada. This mentality, as much as any element we glibly recall in the Columban Quincentenary, explains the ability of this people to construct an empire, whether in the Old World or the New. Thus the crucible of the twelfth century fuses its resources into the hard alloy of the sixteenth.

---

[30] Powers, *Society*, pp. 164–87.

The Medieval German City under Siege

Michael Toch
Hebrew University of Jerusalem

Some time ago, while working on the political history of thirteenth-century Germany for a new edition of the *Cambridge Medieval History*, I was struck by an odd grouping of facts:[1] namely the high intensity of military conflict and war, most of which, at some stage or the other, involved sieges. Such sieges, however, almost never led up to the conquest of the city concerned. Moving from political to military history allows rephrasing of the problem: why, in thirteenth-century Germany, did hardly any of the many military operations involving the siege of a city result in taking the objective? Why were there so many cities besieged and so few conquered? The general answer to the problem is, of course, well-known: the overall predominance of defense over attack during the Middle Ages.[2] The consequence for military tactics has also been noticed: namely the preponderance of the pitched cavalry battle as the way to decide the military issue. For the historical imagination, the flowering of chivalry, with all its ramifications for society and culture, has, of course, been the main occupation, much more than the technical aspects of warfare and tactics. It has been taken as something so ingrained in medieval society and spirit as to be an almost unchanging feature. Such a view, even if generally true, disregards chronology and historical change, which will be the focus of this study. I would like to examine the thirteenth-

---

[1] For the sequence of the political history of thirteenth-century Germany, see my chapter in the forthcoming Vol. 5 of the *New Cambridge Medieval History*, ed. David Abulafia. There is no modern comprehensive military history of medieval Germany available, but see Hans Delbrück, *Geschichte der Kriegskunst im Rahmen der politischen Geschichte*, Part 3 (Berlin: G. Stilke, 1907). For an excellent introduction to the problems of German urban history, see A. Haverkamp, "Die 'frühbürgerliche' Welt im hohen und späten Mittelalter," *Historische Zeitschrift* 221 (1975), 572–602.

[2] Delbrück, p. 335; C. Oman, *A History of the Art of War in the Middle Ages*, Vol. 2 (London: Methuen, 1927), p. 43; J. F. Verbruggen, *The Art of Warfare in Western Europe during the Middle Ages. From the Eighth Century to 1340*, Europe in the Middle Ages, 1 (Amsterdam: North-Holland Publishing Company, 1977), p. 285; Philippe Contamine, *War in the Middle Ages*, trans. Michael Jones (Oxford: Basil Blackwell, 1984), p. 219.

HOLY ROMAN EMPIRE *c.* 1300.

century German conditions and developments leading to the ubiquity of siege warfare, its futility, and, as a corollary, the fact that most military issues were decided in pitched battles of mounted fighters.

I

This study will make a quick tour of the thirteenth-century German military operations. In a first run, it will confine itself to wars at the highest level, between the contenders for the German throne. Such wars occurred at several junctures: after the death of Emperor Henry VI; during the long absences of

Emperor Frederick II; at the time of that rulers final struggle against the papacy; and after the demise of the Staufer dynasty; in short, throughout the thirteenth century. At some point this study will lower its sights and look at an even more rampant form of military rivalry, the one between regional powers.

After Emperor Henry VI's death (1197), the fight for the German crown opened with sorties of both contenders, Otto the Welf and Philip the Staufer, against towns allied to the opponent.[3] None of the objectives of this very first rush – Strasbourg, Goslar, Cologne and Brunswick – were taken. Philip's coronation had to be put off because of his inability to conquer Aachen. The year 1200 saw unsuccessful attempts against the Welf's strongholds, Cologne and Brunswick. In 1201 Otto, in turn, besieged Philip in Speyer, and twice in Erfurt in 1203. Otto was unable to win Halle, Halberstadt and Goslar. Goslar was again besieged, without outcome, in 1204. Only small Weissensee fell to Philip's determined effort in the summer of the same year. In late summer 1205, the Staufer, by now dominant, concentrated a huge effort to subdue Otto's main stronghold, Cologne. Frontal assault being of no avail, a number of rings were laid around the town, the countryside devastated, and a fleet dispatched on the Rhine to cut supplies. Only in the fall of 1206 did Cologne finally submit on honorable terms, which included permission to maintain and extend its fortifications. The town's decision came only after the defeat suffered by its lord, Otto IV, in the pitched battle of Wassenberg (end of June 1206). Thus the first series of thirteenth-century military campaigns, consisting almost exclusively of siege operations, was decided in a field battle of heavily armoured knights and consolidated in an ensuing round of diplomacy.

The next sequence of rivalry, after the assassination of Philip in 1208, was nipped in the bud when the German magnates quickly decided to acknowledge Otto. The transfer of power was effected, in the words of a contemporary source, by turning over "the imperial insignia, the towns, the fortified places and the castles."[4]

The following set of campaigns, after Philip's assassination in 1208, involved Otto IV – now crowned emperor but fallen from papal grace – and Pope Innocent III's client, young Frederick of Sicily, the future emperor. The season of 1213, mainly fought by Otto against Frederick's partisans in the north, was a dreary one. To quote one historian who knew his sources well, "it seldom came to an engagement in the open field; the campaign for the most part consisted of the usual ineffective plundering raids, devastations of property, sieges, but rarely

---

[3] A detailed account of the struggles over the throne can be found in A. L. Poole, "Philip of Swabia and Otto IV," in *Cambridge Medieval History of Europe*, eds. H. M. Gwatkin and J. P. Whitney, Vol. 6 (New York: Macmillan; Cambridge: Cambridge University Press, 1936), pp. 44–79, and Bernhard Töpfer and Evamaria Engel, *Vom staufischen Imperium zum Hausmacht-königtum. Deutsche Geschichte vom Wormser Konkordat 1122 bis zur Doppelwahl von 1314* (Weimar: Bohlau, 1976).

[4] *Chronica S. Petri Erfordensis moderna*, ed. O. Holder-Egger, in *Monumenta Erphesfurten-sia* (Hanover: Hahn, 1899) (=*Monumenta Germaniae Historica. Scriptores rerum Germanica-rum in usu scholarum*, Vol. 31), cited by Töpfer and Engel, p. 176.

captures, of castles."[5] This round of struggle over the throne, although of little appeal to the chronicler then or now, was determined in yet another pitched battle exciting enough to tempt an eminent medievalist into writing a whole book devoted to just that one day, Sunday, July 27, 1214. The reference is, of course, to the day of Bouvines, where in addition to the German side-show, much greater issues were decided.[6] Thus, again, there is a strain between long and muddled series of indecisive sieges and the one short, explosive action in the open field. There is a similar tension, on the level of historical method and understanding, between the tedious tracking of a multitude of actors and actions and the concentration of all forces, albeit intellectual, into the one flash through which everything is resolved.

After Frederick II's ascendancy in 1214–15 there was a prolonged lull in military operations.[7] When he left for Italy and the crusade, a regency government was established, but regional powers came to the fore again, and with them war. Thus in 1227 the regent, the duke of Bavaria, and adolescent King Henry joined forces to occupy the Welf inheritance. Against the Brunswick citizens' determined resistance, these two foremost German magnates were forced to break off their siege.[8] Two years later King Henry was fighting for his father against the papal ban. He managed to confine the papal envoy in Strasbourg but failed twice to take the city. Both times Henry had to dismiss his forces before the supplies could be cut off.[9] In 1235 the young king was finally ranged against his father, who had tired of Henry's unceasing confrontations with the magnates. Henry's last attempt at armed resistance was aimed at the city of Worms, but his army of 5000 men failed in the siege against the town burghers.[10]

Eleven years later, in 1246, when Emperor Frederick's partisans and the German papal allies confronted each other, the bishop of Strasbourg led his forces against the Staufer strongholds in the Alsace. He succeeded in taking Offenburg and a number of castles but failed at the sieges of smaller Schlettstadt and Waisersberg.[11] The summer of the same year, 1246, saw two other contenders, Konrad, son of the emperor, and anti-king Henry Raspe, racing each other for the possession of Frankfurt, the traditional site for holding the imperial

---

[5] Poole, p. 67.

[6] G. Duby, *Le dimanche de Bouvines* (Paris: Gallimard, 1973); English trans. *The Legend of Bouvines: War, Religion, and Culture in the Middle Ages*, trans. Catherine Tihanyi (Berkeley: University of California Press, 1990).

[7] For the latest on Frederick II, see D. Abulafia, *Frederick II: A Medieval Emperor* (London: Allen Lane, Penguin Press, 1988); on the emperor's German activities, see Eduard Winkelmann, *Kaiser Friedrich II*, 2 vols., Jahrbücher der Deutschen Geschichte (Leipzig: Duncker & Humblot, 1889–97) and A. L. Poole, "Germany in the Reign of Frederick II," in *Cambridge Medieval History of Europe*, Vol. 6, pp. 80–109.

[8] Winkelmann, Vol. 1 (1989), pp. 508–09.

[9] Winkelmann, Vol. 2 (1997), pp. 74–76.

[10] Heinrich Boos, *Geschichte der rheinischen Städtekultur mit besonderer Berücksichtigung von Worms*, Vol. 1 (Berlin: J. A. Stargardt, 1897), p. 505.

[11] J. Kempf, *Geschichte des Deutschen Reiches während des grossen Interregnums 1245– 1273* (Würzburg: A. Stuber, 1893), pp. 33–34.

parliamentary assembly (*Reichstag*). When both armies assembled nearby, Henry's military superiority became obvious. After a standoff of some days, Konrad was forced against odds to accept battle and was decisively defeated. He made a run for Frankfurt, followed at the heels by the enemy. Once behind the walls he easily held the city, even though he had previously been beaten in the field.[12] The following winter, which was very cold, his adversary Henry Raspe besieged Ulm, "a strange idea" according to some contemporaries.[13] Lacking provisions, he failed, fell ill and was forced to raise the siege after a couple of weeks. Shortly thereafter he died.

Henry Raspe's successor as papal anti-king was Count William of Holland. His record of sieges is the most complete, including some successes instructive in the long list of failures. I have tabulated his siege operations directed against towns:[14]

Siege	Dates – Duration	Outcome
Kaiserswerd	1½ months	None
Kaiserswerd	2 weeks	None
Aachen	½ year	Surrender
Kaiserswerd	6–8 weeks	Surrender
Boppard	6.2.1249–?	Truce
Castle Ingelheim	6 weeks	Taken
Sachsenhausen	1 week	Taken
Frankfurt	After 15.7.1249	None
Boppard	1–2 weeks	None
Boppard	3 weeks	None
Gelnhausen	Late September 1250	None
Oppenheim		
Boppard	Late August 1251–?	Taken

William's operations, in a very confined theatre of war, up and down the middle Rhine, show a different, very much determined approach to the problem. Yet they also prove the rule: for a full encirclement of Aachen – not an ordinary place but the highly desirable site of legitimate coronation – he needed a crusade preached by the papal envoy to enlist enough troops, which, moreover, had to be kept in the field for a full six months. The moderately sized town of Kaiserswerd was only taken at the third attempt. Boppard fell at the fourth effort, *multis laboribus et expensis*, with troops that, again, had to be recruited through the preaching of a crusade.[15] Some years later, the same Boppard once more held

---

[12] Kempf, pp. 26–27.
[13] Kempf, p. 35.
[14] Kempf, pp. 54–7, 69, 77–87, 84–87, 120.
[15] J. F. Böhmer, *Regesta Imperii*, V, I (Hildesheim: G. Olms, 1971), p. 948, ns. 5048a, 5050a. For political crusades, see J. R. Strayer, "The Political Crusades of the Thirteenth Century," in *A*

out, for about seven weeks, against another contender for the German throne, Richard of Cornwall.[16]

Our last sequence of siege operations concerns King Rudolf of Habsburg, an experienced fighter and tactician, who used siege warfare in a sophisticated way as a means of applying political pressure.[17] In 1276 Rudolf, with an imposing army, besieged Vienna in order to force King Ottokar II of Bohemia into subjection. In 1281 the king's sons did the same to the town and count of Freiburg. 1285 saw King Rudolf in Alsace besieging places both small and big. For the year 1289, a sympathetic chronicler has credited the king with the capture of seventy castles, towns and fortresses in Thuringia.[18] This is undoubtedly an exaggeration, but indicative of the systematic way a resourceful king would go about strengthening his grip on the land. Still, his greatest victory, over King Ottokar of Bohemia, was won at the pitched battle of Dürnkrut (26 August 1278).[19] Rudolf's son, Albrecht, has a similar record as a capable besieger of cities and castles, yet he won his kingship by beating his predecessor at the battle of Göllheim, a pure knights' combat if there ever was one.[20]

A preliminary summing up will thus point to the following features. With contenders more or less evenly matched, such as during the struggles between Otto IV and Philip, sieges of cities were most frequent but to practically no avail. The case was similar after the demise of strong kingship and the rise of regional rivalries following Emperor Frederick's departure from Germany. Sieges could succeed sometimes, as shown by William of Holland's record, but only by great persistence and investment of much time and effort. This was possible only in a limited theatre of war where one could tilt the local balance of power, or with a lot of help from one's papal friend who would go to the extent of preaching a crusade. Siege operations could also be part of a broader strategy, such as the one used by the first Habsburgs, Rudolf and Albrecht. But all through the thirteenth century, the real military decisions were achieved in very limited actions involving a few hundred to a thousand cavalry and some infantry. Yet towns were clearly perceived to be a key factor in the political structure and were thus besieged time and again.

History of the Crusades, ed. K. M. Setton, Vol. 2 (Philadelphia: University of Pennsylvania Press, 1962), pp. 343–76.

[16] A. L. Poole, "The Interregnum in Germany," in *Cambridge Medieval History of Europe*, Vol. 6, p. 119.

[17] On King Rudolf, see O. Redlich, *Rudolf von Habsburg: das deutsche Reich nach dem Untergange des alten Kaisertums* (Innsbruck: Wagner, 1903).

[18] Fritsche Closener, in C. Hegel, *Die Chroniken der deutschen Städte*, Vol. 8 (Leipzig: S. Hirzel, 1870), p. 53.

[19] For an account of the battle, see Oman, pp. 515–26.

[20] Delbrück, p. 434; on Albrecht of Habsburg, see A. Hessel, *Jahrbücher des Deutschen Reiches unter König Albrecht I. von Habsburg*, Jahrbücher der Deutschen Geschichte (München: Duncher & Humblot, 1931).

II

Leaving the upmost level of politics and war, this study will now turn to events on the local and regional level. For this purpose the ongoing feud between the archbishop and city of Cologne was chosen. Their rivalry goes back to the eleventh century and was fought over a host of issues, be it the right to coinage, market, justice, and appointment of urban magistrates.[21] But time and again such constitutional arguments boiled down to the simple question of holding power in the city, the control of gates, ramparts and towers, and the stationing of soldiers. Although mostly a local affair, it involved two major powers, the archbishop – one of the foremost magnates of his day – ranged against the richest and biggest city in Germany. Cologne has already been shown to withstand concentrated assaults during the throne struggle of the early century. There were to be many more sieges under the rule of two archbishops, Konrad von Hochstaden (1238–61) and his successor Engelbert von Falkenburg (1261–74).[22] The following is a purely one-sided account, based on contemporary and later chronicles emanating from the citizenry of Cologne.[23] By the mid-thirteenth century, the old-established rivalry with the archbishop had once again come to a head, the issue being this time the right to coinage. After a breakdown of negotiations in March 1252, Archbishop Konrad left the city in anger and organized his forces upriver in Andernach, including fourteen ships of war which were to transport the soldiers down the Rhine to the city. Cologne, too, prepared for war, entering into an alliance with the count of Jülich. The landing was foiled by the city's fleet anchoring at the embankment, forcing the archbishop to disembark downstream. From there Cologne was bombarded, with some damage to one house which was penetrated by a stone to the depth of five roof slates. Such efforts were greeted with scorn by the chronicler:

> he [the archbishop] imagined to win Cologne by throwing.[24]

As a last resort a wooden belfry fitted with a device of Greek fire was put on a deep-bottomed wine-barque, which was to be sent into the thick tangle of ships defending the embankment. But somehow this, too, failed: the wine-ship

---

[21] For the political background it is still worthwhile to consult the introduction by C. Hegel, Vol. 12 (1875), pp. i–liii. For the institutional structure, see F. Lau, *Entwicklung der kommunalen Verfassung und Verwaltung der Stadt Köln bis zum Jahre 1396*, Gesellschaft für Rheinische Geschichtskunde (Bonn: H. Behrendt, 1898).

[22] On the two archbishops, see M. Groten, "Konrad von Hochstaden," *Lexikon des Mittelalters* 5 (1991), 1351–52, and K. Militzer, "Engelbert II. von Falkenburg," *Lexikon des Mittelalters* 3 (1986), 1918.

[23] All of them printed in Vols. 12 (1875) and 13 (1876) of Hegel, and thence forth cited by the name of the chronicler. For an evaluation of contemporary historiography, the introduction of H. Cardauns in Hegel, Vol. 12, pp. liv–xciv, is still worthwhile reading.

[24] Hagen, *Boich van der stede Colne*, in Hegel, Vol. 12, p. 43: "hei wainde mit werpene Colne gewinnen."

itself burned down and the Greek fire spilled onto the river and dispersed. The chronicler's comment:

> some man thinks: thus it shall go,
> but God let it go differently.[25]

Leading nowhere, this round ended in compromise, mediated by none less than Albertus Magnus, the Dominican lector at Cologne.

The next encounter in 1257 returned to regular warfare. A personal feud between a relative of the archbishop and one of the patrician families ruling Cologne escalated into full-scale war which the patricians were, however, able to turn into a fight for urban freedom. The military moves appear to have been the following. The archbishop moved his forces from Bonn to a camp in the vicinity of the city. A force of four hundred, most probably cavalry, made an attempt at one of the gates, but was thrown back. The defenders of Cologne are called by a contemporary source *die betschelere van Colne*, the bachelors, meaning either the younger members of the patriciate or hired mounted soldiers. A later source names *die burger mit iren souldeneren*, the citizens and their soldiers, a denotation which would support our reading of mercenaries.[26] Not a big clash, as the only victim was one of the archbishop's knights taken prisoner. But it was the opening to a long siege, in which all surface and river approaches to the city were cut. Finally the city's mounted forces, under the experienced leadership of Count Dietrich von Falkenburg, sought battle and prevailed at Frechen, a village in the vicinity.[27] The sequence to this victory was again political, mediation by five clerics of Cologne, led as before by Albertus Magnus. In the end Archbishop Konrad did, indeed, make his entrance into the city, not by military means, but rather as an ally of the middling guild artisans, whom he helped to power against the patricians.

Such concord was not maintained by the next archbishop, Engelbert of Falkenburg, a brother of the town's military commander seen in action a few years earlier. Engelbert, a man of violent character, pushed the popular party into the arms of the patricians. Thus one day in early summer 1262, the burghers were summoned by alarm-bells rung all over the town. The chroniclers are insistent that everyone, rich and poor, men and women, assembled in the streets. Using the equipment from the town's arsenal, the burghers dug for three days under the walls of the archbishop's main stronghold, the Bayenturm near the Rhine, and then stormed this as well as its twin tower on the other side of town and the gates held by the archbishop's garrison.[28]

The archbishop reacted, instinctively one might guess, by besieging the town.

---

[25] Hagen, p. 44:
> mennich mensche denkit: dus sal it gain,
> und got deit it in anders gain.

[26] Hagen, p. 48; *Köhlhoffsche Chronik* in Hegel, Vol. 13, p. 555.

[27] Delbrück, pp. 381–82.

[28] Hagen, pp. 89–97; *Köhlhoffsche Chronik*, pp. 584–87.

Upon consideration, however, he allowed himself to be persuaded by his allies to break off operations. Their argument, attributed by our chronicler to the count of Guelder, goes as follows:

> you shall lie before Cologne seven years . . .
> without damaging one of her hairs
> you will eat up everything Saint Peter (the
> archbishopric) can provide
> before you are able to win her[29]

This is reminiscent of the famous advice given to Count Geoffrey Martel of Anjou by his seneschal, while besieging Tours in 1044:

> Leave the city which you are besieging.
> Sieges waste time, and the town is rarely taken.[30]

An accord signed in June 1262 reestablished the patrician government of Cologne. The archbishop was unable to abide by these facts of power but also equally unable to change them. Our chroniclers, careful as usual not to offend the adversary too much, make use of the device of the evil counsellor and tell of yet another scheme whispered into the archbishop's ear: to invite the ruling families of Cologne to a judicial deliberation in his great hall and then let his brother (the same former military leader of Cologne) take them all prisoner. This scheme lead instead to the capture, in 1263, of both the archbishop and his brother, the count. Next came, probably in 1264, a new attempt to gain power by helping the commons to oust the patricians. This was prevented by the victory of the patricians in a number of street battles (this is, indeed, amidst a heavy stretch of political fighting within the city). Next, in September 1265, there was yet another effort to gain the city by treason, the failure of which led to a new siege. It was foiled in the following manner: the count of Cleve, one of the archbishop's allies, present with his troops in the besiegers camp, was sleeping in his tent. He dreamt of Saint Ursula and her eleven thousand virgins keeping watch on the city's walls. This was enough to convince the count and his brethren-in-arms to leave the archbishop's camp, thus perforce terminating the siege. In a last attempt, in 1268, the archbishop and the duke of Limburg allied themselves with a patrician faction exiled from the city. They hired a man, disguised as a beggar, to dig a tunnel under the wall near the monastery of St. Pantaleon. This passageway, almost finished, was discovered, however, and the citizens made

---

[29] Hagen, p. 101:

> ain leicht ir vinr Colne seven jair
> dat sain ich inch sunder vair
> ir enmoicht eme schaden neit ein hair
> ir soilt dat minste zo dem meisten,
> wat sen Peter maich geleisten,
> verzeren e ir si moicht gewinnen, . . .

[30] *Chroniques des comtes d'Anjou et des seigneurs d'Amboise*, eds. L. Halphen and R. Poupardin, pp. 55–56, cited by Verbruggen, p. 251.

ready. In the ensuing scuffle the archbishop's brother, who really must have been an intrepid fighter, was killed together with six hundred more.

So much for Cologne. Here siege operations were a central part of the enduring and usually unsuccessful effort by the archbishop to regain control of his unruly, rich and powerful city. The town itself was heavily fortified, prepared to withstand attacks from land and river. In case of need, it allied itself to other regional powers, and it felt sure of the protection by God and the saints. State-of-the-art attack technologies, such as catapults and Greek fire, made little impression. With forces evenly matched, sieges were expensive because they took such a long time and necessitated great numbers of paid troops. Thus recourse must necessarily be had to other means – treason and secret schemes, alliances with factions within the city. In most cases the meager outcome led to negotiations which allowed for a withdrawal from confrontation and restored the status quo. But there was also pitched battle, initiated by the besieger as part of a sudden attack, or by the besieged because of their reluctance to suffer a lengthy blockade so damaging to trade. Indeed, town and archbishop finally parted ways in 1288, when the citizens of Cologne, allied to the duke of Brabant, were victorious against their lord and his helpers at the battle of Worringen.[31] This most important military engagement in the medieval history of Cologne was again a pitched battle of mounted fighters.[32]

II

I believe I am now in a better position to answer the questions posed at the beginning of this study. First, the ubiquity of siege operations should be viewed as a by-product of the fractured political landscape into which Germany and its sub-regions developed by the thirteenth century.[33] Few of the contenders for the German throne or the regional and local forces were able, for longer periods of time, to tilt the balance of power in any given area, be it Germany as a whole or one of its territories: thus the universality of the pitched battle as a device to break stalemate. It is of course possible to view such battles as belonging to the order of the sacred, as something of a duel, the "remedy applied to war when it worsens."[34] But not all contenders were as eager as the historian of mentalities to acknowledge such divine judgment. Before or after the trial, contemporaries,

[31] For the political background and consequences of the battle of Worringen, see the special volume of *Blätter für deutsche Landesgeschichte* 124 (1988), 1–453. The latter also appeared as a separate issue, see W. Janssen and H. Stehkämper, *Der Tag bei Worringen. 5. Juni 1288* (Düsseldorf: Selbstverlag des Nordrhein-Westfälischen Hauptstaatsarchivs, 1988).

[32] For a concise account of the battle, see Verbruggen, pp. 237–48.

[33] The most convincing newer assessments of central and late medieval Germany are A. Haverkamp, *Medieval Germany 1056–1273* (Oxford: Oxford University Press, 1988) and P. Moraw, *Von offener Verfassung zu gestalteter Verdichtung. Das Reich im späten Mittelalter 1250 bis 1490*, Propyläen-Studienausgabe (Frankfurt-am-Main-Berlin: Ullstein, 1989).

[34] Duby (English trans.), pp. 108, 110–13.

rather than admit defeat, preferred to fall back on fortified places, just as King Konrad did when he fled into Frankfurt after his defeat by Henry Raspe in 1246. With combatants seeking shelter behind city walls, sieges were inevitable. Thus every war contained at least an element of siege warfare, and many campaigns were just a series of sieges. There was also the relative poverty of protagonists to reinforce the ubiquity of siege warfare (except maybe for the rare figure of Frederick II at the height of his power, who had no need of an army at all to subdue resistance). By relative poverty I mean the inability of most contenders to afford to keep armies in the field for any long period of time. Sheltering in a town enabled one to discharge part of the troops, making use instead of the fortifications, the inhabitants and their military equipment. One need not mention the relative comfort of lodging in town rather than sleeping out in camp.

Why did most sieges fail? For this I believe a number of factors to be responsible: first, technology. No revolutionary attack weapons are to be found in thirteenth-century Germany. Catapults, belfries, battering rams, the different techniques of mining, and Greek fire were all well-known. The only new weapon was the trebuchet, introduced in 1213 by Otto IV from Italy, where he had been campaigning in the previous years.[35] It proved devastating only to old-style fortifications, those builde of wood and earth. What was needed for a successful siege of a modern town were large numbers of troops and a sizable work force. To come back to William of Holland besieging Aachen from April to October 1248: only the arrival of new crusaders from William's own homeland of Holland and Frisia made possible the full encirclement of Aachen. While hunger took its slow toll on the defenders, the attackers dammed a stream to flood the besieged city and submerge a whole third of its area. With all this devastation, the town still held out for half a year, giving in only after a false rumour spread regarding the death of Emperor Frederick II. It took a lot of besieging to make one's way into a town.

Now for defense technology. The building of walls is just one aspect of the very long process of urban growth.[36] But this process was considerably accelerated and extended during the thirteenth century. In that time most of the older German towns replaced their earth and wood works with stone walls. Over time, fortifications were extended by moats, towers and gates, and newer quarters and suburbs included within the significantly enlarged ring of walls. Again Cologne provides a good example, but many other cities, too, were widely extended in

---

[35] Contamine, p. 104; Bern Ulrich Hucker, *Kaiser Otto IV,* Monumenta Germaniae Historica, Schriften Band 34 (Hanover: Hahn, 1990), pp. 555–57; on the trebuchet itself, see D. Hill, "Trebuchets," *Viator* 4 (1973), 99–114; on other attack technologies, see *Lexikon des Mittelalters*, entries "Antwerk," "Blide," "Katze."

[36] For the following, see C. Haase, "Die mittelalterliche Stadt als Festung. Wehrpolitisch-militärische Einflußbedingungen im Werdegang der mittelalterlichen Stadt," in *Die Stadt des Mittelalters*, ed. C. Haase, Vol. 1, Wege der Forschung, 243–45 (Darmstadt: Wissenschaftliche Buchges., 1969), pp. 377–407; Hans Planitz, *Die deutsche Stadt im Mittelalter* (Wien: Boehlau-Verlag, 1965), pp. 229–49.

the thirteenth century.[37] Such shiny new walls could, indeed, serve as a powerful symbol and focus of urban self-consciousness.[38] They were long-lived enough to be still seen exactly in such a way by nineteenth-century liberals, as witnessed for instance by the illustrations to Boos' very influential volume *Geschichte der rheinischen Städtekultur*.[39] Many of the numerous smaller new towns, founded during that century as military outposts rather than as centers of trade and industry,[40] could boast from their very beginnings expensive stone works.

Who initiated and financed these modernizations? Since the end of the twelfth century, the control over fortifications in the older towns was increasingly transferred from the lords, that is king, bishops and lay aristocracy, to the urban magistrates.[41] Indeed, such control served as a powerful engine for the development of yet other aspects of independent town government: taxation geared specifically towards the building and upkeep of new defenses; urban forces commanded by patricians; town arsenals; and the whole machinery of alliances and mercenaries seen in action in the case of Cologne. All this necessitated large sums of money, to which in our period, the time of the commercial revolution in Germany, only towns with their merchant and artisan classes had access.[42] Even where lords remained in control of towns, the practical task of funding such increasingly expensive fortification works was transferred to the citizenry and its representatives. Thus in an extant tax-list of 1241–42, rebates are granted to a large number of royal towns expressively for the building of walls.[43]

I have mentioned the military leadership of urban forces recruited from the traditional warring classes. Indeed, hired knights appear time and again as important elements in the major military engagements fought by towns. Organized units of foot soldiers – what one might expect to be the main military asset put in the field by towns – are almost absent during our period. I have found only one engagement of the thirteenth century in which urban foot-soldiers played any considerable role: the battle of Hausbergen between the city of Strasbourg and its bishop (1262). Here a corps of archers from Strasbourg, under the command of two knights, by rapid and disciplined cross-bow fire, cut off the enemy's cavalry from its supporting infantry, thus enabling the decisive horse charge to be delivered. This charge was supported by another corps of

---

[37] Planitz, p. 15.

[38] H. Koller, "Die mittelalterliche Stadtmauer als Grundlage städtischen Selbstbewußtseins," in *Stadt und Krieg*, eds. B. Kirchgässner and G. Scholz (Sigmaringen: Thorbecke, 1989), pp. 9–25.

[39] Boos, Vol. 3 (1899), after p. ix.

[40] Haase, p. 390.

[41] Haase, p. 396.

[42] For the thirteenth century the most detailed accounts were preserved for the town of Koblenz, see Max Bär, *Der Koblenzer Mauernbau Rechnungen 1276–1289*, Publikationen der Gesellschaft für Rheinische Geschichtskunde, 5 (Leipzig: Gesellschaft für Rheinische Geschichtskunde, 1888). For later periods, see below n. 49.

[43] *Monumenta Germanicae Historica. Constitutiones et acta publica imperatorum et regum*, ed. J. Schwalm, Vol. 3 (Hannover: Hahn, 1904), p. 1ff.

pikemen who outflanked the enemy and cut down the bishop's horses.[44] In general, companies of archers, pikemen and engineers marching under the banners of their craft-guilds, the military drill, the archery competitions and all the other manifestations of burgher bellicosity were yet to come. They were a by-product, I believe, of the intense political struggles between patricians and artisans in the fourteenth century. What warlike spirit originally developed in the towns belonged to the patrician clans, part of which had their origins in the fighting ministeriales class of the twelfth century.[45] Some of them were living in fortified towers, many of them aspired to a knightly way of life, and all of them were rich enough to equip themselves for mounted warfare.[46] In our period the ordinary citizenry seems to have been organized mainly for defensive purposes, manning the walls, in addition to their main contribution of paying taxes. Thus I again come back to money, the sinews of war. In Worms, for instance, there was a clear division of tasks: the citizens financed the building and upkeep of walls by a regular tax levied on the sale of wine (the *Ungeld*), while the Jews paid special taxes for the military campaigns undertaken by their town.[47]

Stone fortifications, the very size of cities, the sheer numbers of population, ruling patricians aspiring to a knightly way of life, urban arsenals, access to military alliances – all these together made the towns of the thirteenth century into military powers in their own right. Therefore the main factor appears to have been not military technology as such, but the social and economic growth of which the thirteenth-century towns were the outriders and main beneficiaries. This is what provided them, rather than other social forces, with almost exclusive access to the means of acquiring military defense technology and fighting forces. And this is what made towns so hard to conquer. Such urban dynamism was, on the one hand, rooted in century-long processes of institutional, social, and economic growth. But, on the other, the strength of the German urban movement is also directly attributable to the weakness of kingship during the thirteenth century, to the need of town populations for secure trade routes, to the will of urban oligarchies to preserve and extend their freedom of action against other aggressive forces – such as the scheming archbishop of Cologne. Thus a phenomenon like the Rhenish town-league, founded in 1254 as an alliance between Mainz and Worms, grew to encompass over seventy towns. It was equipped with a river-fleet of armed ships and appeared so formidable that the

---

[44] Verbruggen, pp. 196–97; Delbrück, pp. 383–88.

[45] The problem of *ministeriales* has been a pet question of scholarship: Benjamin Arnold, *German Knighthood 1050–1300* (Oxford: Clarendon Press, 1985). For their place in towns, see E. Maschke and J. Sydow, *Stadt und Ministerialität. Protokoll der IX. Arbeitstagung des Arbeitskreises für Südwestdeutsche Stadtgeschichtsforschung, Freiburg i. Br., 13.–15. November 1970* (Stuttgart: W. Kohlhammer, 1973); and Josef Fleckenstein, *Herrschaft und Stand. Untersuchungen zur Sozialgeschichte im 13. Jahrhundert*, Veröffentlichungen des Max-Planck-Instituts für Geschichte 51 (Göttingen: Vandenhoeck & Ruprecht, 1977).

[46] On fortified towers in towns, see Herwig Ebner, "Die Burg als Forschungsproblem mittelalterlicher Verfassungsgeschichte," in *Die Burgen im deutschen Sprachraum*, ed. H. Patze, Vol. 1, Vorträge und Forschungen 19 (Sigmaringen: J. Thorbecke, 1976), p. 13.

[47] Boos, Vol. 2 (1898), p. 26.

Rhenish archbishops and bishops, magnates and nobles, and finally also the king, thought it wise to join on.[48]

One might rejoice at the ascendancy of the forces of historical progress. In the following late medieval centuries towns were to expend even greater sums of money on their fortifications.[49] Urban forces, too, became much better organized, but the old pattern of reliance on aristocratic military leadership and the hiring of mounted knights prevailed. Still, the superiority of urban military might, founded during the thirteenth century and augmented in the following period, was to be short-lived. Territorial lords also learned to employ their towns as military strongholds, and castle building was to go on throughout the entire Middle Ages. Most important, during the fourteenth century the development of the financial machinery of territorial lords bridged the gap of wealth created by town burghers in the previous period.[50] By the end of the fourteenth century, the ascendancy of towns, urban forces and urban defences was coming to an end, as witnessed by the sweeping defeats of town-leagues. Gunpowder and cannonry only came slowly and late and cannot be held responsible for the long-term shift in the balance of power. In the longer view, the situation created during the thirteenth century and described in detail here was to be but an interlude between much more extended periods of aristocratic superiority. Politically, as well as militarily, the Swiss syndrome was not to hold for the German towns, most of which were again to become subjects, not of one distant king, but of much nearer and therefore much mightier lords.

---

[48] See the map of the league in Moraw, p. 207. See also Arno Buschmann, "Der Rheinische Bund von 1254–1257. Landfriede, Städte, Fürsten und Reichsverfassung im 13. Jahrhundert," in *Kommunale Bündnisse Oberitaliens und Oberdeutschlands im Vergleich*, ed. H. Maurer, Vorträge und Forschungen 33 (Sigmaringen: J. Thorbecke, 1987), pp. 167–212.

[49] See the latest contribution to the large literature on late medieval urban war-finances: Gerhard Fouquet, "Die Finanzierung von Krieg und Verteidigung in oberdeutschen Städten des späten Mittelalters (1400–1500)," in *Stadt und Krieg*, pp. 41–82.

[50] H. Patze, *Der deutsche Territorialstaat im 14. Jahrhundert*, 2 vols, Vorträge und Forschungen, 13–14 (Sigmaringen: J. Thorbecke, 1970–71).

Siege Warfare and the *Bonnes Villes* of France during the Hundred Years War

Michael Wolfe
The Pennsylvania State University, Altoona Campus

Towns generally do not spring to mind when thinking about the Hundred Years War; instead we recall the dramatic battles of Crécy, Poitiers, and Agincourt; the dynastic personalities later immortalized by Shakespeare; or the chivalrous sentiments and encounters celebrated by Froissart and Christine de Pisan.[1] However, it was precisely during this long complicated struggle that the *bonnes villes* (medium-sized cities) of France came into their own politically and militarily, helping in the process to define the nascent outlines of modern France, a country at once more unified yet still enjoying a considerable measure of local self-rule until the triumph of absolutism later in the seventeenth century.[2] War more than royal decree spurred these changes forward; indeed, while dynastic rulers could start a war fairly easily, they found it very difficult to retain control over the armies they unleashed. Rather than increase royal control, the demands of war created strains that militarized society in ways which altered

---

[1] M. G. A. Vale, *The Angevin Legacy and the Hundred Years War, 1230–1340* (Oxford: Blackwell, 1990); J. Maddicott, "The Origins of the Hundred Years War," *History Today* 36 (1986), 31–37; Peter F. Ainsworth, *Jean Froissart and the Fabric of History: Truth, Myth and Fiction in the "Chroniques"* (Oxford: Clarendon, 1990); P. Contamine, "Froissart. Art militaire, pratique et conception de la guerre," in *Froissart: Historian*, ed. J. J. N. Palmer (Totawa NJ: Boydell Press, 1981), pp. 132–44. Christine de Pisan, *Le livre de fais et bonnes meurs du sage roy Charles Quint*, ed. S. Solente, 2 vols. (Paris: H. Champion, 1936–41) and *The Book of Fayttes of Armes and of Chyvalrye*, trans. W. Caxton, ed. A. T. P. Byles, Early English Texts Society, 189 (London: Early English Texts Society, 1932); C. Gauvard, "Christine de Pisan, a-t-elle eu une idée politique?," *Revue historique* 250 (1973), 417–30.

[2] Bernard Chevalier, *Les bonnes villes de France du XIVe au XVIe siècles* (Paris: Aubier & Montaigne, 1982), lists some 240 such towns in his index. See also G. Maudvech, "La 'bone ville': origine et sens de l'expression," *Annales économies, sociétés et civilisations* 27 (1972), 1441–48. Numerous individual studies exist, including J-P Leguay, *Un réseau urbain au Moyen Âge: les villes du duché de Bretagne aux XIVe et XVe siècles* (Paris: Maloine, 1981); A. Castaldo, *Seigneurs, villes et pouvoir royal en Languedoc: le consulat médiéval d'Agde (XIIe–XIVe siècles)* (Paris: A. & J. Picard, 1974); P. Desportes, *Reims et les rémois aux XIIIe et XIVe siècles* (Paris: A. & J. Picard, 1979); and A. and S. Plaisse, *La vie municipale à Evreux pendant la guerre de Cents Ans* (Evreux: Connaissance de l'Eure, 1978).

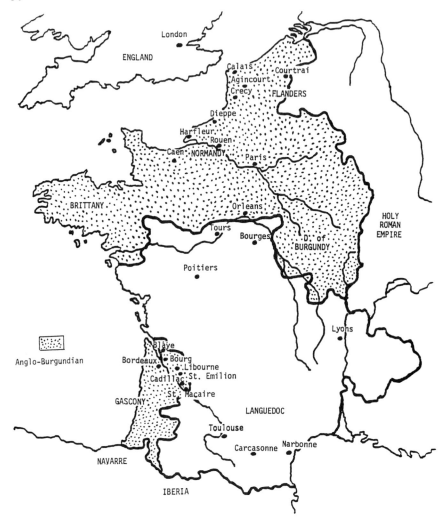

FRANCE *c.* 1429.

both the rule of kings and the social order. Nowhere did the forces of change during the Hundred Years War come together more completely than in siege warfare – be they reflected in the massive walls that cities constructed or the daunting logistics of attack. Indeed, as a result of this long conflict, the *bonnes villes* realized a degree of independence and regional sway which the crown had to include in its future calculations to achieve greater power.[3]

---

[3] Recent studies of the Hundred Years War include Jonathan Sumption, *The Hundred Years War: Volume I. Trial by Battle* (London: Faber & Faber, 1990); C. T. Allmand, *The Hundred Years War: England and France at War, c. 1300–c. 1450* (Cambridge: Cambridge University Press, 1988) and *Society at War. The Experience of England and France during the Hundred Years War*

Hundreds of sieges, large and small, took place during the Hundred Years War because towns held a new strategic importance that changed the way kings fought for as well as defined their dynastic objectives. Towns provided a place to garrison soldiers and muster companies, stockpile food and armaments, assemble a skilled work force, and procure a ready source of cash with which to underwrite a campaign. Sieges punctuated the various stages of this protracted war by redefining both territorial holdings and the respective resources each side commanded. The military significance of cities quite naturally derived from their position as commercial and population centers, which since the eleventh century had grown to dominate the regional economy of much of medieval France. So much so, in fact, that by 1300, however much crowned heads and feudal princes may have aspired to rule the territories listed in their lengthy titles, they increasingly found effective control over their domains required cooperation from the towns. We need here merely recall the contrasting fortunes of the dukes of Burgundy, who prospered by playing to the urban crowd, and the dukes of Flanders, who did not.[4] The English enjoyed so much success against the French, at least until the siege of Orléans in 1429, not least because they, too, had early on adjusted to the new power represented by cities. When Charles VII successfully followed suit after 1430, French resurgence became nearly irresistible.[5]

French kings up to Charles VII failed to acknowledge the new importance of towns in part because they shared the disdain heaped by French aristocrats on bourgeois culture. The memoirs of Boucicaut, Jean de Bueil's *Le Jouvencel* and Froissart's *Chroniques* mention many sieges, but rarely beyond their symbolic value as prizes to be won by noble *gens d'armes* (men-at-arms).[6] As we all

(New York: Barnes & Noble Books, 1973); Kenneth Fowler, *The Age of Plantagenet and Valois: The Struggle for Supremacy 1328–1498* (New York: Putney, 1967); J. Favier, *La guerre de Cent Ans* (Paris: Fayard, 1980); A. Leguai, *La guerre de Cent Ans* (Paris: Nathan, 1974).

4 Guy Llewelyn Thompson, *Paris and Its People Under English Rule: The Anglo-Burgundian Regime 1420–1436* (Oxford: Clarendon Press, 1991); P. Bonenfant, "Bruxelles et la Maison de Bourgogne," in *Bruxelles au XVe siècle* (Brussels: Pro Civitate, 1953), pp. 21–32; Bernard Doumerc, "La politique des 'rois-marchands' au XVe siècle: l'enjeu des Flandres," in *La 'France Anglaise' au Moyen Âge. Congrès national des Sociétés Savants*, Vol. 1 (Paris: Édition du CTHS, 1988), pp. 61–71; Richard Vaughan, *John the Fearless. The Growth of Burgundian Power* (New York: Barnes & Noble Books, 1966) and *Philip the Good. The Apogee of Burgundy* (Harlow: Longmans, 1970); Henry S. Lucas, *The Low Countries and the Hundred Years War* (Ann Arbor: University of Michigan Press, 1929).

5 A. Leguai, "The Relations between the Towns of Burgundy and the French Crown in the Fifteenth Century," in *The Crown and Local Communities in England and France in the Fifteenth Century*, eds. J. R. L. Highfield and R. Jeffs (Gloucester: Alan Sutton, 1981), pp. 23–46, and R. H. Hilton, *English and French Towns in Feudal Society: A Comparative Study* (Cambridge: Cambridge University Press, 1992).

6 Philippe Contamine, "The French Nobility and the War," in *The Hundred Years War*, ed. Kenneth Fowler (London: Macmillan, 1971), pp. 135–62; J. B. Henneman, "The Military Class and the French Monarchy in the Late Middle Ages," *American Historical Review* 83 (1978), 946–65; Maurice Keen, *Chivalry* (New Haven: Yale University Press, 1984); M. G. A. Vale, *War and Chivalry: Warfare and Aristocratic Culture in England, France and Burgundy at the End of the Middle Ages* (Athens: University of Georgia Press, 1981); *Le livre des fais du bon messire*

know, this premium on noble *élan* led to the French disasters at Crécy, Poitiers, and Agincourt. Yet while such battles obviously affected the course of the war, they were exceptional encounters that did not determine its final outcome. This lay rather in the dynamics involved in siege warfare, which required both the attacker and defender to bring to bear a sustained concentration of resources, technologies, and new forms of organization that taken together transformed the nature of war.[7] Major battles naturally affected the fate of towns in that the large forces so involved – upwards of 25,000 fighters at Agincourt alone – could only be assembled by draining garrisons of men and materiel, thus leaving the towns relatively unprotected. Both sides thus ran the risk of losing substantial territory in the event of defeat, which visited the French more often than not until 1430. Over time towns took steps to avoid such an eventuality, not only by responding halfheartedly to the crown's call to arms, but also by organizing their own militias – a trend increasingly apparent after 1370.[8] These moves explain in part why the French defeat at Poitiers, which resulted in the capture of King John the Good, did not lead to the same loss of territory suffered earlier after Crécy.[9] If control of territory hinged on control of its towns, then a town's ability to resist a siege ultimately determined who controlled that territory. One measure of the changing balance of power in siege warfare can be found by looking at city walls. Urban fortifications in France had developed sporadically up to the four-teenth century, in large part because there was no pressing need before the Hundred Years War for towns to invest in their own defense.[10] Philip Augustus' decision back in the late twelfth century to enclose Paris within a ring of walls

---

Jean le Maingre, dit Bouciquaut, mareschal de France et gouverneur de Jennes, ed. D. Lalande (Geneva: Droz, 1985); D. Lalande, *Boucicaut: étude d'une biographie heroïque* (Geneva: Droz, 1988); J. Vale, *Edward III and Chivalry: Chivalric Society and Its Context, 1270–1350* (Wood-bridge: Boydell Press, 1982); A. Artonne, "Froissart historien. Le siège et la prise de la Roche-Vendeix," *Bibliothèque de l'école des Chartes* 110 (1952), 89–107; G. T. Diller, "Froissart's *Chroniques*: Knightly Adventures and Warrior Forays. Que chascun se retire en sa chascunière," *Fifteenth Century Studies* 12 (1987), 17–26.

   [7] A lengthy list of all the equipment necessary for a successful siege can be found in Jean de Bueil, comte de Sancerre, *Le Jouvencel*, eds. Camille Favre and Léon Lecestre, Vol. 2 (Paris, 1887), pp 31–54. See also Philippe Contamine, *Guerre, état et société à la fin du Moyen Âge. étude sur les armées des rois de France, 1337–1494* (Paris: La Haye–Mouton, 1972), and Michael Powicke, *Military Obligation in Medieval England* (Oxford: Clarendon Press, 1962).

   [8] Such moves received justification by reference to the right of self-defense. Philippe Contamine, "L'idée de guerre à la fin du Moyen Âge: aspects juridiques et éthiques," in *La France aux XIVe et XVe siècles. Hommes, mentalités, guerre et paix* (London: Variorum Re-prints, 1981), ch. 13. M. Garsonnin, *Le guet et les compagnies du guet à Orléans. études historiques précédées de notes sur le guet de Paris* (Orléans, 1898); and G. Jarousseau, "Le guet, l'arrière-guet et la garde en Poitou pendant la guerre de Cents Ans," *Bulletin de la société des antiquitaires de l'Ouest* 8 (1965), 159–202.

   [9] J. E. Morris, "The Archers at Crécy," *English Historical Review* 12 (1897), 427–36; J. Viard, "La campagne de juillet-août 1346 et la bataille de Crécy," *Le Moyen Âge*, 2nd series 27 (1926), 1–84; R. Cazelles, *Société politique, noblesse et couronne sous Jean le Bon et Charles V* (Geneva: Droz, 1982).

   [10] J. Scheider, "Problèmes d'histoire urbaine dans la France médiévale," *Bulletin philol-ogique et historique* 3 (1977), 23–54.

was exceptional, yet even here urban growth in the capital soon burst out of its new confines.[11] Many towns in France simply did not have walls; those that did often had walls dating back to Gallo-Roman times which did little more than define the city's original core. Much the same can be said of the ecclesiastical precincts in and around the cathedral, which offered at best very limited protection in cases of emergency. Even the handful of towns which had walls of fairly recent construction often let them fall into disrepair given the sizeable ongoing costs required for their upkeep.[12] Several reasons explain why the *bonnes villes* displayed such patent disregard for their safety: the lack of immediate threats; the ill-defined nature of municipal government and jurisdiction, particularly in relation to the competing claims of the crown, church, and local seigneurs; underdeveloped revenue sources to provide the necessary capital for fortifications; uncertainty as to where to draw the line between the city, with its sprawling *faubourgs* (suburbs), and the outside world; and, lastly, a willingness on the part of the citizenry to shoulder the enormous burdens entailed by self-defense.

These hidden vulnerabilities became all too apparent during the early stages of the Hundred Years War. Overcoming them required not just a change in the towns, but also a break with the military policies put in place earlier by Philip IV and his sons. No one need be reminded that the Achilles heel of the French monarchy, all the way down to Louis XVI, was taxation. Although innovative, the encouragement of representative institutions after 1300, from the Estates General down to regional assemblies, did not appreciably improve the crown's ability to raise money to wage war, as witnessed in their various disastrous conflicts with the Flemings, most notably Courtrai (1302).[13] Such policies raised suspicions that tended to alienate the two groups in French society who could provide immediate cash to finance the monarchy's adventures, namely, the church and the towns. While France eagerly sought war with the English later in the 1330s, it could hardly hope to prosecute it effectively without its financial house in order. Excessive borrowing and periodic currency devaluations offered momentary solutions that exacerbated the long-term problem of war finance for the French.[14] Only after the setbacks of the 1340s did Philip VI's government begin to address these shortcomings by linking reform of the antiquated and unwieldy feudal host with a new, cooperative relationship with the towns.[15] The

---

[11] Roger Rottmann, *Murs et mémoires: la construction de Paris* (Paris: Syros-Alternatives, 1988); A. Bonnardot, *Dissertations archéologiques sur les anciens enceintes de Paris, suivies de recherches sur les portes fortifiées qui dependaient de ces enceintes* (Paris, 1852).

[12] F. L. Ganshof, *Étude sur le développement des villes entre Loire et Rhin au Moyen Âge* (Paris: Presses Universitaires de France, 1943), pp. 39–45.

[13] P. S. Lewis, "The Failure of the French Medieval Estates," *Past and Present* 23 (1962), 3–24; J. R. Strayer and C. H. Taylor, *Studies in Early French Taxation* (Cambridge MA: Harvard University Press, 1931), pp. 22–94.

[14] J. Lafaurie, *Les monnaies des rois de France* (Paris: E. Bourgey, 1951); H. Miskimin, *Money, Prices and Foreign Exchange in Fourteenth-Century France* (New Haven: Yale University Press, 1963); R. Cazelles, "Quelques réflexions à propos des mutations de la monnaie royale française (1295–1360)," *Le Moyen Âge* 72 (1966), 83–105, 251–78.

[15] J. B. Henneman, *Royal Taxation in Fourteenth-Century France. The Development of War*

French crown worked to commute the troop contingents contributed by towns into straight cash payments to be used to hire foreign mercenaries, first the Scots and then Swiss pikemen later in the fifteenth century.[16] Needless to say, it was a task much more easily said than done.

In contrast to the many structural weaknesses plaguing the French effort, the English entered the war with a number of distinct advantages beyond the much vaunted longbow – advantages which allowed them to prosecute siege warfare, in terms of both offense and defense, much more effectively. First off was the crown's fairly sound financial footing. Like his immediate predecessors, Edward III was able through Parliament to milk the profitable wool trade quite regularly to support his campaigns against not only the French, but also the Welsh and Scots.[17] Secondly, these long hostilities with the Welsh and Scots – in which sieges mattered as much as pitched battles – meant that fortifying a frontier was not something new for the English when it came time to secure their holdings on the continent against the French by garrisoning strategic small towns, building *bastides* (small, fortified towns), and reinforcing castles.[18] Such moves compelled the enemy to disperse his force to secure supplies and forestall rearguard actions. Lastly was the early recognition that control of Normandy and Gascony – and any other territory which might be conquered in the future – began in the major towns like Bordeaux, Rouen, and Caen, where since Edward I's reign, if not earlier, English rulers had developed a resilient partnership with urban elites that served them well until the very end of the Hundred Years War.[19]

Financing, 1322–1356 (Princeton: Princeton University Press, 1971) and M. Rey, *Le domaine du roi et les finances extraordinaires sous Charles VI* (Paris: SEVPEN, 1965).

16 B. Chevalier, "Les Écossais dans les armées de Charles VII jusqu'à la bataille de Verneuil," in *Jeanne d'Arc. Une époque, un rayonnement. Colloque d'histoire médiévale. Orléans, Octobre 1979* (Paris: Édition du Centre National de la Recherche Scientifique, 1982), pp. 47–62 and J. Campbell, "Scotland and the Hundred Years War in the Fourteenth Century," in *Europe in the Late Middle Ages*, eds. J. R. Hale, R. Highfield and B. Smalley (Evanston: Northwestern University Press, 1965), pp. 184–216.

17 E. B. Fryde, "Edward III's Wool Monopoly: A Fourteenth-Century Royal Trading Venture," *History* 37 (1952), 8–24; "Financial Resources of Edward III in the Netherlands, 1337–40," *Revue belge de philologie et d'histoire* 45 (1967), 1142–216; T. H. Lloyd, *The English Wool Trade in the Middle Ages* (Cambridge: Cambridge University Press, 1977); John H. Munro, *Wool, Cloth, and Gold: The Struggle for Bullion in Anglo-Burgundian Trade, 1340–1478* (Toronto: University of Toronto Press, 1973); E. Miller, "War, Taxation and the English Economy in the Late 13th and Early 14th Centuries," in *War and Economic Development. Essays in Memory of David Joslin*, ed. J. M. Winter (Cambridge: Cambridge University Press, 1975), pp. 11–31; M. Prestwich, *War, Politics and Finance Under Edward I* (Totawa NJ: Rowman & Littlefield, 1972).

18 M. Prestwich, *The Three Edwards. War and the State in England, 1272–1377* (New York: St. Martin's Press, 1980); H. J. Hewitt, *The Organisation of War Under Edward III, 1338–1362* (New York: Barnes & Noble Books, 1966); N. B. Lewis, "Recruitment and Organisation of a Contract Army: May to November 1337," *Bulletin of the Institute of Historical Research* 37 (1964), 1–19.

19 J. Barnie, *War in Medieval Society: Social Values in the Hundred Years War, 1377–1399* (Ithaca: Cornell University Press, 1974); J. G. Black, "Edward I and Gascony in 1300," *English Historical Review* 27 (1902), 518–25; L. Drouyn, *La Guyenne militaire*, 3 vols (Paris, 1865); J. Le Patourel, "Edward III and the Kingdom of France," *History* 43 (1958), 173–89; M. W.

For both the French and English crowns, such a partnership with the towns depended on developing mutual self-interests and equitably dividing the shared responsibilities entailed by local defense. Only in this way could a siege be successfully resisted and a territory thus secured. Such a relationship usually revolved around the questions of money and municipal liberties. Distance as much as foresight explain why the English initially proved more generous than the French when it came to upgrading a town's standing.[20] Longstanding commercial advantages, carefully nurtured over the years by exemptions and preferments (often to the chagrin of London merchants), inspired the allegiance of Gascon and Norman towns to the Plantagenets; wine producers and shippers in the Bordelais depended on the English market for their livelihood, as did cloth merchants in Rouen.[21] Soon after the capture of Calais in 1347, for example, Edward III granted the city numerous commercial incentives designed to make it the chief port through which English cloth, lead, and tin passed to the Continent. As a result, Calais quickly displaced Dieppe as the major transit point between England and France – a position the city still holds today.[22]

This high volume trade between England and its major continental towns influenced the evolution of urban fortifications in English continental holdings during the Hundred Years War. First off, it enriched urban oligarchs, who tolerated a surprising degree of English interference in municipal matters, especially in the areas of justice and police.[23] Secondly, it raised the overall level of economic activity and exchange among local producers, thus providing additional opportunities for indirect taxation. Much of this money eventually went into fortification construction. Surrounding villages and small towns also found

Beresford, *New Towns of the Middle Ages: Town Plantation in England, Wales and Gascony* (London: Lutterworth, 1967).

[20] Kenneth Fowler, *The King's Lieutenant: Henry of Grosmont Duke of Lancaster, 1310–1361* (New York: Barnes & Noble Press, 1969); J. P. Trabut-Cussac, *L'administration anglaise en Gascogne sous Henri III et Edward I de 1254 à 1307* (Geneva: Droz, 1972). Brittany tried to play both sides off against the middle. Michael C. E. Jones, *Ducal Brittany, 1364–1399: Relations with England and France during the Reign of Duke John IV* (Oxford: Oxford University Press, 1970).

[21] A. R. Bridbury, "The Hundred Years' War: Costs and Profits," in *Trade, Government and Economy in Pre-Industrial England. Essays presented to F. J. Fisher*, eds. D. C. Coleman and A. H. John, (London: Weidenfeld & Nicolson, 1976), pp. 19–34; K. B. McFarlane, "War, the Economy and Social Change. England and the Hundred Years War," *Past and Present* 22 (1962), 47–64; E. M. Carus-Wilson, "The Effects of the Acquisition and Loss of Gascony on the English Wine Trade," *Bulletin of the Institute of Historical Research* 21 (1947), 145–54.

[22] S. J. Burley, "The Victualling of Calais, 1347–1365," *Bulletin of the Institute of Historical Research* 31 (1958), 49–57; J. Le Patourel, "L'occupation anglaise de Calais," *Revue du Nord* 33 (1951), 228–41; J. Viard, "Le siège de Calais: 4 septembre 1346–4 août 1347," *Le Moyen Age*, 2nd series 30 (1929), 9–189.

[23] J. A. Kicklinger, "English Bordeaux in Conflict: The Execution of Pierre Vigier de la Rousselle and Its Aftermath," *Journal of Medieval History* 9 (1983), 1–14; E. C. Lodge, "The Constables of Bordeaux in the Reign of Edward III," *English Historical Review* 1 (1935), 225–41; Y. Renouard, *Bordeaux sous les rois d'Angleterre* (Bordeaux: Fédération historique du Sud-Ouest, 1965); Benedicta J. H. Rowe, "Discipline in the Norman Garrisons under Bedford, 1422–1435," *English Historical Review* 46 (1931), 54–76.

it increasingly difficult to resist economic and political pressures from those cities, like Bordeaux and Rouen, and to a lesser degree Caen and Calais, that served as major bases for the English. Commercial privileges, the right to mint money, tax exemptions, letters of protection, as well as extended jurisdictional competence enabled these cities to knit the smaller towns which relied upon them together into networks that made them their "little sisters" or *filleules*.[24] Later, in the 1380s and 1390s, as English power briefly waned in France, these networks gradually became paramilitary organizations committed to regional defense. Even after Henry V's invasion of northern France in 1415, Gascony still depended on the urban league organized by Bordeaux rather than an English army for its protection against the Dauphinists. In 1424, urban militias from Blaye, Bourg, Libourne, Saint-Émilion, Castillon, Cadillac, Saint-Macaire, and Rions, marching under the banner of Bordeaux, beat back a French invasion.[25] Ten years later, the Duke of Bedford tried, less successfully as it turned out, to simulate these defensive arrangements in Normandy and the adjoining *pays de conquête* (conquered territory) by bolstering the regional authority of Caen and Rouen.[26] Accepting the leadership of major provincial cities could be made more palatable for smaller towns by extending to them the same export privileges, although places like Bordeaux complained quite bitterly about such practices. By the same token, when Anglo-Gascon towns fell to the French, they occasionally had the temerity to seek indemnities from Paris to cover the additional cost of shipping their wine through Bordeaux to England.[27] The laws of war at the time accorded urban officials and local royal commanders considerable leeway when pursuing a town's defensive interests.[28]

Encouraging the regional preponderance of larger cities did not always

24 Eleanor Lodge, *Gascony Under English Rule, 1152–1453* (London: Methuen, 1926), pp. 158–62.

25 M. G. A. Vale, *English Gascony, 1399–1453: A Study of War, Government and Politics in the Later Stages of the Hundred Years War* (Oxford: Oxford University Press, 1970); Robert Boutruche, *La crise d'une société. Seigneurs et paysans du Bordelais pendant la guerre de Cents Ans* (Paris: Aubier, 1959), pp. 153–61, 219–31.

26 C. T. Allmand, *Lancastrian Normandy, 1415–1450: The History of a Medieval Occupation* (Oxford: Clarendon Press, 1983); R. Jouet, *La résistance à l'occupation anglaise en Basse-Normandie, (1418–1450)* (Caen: Annales de Normandie, 1969); R. Cazelles, "La rivalité commerciale de Paris et de Rouen au Moyen Âge: compagnie française et compagnie normande," *Bulletin de la société de l'histoire de Paris et de l'Ile de France* 96 (1969), 99–112; A. E. Curry, "The First English Standing Army? Military Organisation in Lancastrian Normandy, 1420–1450," in *Patronage, Pedigree and Power in Later Medieval England*, ed. C. D. Ross (Gloucester: 1979), pp. 193–214.

27 M. Mollat, "Anglo-Norman Trade in the Fifteenth Century," *Economic History Review* 17 (1947), 54–76.

28 M. Keen, *The Laws of War in the Late Middle Ages* (London: Routledge & Kegan Paul, 1965); S. H. Cuttler, *The Law of Treason and Treason Trials in Later Medieval France* (Cambridge: Cambridge University Press, 1981); M. Jones, "Bons brétons et bons françoys. The Language and Meaning of Treason in Late Medieval France," *Transactions of the Royal Historical Society*, 5th series 32 (1982), 92–112; and Y. Lanhers, "Deux affaires de trahison défendues par Jean Jouvenel des Ursins (1423–1427)," in *Mélanges Pierre Tisset* (Montpellier: Recueils, Mémoires et Travaux de la société de l'histoire du droit, 1970), pp. 317–28.

proceed smoothly, in part because they tried to shift the burden of their own defense, such as the cost of building fortifications, garrisoning troops, stockpiling food supplies, and manufacturing armaments, onto smaller towns and villages. This led to inter-communal disputes as members of these smaller towns and villages often went over the heads of Anglo-Gascon and Anglo-Norman authorities by invoking feudal laws to appeal to the Parlement of Paris. Paris usually obliged such resentments by extending to plaintiffs, like the Bordelais towns of Libourne and Saint-Émilion during the 1340s and 1350s, various concessions such as municipal privileges, subsidies to fortify their own walls, the right to hold fairs, and tax preferments.[29] Ultimately, of course, the French crown had to back up such pronouncements militarily for them to be effective – a condition rarely met until the final stages of the war. From the outset, the competition over town loyalties – and by extension surrounding territory – often took place as much in the courtroom as in a siege operation. In both instances, in fact, the *bonnes villes* commonly worked – sometimes together, sometimes against each other – to win greater independence from outside interference as symbolized by their parchment charters and high stone walls.[30]

When circumstances finally compelled townspeople to begin building walls, they did so in earnest after the mid-fourteenth century. The age of cathedrals then gave way to the age of urban fortifications which permanently changed the country's political landscape. The actual construction of urban fortifications is the least well known aspect of siege warfare during the Hundred Years War.[31] Town councils, it seems, usually appointed a comptroller to oversee the project, subcontracting different tasks to specialized groups, like masons, carpenters, ropemakers, and haulers. Unfortunately, only gross expenses paid out by the city

---

[29] J. A. Kicklinger, "Appeal, Negotiation, and Conflict: The Evolution of the Anglo-French Legal Relationship Before the Hundred Years War," *Proceedings of the Western Society for French History* 18 (1991), 45–59, and "French Jurisdictional Supremacy in Gascony: An Aspect of the Ducal Government's Response," *Journal of Medieval History* 3 (1979), 127–34; *English Suits Before the Parlement of Paris, 1420–1436*, eds. C. T. Allmand and C. A. J. Armstrong, Camden 4th Series, 26 (London: Royal Historical Society Publications, 1982); A. Bossuat, "L'idée de nation et la jurisprudence du Parlement de Paris au XVe siècle," *Revue historique* 204 (1950), 54–59, and "Le Parlement de Paris pendant l'occupation anglaise," Revue historique 229 (1960) 102-14; and R. G. Little, *The Parlement of Poitiers: War, Government and Politics in France 1418–1436* (London: Royal Historical Society Publications, 1984).

[30] Claude Gaier, "La fonction stratégico-défensive du plat-pays au Moyen Âge dans la région de la Meuse moyenne," *Le Moyen Âge* 64 (1963), 752–71; François Bibolet, "Le rôle de la Guerre de Cents Ans dans le développement des libertés municipales à Troyes," *Mémoires de la société académique de l'Aube* 94 (1939–42), 11–27.

[31] S. Roux, "La construction courante à Paris au milieu du XIVe siècle à la fin du XVe siècle," in *La construction au Moyen Âge*, Association des historiens médiévistes de l'enseignement supérior public (Paris: Les Belles Lettres, 1973), pp. 175–89; A. Champollion-Figeac, *Droits et usages concernant les travaux de construction, publics ou privés sous la troisième race des rois de France (987–1380)* (Paris, 1860); Marcel Le Port, "La charpente du XIe au XVe siècle. Aperçu du savoir du charpentier," in *Artistes, artisans et production artistique au Moyen Âge. Colloque international, Rennes, 2–6 mai 1983*, Vol. 2: *Commande et travail*, ed. Xavier Barral i Altet (Paris: Picard, 1987) pp. 365–84; and M. Aubert, "La construction au Moyen Âge," *Bulletin médiévale* 118 (1960), 241–59, 119 (1961), 7–42, 82–120, 181–209, 297–323.

to these subcontractors are found in municipal account books, thus leaving us very much in the dark as concerns the actual organization and execution of the project in terms of materials used, costs incurred, and wages paid out. The end results nevertheless reflected the impressive capacity of urban authorities to mobilize the vast resources necessary for self-defense.[32]

From the outset of the Hundred Years War, a close connection existed between a town's jurisdictional authority, especially in fiscal matters, and its walls. A town's walls and related defensive emplacements required for their construction the mobilization and organization of enormous resources in a society wracked by the horrors of war, the Black Death, and all their accompanying economic traumas.[33] Given their vulnerability, towns needed little prompting from the crown to initiate these projects as royal wishes coincided with local needs. The key development here lay in the new cooperative arrangements made to defray the considerable costs of wall construction and upkeep. Despite their haphazard nature, it seems clear that after the 1340s the crown, along with local feudatories and church officials, ceded to the towns the right to levy taxes and surcharges to finance wall construction and upkeep. At first limited to set periods of time, these tax concessions eventually became perpetual, thus allowing the towns to gain more power over the labor and property of residents in and around the community.[34] Even if it had wished, the crown could do little to monitor how local authorities actually used the monies so raised so long as the walls went up. And went up they did, judging from the frenzied building activity evident throughout urban France during the late Middle Ages.[35]

The resources used to upgrade urban fortifications took not just tangible forms, like stone and mortar, but also intangible ones related to changing notions about community membership, which some historians point to as akin to the civic republicanism then developing in Italy.[36] If such was the case, it had its

---

[32] A. Rigaudière, "Le financement des fortifications urbaines en France du milieu du XIVe siècle à la fin du XVe siècle," *Revue historique* 273 (1985), 19–95. Considerable building had already gone on in England. See H. L. Turner, *Town Defenses in England and Wales. An Architectural and Documentary Study A.D. 900–1500* (London: Longmans, 1970).

[33] G. Bois, *Crise de féodalisme. économie rurale et démographie en Normandie orientale du début du XIVe siècle au milieu du XVIe siècle* (Paris: Éditions de la Maison des sciences de l'homme, 1976); J. B. Henneman, "The Black Death and Royal Taxation in France, 1347–1351," *Speculum* 43 (1968), 405–28; J. Hatcher, *Plague, Population and the English Economy, 1348–1530* (London: Macmillan, 1977).

[34] E. A. R. Brown, "*Cessante causa* and the Taxes of the Last Capetians: The Political Applications of a Philosophical Maxim," *Studia Gratiana* 15 (1972), 565–87, and "Customary Aids and Royal Fiscal Policy under Philip VI of Valois," *Traditio* 30 (1974), 191–258; J. B. Henneman, "Financing the Hundred Years War: Royal Taxation in France in 1340," *Speculum* 42 (1967), 275–98.

[35] Philippe Contamine, "Les fortifications urbaines en France à la fin du Moyen Âge: aspects financiers et économiques," *Revue historique* 260 (1978), 23–47.

[36] Hans Baron and J. G. A. Pocock, among others, discuss the development of Italian civic republicanism and its diffusion in, respectively, *The Crisis of the Early Italian Renaissance: Civic Humanism and Republican Liberty in an Age of Classicism and Tyranny* (Princeton: Princeton University Press, 1955) and *The Machiavellian Moment: Florentine Political Thought and the Atlantic Republican Tradition* (Princeton: Princeton University Press, 1975).

origins in the fear of sack and pillage more than the revival of classical antiquity, especially with the later emergence of the Free Companies and the *Écorcheurs* (Flayers), who spread terror throughout France.[37] With payments perpetually in arrears, company captains, like le Jouvencel, relished attacking towns for the rich spoils they offered.[38] The 1355 *chevauchée* (campaign) by the Black Prince was fairly typical. In mid-summer, he set out with several hundred men from Bordeaux to ravage Languedoc, then worked his way back through southern Gascony laying waste to towns, such as Carcassonne and Narbonne, and villages not loyal to England. Fernand Lot estimates that the Black Prince burned or devastated upwards of 500 localities during this expedition.[39] French soldiers did much the same to Burgundy eighty years later. The fear of marauding troops gripped French communities from one end of the country to another from the 1340s onward, and provided civilians a powerful incentive to fortify, whatever the cost might be.

Although in principle delegated by royalty, the increasing powers of town governments to undertake such large-scale projects hinged on the willingness of residents to make these tremendous ongoing investments of capital and labor. In this way, a town's walls stood first and foremost as evidence of local public spiritedness that gave real life to the puffed-up rhetoric about civic liberty long found in municipal charters. Such communal cooperation was by no means confined to the towns; indeed, throughout this period, the need for self-defense extended to the countryside and resulted in the construction of fortified peasant villages and small towns known as *bastides*.[40] This massive investment in protection, while not a guarantee against a successful siege, raised considerably the

---

[37] Philippe Contamine, "Les compagnies d'aventure en France pendant la guerre de Cent Ans," in *La France aux XIVe et XVe siècles*, ch. 7; H. Denifle, *La Guerre de Cent Ans et les désolations des églises, monastères et hôpitaux en France*, Vol. 1 (Paris, 1899); M. Keen, "Chivalry, Nobility and the Man-at-Arms," in *War, Literature and Politics*, ed. C. T. Allmand (Liverpool: Liverpool University Press, 1976), pp. 32–45; A. H. Burne, "John of Gaunt's *Grande Chevauchée*," *History Today* 9 (1959), 113–21; Brian G. H. Ditcham, " 'Mutton Guzzlers and Wine Bags': Foreign Soldiers and Native Reactions in Fifteenth-Century France," in *Power, Culture and Religion in France, c. 1350–1550*, ed. C. T. Allmand (Woodbridge: Boydell Press, 1989), pp. 1–13.

[38] Philippe Contamine, "Rançons et butins dans la Normandie anglaise (1424–1444)," in *Actes du 101e Congrès national des sociétés savantes. Lille 1976* (Paris: Bibliothèque Nationale, 1978), pp. 119–32; N. A. R. Wright, " 'Pillagers' and 'Brigands' in the Hundred Years War," *Journal of Medieval History* 9 (1983), 15–24; K. A. Fowler, "Les finances et la discipline dans les armées anglaises en France au XIVe siècle," *Les Cahiers Vernonnais* 4 (1964), 55–84; D. Hay, "The Division of the Spoils of War in Fourteenth-Century England," *Transactions of the Royal Historical Society*, 5th series 4 (1954), 91–109.

[39] R. Barber, ed. *The Life and Campaigns of the Black Prince* (Woodbridge: Boydell Press, 1986); H. J. Hewitt, *The Black Prince's Expedition of 1355–1357* (Manchester: Manchester University Press, 1958); R. Barber, *Edward, Prince of Wales and Aquitaine. A Biography of the Black Prince* (Woodbridge: Boydell Press, 1978).

[40] C. Higounet, "Bastides et frontières," *Le Moyen Age* 49 (1948), 113–30; Alain Giradot, "Les forteresses paysannes dans le duché de Bar aux XIVe et XVe siècles," *Annales de l'Est* 38 (1986), 3–55; R. Truttmann, "Églises fortifiées de l'Est de la France," *Le pays lorrain* 1 (1959), 1–46; A. Columbet, "Les églises fortifiées de Bourgogne," *Annales de Bourgogne* 61 (1959), 250–58.

stakes of such an undertaking by the enemy, be he a local seigneur, marauding mercenary commander, or the king. No change in behavior fostered by these insecurities proved more long lasting than a readiness to accept new forms of taxation levied by local authories for the community's fortifications. Granted, there were occasionally violent instances of fiscal resistance against agents of the crown, like the rural Jacqueries and urban uprisings of the 1350s and 1360s; and there was no doubt plenty of less dramatic, though no less costly, taxing dodging on the part of individuals.[41] Such deviance should not blind us to the equally significant evidence of compliance embodied in the walls and towers that ringed most French towns by the mid-fifteenth century. The principle of royal taxation was very much in its infancy during this period, especially in the towns; if anything, in fact, this principle only became solidly established once the crown conceded to municipal authorities intermediate control over direct and indirect levies for the express purpose of building fortifications.[42] Any other route was fraught with difficulty and higher costs: the drastic hikes of the 1380s in the *fouage* (hearth tax), for example, led to so much resistance that Charles VI, for a short while at least, contemplated abolishing it and all other direct taxes; having the Estates General raise revenue at first appealed to few besides the king, until, of course, the 1350s when under the leadership of Étienne Marcel there was a move to make it virtual co-ruler with the king.

This left the tried and true policy – to be maintained, it should be added, on through to the end of the ancien régime – of establishing broad principles of royal sovereignty but relying on negotiation with corporate groups when it came to actual policy, especially in the sensitive area of taxation. Already under Philip IV, attempts – most of them failures – had been made to tap urban wealth, either through direct taxes, like the *taille*, or indirect levies, like excises (*impôts indirects*).[43] Given the limited administrative capabilities of the monarchy – limits that would remain in place for centuries to come – the crown had to cajole and negotiate with representatives of the towns (as well as clergy and nobility) when determining subsidy.[44] After the disasters of the 1340s, such an approach proved to be too cumbersome and time consuming, so the French crown gradually transferred to the towns not only the right to levy all such taxes, but also

[41] G. Fourquin, *Les campagnes de la région parisienne à la fin du Moyen Âge* (Paris: Presses Universitaire de France, 1964); E. B. Fryde, "The Financial Policies of the Royal Government and Popular Resistance to them in France and England, c. 1270–1420," *Revue belge de philologie et d'histoire* 57 (1979), 824–60; Marie-Thérèse de Medeiros, *Jacques et chroniqueurs: une étude comparée de récits contemporains relatant la Jacquerie de 1358* (Paris: H. Champion, 1979); and A. Leguai, "Les révoltes rurales dans le royaume de France, du milieu du XIVe siècle à la fin du XVe," *Le Moyen Âge* 88 (1982), 42–65.

[42] J. Favier, "Les rôles d'impôts parisiens du XVe siècle," *Bibliothèque de l'école des Chartes* 130 (1972), 467–91; J. Guerout, "Fiscalité, topographie et démographie à Paris au Moyen Âge," *Bibliothèque de l'école des Chartes* 130 (1972), 33–129, 383–465.

[43] Martin Wolfe, *The Fiscal System of Renaissance France* (New Haven: Yale University Press, 1972), pp. 15–21.

[44] C. H. Taylor, "Assemblies of Towns and War Subsidies, 1313–1319," in Strayer and Taylor, pp. 109–171.

gave the them greater control over assessment. The bulk of all such revenues went into local fortifications, although the monarchy still occasionally demanded outright cash payments, such as *aides* and forced loans. While still more onerous than the situation in English-held towns, these new arrangements underwrote the emergence of the *bonnes villes* as a force to be reckoned with in late medieval France. Even Charles VII, hoping to capitalize on French military successes in the 1430s, recognized this state of affairs by prudently concentrating on the countryside rather than the cities when revamping the crown's fiscal machinery to support his new standing army.[45]

A variety of different revenue sources could be tapped by municipal authorities to pay for fortifications, and while certain patterns eventually emerged, every town apparently tailored its fiscal policies to its own particular commercial strengths. Again, it is worth recalling that these massive investments began at a time when France entered a prolonged period of relative economic stagnation which lasted until the sixteenth century. This is probably another reason why the crown found it more convenient to encourage local communities to assume more of the direct costs entailed by defense. Municipal independence thus brought with it considerable financial obligations; indeed, the appearance of urban budgetary records, which prior to the Hundred Years War are fairly scarce, directly resulted from these moves to prevent a siege.[46] Start-up costs represented the first and perhaps most formidable obstacle to overcome. Towns usually defrayed these by selling life annuities (*rentes viagères*), which attracted primarily wealthy investors whose rate of return was commonly around 3% to 5%. Managing this large, long-term debt required urban authorities to receive the right to collect royal levies, like the *taille*, as well as exploit new revenue sources, particularly excise taxes.[47] Besides arranging ongoing levies to meet annual obligations was the need to set up administrative agencies to handle assessment, collection, and disbursement. This naturally led to an increase in the size and jurisdictional competence of municipal government, whose responsibilities soon went beyond the immediate construction of walls. All sorts of urban projects soon found their way into the expenditures originally earmarked for fortifications – a conflation that makes it very difficult to identify how much of a town's annual budget actually went into its defenses. Of course, a case could be made – and probably was – that civic buildings, street improvements, new fountains, and market places all encouraged local commerce and thus enhanced

[45] B. Chevalier, "Pouvoir royal et pouvoir urbain à Tours pendant la Guerre de Cent Ans," *Annales de Bretagne* 81 (1974), 365–92, 681–707.

[46] François Humbert, *Les finances municipales de Dijon du milieu du XIVe siècle à 1477* (Paris: Société les Belles Lettres, 1961); J-P Leguay, "Rennes au XVe siècle à travers les comptes municipaux," *Annales de Bretagne* 75 (1968), 52–6.

[47] J. Glénisson and Charles Higounet, "Remarques sur les comptes et sur l'administration financière des villes françaises entre Loire et Pyrenées (XIVe–XVIe siècles)," in *Finances et comptabilité urbaine du XIIe au XVIe siècle*, Pro Civitate, Collection Histoire, 7 (Brussels: Pro Civitate, Crédit communal de Belgique, 1964), pp. 38–69.

the town's ability to raise more indirect taxes.[48] These efforts to resist a siege thus altered not only a town's relationship with the outside world, but also its entire physical aspect beyond the imposing sight of its ramparts and towers.

Urban fortification projects necessarily entailed rethinking a city's layout and ultimately identity. Many considerations entered such calculations. Determining the wall's circumference meant balancing projected costs with anticipated revenues; deciding which *faubourgs*, if any, could be incorporated within the walls; and arranging the unpleasant expropriations to clear away private residences and church buildings standing in the way.[49] Construction costs could be kept down if the materials of razed buildings were recycled into the fortifications; stones from the old wall, if such existed, could also be reused. The new walls built for both Orléans and Bourges during this period contain boulders that go back to the original Roman settlement.[50] Law suits could hold up construction if property owners sought either to block expropriations or win higher indemnities. Recent studies have suggested that such obstructionism was rare, that city inhabitants so affected, including – perhaps surprisingly – the clergy, accepted these sacrifices *pro bono publico*. Altogether, the growth of state authority at the local level and in local hands increased considerably as a result of the need to fortify towns.[51]

Direct taxes on property owners provided a fairly insubstantial part of the funds necessary for building, in large part because those who held wealth usually enjoyed various exemptions which the crown confirmed in a town's charter. In lieu of paying taxes, urban clergy and notables alike often arranged to make periodic "gifts" to the town, which could be either voluntary or in the form of forced loans. Even so, such amounts – as best as can be reconstructed from the available evidence – in no way approached the sums generated by excise taxes on such essentials as wine, salt, and foodstuffs, like bread and

---

[48] R. Favreau and J. Glénisson, "Fiscalité d'état et budget à Poitiers au XVe siècle," in *L'impôt dans le cadre de la ville et de l'État* (Brussels: Pro Civitate, Crédit communal de Belgique, 1966), pp. 114–49; Philippe Wolff, *Commerces et marchands de Toulouse (vers 1350–vers 1450)* (Paris: Plon, 1954).

[49] A. Higounet, "Le financement des travaux publics à Périguieux au Moyen Âge," in *Les constructions civiles d'intérêt public dans les villes d'Europe au Moyen Âge et sous l'Ancien Régime et leur financement* (Brussels: Pro Civitate, 1971), pp. 147–73.

[50] H. Boyer, "Les enceintes de Bourges," *Mémoires de la société historique, littéraire, artistique et scientifique du Cher 4* (1888–89), 108–43.

[51] J. Mesqui, *Provins. La fortification d'une ville au Moyen Âge* (Geneva: Droz, 1979); J-L Mestre, "La contribution des droits romain et canonique à l'élaboration du droit administratif," *Annuaire européen d'administration publique 5* (1982), 916–43; E. Kantorowicz, "*Pro patria mori* in Medieval Political Thought," *American Historical Review* 56 (1951), 472–92. Some towns were deeply divided over which side to support. M. Guyard, "Langres pendant la guerre de Cent Ans (1417–1435). Les Langrois 'Bourguignons' ou 'Armagnacs'?," *Les Cahiers Haut-Marnais* 80 (1965), 24–33. Nobles also wrestled with the same dilemma. See Arie Johan Vanderjagt, *"Qui sa vertu anoblist": The Concepts of 'Noblesse' and 'Chose Publique' in Burgundian Political Thought* (Gronigen: Verdingen, 1981).

meat.[52] The inelasticity of these products together with a town's role as regional market center put urban officials in a privileged position to reach into the pockets of consumers, rich and poor alike.[53] Wine taxes alone provided in some cases upwards of 50% of a town's revenues. Municipal surveillance of markets and taverns insured compliance, which authorities reinforced by spelling out in statutes the penalties to be enforced against those who tried to evade the *impôts indirects*. Ironically, the very walls which these taxes helped to build furthered their collection, since gateways served as toll stations for goods brought into the city by rural producers. Given their regressive character, excise taxes worked to broaden the boundaries of the urban community when it came to preparing for a siege, since collective self-defense was supposedly in everyone's best interest. The same communal rationale lay behind the conscription of labor gangs, known as pioneers, from among the urban poor and the forced contributions of surrounding peasant villages to help build a town's walls.[54]

This all-embracing sense of the public good did not hold up when it came to a protracted siege, however. When such occurred, as at the 1446 siege of Rouen, the boundaries of the urban community shrank as city officials, anxious to stretch vital food supplies, frequently expelled peasant refugees, women, children, and the urban poor whom they considered to be *bouches inutiles*, or useless mouths.[55] Rarely did the besieging army allow such persons to pass through their lines unhindered, since to do so enabled the defenders to hold out longer. The fate of such *bouches inutiles* was consequently a piteous one, trapped between the city walls they had helped build and enemy trenches. Nowhere were the brutal contradictions of urban warfare more apparent.[56]

As towns raised walls, stockpiled food supplies, and organized militias after 1340, they naturally improved their position against outside attack. Such remained the case until *c.* 1410 when the nature – and costs – of urban defense again rose dramatically as a result of further refinements in the manufacture and tactical use of artillery. Ironically, the cities had very much pioneered the new gunpowder technology because they possessed the finances, skilled craftsman,

[52] A. Rigaudière, *Saint Flour ville d'Auvergne au bas Moyen Âge. Étude d'histoire administrative et financière*, 2 vols. (Paris: Presses Universitaire de France, 1982).

[53] Riguadière, "Le financement," pp. 75–86, and M. J. James, *Studies in the Medieval Wine Trade* (Oxford: Oxford University Press, 1971).

[54] M. Bécet, "Comment on fortifiait une petite ville pendant la Guerre de Cent Ans," *Annales de Bourgogne* 21 (1919), 3–39; G. Fournier, "Chartes de franchises et fortifications villageoises en Basse Auvergne au XIIIe siècle," in *Les libertés urbaines et rurales du XIe au XIVe siècle* (Brussels: Pro Civitate, 1968), pp. 211–53; J. Mallet, "Les enceintes médiévales d'Angers," *Annales de Bretagne* 72 (1965), 237–72.

[55] C. T. Allmand, "War and the Non-Combatant," in *The Hundred Years War*, ed. K. A. Fowler (London: Macmillan, 1971), pp. 163–83; Michel Mollat, *Les pauvres au Moyen Âge. Étude sociale* (Paris: Hachette, 1978).

[56] This can be seen most strikingly in the lack of protection afforded peasants, who directly and indirectly had contributed so much to urban fortifications. R. Boutruche, "The Devastation of Rural Areas during the Hundred Years War and the Agricultural Recovery of France," in *The Recovery of France in the Fifteenth Century*, ed. P. S. Lewis (New York/London: Blackwell, 1971), pp. 23–59.

and ability to procure raw materials to transform into cannon, shot, and gun-powder.[57] The architectural response to artillery had to wait another hundred years, however, before new methods of construction, many imported from Italy, began to leave their mark on urban fortifications in France.[58] In the meantime, heavy artillery in the form of bombards and mortars, which complemented rather than supplemented traditional siege engines like the battering ram and trebuchet, gradually tipped the scales in favor of the attack, provided the besieg-ing force was able to deploy and supply sufficient numbers of guns to pulverize a town's thick walls. Henry V recognized this advantage first during his 1415 invasion of Normandy when, beginning with Harfleur, he blasted his way into town after town, driving French forces from the province.[59] Such was not the case later at the crucial siege of Orléans in 1429, when the Duke of Bedford opted to try to starve out the Dauphinist garrison rather than pummel them into submission.[60] This misdirected siege strategy, of course, set the stage for Jeanne d'Arc's dramatic rescue of the city. Thereafter, the initiative lay with the French as Charles VII improved upon Henry V's methods, thanks to the tireless efforts of Pierre Bessoneau, France's first *maître de l'artillerie*, and then the Bureau

[57] Claude Gaier, *L'industrie et le commerce des armes dans les anciennes principautés belges du XIIIe à la fin du XVe siècle* (Paris: Presses Universitaires de France, 1973); Philippe Contamine, "Les industries de guerre dans la France de la Renaissance: l'exemple de l'artil-lerie," *Revue historique* 271 (1984), 249–80; A. Basset, "Essai sur l'histoire des fabrications d'armement en France jusqu'au milieu du XVIIIe siècle," *Mémorial de l'Artillerie Française* 14 (1935), 881–1280; J. F. Finò, "Notes sur la production du fer et la fabrication des armes en France au Moyen Âge," *Gladius* 3 (1964), 47–66; L. Lacabane, "De la poudre à canon et de son introduction en France," *Bibliothèque de l'école des Chartes*, 2nd series 1 (1844), 28–57; R. C. Clephan, "The Ordnance of the Fourteenth and Fifteenth Centuries," *Archeological Journal* 68 (1911), 49–138; M. G. A. Vale, *War and Chivalry*, pp. 129–46; B. H. St. J. O'Neil, *Castles and Cannon: A Study of Early Artillery Fortifications in England* (Oxford: Clarendon Press, 1960), pp. 1–40.

[58] J. F. Finò, *Forteresses de la France médiévale*, 3rd ed. (Paris: A. & J. Picard, 1967), pp. 253–98; Horst de la Croix, *Military Considerations in City Planning: Fortifications* (New York: G. Braziller, 1972); J. R. Hale, "The Early Development of the Bastion: An Italian Chronology, c. 1450–c. 1534," in *Renaissance War Studies*, ed. J. R. Hale (London: Longmans, 1983), ch. 1. Simon Pepper and Nicholas Adams, *Firearms and Fortifications: Military Architecture and Siege Warfare in Sixteenth Century Siena* (Chicago: University of Chicago Press, 1986); Christopher Duffy, *The Fortress in the Early Modern World, 1494–1660* (London: Newton Abbot, 1979); B. Gille, *Les ingénieurs de la Renaissance* (Paris: Hermann, 1964).

[59] C. T. Allmand, "Henry V the Soldier and the War in France," in *Henry V: The Practice of Kingship*, ed. G. L. Harriss (Oxford: Oxford University Press, 1985), pp. 117–35; E. F. Jacob, *Henry V and the Invasion of France* (London: Hodder & Stoughton, 1947); R. A. Newhall, *The English Conquest of Normandy, 1416–1424* (New Haven: Yale University Press, 1924); F. Dupuis, *Mémoire sur le siège de Montargis en 1427* (Orléans, 1853). The English never could take Le Mont Saint-Michel despite a long siege because the citadel was out of range of enemy gun emplacements on the mainland. See C. de Merindol, "Saint Michel et la monarchie fran-çaise à la fin du Moyen Âge dans le conflit franco-anglais," in *La 'France anglaise' au Moyen Âge*, pp. 513–42.

[60] Bedford apparently decided against taking heavy guns in English-held towns for the siege of Orléans. C. T. Allmand, "L'artillerie de l'armée anglaise et son organisation à l'époque de Jeanne d'Arc," in *Jeanne d'Arc: Une époque*, pp. 73–81; L. Douët d'Arcq, ed., "Inventaire de la Bastille de l'an 1428," *Revue archéologique* 12 (1855–56), 321–49.

brothers to lay hold of urban artillery for the king. In the 1450 campaign of Normandy, for example, French troops with substantial artillery support were able in one year to capture over 60 fortified towns and castles, some of which had taken the English months to seize a generation before. In fact, Caen, despite its sizeable garrison, capitulated immediately after the first barrage of Charles VII's heavy guns. Not that some English strongholds did not attempt to mount a credible defense. In a foreshadowing of future trends in urban fortification, Bordeaux, for example, tried in 1450–51 to fend off the threat of French cannon by throwing up earthworks, known as *boulevards* (after the German word, *Bollwerk*), around the city's gates. Such labors went unrewarded as the city fell in early 1451.[61] Excessive cost and lack of time prevented these innovations from being permanently incorporated into urban defenses before the end of the Hundred Years War. Even so, such developments reflected the growing premium not only on mobile artillery for the attack, but also the malleability of defensive fortifications to parry the new technologies of war in the centuries ahead.

Artillery henceforth became a key part of the French royal army, both in Louis XI's later assertion of control against the nobility in the 1470s and 1480s and in Charles VIII's celebrated invasion of Italy in 1494.[62] This new technology underscored the crucial role assumed by the *bonnes villes* of France during the Hundred Years War. Together these urban centers, now more independent yet in prudent partnership with the crown, provided the infrastructure upon which French military power rested in the centuries ahead, complementing rather than countering the monarchy's moves under Charles VII and his successors to build a standing army and strengthen the crown's fiscal hold on the peasantry. In meeting the challenge of siege warfare, town governments throughout France had secured greater control over the local population and economy, marshalling the resources necessary to build walls, develop armament industries, form urban militias, and requisition food supplies from the countryside for the king's army. In exchange, the crown acknowledged the towns' new measure of autonomy.[63]

---

[61] M. H. Keen, "English Diplomacy and the Sack of Fougères in 1449," *History* 59 (1974), 3–27; V. Hunger, "Le siège et la prise de Vire par Charles VII en 1450," *Annales de Normandie* 21 (1971), 52–67; J. Le Patourel, "Le rôle de la ville de Caen dans l'histoire de l'Angleterre," *Annales de Normandie* 11 (1961), 11–31; M. G. A. Vale, "New Techniques and Old Ideals: The Impact of Artillery on War and Chivalry at the End of the Hundred Years War," in *War, Literature and Politics*, pp. 57–72.

[62] J. R. Lander, "The Hundred Years War and Edward IV's 1475 Campaign in France," in *Tudor Men and Institutions: Studies in English Law and Government*, ed. A. J. Slavin (Baton Rouge: Louisiana State University Press, 1972), pp. 23–41; Philippe Contamine, "L'artillerie royale à la veille des guerres d'Italie," *Annales de Bretagne* 71 (1964), 221–61.

[63] *The Recovery of France in the Fifteenth Century*, ed. P. S. Lewis (London: Blackwell, 1971); P. Cambier, *La vie économique en France à la fin de la guerre de Cent Ans* (Paris: Librairie du Recueil Sirey, 1942); Philippe Contamine, "Guerre, fiscalité royale et économie en France (deuxième moitié du XVe siècle)," in *Proceedings of the Seventh International Economic Congress*, ed. M. Flinn, Vol. 2 (Edinburgh: Edinburgh University Press, 1978), pp. 266–73; Paul Solon, "Popular Response to Standing Military Forces in Fifteenth-Century France," *Studies in the Renaissance* 19 (1972), 78–111.

These developments at the end of the Hundred Years War not only enabled the monarchy to expel the English, but also inaugurated an era of French expansionism that, while proceeding in fits and starts, lasted down to the nineteenth century.[64]

[64] I gratefully acknowledge the generous support of the National Endowment for the Humanities, which helped make the research for this essay possible.

Siege Technologies and Urban Fortifications

Town Defences in the Crusader Kingdom of Jerusalem

Denys Pringle
Edinburgh

I. Introduction

Some twenty years ago, it was remarked by the late Joshua Prawer that a study of the problem of Crusader urban fortifications had yet to be made.[1] Despite the amount of attention that has been devoted in the meantime to Crusader castles, the situation today regarding town defences has hardly changed. In part this is due to the fact that comparatively little survives of most of the major town walls that once existed in the Kingdom of Jerusalem. Yet it is perhaps a curious reflection on the priorities of archaeologists working in the Holy Land that even where considerable remains of medieval defences do survive, as at Ascalon, Arsuf, Caesarea and even Jerusalem itself, we still seem to know little more about them than did the officers of the Survey of Western Palestine, who surveyed them more than a century ago.[2] I make no claim, therefore, that this chapter will satisfy the outstanding need for a detailed field study of surviving town defences. I hope, nonetheless, that it may at least highlight some aspects of the subject that deserve attention, besides contributing to the general theme of this volume on the medieval city under siege.

Before considering the methods used for defending towns in the Kingdom of Jerusalem in the twelfth and thirteenth centuries, we must first define what – for present purposes, at least – constituted a town.

Palestine was already urbanized long before the arrival of the First Crusade in 1099. But although much of the physical fabric of the Muslim towns and cities that were captured by the Franks survived intact, in most cases their populations

Abbreviations. See p. 102.

I am grateful to David Jacoby and Benjamin Kedar for their comments on an earlier draft of this paper.

[1] *The Latin Kingdom of Jerusalem: European Colonialism in the Middle Ages* (London: Weidenfeld and Nicolson, 1972), p. 319, n. 36.

[2] C. R. Conder and H. H. Kitchener, *The Survey of Western Palestine: Memoirs of the Topography, Orography, Hydrography and Archaeology*, 3 vols. (London, 1881–83).

and urban institutions did not. The Crusader towns that developed in their place nevertheless had certain characteristics which distinguished them from contemporary towns in the West and affected the way in which they were defended.[3]

First, throughout the period of the Latin Kingdom (1099–1291), towns and cities remained subject to their lords, who, in the case of Jerusalem, Acre and (until 1240) Tyre, was the king. Although there were abortive communal movements in Tyre in 1187 and in Acre in 1231, these were not specifically urban in character;[4] and the communes that were established by Italian and Provençal merchant colonies in the coastal cities were dependent on their home cities in the West, rather than forming a political part of those in which they found themselves. Thus, while there is evidence from thirteenth-century Acre for the Italian communes, and also the military orders, defending their own quarters of the city with gates and towers, besides contributing to the defence of the town walls, overall responsibility for urban defence remained with the king.

A second difference between Crusader towns and those in the West concerns the legal status of their inhabitants. Burgage tenure, which is often taken by historians of the medieval West to distinguish a town-dweller on the one hand from castle- or village-dwellers on the other, is of less help as an indicator of urban status in the Crusader East. In the Kingdom of Jerusalem virtually all Franks who were not knights or clerics were legally classed as burgesses. Thus we find burgage tenure existing in a settlement such as Sinjil, north of Jerusalem, which in terms of its size and economy cannot have been anything more than a village;[5] on the other hand, in addition to burgage tenure, a variety of feudal tenures also existed in a major city such as Acre.

The legal and institutional distinctions between urban and non-urban settlements in the Crusader Kingdom of Jerusalem are, therefore, far from clear cut. Other criteria may of course be considered. In the West, for instance, towns are often distinguished by the relative size of their population, though in practice absolute sizes could vary considerably. They may also be characterized by their specialized functions, whether economic, social, political, administrative, religious, or cultural. All of these factors may be expected to have played a part in the physical layout of a town's buildings, streets, markets, and fortifications. Unfortunately to apply such a broadly based approach to the settlements of the

---

3 See Joshua Prawer, "Crusader Cities," in *The Medieval City*, ed. H. A. Miskimin, D. Herlihy and A. L. Udovitch (New Haven: Yale University Press, 1977), pp. 179–201, and his *Crusader Institutions* (Oxford: Clarendon Press, 1980), chs. 4, 5, 8–13. On the physical aspects of towns and cities, see also M. Benvenisti, *The Crusaders in the Holy Land* (Jerusalem: Israel Universities Press, 1970), pp. 25–209.

4 H. E. Mayer, "On the Beginnings of the Communal Movement in the Holy Land: The Commune of Tyre," *Traditio* 14 (1968), 443–57 (rpt. in his *Kreuzzuge und lateinische Osten* [London: Variorum, 1983], ch. XIII); J. Prawer, "The Earliest Commune of Tripoli," in *Studies in Memory of Gaston Wiet*, ed. M. Rosen-Ayalon (Jerusalem: Institute of Asian and African Studies, Hebrew University of Jerusalem, 1977), pp. 171–79; Prawer, *Crusader Institutions*, pp. 46–82.

5 *RRH*, pp. 77–78, n. 302; cf. J. S. C. Riley-Smith, *The Feudal Nobility and the Kingdom of Jerusalem, 1174–1277* (London: Macmillan, 1973), pp. 81–82.

Kingdom of Jerusalem would require a separate study, and possibly more archaeological evidence than is currently available. It might not, in any case, provide a very convenient yardstick for determining what was and what was not a town; and to single out the existence of a particular material feature, such as a circuit of walls, as a specifically urban characteristic also risks circularity of argument in the present context.

For the purposes of the present study, I therefore propose to adopt a more convenient, if less methodically rigorous, definition of what constituted a town. In the Kingdom of Jerusalem, wherever sufficient numbers of burgesses were gathered together there is often evidence for a burgess court, separate from the lord's own court. The law book of John of Ibelin, drawn up in the mid-thirteenth century, lists 37 such places by name, though the author admits that there may have been others that had slipped his memory.[6] To these we may add another three places, Mirabel (Majdal Yaba), Qaqun and Qalansuwa, where a viscount and burgesses are recorded;[7] and seven "new towns," which, although agriculturally based and unlikely to have numbered more than 500–750 inhabitants each, were socially, economically and institutionally towns in the making.[8] It is these 47 settlements (shown in Table 1 and Fig. 1; all tables and figures are found at the end of this article) whose defences we shall be considering in the following pages.[9]

II. Towns without Walls

More than half of the towns listed in Table 1 lacked town walls; indeed, four of them appear to have lacked fortifications altogether. Each of these, however, depended on a cathedral church which was itself fortified, and provided a measure of security for the inhabitants at its gate.

The church of the Nativity at Bethlehem, for example, was surrounded in the twelfth century by a strong wall, with a projecting gatehouse and towers, one of which took the form of a tower-keep or *donjon* and may have been the bishop's own residence.[10] At Lydda, the bishop's *monasterium* was likewise fortified by May 1102, when Egyptian raiders declined to attack it on account of its

---

[6] *Le Livre de Jean d'Ibelin*, ch. CCLXX, ed. A. A. Beugnot, in *RHC Lois*, Vol. 1, pp. 419–21.

[7] Prawer, *Crusader Institutions*, pp. 327–39; D. Pringle, *The Red Tower (al-Burj al-Ahmar): Settlement in the Plain of Sharon at the Time of the Crusaders and Mamluks, A.D. 1099–1516*, British School of Archaeology in Jerusalem Monograph Series, 1 (London: British School of Archaeology in Jerusalem, 1986), pp. 42–43, 58–59.

[8] Prawer, *Crusader Institutions*, pp. 126–42.

[9] Detailed bibliographies for the archaeological evidence for fortification works surviving at these sites will be found in D. Pringle, *Secular Buildings in the Crusader Kingdom of Jerusalem: An Archaeological Gazetteer* (Cambridge: Cambridge University Press, in preparation).

[10] D. Pringle, *The Churches of the Crusader Kingdom of Jerusalem: A Corpus*, Vol. 1 (Cambridge: Cambridge University Press, 1993), pp. 153–54, fig. 46, pl. XCIV.

strength;[11] and in 1177 the inhabitants took refuge on the church roof.[12] In Nazareth, the church of the Annunciation was used as a refuge by the population when Saladin attacked in 1183,[13] and again, *causa munitionis*, in 1187 – though on the latter occasion the defences failed them.[14] The bishop of Sabastiya also seems to have assumed a protective role towards his flock in 1184, when we find him gaining them a temporary respite by buying Saladin off.[15] In each of these cases it may be supposed that the resources for building the churches and their surrounding complexes would have left little over for additional defence works.

In a number of the "new towns" established by ecclesiastical and other landowners in the twelfth century, provision for defence was made from the start. At Dabburiya (Buria), where a *suburbium* with its own "customs" had developed at the foot of Mount Tabor, dependent on the Benedictine abbey on its summit, the inhabitants fled into a tower when faced by an unexpected Muslim attack in 1182.[16] In 1124, when Muslims from Ascalon raided al-Bira (Magna Mahumeria), a new town founded by the canons of the Holy Sepulchre north of Jerusalem, the old men, women and children also escaped into a tower, which had only recently been built there;[17] this building was subsequently expanded by the addition of an outer wall and vaults into the *curia*, or courthouse, where the inhabitants were obliged to pay their rents and tithes to the canons' steward.[18] Otherwise, the settlement appears to have been unfortified.[19] Similar developments are recorded archaeologically at ar-Ram (Rama, Ramatha) and al-Qubaiba (Parva Mahumeria), two other new towns of the Holy Sepulchre, though at the latter the nucleus of the *curia* seems to have been a first-floor hall-house rather than a tower.[20] This and the relative sizes of the towers

---

11 Fulcher of Chartres, *Historia Hierosolymitana (1095–1127)*, II.15.3–4, ed. H. Hagenmeyer (Heidelberg: C. Winter, 1913), pp. 426–27.

12 William of Tyre, *Chronicon*, XXI.20 (21), ed. R. B. C. Huygens, in *Corpus Christianorum, Continuatio Mediaeualis*, Vols. 63–63a (Turnholt: Brepols, 1986), p. 989; *A History of Deeds Done Beyond the Sea*, trans. E. A. Babcock and A. C. Krey, Vol. 2, Records of Civilization, Sources and Studies, 35 (New York: Columbia University Press, 1941), p. 428.

13 William of Tyre, XXII.27, p. 1052.

14 Ralph of Coggeshall, *Chronicon Anglicanum*, ed. R. J. Stevenson, in *RS*, Vol. 66, p. 231.

15 Ralph of Diss, *Opera Historica*, ed. W. Stubbs, in *RS*, Vol. 68.2, p. 28; Roger of Wendover, *Flores Historiarum*, ed. H. G. Hewlett, in *RS*, Vol. 84.1, p. 133.

16 William of Tyre, XXII.15 (14), pp. 1027–28; cf. Prawer, *Crusader Institutions*, p. 136.

17 Fulcher of Chartres, III.33.1–2, in *RHC Occ*, Vol. 3, p. 465; William of Tyre, XIII.12, p. 600.

18 *Le Cartulaire du chapitre du Saint-Sépulcre de Jérusalem*, ed. G. Bresc-Bautier, DRHC, 15 (Paris: Geuthner, 1984), pp. 249–50, n. 123; *RRH*, p. 95, n. 362; D. Pringle, "Magna Mahumeria (al-Bīra): The Archaeology of a Frankish New Town in Palestine," in *Crusade and Settlement*, ed. P. Edbury (Cardiff: University College Cardiff Press, 1985), pp. 147–68 (at. pp. 151–57).

19 Pringle, *Churches*, p. 161.

20 B. Bagatti, *I Monumenti di Emmaus el-Qubeibeh e dei dintorni*, Studium Biblicum Franciscanum, Collectio Maior, 4 (Jerusalem: Franciscan Printing Press, 1947), pp. 87–94; D. Pringle, "Two Medieval Villages North of Jerusalem: Archaeological Investigations in al-Jib and ar-Ram," *Levant* 15 (1983), 141–77 (at pp. 160–74); *The Atlas of the Crusades*, ed. J. S. C. Riley-Smith (London: Times Books, 1991), pp. 40–41.

surviving at al-Bira and ar-Ram suggests that such towers were not intended simply as refuges, but were at least partly residential from the start.[21]

In a score or more cases, a tower or castle seems to have represented the only defensive provision made for the inhabitants of a town. This was the case at Qaqun (Caco), where a castle is first mentioned in 1123 and a viscount, presumably the castellan, in 1131.[22] In Baisan (Bet She'an, Bethsan), a large tower over 17 m. square probably represented the nucleus of the castle (*praesidium*) in whose defences the inhabitants of the little town had little faith when they abandoned it in 1183.[23] Even a large town like Nablus, whose public buildings included at least four major churches and a hospital, seems to have had no town walls in the twelfth century, though it had a castle, variously described as *praesidium* and *palatium regis*, remains of which still survive.[24]

Other towns grew up around existing castles. At Bait Jibrin (Bethgibelin) a roughly square castle with rectangular corner-towers was built as an outpost against Muslim-held Ascalon and was granted by King Fulk to the Hospitallers in 1136.[25] After the fall of Ascalon in 1153, and before 1160, the civilian settlement outside the castle, numbering some 32 families, was given a charter by the master, Raymond of Le Puy.[26] It may have been at this time that an aisled church, evidently too large to have been the castle chapel, was constructed against the outer face of the original castle, entailing the demolition of its south-east corner-tower.[27] Traces of an outer enceinte survive north of the castle, but it is uncertain whether this wall continued around the whole settlement, or simply enclosed an outer bailey.

At Yibna (Ibelin) and Darum (Dair al-Balah), we also find civilian settlements with their own churches and burgess courts developing beside castles established primarily for military reasons. Yibna was built in 1141, like Bait Jibrin as an offensive fortress opposing Ascalon.[28] William of Tyre gives its first lord, Balian I, the credit for establishing the town, and the mention, in 1158, of a viscount suggests that the burgess court recorded by John of Ibelin existed by then.[29] However, the site has yet to be excavated, and although the positions of

---

[21] D. Pringle, "Towers in Crusader Palestine," *Château Gaillard: Études de castellologie médiévale* 16 (1992), 335–50 (at pp. 337, 342).

[22] Fulcher of Chartres, III.18.1, pp. 664–65; *CGOH*, Vol. 1, pp. 83–84, n. 94, cf. p. 97, n. 115; *RRH*, p. 35, n. 139 and p. 39, n. 159; Pringle, *Red Tower*, pp. 58–71.

[23] William of Tyre, XXII.27 (26), p. 1051; I. Ben-Dor, *Guide to Beisan* (Jerusalem: Govt. of Palestine, Dept. of Antiquities, 1943), p. 9; A. Boaz, "Bet Shean, Crusader Fortress – Area Z," *ESI* 9 (1989–90), 129.

[24] William of Tyre, XIV.27, p. 667 (1137); *RRH*, p. 50, n. 201 (1141); F. M. Abel, "Chronique, IV – Naplouse. Essai de topographie," *Revue biblique* 32 (1923), 120–32 (at pp. 123; 130–31; fig. 9).

[25] William of Tyre, XIV.22, pp. 659–61; *CGOH*, Vol. 1, p. 97, n. 116; *RRH*, pp. 40–41, n. 164.

[26] *CGOH*, Vol. 1, pp. 272–73, n. 399; p. 350, n. 509; Prawer, *Crusader Institutions*, pp. 119–26.

[27] Pringle, *Churches*, I, pp. 95–101, n. 32.

[28] William of Tyre, XV.24, pp. 706–07.

[29] *Cartulaire*, pp. 136–38, n. 51; *RRH*, p. 87, n. 333.

the castle and church are known, the extent of the defences is not fully understood; probably they were not very strong, for the place was easily sacked in 1177 and taken and burnt in 1187.[30] The castle and town of Darum were established by Amalric I (1163–74) after the fall of Ascalon, as an outpost against Egypt.[31] Here the royal castle served as the town's defence, and when Saladin attacked, in 1170, it was in the castle that the inhabitants took refuge until help arrived.[32]

Other examples of castles giving protection to civilian settlements, often with a church, included: Hebron, where the castle was annexed to the Herodian precinct enclosing the cathedral church of St. Abraham;[33] Mi'iliya (Castellum Regis), where the castle, first mentioned in 1160, occupied a hilltop dominating the settlement, with the church of St. Mary Magdalene beside it;[34] and Tibnin (Toron), where the constable of the kingdom, Humphrey of Toron, was buried in April 1179 in the church of St. Mary, "apud nobile et famosum castrum eius" (at his renowned and famous castle).[35]

In certain cases we also find Frankish settlements, which eventually developed their own burgess courts, being established from the start inside rather than adjacent to castles. Baldwin I founded the castle (*praesidium*) of Montreal (ash-Shaubak) in Transjordan in 1115; and William of Tyre tells us, "he placed as inhabitants both knights and footsoldiers, granting them extensive possessions; and the town (*oppidum*) was well fortified with a wall, towers, an outer wall and a ditch (*antemurali et vallo*), arms, food and machines."[36] Archaeological investigation of the site suggests that the *oppidum* and *praesidium* were the same thing, a large oval castle with a double wall, which despite extensive rebuilding by the Ayyubids and Mamluks still occupies the summit of a conically shaped hill.[37] By the 1180s, a *suburbium*, inhabited largely by native Christians and apparently undefended, had developed down the valley to the east. But the existence within the castle in 1152 of houses belonging to the Hospitallers and to the viscount of Nablus respectively, and of a three-aisled

30 J. Prawer, *Histoire du royaume latin de Jérusalem*, Vol. 1, 2nd ed. (Paris: Centre National de la Recherche Scientifique, 1975), pp. 553, 668; and Prawer, *Crusader Institutions*, p. 106.

31 William of Tyre, XX.19, p. 937.

32 William of Tyre, X.19, pp. 936–37; Prawer, *Crusader Institutions*, pp. 107–09; Pringle, *Churches*, p. 195.

33 L. H. Vincent, E. J. H. Mackay and F. M. Abel, *Hébron: le Ḥaram al-Khalîl: sépulture des Patriarches*, Vol. 1 (Paris: E. Leroux, 1923), p. 163; Pringle, *Churches*, p. 224.

34 B. Bagatti, *Antichi villaggi cristiani di Galilea*, Studium Biblicum Franciscanum, Collectio Minor, 13 (Jerusalem: Franciscan Printing Press, 1971), pp. 210–16; D. Pringle, "Survey of Castles in the Crusader Kingdom of Jerusalem, 1989: Preliminary Report," *Levant* 23 (1991), 87–91 (at p. 90, n. 10).

35 William of Tyre, XXI.26 (27), p. 999.

36 William of Tyre, XI.26, p. 535; cf. Prawer, *Crusader Institutions*, pp. 109–11.

37 R. M. Brown, "Summary Report of the 1986 Excavations. Late Islamic Shobak," *Annual of the Department of Antiquities of Jordan* 32 (1988), 225–45.

church, dated by an inscription to 1118, supports William of Tyre's testimony that the nucleus of the Frankish settlement lay inside the castle.[38]

A rather similar situation seems to have obtained in Jaffa, where the twelfth-century defences consisted of a castle, or citadel, situated on a hill overlooking the harbour, and a defended lower town, or *faubourg*, enclosing it on the three landward sides.[39] Within the castle stood the parish church of St. Peter, serving the town, as well as two chapels, whose chaplain in 1176 was granted parish rights within the castle itself.[40] In the later thirteenth century, the castle also contained the residences of the count of Jaffa and of the patriarch of Jerusalem, besides other private properties.[41]

At Haifa the *castrum* (or *castellum*) was also more than just the residence of the lord of the city. In fact it seems to have represented the nucleus of a new town that had been established in the later eleventh century by the Fatimids, some distance to the west of Old Haifa, which was thereafter deserted.[42] Old Haifa, which had evidently once had a wall and gates,[43] was still being distinguished from New Haifa as late as c. 1172, when Theodoric describes the latter as "castellum ingens."[44] It was probably within the Castle of Haifa that the parish church of St. Mary stood; this may explain the somewhat anomalous status of its priest, Boniface, who in 1164/65 was denoted both as chaplain of Haifa and as a canon of Caesarea.[45] The castle ("castru[m] nomine Cayphasi") also contained a square, a church, houses, ovens and a mill, that were granted to the abbey of St. Mary of Josaphat by Tancred, prince of Galilee, in 1115.[46] As in Jaffa, it may be assumed that the lord of Haifa would have had his own residence, no doubt also fortified, within the castle. Indeed, the reverse of the seal of García Álvarez (c. 1250), which is inscribed "CASTRVM CAIFE," appears to show three castles: one on a hilltop (evidently the Templar castle on Mount Carmel), another (unidentified) near its foot, and a third (Haifa itself) in the plain, from which the lord's banner is shown flying.[47]

At Mi'iliya (Castellum Regis) there is also evidence for the existence of private houses within the castle. Thus, in October 1179, we find Baldwin IV

[38] *RRH*, p. 71, n. 279, cf. pp. 146–47, n. 551; Pringle, *Churches*, Vol. 2, forthcoming; S. de Sandoli, *Corpus Inscriptionum Crucesignatorum Terrae Sanctae (1099–1291)*, Studium Biblicum Franciscanum, Collectio Maior, 21 (Jerusalem: Franciscan Printing Press, 1974), p. 332, appx. n. 4.

[39] F. M. Abel, "Jaffa au Moyen-âge," *Journal of the Palestine Oriental Society* 20.1 (1946), 6–28; Pringle, *Churches*, pp. 264–66, fig. 79.

[40] Pringle, *Churches*, pp. 267–68, n. 110 and p. 270, ns. 111–12.

[41] Pringle, *Churches*, pp. 266–67.

[42] J. Prawer, *The History of the Jews in the Latin Kingdom of Jerusalem* (Oxford: Clarendon Press, 1988), pp. 35–40; Pringle, *Churches*, pp. 222–23.

[43] *Cartulaire*, pp. 268–69, n. 137; *RRH*, pp. 108–09, n. 418 (1164/65).

[44] Theodericus, *Libellus de Locis Sanctis*, XL, LI, ed. M. L. and W. Bulst, Editiones Heidelbergenses, 18 (Heidelberg: Winter, 1976), pp. 43, 51.

[45] *Cartulaire*, p. 261, n. 134 and p. 269, n. 137; Pringle, *Churches*, p. 223, n. 96.

[46] Pringle, *Churches*, p. 223, n. 97.

[47] de Sandoli, *Corpus Inscriptionum*, pp. 279–80, n. 377.

confirming to Count Joscelin, his seneschal, "the houses that [Petronilla, vi-
scountess of Acre] possessed in my castle, which is called the New Castle, and
all the vines and gardens, and every possession that she was seen to possess by
hereditary right both in the aforesaid castle and in its territory, both in land and
in houses, vines, and gardens."[48]

Whatever the legal distinction between a castle and a town, the relation of this
to the physical structures of either is, therefore, not always easy to draw. Indeed,
it may not have been obvious even to contemporaries, hence William of Tyre's
description of Montreal as *castrum*, *praesidium* and *oppidum* within a few lines,
and the descriptions of Haifa as *castrum*, *castellum* and *oppidum*.[49] In the West,
too, we find instances of houses and churches being located inside castle walls,
and a general toing and froing of town or village folk through castle gates.[50]
Certainly there were legal distinctions to be made, as for example those relating
to the delimitation of parish rights.[51] The one distinction between a castle and a
town wall that would have been as intelligible to contemporaries as to us today,
however, would have been the size of the area enclosed.

III. Towns Defended by Town Walls

While some Crusader towns relied for their defence on a citadel, a castle, a
refuge tower, or simply a strong building such as a church, others had town walls
enclosing the entire settlement or a major part of it.

Three factors in particular seem to have influenced the size of the area
enclosed. First, in many cases it was determined by the extent of fortifications
which already existed when the Franks took control of a place; indeed, we know
for certain of only two town walls built *de novo* by the Crusaders in the
Kingdom of Jerusalem: that enclosing the Montmusard suburb at Acre, and that
surrounding the *faubourg* of 'Atlit. Secondly, town walls were extremely expensive to build and maintain. Even in the medieval West, a city such as
Coventry took two centuries to complete its full circuit of walls, longer than the
Kingdom of Jerusalem lasted; and in Southampton, the sectors of town wall
built by the city authorities appear fairly ramshackle compared to those built by
the king.[52] Thirdly, whereas in the West town walls were often built as much as
an expression of civic pride as for defence, in the Kingdom of Jerusalem the
more or less constant military threat often demanded a more pragmatic approach
to security.

---

48 *TOT*, pp. 11–12, n. 11.

49 *Itinerarium Peregrinorum et Gesta Regis Ricardi*, IV.11, ed. W. Stubbs, in *RS*, Vol. 38.1, p.
252.

50 N. G. Pounds, *The Medieval Castle in England and Wales: A Social and Political History*
(Cambridge: Cambridge University Press, 1990), pp. 24–25.

51 B. Hamilton, *The Latin Church in the Crusader States: The Secular Church* (London:
Variorum, 1980), pp. 92–93.

52 C. Platt, *The English Medieval Town* (London: Secker and Warburg, 1976), pp. 41–44.

In some Crusader towns even the maintenance of an existing circuit of walls would have been impracticable, for even if the finance could be found there still would not have been enough people to defend it. In a number of cases town walls were, therefore, reduced in extent or simply abandoned after the Frankish occupation. In 1047, for example, the Persian traveller Nāsir-i Khusraw described Ramla as "a great city, with strong walls built of stone, mortared, of great height and thickness, with iron gates opening therein."[53] When the army of the First Crusade entered Syria, William of Tyre tells us that Ramla was still "a populous city, surrounded by a wall with towers . . . But it had neither outer defences (*antemurali*) nor a moat."[54] The Muslim inhabitants, therefore, fled to Ascalon, which was more securely defended. In 1099, when a Christian settlement was established in Ramla, under the lordship of the newly installed bishop of Lydda, Robert of Rouen, the city was virtually deserted. "It would have been difficult to occupy the entire city when the inhabitants were so few. They therefore newly fortified a stronghold with walls and a moat in one part of it."[55] The principal element of this stronghold seems to have been a tower, from which in May 1102 King Baldwin I barely escaped with his life when it was attacked and undermined by the Ascalonites.[56]

At Karak in Transjordan, it is not clear whether the town had any walls to speak of in the Crusader period, those that exist today being largely Ayyubid and Mamluk in date. The town, containing the cathedral of the bishop of Petra and a number of other churches, occupied a plateau, with cliffs providing a natural defence in all but two places. At the south end, a triangular promontory, detached by a rock-cut ditch, was the site of the castle, built by Pagan the Butler in 1142, and enlarged by his successors, Maurice and Philip of Milly.[57] In 1183, when Saladin attacked Karak, its lord, Reynald of Châtillon, attempted to defend the entire plateau and refused to allow the inhabitants into the castle; but the Muslims took the town and almost penetrated the castle itself, into which as many of the townsfolk as were able had by then fled.[58]

At Gaza the story was similar. In Byzantine times this had been a fortified city; but in 1149, when Baldwin III decided to fortify the place, it was in ruins. Seeing that he had insufficient men or resources to enclose the whole area, Baldwin contented himself with building a castle with stone walls and towers in

[53] G. Le Strange, *Palestine under the Moslems* (London, 1890), p. 306.

[54] William of Tyre, X.16 (17), p. 472; trans. from *A History of Deeds*, Vol. 1, pp. 438–39.

[55] William of Tyre, X.16 (17), p. 472; trans. from *A History of Deeds*, Vol. 1, pp. 438–39.

[56] Albert of Aachen, *Liber Christianae expeditionis*, IX.2–6, in *RHC Occ*, Vol. 4, pp. 591–94; Fulcher of Chartres, II.15.1–5, II.19.1–5; *RHC Occ*, Vol. 3, pp. 424–28, 441–44; Prawer, *Crusader Institutions*, pp. 112–16; S. Runciman, *A History of the Crusades*, Vol. 2 (Cambridge: Cambridge University Press, 1952), pp. 76–78.

[57] On the history and topography of Crusader Karak, see P. Deschamps, *Les Châteaux des croisés en Terre Sainte*, II, *La défense du royaume de Jérusalem*, Bibliothèque archéologique et historique, 34 (Paris: Geuthner, 1939), pp. 36–98; and his *Terre Sainte romane*, La Nuit des Temps, 21 (La Pierre-qui-Vire: Zodiaque, 1964), pp. 44–72; Pringle, *Churches*, pp. 286–96.

[58] William of Tyre, XXII.29 (28), pp. 1055–57.

just part of it. This he granted, when finished, to the Templars.[59] By 1170, however, a civilian settlement had been attracted to the area outside the castle, which was defended by some low rather feeble walls, with gates. But these proved ineffectual against Saladin, who that year raided the suburb and killed the townsfolk, who had been shut out of the castle by the temporary castellan, Miles of Plancy.[60]

At Beaufort (Qal'at ash-Shaqif Arnun), the town probably occupied the plateau that extends south of the castle (occupied 1129–90 and 1240–68); but the traces of walling with rounded towers shown on the plan made by E. G. Rey in the 1860s are of uncertain date.[61] Similarly at Hunin (Castrum Novum) the town walls recorded by the Survey of Western Palestine in the 1870s appear to have been Ottoman, though possibly overlying earlier defences.[62] At Qaimun (Caymont), some crude walls without towers that have been revealed by excavation surrounding the top of the tell may also have provided some defence, in addition to the castle (*munitio*) that was built on another part of the site by Baldwin I (1100–18).[63]

Only 14 towns in the Kingdom of Jerusalem are recorded as having had full circuits of stone-built defences (see Table 2 and Fig. 1). These towns have a number of things in common. First, all but three of them are on the Mediterranean coast. Secondly, despite some notable exceptions, such as Nablus, which had no walls, and 'Atlit, which did, the towns with walls tended as might be expected to be the larger and more important urban centres. Thirdly, all the walled towns except 'Atlit and the Montmusard suburb of Acre, which were new foundations, already had walls before they fell to the Franks. When we look at the documented chronology for the construction of town walls, it also becomes clear that most of the building activity was concentrated in the period after the Third Crusade, when the Kingdom was reduced to little more than a coastal strip and was very much on the defensive; indeed, much of the work was carried out at this time under the patronage of Western Crusading leaders.

The walls of Jerusalem that were stormed by the Crusaders in July 1099 followed much the same course as those of Sulayman the Magnificent that stand today (Fig. 2).[64] The city thus enclosed was, therefore, somewhat smaller than that walled by the empress Eudocia in the mid-fifth century. In particular the

59 William of Tyre, XVII.12, p. 776; XX.20, p. 938.

60 William of Tyre, XX.20, pp. 938–39. On the topography, see Pringle, *Churches*, pp. 208–09, fig 59.

61 *Étude sur les monuments de l'architecture militaire des croisés en Syrie* (Paris, 1871), pp. 127–39, pl. XIII; cf. Deschamps, *Châteaux*, II, pp. 176–208.

62 Conder and Kitchener, Vol. 1, pp. 123–25; Deschamps, *Châteaux*, II, p. 130.

63 Bartolf of Nangis, *Gesta Francorum expugnantium Hierusalem*, in *RHC Occ*, Vol. 3, p. 543n.; A. Ben-Tor and R. Rosenthal, "The First Season of Excavations at Tel Yoqne'am, 1977," *IEJ* 28 (1978), 57–82; A. Ben-Tor, Y. Portugali and M. Avissàr, "The Second Season of Excavations at Tel Yoqne'am, 1978: Preliminary Report," *IEJ* 29 (1979), 65–83.

64 See *The Atlas of the Crusades*, pp. 44–45; cf. A. Cohen, "The walls of Jerusalem," in *Essays in Honor of Bernard Lewis*, eds. C. E. Bosworth et al., (Princeton: Princeton University Press, 1989), pp. 467–77.

southern parts of Byzantine Jerusalem – Mount Sion, Ophel and the Pool of Siloam – were now excluded. This contraction of the walled city seems to have occurred in the early eleventh century. Around 1033 the walls had been badly damaged by an earthquake, and Yaḥḥyā Ibn Saʿīd of Antioch records stone being taken from the ruined church of Mount Sion to rebuild them in that quarter. The rebuilding of the wall around the north-western or patriarch's quarter is also attested in 1063, when the Christian community, upon whom the financial burden fell, appealed to the Byzantine emperor for assistance. And the walls were probably further strengthened in the 1070s by the Seljuks, who may have been responsible for the forewall (*barbicana*, *antemurale*) and the ditch that are mentioned in the accounts of the siege of 1099 as having enclosed the northern part of the city, from David's Gate on the west to the Josaphat Gate on the east, and the south side of the city facing Mount Sion. Traces of a double wall have also been recorded archaeologically around the north-west side of the city; and the rock-cut ditch may still be seen at the north-west corner and at the northern end of the east wall.[65]

The walls that were described by Theodoric around 1172 were probably little different from those captured in 1099:

> [The city] is most strongly fortified by towers, walls and foreworks (*propugnaculis*) on the heights of the hill above the . . . valleys [Hinnom and Cedron]. A dyke (*vallum*) or ditch (*fossatum*) is also placed outside the wall, defended by a wall and foreworks with loopholes (*minis*), which they call a barbican (*barbicana*).[66]

On the west, the ditch entered the city to enclose the citadel, or David's Tower; while another rectangular tower of pre-Crusader date (Tancred's Tower, or the Tower of Goliath) occupied the north-west corner. In the south-east the city wall followed the south and east walls of the Temple Mount. There were seven principal gates and at least five posterns, including one near the church of St. Mary Magdalene in the north-east which opened into the space between the walls.[67]

There is scant record of any building work on the walls in the twelfth century,

---

[65] J. Prawer, "The Jerusalem the Crusaders Captured: A Contribution to the Medieval Topography of the City," in *Crusade and Settlement*, ed. P. Edbury (Cardiff: University College Cardiff Press, 1985), pp. 1–16; D. Bahat and M. B. Ben-Ari, "Excavations at Tancred's Tower," in *Jerusalem Revealed: Archaeology in the Holy City 1968–74*, ed. Y. Yadin (Jerusalem: Israel Exploration Society, 1975), pp. 109–10; G. Wightman, *The Damascus Gate, Jerusalem: Excavations by C.-M. Bennett and J. B. Hennessy*, BAR International Series, 519 (Oxford: BAR, 1989), fig. 24.

[66] Theodericus, III, p. 11.

[67] F. M. Abel, "L'état de la cité de Jérusalem au XII siècle," in *Jerusalem 1920–1922: Being the Records of the Pro-Jerusalem Council during the First Two Years of the Civil Administration*, ed. C. R. Ashbee (London: J. Murray for the Council of the Pro-Jerusalem Society, 1924), pp. 32–40; cf. H. Vincent and F. M. Abel, *Jérusalem: Recherches de topographie, d'archéologie et d'histoire*, II, *Jérusalem nouvelle*, 4 fascs. + album (Paris: Gabalda, 1914–26), pp. 945–73; D. Pringle, "Crusader Jerusalem," *Bulletin of the Anglo-Israel Archaeological Society* 10 (1990–91), 105–13.

beyond repairs in 1116 and 1177.[68] Following his capture of the city in August 1187, Saladin initiated an extensive rebuilding programme in 1192, giving his amirs individual responsibility for rebuilding sectors of the wall and its towers.[69] It may have been at this time that Mount Sion was enclosed by a wall, partly following the line of an earlier one of the Roman-Byzantine period that was excavated in the 1870s and '90s and appears to be that represented, albeit anachronistically, on Marino Sanuto's map of the city, drawn around 1321.[70] The building work continued under al-Muʿaẓẓam ʿĪsā (1202–12), but now excluded Mount Sion; it seems to have included the series of at least four massive towers, some 23 m. square, whose foundations have been excavated along the south side of the city.[71] In 1219–20, however, these and the rest of Jerusalem's defences were dismantled by the same sultan just ten years before the city was returned once more to Christian hands. During this second Crusader occupation, work is recorded being carried out on the Citadel, St. Stephen's Gate and Sion Gate; but in 1239 al-Nāsir Dāwūd took the Citadel and destroyed it. Thereafter construction work continued under the Templars in 1243–44; but in August 1244 the city was finally lost.[72]

A general archaeological assessment of Jerusalem's medieval walls has still to be made.[73] Excavations carried out at St. Stephen's Gate (the present Damascus Gate) in the 1960s, however, have shed some light on the character of the twelfth- and thirteenth-century defences.[74] The gate was found to be Roman in origin, built between the mid-first and mid-third century A.D. It consisted of a central archway, flanked by smaller arched gates for pedestrians and two

68 Benvenisti, p. 49.

69 Deschamps, *Châteaux*, II, p. 7; D. Pringle, "King Richard I and the Walls of Ascalon," *Palestine Exploration Quarterly* 116 (1984), 133–47 (at p. 138); M. Rosen-Ayalon, "Art and Architecture in Ayyubid Jerusalem," *IEJ* 40 (1990), 305–14 (at. pp. 306–07).

70 D. Bahat, "Sanuto's Map and the Walls of Jerusalem in the Thirteenth Century," *Eretz Israel* 19 (1987), 295–89, 83* [in Hebrew, with English summary; title here given in English translation]; cf. C. Warren and C. R. Conder, *The Survey of Western Palestine: Jerusalem* (London, 1884), pp. 271, 393–97; F. J. Bliss and A. C. Dickie, *Excavations at Jerusalem 1894–1897* (London, 1898).

71 N. Avigad, *Discovering Jerusalem* (Jerusalem: Shikmona, 1983), pp. 251–55; M. Ben-Dov, *Jerusalem's Fortifications: The City Walls, the Gates and the Temple Mount* (Tel Aviv: Zemorah, Bitan, 1983) [in Hebrew; title here in English translation]; M. Broshi, "Al-Malek al-Muazzam Isa – Evidence in a New Inscription," *Eretz Israel* 19 (1987), 299–302, 82* [in Hebrew, with English summary; title here in English translation]; M. Broshi and Y. Tsafrir, "Excavations at the Zion Gate, Jerusalem," *IEJ* 27 (1977), 28–37; M. Rosen-Ayalon, "Art and Architecture," pp. 309–13; Y. Margovsky, "Jérusalem: Bordj Kabrit et environs," *Revue biblique* 78 (1971), 597–98, pl. XXXII; M. Sharon, "The Ayyubid Walls of Jerusalem: A New Inscription from the Time of Al-Muʿazzam ʿĪsā," in *Studies in Memory of Gaston Wiet*, pp. 179–93.

72 Deschamps, *Châteaux*, II, pp. 7–8, 18; C. N. Johns, "The Citadel, Jerusalem: A Summary of Work since 1934," *Quarterly of the Department of Antiquities of Palestine* 14 (1950), 121–90 (esp. pp. 167–70); Benvenisti, p. 51.

73 But see G. J. Wightman, *The Walls of Jerusalem, from the Canaanites to the Mamluks* (Mediterranean Archaeology, Supplement 4: Sydney 1994), pp. 259–98.

74 B. Hennessy, "Preliminary Report on Excavations at the Damascus Gate, 1964–6," *Levant* 2 (1970), 22–27; Wightman, *Damascus Gate*; cf. M. Magen, "Recording Roman Jerusalem – The entry beneath Damascus Gate," *Biblical Archaeology Review* 15.3 (1988), 48–56.

massive quadrangular towers. By the twelfth century only the central gateway remained in use. In the early years of the century, however, a gatehouse, or barbican, containing a bent entrance was constructed in front of it on the line of the outer wall. Later on, other buildings were constructed to either side of and apparently over the road leading between the two gates; that on the west included a small chapel containing a wall-painting representing the Annunciation, executed around 1140.[75] It seems possible that this was part of the hospital belonging to the abbey of St. Mary Latin that is recorded within the gate in 1158.[76] After a phase of destruction, which may perhaps be associated with that of al-Mu'azzam 'Īsā in 1219–20, there is evidence for a partial *mise-en-valeur* before a final destruction, dated by a coin to after 1212/25 and plausibly associated with that of al-Nāṣir Dāwūd in 1239.[77]

Acre was the second largest city in the kingdom after Jerusalem itself, almost equalling it in size in the thirteenth century; and by the time of its fall to the Mamluks it had the most complex system of fortifications of any city in the Crusader states. Frankish occupation lasted from 1104 to 1187, and then from 1191 to 1291.

The nucleus of the city lies on a promontory of marine sandstone, aligned north-south, which defines the north end of the bay of Acre. The plan of the twelfth-century city was determined by that of its Muslim predecessor, with a wall and ditch on the north and east enclosing a roughly rhomboid area. Such is also how the city appears on the early fourteenth-century maps of Pietro Vesconte and Paolino Veneto (see Fig. 3).[78] The scale of these maps when related to the local topography, however, is difficult to determine, for although remains of the north city wall can still be seen, incorporated into the inner north Turkish wall of *c.* 1745–75, and although excavations in 1984 showed the battered base of this wall to have continued eastward beyond the present Turkish east wall of 1799,[79] opinions differ as to how far east it went. D. Jacoby has suggested no more than about 50 m., allowing its southern return to be aligned with the east harbour mole (as it appears to be on the fourteenth-century maps), of which underwater remains are attested. This would make the wall some 700 m. long on the north, and 350 m. on the east, enclosing about 33 ha.[80] Recent research, however, both archaeological and cartographic, supports an earlier theory that

[75] L.-A. Hunt, "Damascus Gate, Jerusalem, and Crusader Wallpainting of the Mid-Twelfth Century," in *Crusader Art in the Twelfth Century*, ed. J. Folda, BAR International Series, 152 (Oxford: BAR, 1982), pp. 191–214.

[76] *Vorarbeiten zum Oriens Pontificius*, III, *Papsturkunden für Kirchen im Heiligen Lande*, ed. R. Hiestand, Abhandlungen der Akademie der Wissenschaften in Göttingen, Phil.-hist. Klasse, series 3, 136 (Göttingen: Vandenhoeck & Ruprecht, 1985), pp. 218–22, n. 79; cf. *RRH*, pp. 85–86, n. 331; Theodericus, XXVI, p. 34; Pringle, "Crusader Jerusalem," pp. 106–07.

[77] Wightman, pp. 59–60.

[78] D. Jacoby, "Crusader Acre in the Thirteenth Century: Urban Layout and Topography," *Studi medievali*, 3rd ser., 20.1 (1979), 1–45 (at pp. 2–4).

[79] A. Druks, "Akko, Fortifications," *ESI* 3 (1984), 2–4.

[80] Jacoby, "Crusader Acre," pp. 40–41.

the wall continued east by another 450 m. or so, and thus enclosed an area of some 51.5 ha.[81]

When Baldwin I unsuccessfully attacked Acre in 1103, it was very strongly defended by a wall and forewall ("muro et antemurali fortis erat ualde").[82] There is scant mention of building works in the twelfth century, though repairs were carried out by Saladin after his capture of the city in 1187, and by the Franks when they retook it in 1191.[83] In 1193, however, when Henry of Champagne, count of Troyes, granted the Hospital part of the east wall extending northward from the postern next to the Gate of Geoffrey de Tor[84] up to (but excluding) the Gate of St. Nicolas, the grant included the forewall (*antemuralis*), land and ditch, and the land in front of the forewall as far as the River Belus.[85] In a simultaneous grant to the Teutonic Order of the sector of fortification extending immediately north of this one and including St. Nicolas' Gate, the defences are described as "totam barbacanam, turres quoque et muros et fossatum" (the whole barbican, also the towers, the walls and the ditch").[86]

On the north side of the city there is mention in January 1194 of a barbican outside the wall at the point where the Hospital's New Gate was to be built;[87] and in October 1198 there is record of a house sited between the wall and the barbican near to the *porta Boueriae Templi*, or St. Michael's Gate, further west.[88] Even in the thirteenth century, when the suburb of Montmusard, which lay immediately north of this, was enclosed by its own wall, there still survived a ditch and an outer wall ("doga fossati civitas") in front of the by then largely defunct inner north wall of the city.[89] It seems, therefore, that in the twelfth century the city was already defended on the north and east by a wall with towers and gates, preceded in sequence by a ditch, a berm or lists (*barbacana*), and finally a forewall (*antemuralis, doga*).

In January 1194, the Hospital's New Gate in the north wall still marked the

---

[81] See W. M. Müller-Wiener, *Castles of the Crusaders* (London: Thames and Hudson, 1966), p. 73, plan 23; B. Dichter, *The Maps of Acre: An Historical Cartography* (Acre: Municipality of Acre, 1973), p. 99. I am also grateful to Professor B. Z. Kedar for discussion of his forthcoming paper on this subject.

[82] Fulcher of Chartres, II.22.1, pp. 456–57; D. Jacoby, "Montmusard, Suburb of Crusader Acre: The First Stage of its Development," in *Outremer: Studies in the History of the Crusading Kingdom*, ed. B. Z. Kedar, H. E. Mayer and R. C. Smail (Jerusalem: Yad Izhak Ben-Zvi Institute, 1982), pp. 205–17 (at p. 214).

[83] Jacoby, "Crusader Acre," p. 40; and "Montmusard," p. 211.

[84] This postern had been formed sometime before March 1181: *CGOH*, Vol. 2, p. 909, n. 20; cf. Jacoby, "Montmusard," p. 212.

[85] *CGOH*, Vol. 1, p. 594, n. 938; *RRH Ad*, p. 48, n. 716a.

[86] *TOT*, pp. 24–25, n. 28; *RRH*, pp. 191–92, n. 716.

[87] *Codice diplomatico del sacro militare ordine gerosolimitano oggi di Malta*, ed. S. Paoli, Vol. 1 (Lucca, 1733), p. 87, n. 81; *RRH*, p. 192, n. 717.

[88] *Codice diplomatico*, p. 287, n. 8; *RRH*, pp. 198–99, n. 746; Jacoby, "Montmusard," p. 208, n. 20.

[89] *RRH*, p. 270, n. 1036 (1232), cf. pp. 277–78, n. 1063 (1235); *TOT*, pp. 73–74, n. 92 (1242).

city boundary.[90] By 1291, however, as the fourteenth-century maps and the descriptions of the siege of 1291 make clear, the Montmusard suburb had been enclosed by a double wall extending from the sea on the north-west to St. Antony's Gate, opposite the royal castle, in the south-east; from here, the double wall continued east and south, following the line of the twelfth-century defences.

When was Montmusard enclosed? Jacoby argues that the double wall was completed by 1212, when the city's landward side was described by Wilbrand of Oldenburg as

> encompassed by a fine, wide and deep ditch, stone-lined to the very bottom, and by a double wall fortified with towers according to a fine arrangement, in such a way that the first [outer] wall with its towers does not overtop the main [inner] wall and is commanded and defended by the second and inner wall, the towers of which are tall and very strong.

We have seen, however, that a system comprising wall, ditch, "barbican" and outer wall already existed by the 1190s around the whole of the "Old City," but not apparently around Montmusard. Furthermore, Henry of Champagne granted the Teutonic Order part of such a system on the east in 1193, on condition that they repaired and improved it.[92] In August 1217, the Order also received from King John of Brienne another barbican, "infra duos muros ciuitatis" (between the two walls of the city), further south between the gate of Geoffrey de Tor and the Barbican of the Seneschal.[93] It appears possible, therefore, that, at least on the east, the double wall described by Wilbrand may have represented simply a rebuilding and strengthening of a system that had existed in the twelfth century. Could the same have also been true on the north? Against this idea, and in support of Jacoby's view that the wall seen by Wilbrand did, indeed, enclose Montmusard, we may note the lack of any specific evidence for rebuilding of the inner north wall after the 1190s or for two walls (as opposed to a wall and forewall), and the fact that the double wall of Montmusard shown on the fourteenth-century maps appears to have been integral with that around the eastern part of the city. Extensive rebuilding would in any case have been necessary after the earthquake of 1202, in which the town walls and royal castle sustained serious damage.[94] The standard of the walls of Montmusard in 1212, however, may still not have been up to that of the eastern sector, which had a longer history of fortification; for it was precisely the sector enclosing Montmusard that King Louis IX, in 1251, "fortified with walls and ditches . . . beginning

---

[90] *Codice diplomatico*, p. 87, n. 81; *RRH*, p. 192, n. 717.

[91] *Peregrinatio*, ed. J. C. M. Laurent, *Peregrinatores Medii Aeui Quatuor* (Leipzig, 1864), pp. 159–91 (at p. 164); passage trans. in Jacoby, "Montmusard," p. 212.

[92] *TOT*, pp. 24–25, n. 28; *RRH*, pp. 191–92, n. 716.

[93] *TOT*, p. 41, n. 50; *RRH*, p. 241, n. 899.

[94] H. E. Mayer, "Two Unpublished Letters on the Syrian Earthquake of 1202," in *Medieval and Middle Eastern Studies in Honor of S. A. Atiya* (Leiden: Brill, 1972), pp. 295–310 (at pp. 307, 309).

from the Gate of St. Antony [and continuing] towards the sea as far as St. Lawrence."[95]

The question of the location of the walls of Montmusard is now somewhat closer to resolution than it was ten years ago.[96] The foundations of a cylindrical tower, 13.1 m. in diameter with walls 1 m. thick, have been located below high-water level on the foreshore some 800 m. north of the present city walls. This tower appears to be the one shown on one copy of the Paolino map of c. 1220 as marking the termination of the outer wall of Montmusard.[97] The size of the suburb thus enclosed would, therefore, have been about 34 ha. and the course of its walls would have corresponded to the trace of medieval walls shown on maps dating from the time of Napoleon's siege of 1799.[98]

Between the time of the Mamluk raids on the extramural suburbs of Acre in 1263 and 1266 and the fall of the city in 1291, further works were carried out to strengthen the north-eastern corner of the old city wall, which represented one of its weakest points. The Accursed Tower, at the corner of the inner wall, was preceded by an outer New Round Tower of King Henry II (of Cyprus), beyond which was a Barbican of King Hugh.[99] There is also mention of a Tower of the Countess of Blois and of a Tower of the English, or Barbican of the Lord Edward, that were evidently built in the 1270s–80s.[100]

Ascalon, almost taken in August 1099, only fell to the Franks after a siege in August 1153. Its walls ran along the top of a vast earthwork of Middle Bronze Age date, surrounding the city to landward in a semi-circle some 1.5 km. long and enclosing an area of some 50 ha. (Fig. 4). They appear to have been constructed in the late Roman or Byzantine period, but were rebuilt by the 'Umayyads in the seventh century and quite possibly again by the Fatimids in the eleventh and early twelfth. William of Tyre describes the walls in 1153 as strengthened with closely spaced towers, and ringed by forewalls (antemuralia). The four gates, facing Jaffa, Jerusalem, Gaza and the sea respectively, were defended by towers, and the Jerusalem gate was set between towers and was approached by means of certain tortuous paths from three or four smaller gates in the forewall in front of it.[101] Later accounts give the number of towers somewhat implausibly as 53, not counting the smaller ones, and provide names for five of them: the Tower of the Maidens, of the Shields, of Blood, of the

95   F. Boustrone, Chronique de l'Île de Chipre, ed R. de Mas Latrie (Paris, 1885), p. 109; cf. Jacoby, "Montmusard," p. 214, n. 45; P. Deschamps, Les Châteaux des croisés en Terre Sainte, I, Le Crac des Chevaliers, Bibliothèque archéologique et historique, 19 (Paris: Geuthner, 1934), pp. 63–69; and his Châteaux, II, p. 18.

96   Cf. Jacoby, "Montmusard," pp. 214–16.

97   R. Frankel, "The North-West Corner of Crusader Acre," IEJ 37 (1987), 256–61, pls. 31–32.

98   Dichter, pp. 139–52. See also my note 81 above.

99   E. Stickel, Der Fall von Akkon, Geist und Werk der Zeiten, 45 (Frankfurt: Peter Lang, 1975), pp. 15–18.

100   Stickel, pp. 17–18; T. E. Lawrence, Crusader Castles, ed. D. Pringle (Oxford: Clarendon Press, 1988), p. xl. See also below in the section The organization of building work.

101   William of Tyre, XVII.22, pp. 790–93; cf. al-Idrīsī, translation in Le Strange, p. 401.

Amirs, and of the Bedouin.[102] In 1187, Ascalon fell to Saladin, who in 1191 razed its walls and expelled its population. By the time that the Crusaders entered the city both Muslim and Christian sources agree in saying that all the towers had been reduced to ground level. From January to Easter 1192, Richard I rebuilt the walls and towers with the help of Duke Hugh III of Burgundy's French contingent.[103] In September 1192, however, by the Treaty of Jaffa it was agreed by both parties to demolish the walls once more, and this work was carried out by the Muslims and Franks within a year.[104]

In November 1239, Ascalon was recovered by the Franks and was refortified the following year by Richard of Cornwall, the brother of Henry III of England. This work, however, seems to have involved no more than the construction of a castle in the north-west corner of the site. This fell to the Muslims in October 1247, and was destroyed by Baybars in 1270.[105]

The deliberate destruction of the walls in 1191 and 1270, helped by the fact that they were built on a sandy foundation, means that what survives of them today is in an extremely ruinous state. Little is, therefore, known archaeologically of the walls and forewalls that were standing in 1153. The latest major structural phase, however, may be associated with Richard I's rebuilding work of 1192. The work is characterized by narrow courses of smoothly dressed ashlar, set on a battered plinth with horizontal offsets at intervals of 1.2–1.9 m.; the mortar is a strong hydraulic lime, containing crushed pottery or brick and in the wall core some shell and charcoal. The walls and towers, numbering at least 14 and varying in shape from rectangular to rounded and triangular, are built with through-columns. The construction of Richard of Cornwall's castle is similar, though less of it survives. On the north, where its outer wall follows the course of the earlier town wall, its base is strengthened by a thick masonry *talus*, while on the south and east it is enclosed by a rock-cut ditch.[106]

The medieval city of Tyre was sited on a rocky island, triangular in shape and some 48 ha. in extent, connected to the mainland by a low-lying causeway, man-made in origin and a bow-shot wide (Fig. 5).[107] From February to July 1124, during the captivity of Baldwin II, it was besieged by the barons of the kingdom and the Venetians.

> On the sea side – writes William of Tyre – Tyre was surrounded by a double wall with towers of goodly height at equal distances apart. On the east, where the approach by land lies, it has a triple wall with enormously high and massive towers so close together that they almost touch one another. There was also a

---

[102] *Itinerarium Peregrinorum*, V.6, pp. 316–17.

[103] *Itinerarium Peregrinorum*, V.6, V.17–18, pp. 315–16, 329–30.

[104] *Itinerarium Peregrinorum*, VI.27, pp. 428–29; Benvenisti, pp. 114–28; Pringle, "King Richard I."

[105] See Pringle, "King Richard I," pp. 143–46; C. Marshall, *Warfare in the Latin East, 1192–1291*, Cambridge Studies in Medieval Life and Thought, 4th series, 17 (Cambridge: Cambridge University Press, 1992), pp. 102–05; cf. Benvenisti, pp. 120, 126.

[106] Pringle, "King Richard I."

[107] William of Tyre, XIII.4, p. 590.

broad open dyke (*uallum*) through which the citizens could easliy let in the sea from both sides. On the north, its entrance guarded by two towers, was the inner harbour which lay within the walls of the city.[108]

There was also a safe anchorage in the lea of the island, on the north side of the isthmus. While the Christians pounded the land walls with stone-hurling machines, calling in at one point an expert Armenian engineer from Antioch to direct them, the defenders hit back with bows and *ballistae*; but finally the city surrendered on 7 July.[109]

The existence of a double wall on the seaward side is confirmed by a grant, made by Baldwin II to the Holy Sepulchre soon after the city's capture, of "a garden, which is between the wall and the forewall (*antemurale*) of the . . . city, on the side facing the sea."[110] This was associated with a pool (*berquilium*).[111]

Descriptions of Tyre from later in the twelfth century suggest that the walls and towers were subsequently repaired. Theodoric describes the land wall around 1172 as very strongly defended by ditches, barbicans, towers, walls, foreworks (*propugnaculis*) and embrasures (*minis*).[112] Ibn Jubayr, who travelled in 1184, echoes Theodoric's decription of the gates, saying that the city had two, one to landward and one facing the harbour, both of them flanked by towers and the former having three or four gates within it.[113]

The walls were damaged by an earthquake in 1170, and in June 1202 Philip of Le Plessis, master of the Teutonic Order, reported to the abbot of Cîteaux that "all the towers but three, and the walls except for the outer barbican" had collapsed;[114] the master of the Hospital considered the damage caused by this tremor to have been so extensive that it was unlikely to be repaired in a lifetime.[115] However, it is clear that by 1283 the walls had been rebuilt, for in that year Burchard of Mount Sion described the landward side of the city as

> surrounded by a triple wall, strong and high, and 25 feet thick. These walls are moreover fortified with twelve very strong towers, of which I do not recall having seen better in all the world. These towers are linked to the citadel or castle, which is very strongly defended and situated on a rock in the midst of the sea; it is likewise fortified with towers and very strong residences (*palaciis fortissimis*).[116]

[108] William of Tyre, XIII.5, p. 592; trans. (adapted) from *History of Deeds*, Vol. 2, p. 9.

[109] William of Tyre, XIII.6–10, 14, pp. 593–98, 602.

[110] *Cartulaire*, pp. 90–91, n. 28; *RRH*, p. 27, n. 109.

[111] *Cartulaire*, pp. 147–48, n. 56; *RRH*, pp. 97–98, n. 370.

[112] *Libellus*, LI, p. 51.

[113] *Voyages*, trans. M. Gaudefroy-Demombynes, Vol. 3, DRHC, 4–6 (Paris: Geuthner, 1953), p. 357.

[114] Mayer, "Two Unpublished Letters," p. 309, cf. pp. 303, 307.

[115] Mayer, "Two Unpublished Letters," p. 307; cf. D. H. Kallner-Amiran, "A Revised Earthquake-Catalogue of Palestine," *IEJ* 1 (1951), 233–46 (at p. 228); M. Chéhab, *Tyr à l'époque des croisades*, II, *Histoire sociale, économique et religieuse* (Paris: Geuthner, 1979), pp. 710–12.

[116] *Descriptio Terrae Sanctae*, XIII, *IHC*, Vol. 4, p. 130 (*palaciis* might alternatively be interpreted as "palings, fences or enclosures").

The triple walls of Tyre were mentioned by John Poloner in 1422,[117] and traces of them were still visible in the eighteenth century.[118] They had disappeared by the 1870s, though remains of the seaward walls with rectangular towers could be seen on the south and west departing from the western mole of the harbour; these were constructed, like the Crusader defences of Ascalon, with through-columns.[119]

The castle mentioned by Burchard of Mount Sion in 1283 was probably sited at the northern end of the land wall, close to and possibly integral with the eastern mole of the harbour.[120] It is already mentioned in 1190 as being near the walls;[121] and in March 1212 King John of Brienne purchased land "near the Sidon gate . . . next to the new castle that I have begun to build, which land was absolutely necessary for the same castle."[122]

Beirut was in Frankish hands from 1110 to 1291, with a Muslim occupation lasting from 1187 to 1197. It was already defended by strong walls when it first fell to the Franks, so that despite the existence of an ample local supply of timber for building siege engines it took two months to reduce it.[123] We hear little of its walls in the twelfth century; but they were evidently kept in a state of repair, for in 1182 they withstood a siege by Saladin, who despite having overwhelming forces, lacked siege machines.[124] In 1190, however, three years after its recapture by the Muslims, Saladin dismantled Beirut's town walls, though not its castle.[125] The walls were, therefore, in ruins when the city was retaken in 1197; but it was subsequently refortified by its new lord, John of Ibelin, from 1205 onwards.[126]

If we assume that the town walls followed more or less the line of those that still existed in the late nineteenth century (Fig. 6), they would have measured some 570 m. N-S by 370 m. E-W and have enclosed a roughly rectangular area of 19 ha.[127] On the north was the harbour, enclosed by a mole, with a pair of

[117] *Description of the Holy Land (circa 1421 A.D.)*, trans. A. Stewart, PPTS (London, 1894), p. 31.

[118] R. Pococke, *A Description of the East and Some Other Countries*, Vol. 2 (London, 1743–45), p. 82, pl. IX.

[119] Conder and Kitchener, Vol. 1, pp. 72–81, pl. opp. p. 72; cf. V. Guérin, *Description géographique, historique et archéologique de la Palestine*, III, *Galilée*, Vol. 2 (Paris, 1880), pp. 180–95; E. G. Rey, *Les Colonies franques de Syrie aux XIIme et XIIIme siècles* (Paris, 1883), pp. 502–05.

[120] Cf. Rey, pp. 504–05; "Chronique," *BMB* 18 (1965), 111–25 (at pp. 112–13).

[121] *RRH*, pp. 183–84, n. 691, cf. pp. 347–48, n. 1331 (1264).

[122] *Chartes de Terre Sainte provenant de l'abbaye de Notre-Dame de Josaphat*, ed. H. F. Delaborde, Bibliothèque des Écoles françaises d'Athènes et de Rome, 19 (Paris, 1880), pp. 95–96, n. 46; *RRH*, p. 229, n. 857.

[123] William of Tyre, XI.13, pp. 515–16; cf. Le Strange, p. 408.

[124] William of Tyre, XXII.18–19 (17–18), pp. 1032–36.

[125] *L'Estoire d'Eracles empereur*, *RHC Occ*, Vol. 2, p. 140; *La Continuation de Guillaume de Tyr (1184–1197)*, ed. M. R. Morgan, DRHC, 14 (Paris: Geuthner, 1982), p. 98.

[126] *Les Gestes des Chiprois*, *RHC Arm*, Vol. 2, pp. 678–79; cf. Deschamps, *Châteaux*, II, p. 16n.

[127] Pringle, *Churches*, pp. 111–12, fig. 36; Comte du Mesnil du Buisson, "Les anciens défenses de Beyrouth," *Syria* 3 (1921), 235–57, 317–27, pls. XXXV–XL, XLVI–LIII.

towers at its mouth and a chain stretched between them.[128] At the north-eastern corner, where the land wall met the sea, stood the castle. This is described by Wilbrand of Oldenburg in 1212 as having a deep, stone-lined ditch, overlooked by two strong walls, which were provided with strong towers, their masonry held together by iron clamps as a protection against attack by machines; one of these towers, newly built, contained the ornately decorated Ibelin hall or palace (*palacium*).[129] It is not clear what state the walls were in at this time, but in 1231 Frederick II was able to take the town but not the castle.[130] Both the walls and the castle were destroyed when Beirut fell to the Mamluks in 1291.[131]

Sidon, occupying a rocky promontory between Beirut to the north and Tyre to the south, was held by the Franks from December 1110 until July 1187, and from 1197 to 14 July 1291. By the time of its fall to the Mamluks, the land wall ran from sea to sea, enclosing the southern and eastern sides of an area of some 15 ha., with the Land Castle (Qal'at al-Mu'azzam) occupying a mound at the south-east corner (Fig. 7). At the northern end of the east wall, a bridge linked the town with a Sea Castle, sited on an island and defending the entrance to the part-natural, part-manmade harbour.[132]

A stone wall surrounding the town is already attested by Nāsir-i Khusraw in 1047, and by al-Idrīsī in 1153.[133] In 1162, Gerard, lord of Sidon, granted the Hospitallers a gate in the city wall and forewall (*antemurali*), with some land outside, and the whole forewall from Baldwin's Tower up to the Tower of the Sea; it is uncertain whether this Sea Tower stood at the north-eastern or south-western end of the landward defences.[134] However, there is mention in 1126 of a barbican gate facing Tyre on the south;[135] and in 1228 the same is described as "the two gates of the city of Sidon, from which one goes out towards Tyre."[136]

The defences were demolished by Saladin during the Third Crusade.[137] Refortification began with the construction of the Sea Castle by German Crusaders in 1227. The excavation and architectural analysis of this by H. Kalayan have identified three subsequent phases, which he dates respectively to

---

[128] John Phocas, *Ekphrasis*, ch. V, in *PG*, Vol. 133, col. 932; trans. in A. Stewart, *The Pilgrimage of Joannes Phocas*, PPTS, 5 (London, 1896), pp. 9–10.

[129] *Peregrinatio*, I.5, ed. J. C. M. Laurent, *Peregrinatores Medii Aeui Quatuor* (Leipzig, 1864), p. 167; *IHC*, Vol. 3, p. 204; cf. T. S. R. Boase, *Castles and Churches of the Crusading Kingdom* (Oxford: Oxford University Press, 1967), p. 65.

[130] du Mesnil du Buisson, p. 241.

[131] *Gestes des Chiprois*, *RHC Arm*, Vol. 2, p. 817; du Mesnil du Buisson, p. 242.

[132] Müller-Wiener, p. 69, plan 20.

[133] Le Strange, p. 346.

[134] *CGOH*, Vol. 1, p. 218, n. 302; *RRH Ad*, p. 22, n. 376b; cf. *CGOH*, Vol. 2, p. 510, n. 2160; *RRH Ad*, p. 66, n. 1076a (1237).

[135] *Chartes de l'abbaye de N.-D. de la vallée de Josaphat*, ed. C. Kohler (Paris, 1900; reprinted from *Revue de l'Orient latin* 7 [1899], 108–222), pp. 15–16, n. 12; *RRH Ad*, p. 8, n. 114b.

[136] *TOT*, pp. 50–51, n. 62; *RRH*, p. 260, n. 986.

[137] Abū Shāmā, *Le Livre des deux jardins*, in *RHC Or*, Vol. 4, p. 462; Deschamps, *Châteaux*, II, p. 224.

the period of Louis IX (*c.* 1253), some time between then and 1278, and the period of Templar occupation of the castle from 1278 to 1291.[138] The Land Castle, whose remains were recorded by P. Coupel in 1939, before their destruction in the interests of classical and Phoenician archaeology, seems to have dated mostly from the seventeenth century, but excavations have also revealed traces of a Crusader *talus* with a ditch and counterscarp wall on the side where the castle wall and the city wall were the same.[139] No doubt, this was part of the refortification carried out by Louis IX of France from July 1253 to February 1254. Work began under the direction of Simon of Montcéliard, master of crossbowmen, while Louis was still in Jaffa; but a Muslim attack forced the French to retreat into the Sea Castle and succeeded in breaking into the town and killing over 2000 people, "for the town was not completely surrounded by walls."[140] By the time that Louis left for France, however, the town had been "fortified with high walls and towers, and wide moats cleared of mud within and without."[141]

Caesarea was a walled city when it fell to the Franks in May 1101.[142] After its recapture by the Muslims in 1187, Saladin supervised the destruction of its defences in 1191, before abandoning it to the Christians, who entered the town in August the same year. In 1206, Juliana, lady of Caesarea, granted the Teutonic Order the Tower of Mallart and another smaller tower on the east side of the town, and confirmed the order's possession of a garden adjacent to the east city wall; this seems to suggest that the twelfth-century walls had no outworks, beyond perhaps a ditch.[143]

In 1217, King John of Brienne began to refortify Caesarea with the assistance of Leopold of Austria and the Hospitallers; but during the winter of 1219–20, the city was raided by al-Mu'azzam 'Īsā. Work started again in May 1228, and continued until September with the help of German Crusaders under Henry of Limburg. It was carried to completion by Louis IX from March 1251 to May 1252.[144] The city fell to Baybars in 1265, the walled town in February and the

---

[138] "The Sea Castle of Sidon," *BMB* 16 (1973), 81–89; cf. Deschamps, *Châteaux*, II, pp. 225, 229–33.

[139] G. Conteneau, "Mission archéologique à Sidon (1914)," *Syria* 1 (1920), 16–55, 108–54, 198–229, 287–317 (at pp. 108–24); G. Conteneau, "Deuxième mission archéologique à Sidon (1920)," *Syria* 4 (1923), 261–81 (at pp. 261–69); Deschamps, *Châteaux*, II, pp. 227–29, fig. 23; M. Dunand, "Chronique," *BMB* 3 (1939), 77–85 (at pp. 79–81); 4 (1940), 117–25 (at p. 118); 5 (1941), 87–93 (at pp. 88, 90); M. Dunand, "Rapport préliminaire sur les fouilles de Sidon en 1964–1965," *BMB* 20 (1967), 27–44 (at pp. 29–30, pl. I.5).

[140] John of Joinville, *Histoire de Saint Louis*, CVII.551–53, ed. N. de Wailly (Paris: Hachette et Cie. 1906), pp. 232–33; trans. in M. R. B. Shaw, *Chronicles of the Crusades* (Harmondsworth: Penguin, 1963), pp. 161–353 (at p. 303).

[141] Joinville, CXXI.615, p. 258; trans. in Shaw, p. 318; cf. Joinville, CXIII.582, p. 245; trans. Shaw, p. 310.

[142] William of Tyre, X.14 (15), pp. 469–71; cf. Le Strange, p. 474.

[143] *TOT*, pp. 32–33, n. 40, cf. p. 123, n. 128.

[144] Joinville, XCVI.493, XCVII.495, XCVIII.499, C.515, CXXI.616, pp. 207, 208, 210, 216, 259; trans. Shaw, pp. 289–95, 318.

castle in March, whereupon the Mamluks demolished the defences once again.[145]

The city walls enclose three sides of a roughly rectangular area, some 450 m. N-S by 240 m. E-W (*c.* 10 ha.), with the sea on the west (Fig. 8).[146] Their trace was apparently determined by that of the pre-existing Abbasid or Fatimid walls,[147] whose course was in turn influenced by the earlier Roman-Byzantine street grid. In the south-east, the remains of the castle occupy a natural sandstone promontory, which formed the southern side of an otherwise manmade harbour; it seems to have contained a large central rectangular keep, and to have been cut off from the town by a wall flanked by rectangular towers and preceded by a sea-level rock-cut ditch.

The town walls and ditch were cleared of fallen rubble by the Israel National Parks Authority in 1960–62. They are built throughout of sandstone (*kurkar*) ashlar, set in a white lime mortar with a core composed of weaker clay mortar and rubble. The system comprises in its final form a wall (of uncertain height but over 4 m. thick), which in some places, notably on the north and south, contains rows of casemated arrow-slits with sloping sills. Against its outer face, and clearly secondary to it, is a *talus* (or *glacis*), rising some 8 m. from the bottom of a dry ditch, 7–8 m. wide and 4–6 m. deep, with a vertical counterscarp wall following a dog-legged course corresponding to the trace of the curtains and towers. There are remains of 14 rectangular towers (10–17 m. wide, projecting 7–8 m.), including the gates, but it is likely that others once existed on the west where there has been considerable marine erosion.

Each wall contained a gate. That on the north is set in the west side of a square projecting tower and was reached by a bridge, the outer part of which would have been of timber and the inner carried on a masonry arch. The gate, 3.2 m. wide and defended by a portcullis and a pair of wing-doors, possibly preceded by a slit machicolation, led into the tower's ground floor; this was 8.25 m. square and enclosed by a rib-vault of early-thirteenth-century type, springing from hexagonal corner pilasters with foliated capitals. From here another gate, defended by a pair of wing-doors secured by a draw-bar, led through the south wall into the town, while a smaller door in the west wall between the two gates led up within the wall to a guard chamber on the first floor.

The east gate shows at least two phases. The first, which may be pre-Crusader

---

[145] On the history of Crusader Caesarea, see Benvenisti, pp. 135–40; H. W. Hazard, "Caesarea and the Crusades," in *Studies in the History of Caesarea Maritima*, ed. C. T. Fritsch, Bulletin of the American Schools of Oriental Research, Supplemental Series, 19 (Missoula MT: Scholars Press for the American Schools of Oriental Research, 1975), pp. 79–114; M. Sharon, "Kaysariyya," *Encyclopedia of Islam*, 2nd ed., Vol. 4 (Leiden: Brill, 1978), pp. 841–42.

[146] On the archaeological evidence for the walls, see: A. Frova, M. Avi-Yonah and A. Negev, "Caesarea," in *Encyclopedia of Archaeological Excavations in the Holy Land*, ed. M. Avi-Yonah, Vol. 1 (Jerusalem: Israel Exploration Society, 1975), pp. 270–85 (at pp. 282–84); Benvenisti, pp. 140–44; K. G. Holum et al., *King Herod's Dream: Caesarea on the Sea* (New Haven/London: Norton, 1988), pp. 226–31; Y. Porath, Y. Neeman and R. Badihi, "Caesarea," *ESI* 9 (1990), 132–34.

[147] Porath, Neeman and Badihi, pp. 133–34.

in origin, consisted of a gate set between a pair of massive but barely projecting rectangular towers spaced 6.8 m. apart. This system was replaced in the thirteenth century by a bent entrance, set in the north side of an elongated tower (21.65 m. broad, projecting 8.2–10 m.), built in front of the original gate. The bridge crossing the ditch was of timber, with the decking of the inner half carried on four parallel masonry arches. The outer gate was 3.14 m. wide, and consisted of a pair of wing-doors, secured when shut by a draw-bar; these were preceded by a portcullis and a slit-machicolation. The gate opened into a rectangular space (15 by 4.5 m.), covered by three bays of rib-vaults, with a low stone bench along the east side and a well and basin in the south-west corner. The inner gate, in the central bay on the right, had been narrowed to 3.14 m. in the thirteenth-century phase, and consisted of a pair of wing-doors preceded by a slit-machicolation. This gate-tower also had an upper storey (from which the portcullis was no doubt operated); but this was reached by a separate door at the south-west corner of the gate-tower, leading to a stair and passage within its south and east walls.

The south gate is less well preserved than the other two. It appears to date from the thirteenth century and to have consisted of a pair of wing-doors, preceded by a portcullis and slit-machicolation, set on the line of the town wall. This opened into an inward-projecting gate-tower, containing a stair in its east wall. It is uncertain whether the gate passage led straight through or (as seems quite possible) was bent to the west. In a later period (possibly the nineteenth or twentieth century), the tower was demolished and the arch and jambs of the gate rebuilt as an undefended straight-through gateway.[148]

In addition to the principal city gates, three postern gates, sited in the curtain walls immediately adjacent to towers on the north, east and west repectively and approached from inside the town down narrow staircases, opened into the bottom of the ditch; their main purpose, like those at twelfth-century Belvoir Castle,[149] was evidently to allow the defenders to sally forth and set fire to any siege machine or tower that had been brought too close to the wall for comfort.

The Templar castle of 'Atlit (Pilgrims' Castle) was begun in 1217–18, but the *faubourg* which developed outside it probably belongs to the period *c.* 1225–50, after the unsuccessful attack on the castle itself by al-Mu'azzam 'Īsā in October–November 1220.[150] In 1265, Baybars sacked the town, and excavation of the stables in the south-east corner of the defences, carried out in the 1930s, indicates that they were thereafter abandoned; the town church was also left unfinished, even though the castle itself was not abandoned until after the fall of Acre in May 1291. The defences were then destroyed by the Mamluks.[151]

---

[148] Porath, Neeman and Badihi, pp. 132–33.

[149] M. Ben-Dov, "Belvoir," in *Encyclopedia of Archaeological Excavations in the Holy Land*, Vol. 1, pp. 179–84.

[150] C. N. Johns, *Guide to 'Atlit: The Crusader Castle, Town and Surroundings* (Jerusalem: Govt. of Palestine, Dept. of Antiquities, 1947), p. 23.

[151] Johns, pp. 14–31; Deschamps, *Châteaux*, II, pp. 24–29; R. Hartman, " 'Athlith," in *Encyclopedia of Islam*, 2nd ed., Vol. 1 (Leiden: Brill, 1960), p. 737.

The castle was sited on a low-lying sandstone promontory, cut off from the mainland on the east by a sea-level ditch with a masonry counterscarp (Fig. 9). Behind this stood two massive walls, the first defended by three rectangular projecting towers and the second by two even larger ones, placed so as to overlook the curtain between the outer ones.[152]

The town was defended by the sea on the north and west, and by the castle on the north-west. To landward it was enclosed by a wall some 645 m. long on the east and 230 m. on the south, giving an inhabitable area of 9 ha.[153] The wall survives at least 7.25 m. high, measuring from the bottom of the ditch in front of it, and is built, like the castle, of massive limestone blocks with course heights of 0.75 m. and lengths averaging 2.55 m. It had two gates and a postern leading into the ditch on the east side, and one gate on the south. The main gates were set in gate-towers, only the southern of which projected forward from the wall. The system of closure in the north and south gates was of wing-doors secured by a draw-bar and preceded by a portcullis; the east gate apparently had no portcullis, but was enfiladed from either side by arrow-slits at waist level (like the inner east gate at Belvoir). Very possibly the gate-passages were also defended by slit-machicolations, but the towers do not survive high enough for one to tell. The ditch was crossed by timber bridges, carried in the case of the non-projecting towers on a masonry pier in the middle of the ditch. Rectangular towers built in the sea protected the two ends of the wall, and a single rounded open-gorge tower guarded the way into the ditch from the beach on the north and provided flanking cover for the north gate. At the south-east corner, the wall enclosed two sides of an earlier two-storied tower-keep (14.3 by 11.8 m.), whose lower floor was enclosed by four groin-vaulted bays carried on a central pier. The ditch itself was partly rock-cut and partly dug through sand and faced up with a masonry counterscarp wall.[154]

Banyas was held from 1128–32 and from 1140–64. It was already fortified when taken by the Franks. Although the present walls, with their projecting rectangular towers and gates, are mostly Ayyubid and Mamluk in date, they may be presumed to follow the course of the earlier ones, which would thus have enclosed a roughly rectangular area, some 270 by 280 m. (7.5 ha.), with the river providing additional defence on the north and west.[155]

In 1157, when the town was attacked by Nūr al-Dīn, the Muslims forced an

152 On the castle, see C. N. Johns, " 'Atlit," in *Encyclopedia of Archaeological Excavations in the Holy Land*, Vol. 1, pp. 130–40; C. N. Johns, *Guide to 'Atlit*.

153 C. N. Johns, "Excavations at Pilgrims' Castle ('Atlit): The Faubourg and its Defences," *Quarterly of the Department of Antiquities of Palestine* 1 (1932), 111–29, pls. XI–LIII (at p. 112).

154 Johns, "Excavations at Pilgrims' Castle"; Johns, *Guide to 'Atlit*, pp. 74–76, 81–85.

155 M. Van Berchem, "Inscription arabe de Banyas," *Revue biblique* 12 (1903), 421–24 (reprinted in *Opera minora*, Vol. 1 [Geneva: Slatkine, 1978], pp. 297–300); Benvenisti, pp. 152–54; A. Graboïs, "La cité de Baniyas et le château de Subeibeh pendant les croisades," *Cahiers de Civilisation médiévale* 13 (1970), 43–62; M. Ben-Dov, "Banias – A Medieval Fortress Town," *Qadmoniot* 11 (1978), 29–33 [in Hebrew; title here given in English translation].

entry and began to destroy the fortifications while the Franks retreated into the castle.[156] This castle was evidently inside the town, and should not be confused with the Ayyubid castle known as Qal'at al Subayba (and in recent times as Qal'at Nimrūd), which stands on the slopes of Hermon overlooking Banyas and was only begun in 1228.[157] The walls and towers of Banyas were repaired and the forewall (antemuralia) renewed by Baldwin III later in 1157.[158] It may be hoped that some of these features will be elucidated by the excavations now in progress.[159]

Jaffa was taken by the Franks in June 1099 and was immediately refortified.[160] As we have already seen, its twelfth-century defences comprised a castle or citadel, overlooking the harbour and dating at least in part from the Abbasid period, and a defended faubourg below it on the south and east (Fig. 10).[161] A sea gate led from the faubourg to the town quays on the north west.[162] The walls were slighted when the city was taken by al-Malik al-'Ādil in July 1187, but the walls, towers and ditch were partly restored in September 1191 when Richard I retook Jaffa.[163] In July–August 1192, Saladin's engineers destroyed the Jerusalem gate of the faubourg, and two perches of wall to the right of it.[164] These were repaired by Richard on 2–4 August, "sed sine calce et cemento" (but without lime and cement);[165] the work was still unfinished when the Muslims entered the city and were shut in by the Crusaders closing up the breaches.[166]

Between November 1228 and February 1229, the emperor Frederick II rebuilt the walls of the citadel from the foundations, clearing the ditch of debris and revetting it with masonry. This work was continued by Patriarch Gerald of Lausanne (1225–39), who contributed in particular a pair of towers forming his own residence, the so-called Tower of the Patriarch.[167] The defences were completed by John II of Ibelin, lord of Jaffa, with assistance from the Crusading army of Louis IX, between May 1252 and June 1253. In this campaign the faubourg was enclosed from sea to sea by a wall with 24 towers, three gates and a ditch.[168] Work at strengthening the town walls was carried out over the next 15

---

[156] William of Tyre, XVIII.12, pp. 827–28.

[157] R. Ellenblum, "Who Built Qal'at al-Subayba?," Dumbarton Oaks Papers 43 (1989), 103–12; R. Amitai, "Notes on the Ayyūbid Inscriptions at al-Subayba (Qal'at Nimrūd)," Dumbarton Oaks Papers 43 (1989), 113–19.

[158] William of Tyre, XVIII.13, pp. 828–29; cf. Pringle, Churches, p. 108.

[159] See reports in ESI 6 (1987–88), 2–3; 7–8 (1988–89), 10–11; 9 (1989–90), 3–4.

[160] William of Tyre, VIII.9, pp. 397–99; Albert of Aachen, VII.12, in RHC Occ, Vol. 4, p. 515; Deschamps, Châteaux, II, pp. 5–6.

[161] Le Strange, pp. 550–51; Abel, "Jaffa"; Pringle, Churches, pp. 264–66, fig.79.

[162] RRH, p. 178, n. 667.

[163] Itinerarium Peregrinorum, IV.26–27, pp. 284–85.

[164] Itinerarium Peregrinorum, VI.13, pp. 400–02.

[165] Itinerarium Peregrinorum, VI.18, p. 412.

[166] Itinerarium Peregrinorum, VI.22, p. 420.

[167] Les Gestes des Chiprois, ed. G. Raynaud, Publications de la Société de l'Orient latin, Série historique, 5 (Geneva, 1887), p. 77; Joinville, CII.530, p. 222; trans. Shaw, p. 298; Deschamps, Châteaux, II, p. 17; Pringle, Churches, I, p. 266.

[168] Joinville, C.517, CIX.561–62, pp. 217, 236; trans. Shaw, pp. 295, 305.

years and was still in progress in March 1267.[169] But in March 1268, Jaffa fell to Sultan Baybars, whose engineers demolished the castle walls down to the level of the *talus* and removed the more valuable materials to Cairo for use in his building projects there.[170]

Very little is known archaeologically of the medieval defences of Jaffa, though their layout may be largely guessed from the topography and the outline of the Turkish defences that still survived into the early twentieth century. This evidence suggests that the citadel and *faubourg* would each have covered about 3.5 ha., making a total area of 7 ha. Part of the Crusader sea wall was revealed in 1978 on the south-west side; it was built like those of Ascalon and Caesarea with antique through-columns.[171]

Arsuf (Arsur) was occupied from April 1101 to August 1187, and from September 1191 to April 1265, when it was destroyed by Baybars. We hear little of its defences during this period, beyond a notice of fortification by John II of Ibelin in 1241.[172] The existing medieval town walls, which were surveyed by the Survey of Western Palestine in the 1870s,[173] may be assumed to date in origin from the Abbasid or Fatimid periods;[174] certainly they enclose an area somewhat smaller than that occupied in Byzantine and early Islamic times.[175] The area of 5.1 ha. that they describe is roughly quadrangular in shape, some 120/160 m. E-W by 345 m. N-S (Fig. 11). On the west it is defined by the sea cliffs and on the north, east and south by a ditch 12 m. wide, attaining 30 m. on the south. The SWP noted the remains of a "postern" with piers for a drawbridge on the east, and another leading to a spring by the sea on the south. The north-west corner of the enclosure is taken up by the castle, built on a rounded mound, surrounded by an annular ditch and overlooking the harbour on the west.[176]

Tiberias, located on the western shore of the Sea of Galilee, was held by the Crusaders from 1099–87. In 1113, its walls withstood an attack by Mawdūd of Mosul.[177] The Crusader castle, inside its walls, was destroyed by Saladin in 1190, but was refortified by Eûdes of Montbéliard, prince of Galilee, when the

---

169 *RRH*, p. 353, n. 1347.

170 Ibn al-Furāt, *Ayyubids, Mamluks and Crusaders*, ed. and trans. U. and M. C. Lyons, Vol. 2 (Cambridge: Heffers, 1971), p. 108; al-Maqrīzī, *Histoire des sultans mamlouks de l'Egypte*, trans. M. Quartremère, Vol. 1, Part 1 (Paris, 1837–45), p. 51; Pringle, *Churches*, p. 266.

171 Pringle, *Churches*, p. 266, fig. 79.

172 Deschamps, *Châteaux*, II, p. 18.

173 Conder and Kitchener, Vol. 2, pp. 135, 137–40.

174 See Le Strange, p. 399.

175 A. Perkins, "Archaeological News: The Near East," *American Journal of Archaeology* 55 (1951), 81–102 (at. pp. 86–87, fig. 11).

176 On the topography and defences of Crusader Arsuf, see Benvenisti, pp. 130–34; Pringle, *Churches*, pp. 59–61, fig. 18; I. Roll and E. Ayalon, *Apollonia and Southern Sharon – Model of a Coastal City and its Hinterland* (Tel Aviv: Kibbutz Hamanhad, 1988), pp. 93–116 [in Hebrew; title here given in English translation].

177 Z. Razi and E. Braun, "The Lost Crusader Castle of Tiberias," in *The Horns of Hattīn*, ed. B. Z. Kedar (Jerusalem: Yad Izhak Ben-Zvi, Israel Exploration Society; London: Variorum, 1992), pp. 216–27 (at p. 221).

Franks regained control in 1241, and was held thereafter until 1247.[178] Recent archaeological research shows that it was sited in the southern part of the town, beside the lake; what is left of it is now partly overlain by the Jami' al-Bahri, built between c. 1750 and 1882.[179] Less is known, however, of the city's Crusader town walls, apart from the fact that they appear to have enclosed a somewhat smaller area than the existing Turkish walls, and a considerably smaller area than those of the early Islamic city described by Nāṣir-i Khusraw in 1047. Like the latter they would seem to have extended only on the landward side, with the lake giving protection on the east.[180]

The defences of Haifa have already been discussed. The "castle" of Haifa, or New Haifa, had been built some distance west of Old Haifa sometime between 1046–1100.[181] Saladin ordered its defences to be levelled in 1191, just before it was retaken by Richard I.[182] Where they had crumbled, the walls and towers were repaired by Louis IX in c. 1251–52.[183] The town was briefly held by Baybars in 1265, and thereafter remained in Frankish possession until 1291. Nothing is known archaeologically of its defences.

At Iskandaruna (Scandalion), Baldwin I constructed a castle in 1117 as an outpost against Muslim-held Tyre.[184] In 1184, Ibn Jubayr noted that the town was also walled.[185] It was held until 1187, and then from 1192 until 1291. Although the castle was described by Henry Maundrell in 1697 as 120 paces square and enclosed by a ditch,[186] nothing more is known of the town's defences.[187]

IV. Discussion

The characteristics of town walls

From the foregoing some general observations about the form and design of town walls in the Kingdom of Jerusalem may be made. The walled areas of towns varied considerably, from Arsuf at 5 ha. to Jerusalem and thirteenth-

---

[178] Deschamps, *Châteaux*, II, p. 18; Razi and Braun, pp. 217–18.

[179] Razi and Braun, pp. 221–27. The mosque and an adjacent Crusader vault, which once formed part of the castle, are described and illustrated in V. Bernie, M. Milwright and E. J. Simpson, "An Architectural Survey of Muslim Buildings in Tiberias," *Levant* 24 (1992), 95–129 (at pp. 120–29); however, the authors mis-date both buildings and interpret the latter incorrectly as an Ottoman khan.

[180] Le Strange, pp. 336–37; N. Feig, "Tiberias," *ESI* 1 (1982), 110; S. Dar and D. Adnan-Bayewitz, "Tiberias," *ESI* 2 (1983), 103; S. Dar and D. Adnan-Bayewitz, "Tiberias," *IEJ* 33 (1983), 114–15.

[181] Prawer, *History of the Jews*, pp. 35–40.

[182] *Itinerarium Peregrinorum*, IV.11, p. 252.

[183] William of Nangis, *Gesta Ludovici IX*, *RHGF*, Vol. 20, p. 384; Prawer, *Histoire*, Vol. 2, pp. 345–46, n. 53.

[184] William of Tyre, XI.30, p. 543; Bartolf of Nangis, p. 543n.

[185] *Voyages*, p. 356.

[186] "A Journey from Aleppo to Jerusalem at Easter, A.D. 1697," in T. Wright, *Early Travels in Palestine* (London, 1848), pp. 383–512 (at p. 426).

[187] Deschamps, *Châteaux*, II, pp. 9, 118, 236.

century Acre at around 85–86 ha. (see Table 2). The course of walls, however, was often determined by the existence of earlier walls, or by the natural (and in some cases man-made) topography. They are not, therefore, necessarily a reliable indicator of the inhabited area or the size of a town's population; it is known for example that the town walls at Ascalon, Tyre, Acre and Jerusalem also enclosed unoccupied garden areas. At Caesarea, Arsuf, Tiberias and Jerusalem, however, the twelfth-century town walls enclosed a significantly smaller area than those of the Byzantine period. All of the towns with walls also had a castle, usually adjoining the walls. At Arsuf, Ascalon (1244), 'Atlit, Beirut, Caesarea, Sidon, Tiberias, Tyre and possibly Iskandaruna, the castle also stood next to a harbour or quay, thus affording the garrison the option of a speedy escape in time of trouble.

Walls and towers are normally constructed in lime-mortared ashlar, sometimes smooth, sometimes rusticated, and of varying course heights depending on the type of stone and the availability of *spolia* from earlier buildings. Through-columns were used to give extra solidity, both against siege weaponry and also against earthquakes and marine action, at Caesarea, Jaffa, Tyre and Ascalon (1192 and 1244 work). At Beirut and Sidon metal clamps were used for the same purpose.[188] No town walls survive to their full height, and the design of crenellations and wall-walks (or *chemins-de-ronde*) is, therefore, unknown. At Caesarea, however, an enclosed wall-walk below the wallhead leading to casemated arrow-slits survives in places.

Where they survive, towers are usually rectangular in plan and project forward from the walls, though a rounded tower occurs on the town wall at 'Atlit, and rounded and triangular ones at Ascalon. Rectangular towers were easier to build and more functional internally than those of other shapes; however, they were also more susceptible to mining or battering, and their corners left areas of dead ground in front of them. By 1291, the exposed north-east corner of Acre was, therefore, defended by a rounded or polygonal tower (the Accursed Tower), and the outer wall before it by the "turris noua rotunda Regis Henrici" (the New Round Tower of King Henry [II of Cyprus]);[189] even so, it was in this quarter that the Mamluks eventually broke through the outer defences.

City gates seem to have been either flanked by towers, as at Caesarea (east gate, first phase), Tyre, and Jerusalem (St. Stephen's Gate, though on Roman foundations), or sited in gate-towers. At Ascalon, in 1153, the Jerusalem Gate was approached indirectly from a number of gates in the outer wall; and the twelfth-century St. Stephen's Gate in Jerusalem was preceded by a bent entrance set inside a gate-tower on the line of the outer wall. A multiple system of closure is recorded in the main gate of Tyre in 1184, though whether the gate was bent or straight-through is unclear. We find both types of gate in surviving examples. In the town walls of 'Atlit the three gates are all straight-through and set in

188 Deschamps, *Châteaux*, II, pp. 282–83, fig. 25.
189 Stickel, pp. 15–17.

gate-towers; two of them have portcullises, and slit-machicolations may be inferred. At Caesarea, however, two and possibly all three gates were bent; in each case the outer gate seems to have consisted of a sequence of slit-machicolation, portcullis and wing-doors, and the inner one of a slit-machicolation and wing-doors. In the east gate at Caesarea and St. Stephen's Gate in Jerusalem there is also archaeological evidence for the distribution of water to thirsty travellers.

In addition to a curtain wall, towers and gates, we have seen that in most cases there were also outworks of varying types. Most walls were preceded by at least a ditch. At 'Atlit, which may be regarded as fairly typical, this was retained on the inner face by the wall itself, and on the outer by a more roughly constructed counterscarp wall. At Ascalon (1244), Jaffa, Caesarea and Sidon, the walls and towers had a sloping masonry *talus* built against them in the thirteenth century. At Caesarea, Arsuf and 'Atlit, the ditches were crossed by timber bridges leading to the gates, while at Caesarea and 'Atlit there also survive small postern gates (similar to those at Belvoir Castle) leading into the bottom of the ditches. The postern gate of St. Mary Magdalene in Jerusalem likewise gave into the space between the walls.

The question of the existence of outer walls or barbicans is of great interest because of the possible relevance that it has for the development of so-called "concentric" planning in the design of castles and town walls in the West. As we have seen, the Franks encountered town walls with fully developed systems of outworks when they first arrived in Palestine. At Jerusalem a forewall (*antemurale, barbacana*) and ditch existed by 1099 and were maintained in use in the twelfth century. At Acre, the city also had a wall and forewall in 1103, and by 1193–94 the wall was preceded by a ditch, lists (*barbacana*) and a forewall (*antemuralis, doga fossati*); the double wall seen in 1212, therefore, probably represented a reconstruction or up-grading of a concentric system that already existed in the twelfth century. At Tyre, there was a double wall to seaward and a triple wall to landward when the city fell in 1124; and these outworks seem to have been maintained as late as 1283. At Ascalon, a forewall is mentioned at the time of the siege of 1153, though it does not seem to have been rebuilt after Saladin destroyed the defences in 1191. At Sidon, a barbican is mentioned in 1126 and a gate in the forewall in 1162; it is not certain, however, whether the double system extended around the whole circuit of the walls or was merely confined to the gates. At Banyas, the forewalls (*antemuralia*) were rebuilt in 1157; and John of Ibelin's castle at Beirut, in 1212, also had two stone walls and a stone-lined ditch.

The main purpose of such outworks was to keep enemy siege engines and towers at a safe distance from the main wall, where they could be engaged by the defenders' own engines and archers. The development of such systems in the West, as for example at Carcassonne in 1228–39 and Oxford some decades later,[190] was probably in part a response to the increasingly specialized nature of

---

[190] Y. Bruand, "La Cité de Carcassonne: les enceintes fortifiées," *Congrès archéologique de*

warfare and the developing techniques – and technology – for conducting sieges. The experience of those who had travelled to the Crusader states and had seen such defensive systems in action, however, may well have provided an additional stimulus to their later development in the West.[191]

The organization of building work

Accounts of the construction of town defences from the time of the Third Crusade onwards may give the impression that it was often a community activity, in which even kings such as Richard I of England and Louis IX of France participated.[192] In general, however, the work that was done by the army, including Louis (though not perhaps Richard), was unskilled work such as fetching and carrying. It is clear from the accounts of building work at Ascalon in 1192, for example, that masons were required to take charge of the skilled work of cutting the stone and preparing the mortar.[193] At Banyas, in 1157, Baldwin III summoned from other cities in the region and from the whole kingdom "masons and whoever was seen to have any experience of architecture";[194] and King Louis at Sidon, in 1253, "sent for workmen from all the country round" to refortify the city "with high walls and large towers."[195]

Increasingly after the Third Crusade, the Crusader lords and even the king had to rely on charity from the West to assist them in fortifying their towns and cities. At Ascalon, where Richard was reputed to have paid for three-quarters of the wall from his own purse, each noble undertook to rebuild a section of wall proportionate to the means at his disposal;[196] and an inscription referring to the construction of a section of this wall between two gates by Master Philip, clerk of the king's chamber, is material proof that this did, indeed, happen, though we may assume that this section was in fact paid for by Richard himself.[197] At Jaffa, in 1252–53, the papal legate confided to Joinville that a gate and an adjoining section of curtain wall had cost him 30,000 *livres*;[198] while, between the summer of 1250 and that of 1253, King Louis' total expenditure on building works overseas amounted to £95,839 2s.6d., representing roughly 9% of the total cost of the Crusade over that period.[199]

France 131 (1973), 496–515; Lawrence, p. 11; J. R. Kenyon, *Medieval Fortifications* (Leicester/ London: Leicester University Press, 1990), pp. 187–89.

[191] Cf. Lawrence, pp. xxxix–xl.

[192] E.g., *Itinerarium Peregrinorum*, V.6, p. 317; Joinville, C.517, p. 217; trans. Shaw, p. 295.

[193] *Itinerarium Peregrinorum*, V.6, pp. 315–17; cf. Pringle, "King Richard I," pp. 136–37.

[194] "cementariis et quicumque architecture aliquam uidebantur habere experientiam" (William of Tyre, XVIII.13, p. 829).

[195] Joinville, CXIII.582, p. 245; trans. Shaw, p. 310 (adapted).

[196] *Itinerarium Peregrinorum*, V.6, pp. 315–17.

[197] Pringle, "King Richard I."

[198] Joinville, CIX.562, p. 236; trans. Shaw, p. 305.

[199] "Dépenses de Saint Louis," *RGHF*, Vol. 21, pp. 513–15; trans. in L. and J. Riley-Smith, *The Crusades: Idea and Reality, 1095–1274*, Documents of Medieval History, 4 (London: Arnold, 1981), pp. 148–52.

In 1272, Prince Edward while in Acre on Crusade borrowed some 7,000 marks from local merchants for the use of the Hospital;[200] around 1281, after his accession to the throne of England, the Hospital requested payment of a further 254 bezants, "which we still owe to Ibrahim, the money-changer of Acre . . . for the completion of your barbican" ("por le complessement de vostre barrei").[201] This was evidently the outwork ("sbaralium domini Odoardi") that features in accounts of the fall of Acre to the Mamluks in 1291.[202]

Legal, economic and religious aspects of town walls

The works of fortification built or paid for by generous Western patrons did not, of course, remain in their possession. By the time of its fall, sections of Acre's defences had been granted to various groups, including the Venetians, the Pisans, and the military orders, to hold and defend;[203] but the king still retained jurisdiction over them. This is made clear by the terms by which the Teutonic Order was granted a substantial section of the east wall of Acre progressively from 1192 onwards. On 10 February 1192, King Guy gave the order a property next to St. Nicolas' Gate on condition "that you will not make a building or anything else on the wall or next to the wall that has the effect of impeding the people who defend the city from going up or coming down the . . . stairs to the walls."[204] Henry of Champagne in 1193 also granted the order a length of the east wall up to St. Nicolas' Gate, along with the outworks, on condition that they repaired and improved them for the defence of the city.[205] And the order was given the tower over St. Nicolas' Gate by King Amaury, in August 1198,

> in such a way that the same brothers shall have nothing in the gate that is under the tower, through which one comes into and goes out from the town, and may not erect anything de novo in the area about the tower, and shall not be able to give the same tower to anyone, nor sell it nor transfer it; and if their strong religious order should be changed to another [e.g., the Templars], they shall resign the said tower to me or to my successors as lords of the kingdom. Moreover, if on account of war with our enemies or for any other reason that may befall the said tower should be necessary to me or my successors as lords of the kingdom, if we so wish the tower shall be given back to us.[206]

A similar reservation of seigneurial control was made by Juliana, lady of Caesarea, when she granted two towers on the walls of Caesarea to the Teutonic

---

[200] *CGOH*, Vol. 3, pp. 266–67, n. 3445; pp. 272–73, n. 3465; *RRH Ad*, p. 93, n. 1384a and p. 94, n. 1385a.

[201] *CGOH*, Vol. 4, p. 297, n. 3653 bis; *RRH Ad*, p. 100, n. 1443a.

[202] Marino Sanudo, *Liber Secretorum Fidelium Crucis*, ed. J. Bongars (Hanau 1611; rpt. Jerusalem: Massada Press, 1972), p. 230; cf. Lawrence, p. xl. See also now D. Jacoby, "Three Notes on Crusader Acre", *ZDPV*, 109 (1993), 83–96 (at pp. 91–6).

[203] Cf. *CGOH*, Vol. 3, p. 420, n. 3771; *RRH Ad*, pp. 99–100, n. 1442a; Dichter, pp. 16–30 (Paolino map).

[204] *TOT*, pp. 23–24, n. 27; *RRH*, p. 187, n. 701.

[205] *TOT*, pp. 24–25, n. 28; *RRH*, pp. 191–92, n. 716.

[206] *TOT*, pp. 28–29, n. 35.

Order in February 1206, "which . . . towers they must hand over to the lord of Caesarea if they should be necessary against his enemies; but once peace has been established between them, the . . . brothers shall have the towers back again."[207]

The importance of keeping gates clear is also illustrated in Jerusalem in 1151, when Queen Melisende compensated the brothers of St. Lazarus after demolishing a mill of theirs that obstructed David's Gate.[208] In March 1181, Baldwin IV also compensated the abbey of Mount Tabor in kind for a shop that had stood in front of the house of Geoffrey de Tor in Acre, "ubi nunc porta ciuitatis facta est" (where the gate of the city has now been made).[209] Often, however, it was not just a question of keeping gates free of obstruction. For besides their military function gates were also important as marking the legal boundaries of a town. In January 1194, therefore, when Henry of Champagne granted the Hospital permission to make a new gate in the north wall of Acre, he stipulated that while any tower or other construction that the brothers might build above the gate would belong to them, the king should nevertheless have a porter to protect his rights over the gate itself and to open it to let the brothers in and out.[210] Likewise at Tyre, in January 1260, we find John, lord of the city, making an exchange with the Hospitallers in order to take possession for himself of a postern gate on the south wall, facing the sea, which had formerly been conceded to them by King Amaury and Queen Isabella.[211] And at Jerusalem in the 1170s, the city gates were firmly closed from sunset until after sunrise.[212]

The economic function of city gates is illustrated by the references in the twelfth century to the taxes levied on agricultural and other products entering David's Gate in Jerusalem.[213] The customs collectors at the gates of Acre are also described by Ibn Jubayr in 1184:

> We were taken to the customs post, which is a khan intended for the accomodation of the caravan. Before the gate, on benches covered with carpets, sit the Christian secretaries of the customs, with their ebony writing desks ornamented with gold. They can write and speak Arabic, as can their superior, the farmer of customs . . . The merchants set down their loads, and installed themselves on the upper floor. The luggage of those who declared that they had no merchandise was examined, to make sure that nothing was hidden there; then they were allowed to contuinue on their way and take lodgings where they wanted.[214]

Unfortunately no Crusader gates or their associated khans survive at Acre.

From late Roman times, the religious status of town walls was often emphasized

---

[207] *TOT*, pp. 32–33, n. 40.

[208] *RRH*, p. 68, n. 268.

[209] *RRH*, p. 160, n. 601; *CGOH*, Vol. 2, p. 909, n. 20.

[210] *RRH*, p. 192, n. 717.

[211] *RRH*, pp. 336–37, n. 1286, cf. pp. 356–57, n. 1366.

[212] Theodericus, III, p. 11.

[213] *Cartulaire*, pp. 88–89, n. 27 (1120); *RRH*, p. 21, n. 91 (1120), p. 128, n. 487 (1171), p. 146, n. 548 (1177-false?); *RRH Ad*, p. 37, n. 594a (1180).

[214] *Voyages*, vol. 3, p. 354.

by placing them, and their gates and towers, under the protection of saints.[215] In the Crusader states, chapels are found within the castle gatetowers at Belvoir and Saranda Kolones (Cyprus) and in mural towers at Crac des Chevaliers and Montreal. The only chapel certainly associated with a town wall is that in St. Stephen's gate in Jerusalem (see above), though in Jaffa the east end of the church of St. Peter projected from the walls of the citadel and was quite possibly fortified.[216]

The walls of the Holy City itself also served a singular religious function in the twelfth century as a habitation for hermits. We hear, for example, of Cosmas, a Hungarian priest, "enclosed within a narrow cell above the walls of Jerusalem";[217] and around 1170 of a certain woman living in the wall in the Belcaire district on Mount Sion.[218] But in September 1188 the hermits had all gone.[219]

V. Conclusion

From this general survey it would appear that the responses made by the lords of individual towns and cities in the Latin Kingdom of Jersualem to the problem of providing some form of physical defence for their inhabitants varied considerably, depending no doubt on the size of the population to be protected, the resources available, and the seriousness of the perceived enemy threat. In the twelfth century, by no means all major towns had town walls; but this was equally the case in the West in the same period. After the Third Crusade, however, the importance of providing those towns and cities that remained in Crusader hands with adequate circuits of walls assumed a higher priority. Because a large proportion of the resources that were devoted to these building operations came from Western rulers and the military orders, however, the existence, size and elaboration of these thirteenth-century systems of defence possibly tell us less about the state of urban life in this period than about the strategic and political priorities of the kingdom as a whole.

---

[215] W. Seston, "Les Murs, les portes et les tours des enceintes urbaines et le problème des *res sanctae* en droit romain," in *Mélanges d'archéologie et d'histoire offerts à Andre Piganiol*, ed. R. Chevalier, Vol. 3 (Paris: SEVPEN, 1966), pp. 1489–98.

[216] Pringle, *Churches*, p. 268.

[217] Gerard of Nazareth, *De Conuersatione uirorum Dei in Terra Sancta*, cited in B. Z. Kedar, "Gerard of Nazareth: A Neglected Twelfth-Century Writer in the Latin East," *Dumbarton Oaks Papers* 37 (1983), 55–77 (at p. 72, cf. p. 65).

[218] *RRH*, pp. 127–28, n. 483.

[219] *CGOH*, Vol. 1, p. 531, n. 858; cf. Kedar, "Gerard of Nazareth," p. 72, n. 1.

Abbreviations

BAR	British Archaeological Reports.
BMB	*Bulletin du Musée de Beyrouth.*
CGOH	*Cartulaire générale de l'Ordre des Hospitaliers de Saint-Jean de Jérusalem (1100–1310)*, ed. J. Delaville le Roulx, 4 vols. (Paris 1894–1906).
DRHC	Documents relatifs à l'histoire des croisades.
ESI	*Excavations and Surveys in Israel*
IEJ	*Israel Exploration Journal.*
IHC	*Itinera Hierosolymitana Crucesignatorum (saec. XII–XIII)*, ed. S. de Sandoli, 4 vols., Studium Biblicum Franciscanum, Collectio Maior, Vol. 24 (Jerusalem: Franciscan Printing Press, 1978–84).
PG	*Patrologiae Cursus Completus, Series Graeca*, ed. J. P. Migne, 161 vols. (Paris, 1857–).
PPTS	Palestine Pilgrims' Text Society Library.
RHGF	*Recueil des Historiens des Gaules et de la France*, 24 vols. (Paris 1738–).
RHC Arm	*Recueil des Historiens des Croisades. Documents arméniens*, 2 vols. (Paris, 1869–1906).
RHC Lois	*Recueil des Historiens des Croisades. Les Assises de Jérusalem*, 2 vols. (Paris, 1841–43).
RHC Occ	*Recueil des Historiens des Croisades. Historiens occidentaux*, 5 vols. (Paris, 1844–95).
RHC Or	*Recueil des Historiens des Croisades. Historiens orientaux*, 5 vols. (Paris, 1872–1906).
RRH	*Regesta Regni Hierosolymitani*, ed. R. Röhricht (Innsbruck 1893).
RRH Ad	*Regesta Regni Hierosolymitani, Additamentum*, ed. R. Röhricht (Innsbruck, 1904).
RS	*Rerum Britannicarum Medii Aeui Scriptores* (Rolls Series), 99 vols. (London, 1858–97).
TOT	*Tabulae Ordinis Theutonici ex Tabularii Regii Berolinensis Codice Potissimum*, ed. E. Strehlke (Berlin, 1849; rpt. Toronto: University of Toronto Press, 1975).
ZDPV	*Zeitschrift des Deutschen Palästina-Vereins.*

TABLE 1:
URBAN SETTLEMENTS IN THE KINGDOM OF JERUSALEM

Places listed as having a burgess court

Place	Cathedral	Tower	Castle	Town Wall
Acre	x	xxx	x	x
Arsuf			x	x
Ascalon	(x)		x	x
'Atlit		x	x	x
Baisan		x ———	x	
Bait Jibrin			x	
Banyas	x		x	x
Beaufort		x ———	x	(x)
Beirut	x		x	x
Bethlehem	x	x		
Caesarea	x		x	x
Darum			x	
Gaza			x	(x)
Haifa			x ———	x
Hasbiya (Assebebe)		x		
Hebron	x		x	
Hunin (Castrum Novum)			x	
Iskandaruna (Scandalion)			x	x
Jaffa			x ———	x
Jericho		x		
Jerusalem	x		x	x
Karak	x		x	(x)
Lydda	x			
Mi'iliya			x	
Montréal (Shaubak)			x	
Nablus			x	
Nazareth	x			
Qaimun (Caymont)			x	(x)
Ramla			x	
Sabastiya	x			
Safad			x	
Sidon			xx	x
Tantura (Merle, Dor)			x	
Tiberias	x		x	x
Tibnin (Toron)			x	

Place	Cathedral	Tower	Castle	Town Wall
Tyre	x		x	x
Yibna (Ibelin)			x	

Other settlements

Place	Cathedral	Tower	Castle/Curia	Town Wall
Bait Suriq				
al-Bira		x ——————(x)		
Dabburiya		x		
Mirabel		x —————— x		
Palmarea (near Tiberias)				
Al-Qubaiba			x	
ar-Ram		x ——————(x)		
Qalansuwa		x	x	
Qaqun		x —————— x		
az-Zib		x		

TABLE 2:
THE AREAS ENCLOSED BY TOWN WALLS

Town	Area enclosed in ha.
Jerusalem	86
Acre	51.5 < 85.5
Ascalon	50
Tyre	48
Beirut	19
Sidon	15
Caesarea	10
'Atlit	9
Banyas	7.5
Jaffa	7
Arsuf	5
Tiberias	?
Haifa	?
Iskandaruna	?

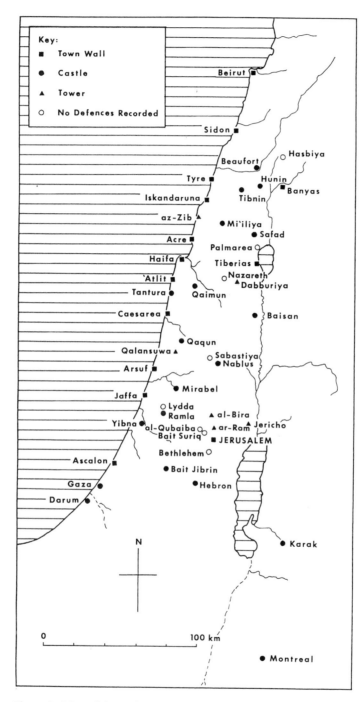

Figure 1. Map of the Latin Kingdom of Jerusalem, showing the location of urban settlements and the nature of their defences.

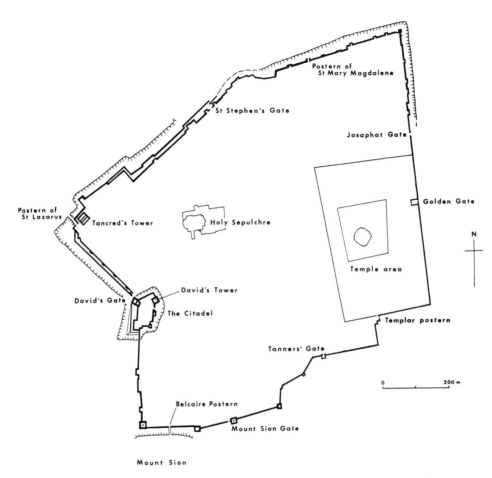

Figure 2. Jerusalem: plan of the town walls in the twelfth and thirteenth centuries.

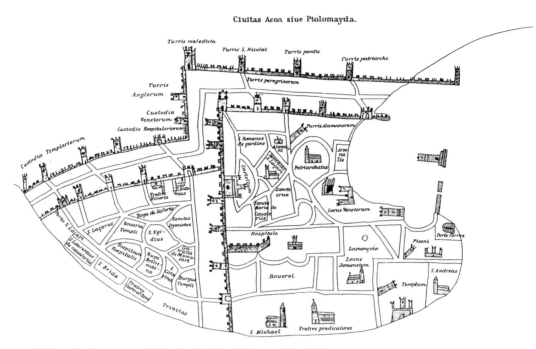

Figure 3. Acre: map of the city by Pietro Vesconte (*c.* 1320) [London, British Library, MS Add. 27 376, fol. 190r], after R. Röhricht, "Karten und Pläne zur Palästinakunde aus dem 7. bis 16. Jahrhundert," *Zeitschrift des Deutschen Palästina-Vereins* 21 (1898), pl. 5 (with amendments).

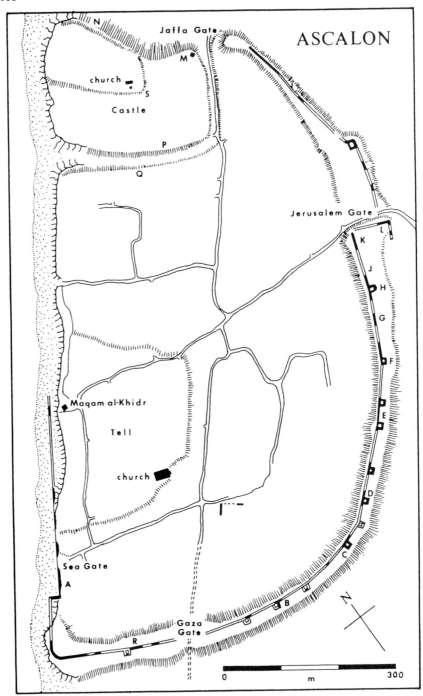

Figure 4. Ascalon: plan of the Byzantine, early Islamic and Crusade city walls.

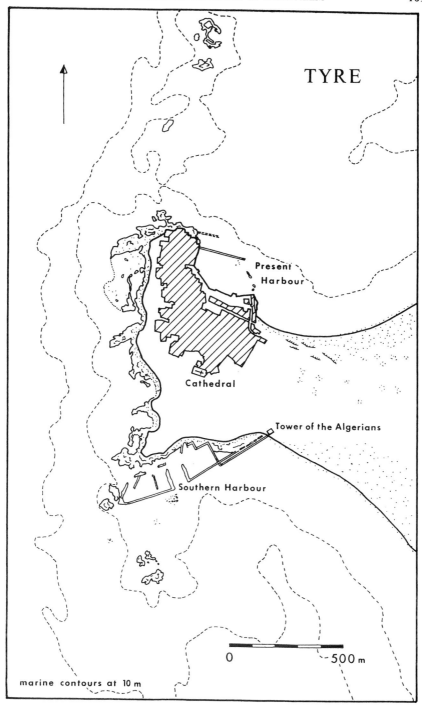

Figure 5. Tyre: plan of the site of the Crusader city in the 1930s (after A. Poidebard,
Un Grand Port disparu: Tyr, Bibl. archéol. et hist., Vol. 29 [Paris: Geuthner, 1939]).
The land wall probably extended between the Tower of the Algerians and the E mole
of the harbour; remains of the sea wall enclosing the eastern side of the peninsula
were recorded in the 1870s.

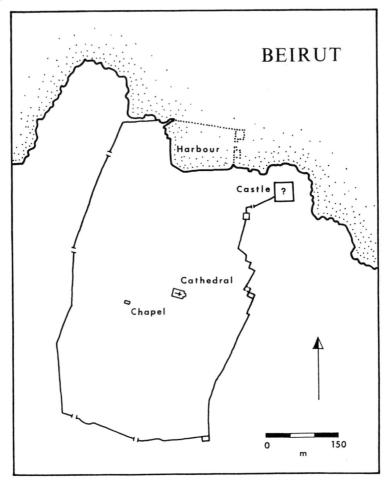

Figure 6. Beirut: plan of the demolished Turkish town walls, which
probably followed the same course as the medieval defences (after comte
du Mesnil du Buisson, "Les anciens défenses de Beyrouth," *Syria* 3
[1921], fig. 3, p. 249).

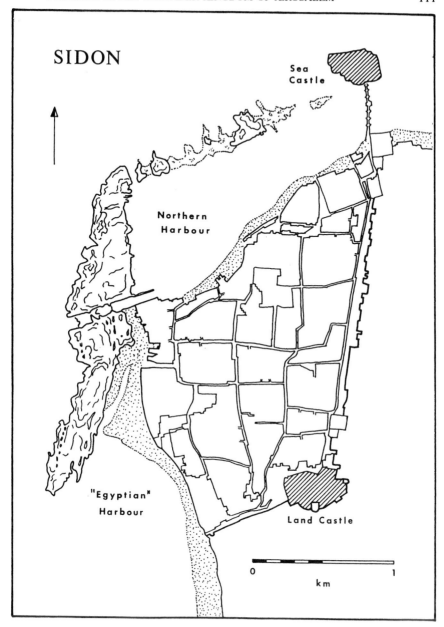

Figure 7. Sidon: plan of the Turkish town walls (1864), showing the position of the Crusader harbour and castles (after E. Renan, in A. Poidebard and J. Lauffray, *Sidon. Aménagements antiques du port de Saida* [Beirut: Ministère des Travaux Publics, 1951]).

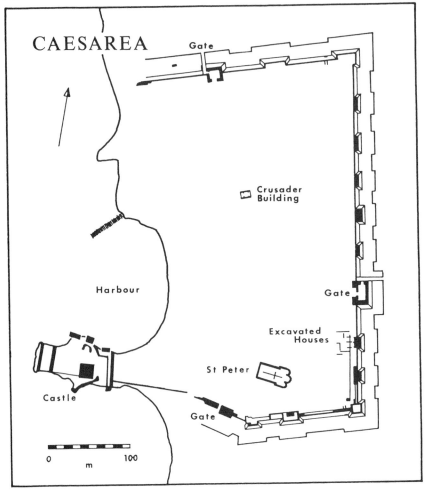

Figure 8. Caesarea: plan of the Crusader city (after M. Benvenisti, *The Crusaders in the Holy Land* [Jerusalem: Israel Universities Press, 1970], p. 140).

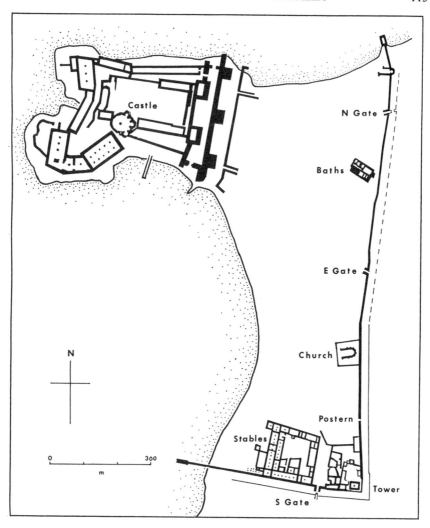

Figure 9. 'Atlit: plan of the Crusader castle and town walls (after C. N. Johns, *Guide to 'Atlit: The Crusader Castle, Town and Surroundings* [Jerusalem: Govt. of Palestine, Dept. of Antiquities, 1947], fig. 25, p. 68).

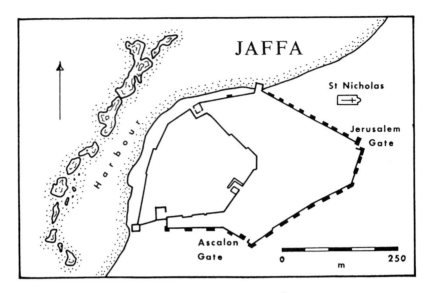

Figure 10. Jaffa: sketch plan of the Crusader town walls.

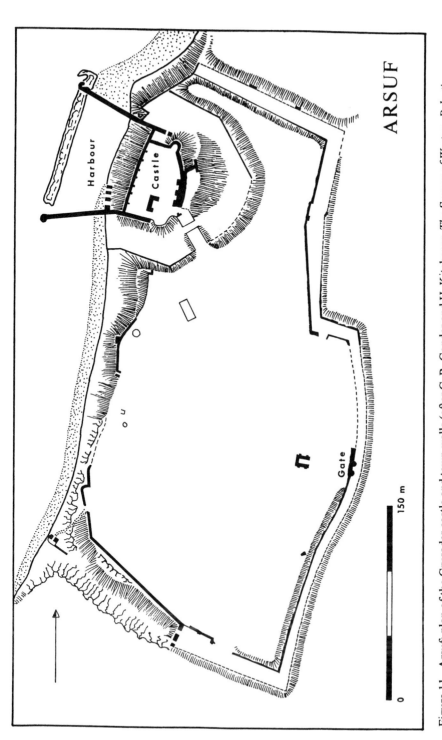

ARSUF

Harbour

Castle

Gate

0   150 m

Figure 11. Arsuf: plan of the Crusader castle and town walls (after C. R. Conder and H. Kitchener, *The Survey of Western Palestine: Memoire*, Vol. 1 [London, 1881], pl. opposite p. 136).

Plate 1. Ascalon: Tower C, one of those inserted into the line of the pre-existing town wall by Richard I in 1192. It was some 10–12 m. wide, rectangular in plan, and incorporated through-columns. The front of the tower has subsequently slumped forward, probably as a result of undermining (photo: D. P. 1983 [40/11]).

Plate 2. Ascalon: Tower H, built by Richard I in 1192. Its plan is D-shaped (11.67 m. wide, projecting 9.7 m.), and it incorporates through-columns (photo: D. P. 1983 [40/15]).

Plate 3. Ascalon: Tower B, build by Richard I in 1192. Only the SW corner survives (photo: D. P. 1983 [40/9]).

Plate 4. Ascalon: The *talus* of the N wall of the castle attributed to Richard of Cornwall (1240–41) (photo: D. P. 1984 [149/19]).

Plate 5. Caesarea: N wall of the town, showing the N gate-tower, looking W (photo: D. P. 1979 [41/3a]).

Plate 6. Caesarea: N gate-tower, from the SW, showing the outer gate (left) and inner gate (right) (photo: D. P. 1979 [40/36]).

Plate 7. Caesarea: N gate-tower, detail of the outer gate showing the slots for its portcullis and draw-bar (photo: D. P. 1980 [50/10]).

Plate 8. Caesarea: E gate-house, the outer gate from inside, showing slit-machicolation, portcullis slot, and the sockets and draw-bar that held the timber gate itself (photo: D. P. 1992 [204/27]).

Plate 9. Caesarea: E gate-house, showing the restored vaulting of the gate-passage and the inner gate (photo: D. P. 1992 [204/31]).

Plate 10. Caesarea: Postern gate in the south wall leading into the ditch. Originally the gate seems to have been lower and covered by an arch (photo: D. P. 1979 [41/11a]).

Byzantine Siege Warfare in Theory and Practice

Eric McGeer
Harvard University

The years between 960 and 1025 stand as the great age of Byzantine military expansion. Led by the great warrior emperors Nikephoros II Phokas, John I Tzimiskes, and Basil II, the Byzantines embarked on their most ambitious campaigns of conquest since the age of Justinian four centuries before. Guiding the Byzantine offensives in east and west was a carefully conceived strategy aimed at isolating and capturing key towns and fortresses, both to consolidate Byzantine control over the surrounding regions and provide stepping stones for subsequent campaigns. To achieve the conquest of Cilicia, Nikephoros Phokas sent an army to capture Adana in 964, to drive a wedge between his next objectives, Tarsos and Mopsuestia; the fall of both towns in the two-pronged assault of 965 opened the way to northern Syria and the ultimate prize, Antioch, which finally fell into Byzantine hands in 969.[1] Four decades later, Basil II took the same systematic approach in his wars against Bulgaria, targeting one crucial stronghold after another (Pliska and the two Preslavs in the east; Berrhoia, Servia, and Vodena in the south; Vidin in the north), to impose a stranglehold on the Bulgars, whose resistance eventually collapsed in 1018.[2] Directed as they were at fortresses and walled towns, the Byzantine campaigns in both theatres naturally entailed extensive siege operations.

Siege tactics and technology must therefore be given considerable scope in the study of Byzantine warfare during the age of conquest, but despite the obvious importance of this subject, the methods and equipment employed by the Byzantines when besieging and defending fortified places have not been examined in detail.[3] My purpose in this study is to offer a preliminary examination of

---

[1] For an account of these campaigns, see M. Canard, *Histoire de la dynastie des H'amdanides de Jazira et de Syrie*, Publication de la Faculté des Lettres d'Alger, Second Series, 21 (Algiers: Imp. "La Typolitho" et J. Carbonel, 1953), pp. 803–25.

[2] G. Ostrogorsky, *History of the Byzantine State*, rev. ed. (New Brunswick NJ: Rutgers University Press, 1969), pp. 307–10.

[3] This is not true of Byzantine fortifications which have been the subject of individual and collective studies; see C. Foss and D. Winfield, *Byzantine Fortifications. An Introduction* (Praetoria: Sigma Press, 1986), with bibliography.

Byzantine siege warfare based on four sources from the tenth and eleventh centuries. Two of these belong to the branch of Greek military literature known as *poliorketika*, or manuals on siege warfare.[4] The first is an illustrated treatise on siegecraft attributed to the pseudonymus Hero of Byzantium, composed about the year 950,[5] while the second is an anonymous, untitled treatise known simply as the *De obsidione toleranda* ("on withstanding sieges"), written most probably in the first half of the tenth century.[6] As compendia derived from ancient manuals, these two treatises pose problems of modernity and realism all too familiar to Byzantinists, but they can be compared with two other contemporary texts to form a reasonably accurate picture of Byzantine siege warfare. These are two treatises written by soldiers who combined knowledge of military literature with firsthand experience of warfare in their writings, and so provide a realistic, practical perspective on siege tactics and technology. The first is Chapter 65 of the *Taktika* of Nikephoros Ouranos (*c.* 1010), in which the author outlines the steps for conducting siege operations in northern Syria;[7] the second is the section on military affairs in the *Strategikon* of Kekavmenos (*c.* 1075), which gives advice on preparing for a siege and relates several campaigns with lessons for prospective besiegers and defenders.[8] A review and comparison of these four sources will enable us to see where the theory and practice of Byzantine siege warfare intersect and to identify the methods and devices which the Byzantines employed in their siege operations.

We begin with the treatise on siegecraft attributed to Hero of Byzantium. In the preface, the unknown author states that he has compiled his text mainly from the poliorcetic manual of Apollodoros (*c.* 100 A.D.), to which he has added various items from other sources. At the same time, he declares that he has reiterated the often complex instructions of the classical manuals in a fuller, clearer style to facilitate the reader's understanding of the construction of the siege devices presented. Further to this end, he has included diagrams with each description "in the knowledge that only a well defined drawing can clarify the murky and inexplicable details of construction."[9] What is striking to observe is that the diagrams, too, have been reworked in an attempt to render them more comprehensible to the beholder. Where the siege devices in the ancient treatise

---

[4] The standard survey of classical and Byzantine military writings is by A. Dain, "Les stratégistes byzantins," *Travaux et mémoires* 2 (1967), 317–92.

[5] The text used here is that published by C. Wescher in *Poliorcétique des grecs. Traités théoriques – récits historiques* (Paris, 1867), pp. 197–279, an outdated edition based on sixteenth-century descendants of the principal witness, the eleventh-century *Vaticanus gr.* 1605. A new edition and translation, based on the *Vaticanus*, complete with reproductions of the original diagrams, is in preparation by Dr. Denis Sullivan.

[6] *Anonymus de obsidione toleranda*, ed. H. van den Berg (Leiden: E. J. Brill, 1947).

[7] Ed. J.-A. de Foucault, "Douze chapitres inédits de la *Tactique* de Nicéphore Ouranos," *Travaux et mémoires* 5 (1973), 281–312, with French translation. On Ouranos' career and the military historical interest of his *Taktika*, see E. McGeer, "Tradition and Reality in the *Taktika* of Nikephoros Ouranos," *Dumbarton Oaks Papers* 45 (1991), 129–40.

[8] Ed. G. G. Litavrin, *Sovety i Rasskazy Kekavmena* (Moscow: "Nauka," 1972), pp. 134–88.

[9] Wescher, pp. 197[1]–99[10].

of Apollodoros were illustrated in flat, one-dimensional representations, the Byzantine copies appear in three-dimensional perspective with human figures added for scale.[10] If nothing else, these textual and pictorial elaborations bear witness to the considerable intellectual investment the Byzantines made in their military efforts during the late tenth century – an investment which, in their eyes, was directed to a practical purpose. As the author states in conclusion to his work, commanders who methodically follow his instructions on the assembly and operation of the siege equipment described in the treatise "will capture cities, especially those of Hagar [the Arabs], with ease."[11]

The siegecraft presented are the devices other than artillery which attackers might employ during an assault on the walls. The repertoire includes protective barriers to be set round the siege camp, tortoises, battering rams, scaling ladders and nets, towers and observatories, tools such as augers and bores, and bridges. Of these devices the most important and versatile are the tortoises (*chelonai*), which are shown in various shapes and sizes. The more intricate models resemble wheeled wooden sheds with sharply peaked roofs and fronts to deflect away heavy objects hurled against them; these heavy structures could be rolled up to the walls by men protected behind or inside them. Peaked huts made of wicker or other stout materials served as portable tortoises, while another kind of tortoise was built in the shape of a lean-to which, when placed against the wall, covered the men underneath. There were also large wooden tortoises supporting and sheltering a swinging ram operated by men working from a smaller tortoise set behind the ram-bearing tortoise.[12] The author describes and illustrates these tortoises from the ancient manuals, but he also interpolates into this section of his treatise descriptions and diagrams of a new type of tortoise ("recently devised"), called *laisai*. This Slavic term, which entered Byzantine Greek in the late ninth century, is found in a number of sources from the tenth through eleventh centuries and refers to mantlets made of interwoven vines and branches.[13]

The author goes on to describe how the tortoises in their various shapes were put to several uses, of which the most important was protecting the besiegers as they advanced with their equipment and tools up to the walls. Once at the base of the walls and sheltered by the tortoises, men in the role of sappers could begin tunnelling to collapse a section of the walls or using battering rams and digging tools to open a breach. These methods will be discussed in greater detail below, but the author's emphasis on tunnelling operations is revealing, suggesting, as it does, that in this period the Byzantines did not possess siege artillery powerful enough to shatter the walls of a fortress – an impression confirmed by the other

[10] Demonstrated by D. Sullivan, "The Reception of Hero of Byzantium in the West and *Vaticanus gr.* 1605," paper read at the XVIth Annual Byzantine Studies Conference, Hellenic College, Brookline MA, 8–10 November 1991.

[11] Wescher, p. 276$^{9-17}$.

[12] Illustrated in Wescher, pp. 211, 215, 218, 228, 259; for the authentic diagrams readers will wish to consult D. Sullivan's forthcoming edition.

[13] On this term, see McGeer, pp. 135–38.

sources – and they therefore relied on this tunnelling technique to take a place by force of arms.

The second poliorcetic manual, the *De obsidione toleranda*, discusses sieges from the perspective of the besieged. A curious text, unfinished and rife with problematic readings, it combines current advice on defensive tactics with recommendations and historical examples derived from ancient sources (Arrian, Polybios, Josephus). Although published in an excellent critical edition nearly fifty years ago, the *De obsidione* has not attracted a great deal of scholarly attention despite the interest of its first section, which issues a fascinating set of instructions to the commander of a town about to be attacked.[14] Opening with the heartening reassurance that "there is no need for the besieged to give up hope, even if the siege threatens to last a long time" (p. 45, ll. 5–6), the anonymous author proceeds to outline the measures essential to conducting a successful defence, occasionally citing historical precedents to justify his advice. The defenders' initial preparations must be to forestall the effects of attrition, starvation, treachery, or carelessness. Once the enemy's intentions have been discerned, the town's inhabitants must gather foodstuffs sufficient to last six months to a year (for distribution by the bishop and other reputable citizens) and evacuate the elderly, children, and the infirm, to reduce the number of mouths to feed. At the same time, they must devastate the surrounding areas to deny provisions to the attackers. Craftsmen skilled in manufacturing armour, weapons, and other useful equipment must be set to work on these items, while the materials necessary for their construction must be stockpiled within the town;[15] the author notes that architects and builders are especially valuable for their ability to repair walls pounded by battering rams. The cisterns and reservoirs must be filled and the water supply strictly rationed. Criminals, a potential source of treachery, should be rounded up and secured, and a system of patrols and counterpatrols maintained to prevent sentries from betraying the town or falling asleep at their stations.

In preparation for the enemy assault, the defenders are advised to increase the height and strength of the walls, and to dig two or three deep, wide trenches around the town. They should also fill these trenches with water and construct a palisade along the inner lip of each one as further obstacles to the besiegers; sharp spikes and caltrops should then be scattered to the outside of the outermost trench. Trebuchets and arrow-shooting instruments are to be set up along the parapets, along with piles of stones, rocks, beams, and logs, with which to bombard the attackers and their tortoises. It is clear from these measures that the defenders were concerned first and foremost with preventing the enemy from reaching the base of the walls and undertaking tunnelling operations, or else

---

[14] *De obsidione*, pp. 45[13]–57[3].

[15] On this interesting inventory of the town's craftsmen and the materials needed for their labours, see J. Teall, "Byzantine Urbanism in the Military Handbooks," in *The Medieval City*, eds. H. A. Miskimin, D. Herilhy, A. L. Udovitch (New Haven: Yale University Press, 1977), pp. 201–05.

from bringing rams to bear on certain parts of the fortifications. Conspicuous by its absence, however, is any fear of enemy artillery. Nowhere in this first, most contemporary section of his treatise does the author express the slightest apprehension about the use or effect of artillery against the walls.

A brief survey of these two poliorcetic manuals reveals little innovation in Byzantine siege tactics and technology during the tenth and eleventh centuries, most notably in the development and use of siege artillery. On the other hand, the methods and devices which they emphasize appear to have been the ones most commonly used during this period, to judge from the two treatises written by veteran soldiers. The most immediate and realistic account of siege tactics is given by Nikephoros Ouranos, a distinguished military and intellectual figure who supervised the eastern frontiers of the Byzantine empire while governor of Antioch (999–1010?). Since Ouranos was also a military writer who distilled his experiences of campaigns in northern Syria into a set of precepts regulating the conduct of a siege from beginning to end, Chapter 65 of his *Taktika* proves to be a very useful source in assessing the balance between the theory and actual conduct of Byzantine siege warfare.

As outlined by Ouranos, a siege campaign required careful planning by the general and the coordination of his forces in a series of operations. The opening stages involved raiding and devastating the outposts and areas around the targeted fortress to destroy its supply of food and bring starvation upon the local populace, forcing them to leave; at the same time, the Byzantine commanders along the frontiers were to prevent all traffic from reaching the fortress once the defenders had sent word of their predicament to their fellow Muslims who would then collect and dispatch money and supplies to their brethren in need. This was not the only source of relief to be cut off, however, since even the local Christian population might be induced "in their love of profit" to sell grain, cheese, and flocks to the Muslim garrison "in return for a high price."[16]

Having arrived at the fortress, the Byzantine besiegers were to set up a secure camp. Before embarking on an assault, however, the commander might first seek to entice the garrison into surrendering by offering generous terms, which, if refused, were to be followed by threats of severe reprisals to those choosing to hold out. The Byzantine commander should also threaten all the Armenian and Syriac Christians, as well as apostates to Islam (*magaritai*), inside the walls with execution unless they deserted to the attackers before the fortress fell. Even if unsuccessful, the alternating offers of mercy and threats of retribution were a useful tool "since it causes dissension and disagreement among them, some favouring this, others that, which is of great benefit to us."[17]

Operations against the fortress began with the construction of "the

---

[16] De Foucault, p. 297. On the shifting allegiances between the various populations along the eastern fringes of the Byzantine empire, see G. Dagron, "Minorités ethniques et religieuses dans l'Orient byzantin à la fin du Xe et au XIe siècle: L'immigration syrienne," *Travaux et mémoires* 6 (1976), 177–216.

[17] De Foucault, p. 299.

implements used in siege warfare, *laisai* made from vine-stalks or from branches of willow or mulberry trees" (p. 299). We have seen that these "recently
devised" mantlets were added to the list of tortoises in Hero of Byzantium;
Ouranos' instructions on their assembly conform closely with their depiction in
the poliorcetic manual. The *laisai* were to be constructed in the shape of a house,
with steep roofs, two entrances, and plaited screens over the front as protection
against enemy projectiles. Light enough to be easily transportable, and spacious
enough for fifteen to twenty men, these mantlets were to be fixed at a distance
of ten or twenty yards from the walls to shelter teams of men as they took turns
fighting and resting through the day. Although Ouranos refers to trebuchets,
these appear to have been used primarily to hurl stones at people rather than
walls and were employed in unison with archers and slingers to keep up a
shower of missiles, which would force the defenders away from the ramparts. To
open a breach in the fortifications, the besiegers pounded the walls with rams
and sledgehammers, but the method which Ouranos deems most effective of all
is tunnelling, an operation which he describes in detail.[18]

Here again, the instructions given by Ouranos are very similar to those in
Hero of Byzantium. Once a suitable place had been located, sappers working
from beneath the *laisai* began digging a tunnel down to the foundations of the
wall. As they progressed, they inserted a series of plaited mats, supported by
wooden posts, to hold the earth over their heads; once at the foundations they
prised the stones loose and replaced them with thick beams to keep the wall
from falling upon them. When they had hollowed out the foundations, they
filled the cavity with dry wood and ignited it so that the fire would consume the
wooden support beams and cause the section of the wall above to collapse.

Ouranos' instructions combine with those in Hero of Byzantium to show that
tunnelling to undermine the foundations was the tactic favoured by the
Byzantines, and the historian Leo the Deacon records its use by Nikephoros
Phokas' army to capture the mighty fortress of Candia during the final conquest
of Crete in 961.[19] Effective as it was, however, tunnelling was a laborious,
time-consuming process. In recognition of this factor, Ouranos advises the
commander to gauge the progress of the siege and offer the garrison the choice
of departing free with their possessions if they surrender the fortress voluntarily,
or enslavement if they continue to resist. The impression conveyed by his advice
is that most sieges were endurance contests in which attrition and the human
element – morale, loyalty, determination – loomed ever larger as the siege wore
on.

The human factor figures even more prominently in Kekavmenos' discussion
of siege tactics. Like the author of the *De obsidione*, Kekavmenos directed his
counsels to the defenders, but he saw siege campaigns (and war generally) as a
contest more of wits than of tactics and technology. In one passage he echoes the

---

[18] De Foucault, pp. 299–301.
[19] *Leonis diaconi Caloensis historiae libri decem*, ed. C. B. Hase (Bonn, 1828), pp. 20–21.

recommendations of the *De obsidione* that the walls be repaired and streng-thened, that trebuchets and projectiles be set out along the parapets, and that ditches festooned with traps be dug around the fortress; he also advises digging countertunnels to intercept enemy sappers and gives instructions on how to increase the height of the walls in case the attackers attempt to raise an earthen mound by which to surmount the fortifications.[20] But the handful of episodes which he relates – drawn mainly from the western frontiers of the empire – record tricks and ruses devised by attackers to gain entry to a fortress or lure the commander out into an ambush, and so emphasize the role of deception, trea-chery, or carelessness over force of arms. In one instance, an enemy feigning friendship sent mules loaded with grain to the unsuspecting commander of an impregnable fortress; once the mule train had passed through the gates, warriors disguised as drivers sprang out and captured the commander and his fortress with him.[21] In another tale, Arab pirates claiming to be traders set up their stations immediately beside the walls of a fortress and bided their time until a rainstorm sent everyone, including most of the sentries, inside their homes, whereupon the Arabs made their way over the walls and captured the town.[22]

It remains now to offer some observations by way of conclusion. This study has concentrated on two objectives: the first to see the relation of theory to practice in the Byzantine treatises on siege warfare, the second to identify the methods which the Byzantines employed in siege operations. It has been seen that the theoretical manuals present a number of methods and devices which, as the soldier's treatises show, were applied in practice; yet where theory and practice intersect is in only the simplest level of technology and tactics. In theory, the repertoire of siegecraft was quite remarkable, but active soldiers made a clear distinction between the realm of ideas and current realities. As Ouranos, steeped in the poliorcetic manuals, declares, "the men of old, in their conduct of siege warfare, constructed many devices such as rams, wooden towers, scaling ladders with various features, as well as tortoises and all kinds of other objects which our generation can hardly imagine . . . many and varied are the means which the men of old contrived forconducting sieges, but I have set down only the methods which our generation currently employs"[23] – which were in fact quite elementary. The sources indicate that Byzantine attackers relied primarily on attrition, ruses, and tunnelling operations to capture a locale; and it is the simplicity of their siege technology – especially in artillery – and the emphasis on ruses and stratagems that emerge from the four sources studied here. The impression remains that in the conduct of siege warfare, as in other military activities, the Byzantines were keener to exploit human weakness than technical devices.

[20] Litavrin, pp. 178^{12}–80^{20}.
[21] Litavrin, pp. 168^{27}–70^{21}.
[22] Litavrin, pp. 184^{17}–86^{16}.
[23] De Foucault, p. 303.

Artillery in Late Antiquity: Prelude to the Middle Ages

Paul E. Chevedden
Salem State College

I. Introduction

One of the unsolved questions pertaining to medieval artillery is whether or not the torsion machines of classical antiquity continued to be used in the Middle Ages. This question has generated a good deal of discussion but remains unresolved. When this question was first addressed in the mid-nineteenth century, the answer was a resounding "No!" In his pioneering work on artillery published in 1840, Guillaume Dufour, while contending that medieval engineers were aware of the force of torsion, stated that, "it must have been difficult to procure the sinews in sufficient quantity and to fabricate the enormous cables which were needed to launch the weights, making these torsion machines increasingly rare, and making the counterweight machines for throwing stones and machines with tension bows for throwing bolts preferable."[1] He concluded that "the catapult or *onager* appears to have been replaced nearly everywhere by the trebuchet."[2] Louis-Napoléon Bonaparte (Napoleon III) echoed this view in his magisterial work on artillery, declaring that, "the artillery pieces used in the Middle Ages, in defending as well as in attacking [fortified] places, were not those of the Romans [i.e., torsion artillery]. . . . The machines of the Middle Ages were trebuchets or else base-mounted tension catapults [*arbalètes à tours*]."[3] At the end of the nineteenth century the question was answered in the affirmative by the experienced artilleryman and military historian General Köhler, who maintained that torsion artillery continued in use from Roman

---

[1] Guillaume Dufour, *Mémoire sur l'artillerie des anciens et sur celle du Moyen Âge* (Paris: Ab. Cherbuliez et Cᵉ, 1840), p. 97.

[2] Dufour, p. 99.

[3] Louis-Napoléon Bonaparte, *Études sur le passé et l'avenir de l'artillerie*, Vol. 2 (Paris: Librairie Militaire de J. Dumaine, 1851), p. 26. In his discussion of medieval artillery, Louis Napoléon uses the term *arbalète à tour* to refer to a large base-mounted tension catapult (p. 27), but he also uses this term to refer to the windlass crossbow (Vol. 1 [1848], pl. 1). Louis-Napoléon argues for a complete break between the artillery of classical antiquity and that of the Middle Ages. For a full discussion of Louis-Napoléon's position on this question, see pp. 38–53.

times through the Middle Ages.[4] In 1910 Rudolf Schneider challenged Köhler's view and argued that discontinuity, rather than continuity, characterized the development of artillery from ancient through medieval times. His findings suggested that the artillery of classical antiquity did not survive the collapse of Rome, and a long period ensued – from the fifth to the ninth century – during which artillery was not used in the Latin West.[5] When artillery was again employed in western Europe, it was radically different from its classical form. The possibility of the continuation of torsion artillery was ruled out by Schneider, because he believed that torsion catapults had fallen out of use long before the appearance of medieval artillery, and this artillery operated on entirely different principles from the torsion machines of antiquity. The Finnish orientalist Kalervo Huuri rendered his judgment on the continuation of torsion artillery in 1941 and concluded that such artillery may have been used in the medieval Mediterranean world, in the form of the one-armed torsion machine of late antiquity, the *onager*. He found no evidence, however, for the survival of the two-armed torsion catapult.[6]

Others have entered the debate on the question of the continuity of torsion artillery, but the works of the above-mentioned scholars remain the fundamental studies on the topic and form the basis for any debate of this issue. Recently, Randall Rogers has reviewed this debate in his excellent monograph *Latin Siege Warfare in the Twelfth Century*.[7] He rightly points out that the "lack of certainty regarding the forms of artillery employed in the early and central Middle Ages reflects fundamental problems with the available evidence."[8] The available evidence consists of narrative accounts, most of which do not provide sufficient detail to identify the type of artillery mentioned, illustrations contemporary to the Middle Ages or the Renaissance which depict artillery, and technical treatises on medieval artillery. Despite the Herculean efforts of Louis-Napoléon, Köhler, Schneider, and Huuri to master this evidence, they fell short of their goal. They missed or improperly understood key texts which clarify the nomenclature of medieval artillery; they gave only limited attention to the vast array of illustrated material on medieval artillery and failed to adequately analyze this evidence; and they did not consult the most significant technical treatises on medieval artillery, written in Arabic. The most important of these treatises have now been published, but major editorial errors and incorrect interpretation of the technical

---

[4] G. Köhler, *Die Entwickelung des Kriegwesens und der Kriegführung in der Ritterzeit von Mitte des II. Jahrhunderts bis zu den Hussitenkriegen*, Vol. 3 (Breslau: Verlag von Wilhelm Koebner, 1890), pp. 139–211.

[5] Rudolf Schneider, *Die Artillerie des Mittelalters* (Berlin: Weidmannsche Buchhandlung, 1910), pp. 10–16.

[6] Kalervro Huuri, "Zur Geschichte des mittelalterlichen Geschützwesens aus orientalischen Quellen," in *Societas Orientalia Fennica, Studia Orientalia* 9.3 (1941), 51–63, 212–14.

[7] Randall Rogers, *Latin Siege Warfare in the Twelfth Century* (Oxford: Clarendon Press, 1992), pp. 254–73.

[8] Rogers, p. 254.

terminology obscure a proper understanding of them.[9] The conflict between the "continuist" and 'discontinuist" schools of thought on medieval artillery may rage indefinitely – with neither side able to claim a decisive victory – unless the full weight of the evidence is brought to bear on this question.

The question pertaining to the continuity of torsion artillery can be approached from many angles. This study will investigate the evidence indicating the continuation or demise of the two-armed torsion catapult in historical and military writings from late antiquity.[10] None of the above-mentioned scholars offered conclusive proof for the disuse of this type of artillery in late antiquity. Moreover, the last systematic examination of the relevant Latin and Greek texts pertaining to this question, completed by E. W. Marsden, concluded that torsion artillery – both single- and double-spring varieties – continued to be produced in late antiquity and that this artillery was comparable in quality to earlier Greek and Roman ordnance.[11] These texts – written by Flavius Vegetius Renatus,[12]

[9] The two most important technical treatises on medieval artillery are the military manual of Mardī b. ʿAlī b. Mardī al-Tarsūsī, *Tabṣirat arbāb al-albāb fī kayfiyat al-najāh fī al-ḥurūb min al-aswāʾ wa-nashr aʿlām al-iʿlām fī al-ʿudad wa-al-ālāt al-muʿīnah ʿalā liqāʾ al-aʿdāʾ* [*Instructions of the Masters on the Means of Deliverance in Wars from Disasters, and the Unfurling of the Banners of Information: Equipment and Engines which Aid in Encounters with Enemies*] (MS 264, Huntington Collection, Bodleian Library, Oxford University, Oxford; MS 2848 mü, Ayasofya Collection, Süleymaniye Library, Istanbul) and *Kitāb anīq fī al-manājanīq (An Elegant Book on Trebuchets)* by Ibn Urunbughā al-Zaradkāsh (MS 3469/1, Ahmet III Collection, Topkapi Saray Müzesi Kütüphanesi, Istanbul). The first treatise contains the earliest full-length description of the counterweight trebuchet and illustrations and descriptions of four different types of traction trebuchets. This treatise was written for Saladin around 583/1187 and is one of the most important military works produced in Islam during the Middle Ages. The section of this treatise dealing with artillery has been published by Claude Cahen ("Un traité d'armurerie composé pour Saladin," *Bulletin d'études orientales* 12 [1947–48], 103–63). The second Arabic treatise is the longest and most profusely illustrated work in any language dealing with the trebuchet. This treatise, written by Ibn Urunbughā al-Zaradkāsh in 867/1462–63, is not only the most important work in any language on the trebuchet, it is one of the most important martial technical treatises produced during the Middle Ages. Two editions of this manuscript have appeared, both entitled *al-Anīq fī al-manājanīq*. The first is edited by Nabīl Muhammad ʿAbd al-ʿAzīz Ahmad (Cairo: Maktabat al-Anglo al-Misrīyah, 1981), and the second by Iḥsān Hindī (Aleppo: Institute for the History of Arabic Science, 1985).

[10] The question of the survival of the torsion-powered *onager* must remain beyond the scope of this paper. Conclusive documentation would require a monographic-length analysis of both late antique and medieval sources.

[11] E. W. Marsden, *Greek and Roman Artillery: Historical Development* (Oxford: Clarendon Press, 1969), p. 198, and his *Greek and Roman Artillery: Technical Treatises* (Oxford: Clarendon Press, 1971), pp. 234–65.

[12] Flavius Vegetius Renatus, *Epitoma rei militaris*, ed. and trans. Leo F. Stelten (New York: Peter Lang, 1990), 4.22. While most scholars agree that the *Epitoma* was produced in the western Empire, its date and the identity of the emperor to whom it was dedicated are still in dispute. Three emperors have been suggested as possible dedicatees: Theodosius I (379–95), Honorius (393–423), and Valentinian III (425–55). For a discussion of the dating problem, see Vegetius, pp. xiii–xv and *Vegetius: Epitome of Military Science*, trans. N. P. Milner (Liverpool: Liverpool University Press, 1993), pp. xxv–xxix. In the most recent assessment of the dating question by Milner (cited above), Theodosius I is judged to be the most likely dedicatee.

Ammianus Marcellinus,[13] the Anonymus who authored *De rebus bellicis*,[14] and Procopius[15] – provide, according to Marsden, "sufficient indirect or implied evidence" to indicate that the standard bolt-projector of late antiquity was the two-armed torsion catapult.[16] If this conclusion stands, the "continuists" may well argue that torsion artillery was used in the Middle Ages, since the manuscript tradition related to this artillery certainly did continue during the medieval period in the Byzantine Empire. If books on torsion artillery continued to be copied and read in the Middle Ages – even if only in one of the three civilizational orders of the Mediterranean world – such artillery may have been built, and, if built, transmitted to other societies by military engineers who operated within an international network of contacts and patronage much as they do today. Before examining these texts, a brief overview of ancient artillery is appropriate.

II. Ancient Artillery

In the Mediterranean world, the Greeks were the first to invent artillery. The earliest piece of artillery is traditionally credited to engineers working under Dionysius the Elder of Syracuse. In 399 B.C. they invented the tension catapult, consisting of a large composite bow fixed to a wooden stock, in which a wooden slider could move back and forth. The top of the slider was grooved to receive a large arrow or bolt. A claw-and-trigger device for grasping and releasing the bowstring was fixed to the top rear of the slider. The slider was pushed forward until the claw could be hooked over the bowstring. To span the weapon, the operator forced the slider to the rear by putting the front of the slider against a stationary surface and pushing against the crescent-shaped butt of the stock with

---

[13] Ammianus Marcellinus, *Res Gestae*, ed. Wolfgang Seyfarth, Vol. 1 (Leipzig: B. G. Teubner, 1978), p. 299 (23.4.1–3), and the ed. and trans. by J. C. Rolfe, Vol. 2 (Cambridge MA: Harvard University Press, 1939), pp. 324–27 (23.4.1–3). The extant books of the history of Ammianus (14–31) cover the years 354 to 378, which fall within the author's own lifetime. His description of artillery forms part of his narrative of Julian's expedition against the Sassanian Empire in the year 363.

[14] E. A. Thompson, trans., *A Roman Reformer and Inventor: Being a New Text of the Treatise "De rebus bellicis"* (Oxford: Clarendon Press, 1952); *De rebus bellicis*, Part 2: *"De rebus bellicis": The Text*, ed. Robert Ireland, B. A. R. International Series, 63 (Oxford: B. A. R., 1979). According to the most recent study of the dating of *De rebus bellicis*, this work was written c. 368–69 (Alan Cameron, "The Date of the Anonymus *De rebus bellicis*," in *De rebus bellicis*, Part 1: *Aspects of the "De rebus bellicis": Papers Presented to Professor E. A. Thompson*, ed. M. W. C. Hassall, B. A. R. International Series, 63 [Oxford: B. A. R., 1979], pp. 1–7).

[15] Procopius, *De Bello Gothico*, in *Procopii Caesariensis opera omnia*, ed. Jacob Haury, re-ed. Gerhard Wirth, Vol. 2 (Leipzig: B. G. Teubner, 1963), p. 106–07 (1.21.14–18), and his *Works*, ed. and trans. H. B. Dewing, Vol. 3 (Cambridge MA: Harvard University Press, 1919), p. 204–07. Procopius, who lived during the reign of Justinian (527–65), was contemporary to the period about which he writes. He describes artillery in his account of the siege of Rome by the Goths in 537–38.

[16] Marsden, *Technical Treatises*, pp. 234–48.

his stomach. A linear ratchet and pawl system locked the slider solidly to the stock and resisted the force of the bow. When the tension was sufficient, the operator placed a bolt in the groove and aimed the weapon at his target. The bolt was discharged by pulling the trigger – a transverse lever – which when forced back allowed the claw to pivot upward, thus releasing the bowstring. Since the operator used his stomach to span the machine manually, it was appropriately called a *gastraphetes* or "belly-bow."[17] This early catapult was a hand-held bolt-projector which could be utilized by foot soldiers. Later, larger catapults were built, mounted on stands, which utilized mechanical pull-back systems, such as a circular ratchet at the rear of the stock, to span the bow. With these improvements, stone-projecting catapults became technically feasible with two slight modifications: widening the groove in the slider and adding a pouch with a loop on its rear side to the bowstring.

By 340 B.C. the improved tension catapult was superseded by the more powerful torsion catapult, which replaced the bow with two vertical springs made of ropes of sinew or hair, each set in a frame on either side of the stock of the machine. A solid wooden arm was inserted horizontally through the middle of each spring and a bowstring was fitted into the notch at the end of each of the arms. The rest of the machine was essentially the same as that of a tension catapult. Hellenistic engineers developed a number of different models of bolt-projecting and stone-projecting, two-armed torsion catapults, but these machines corresponded to two basic types: "straight-spring" (*euthytonos*) bolt-projectors and "back-stretched spring" (*palintonos*) stone-projectors. The palintone engine had springs which extended the forward swing of the arms much further than the euthytone engine, enabling the springs to exert their force on the arms for a longer period than the springs of the euthytone engine. The more powerful palintone torsion catapult was typically a stone-projector, while the less powerful euthytone torsion catapult was always a bolt-projector.

Rome obtained its knowledge of artillery from the Greeks and promoted the development of the catapult, relying on the skilled engineers of the Hellenistic world (fig. 1). From the Republican through the early Imperial period, Rome made several significant improvements in catapult design, including: (1) a more efficient system for tightening the torsion springs, which made it far easier for the operator to tighten the cord bundles and keep them equally balanced; (2) the use of oval, rather than circular, spring holes and washers for stone-projecting catapults which permitted a cord bundle of greater mass to be employed, thereby increasing the power of the machine; (3) the use of curved, rather than straight, arms for bolt-projecting catapults that increased the angle of the twist and gave the machine more power; and (4) the complete plating of the wooden frame of the catapult with metal sheets to protect the machine from the ravages of weather and enemy counter-battery.[18] During the second half of the first century,

---

[17] C. Wescher, *Poliorcétique des grecs* (Paris: Imprimerie Impériale, 1867), pp. 75–81; Marsden, *Historical Development*, pp. 5–12, and *Technical Treatises*, pp. 20–23.

[18] The improved system for tightening the torsion springs can be seen on the catapult found

Roman artillery was radically transformed with the introduction of a new type of catapult having all-metal tension-frames which were both wider and lower than the tension-frames of Hellenistic catapults and more widely-spaced than the tension-frames of earlier artillery (fig. 7). These frames were more durable than wooden ones and could be easily replaced if damaged. The tension-frames were encased in cone-topped metal cylinders to protect them from damp and counter-battery from the enemy, creating a catapult with all-weather capability for the first time. The arms of the catapult had a greater freedom of travel than earlier catapults, giving it considerably more power than wooden-framed catapults of corresponding size. Heron's *Cheiroballistra* and the artillery on Trajan's Column (see below) provide evidence for the new Roman catapult design, and remains of this new artillery have been examined in detail by Dietwulf Baatz.[19] The standard stone-projector of Imperial Rome, which continued in use through the third century, was the two-armed, wooden-framed torsion catapult. It was similar to its Hellenistic counterpart but its tension-frames, like those of the new Roman bolt-projecting catapult, were lower and more widely-spaced than the tension-frames of Hellenistic stone-projectors.[20]

---

in 1912 at Ampurius (ancient Emporion) in Spain which dates from the middle of the second century B.C. On the Ampurius catapult and its system for tightening the torsion springs, see Erwin Schramm, *Die Antiken Geschütze de Saalburg* (1918; reprint, Bad Homburg: Saalburg-museum, 1980), pp. 40–46; Marsden, *Historical Development*,p. 29, and *Technical Treatises*, pp. 53–54; J. G. Landels, *Engineering in the Ancient World* (Berkeley: University of California Press, 1978), p. 115. Similar spanning systems for torsion springs, consisting of a movable spanning washer and a fixed counter-plate, have been studied by Dietwulf Baatz in "Teile Hellenistischer Geschütze aus Griechenland," *Archäologischer Anzeiger* (1979), 68–75, and "Ein Katapult der *Legio IV Macedonica* aus Cremona," *Römische Mitteilungen* 87 (1980), 283–99 and "Hellenistische Katapulte aus Ephyra [Epirus]," *Athenische Mitteilungen* 97 (1982), 211–33, and "Katapultteile aus dem Schiffswrack von Mahdia [Tunesien]," *Archäologischer Anzeiger* (1985), 677–91, and "Eine Katapult-Spannbuchse aus Pityus, Georgien [UDSSR]," *Saalburg Jahrbuch* 44 (1988), 59–64. The spring holes and washers of the stone-projecting *ballista* of Vitruvius are oval rather than circular in order to increase the mass of the cord bundle without increasing the size of the whole machine (Marsden, *Technical Treatises*, pp. 191, 201 n. 28 and fig. 8). Vitruvius' bolt-projecting "scorpion" utilized curved arms to increase the path over which the arms travel (Marsden, *Technical Treatises*, pp. 183–205, 229–30). The covering of the wooden frame of the catapult with metal sheets is confirmed by both archeological and artistic evidence. The sheet of bronze that covered the front of a catapult constructed in A.D. 45 and used in the second battle of Cremona in A.D. 69 has been recovered, as well as sheets of bronze that covered the front and sides of the Hatra *ballista*, dating from the third century A.D. A bas-relief of a bolt-projecting catapult from the tombstone of Vedennius, dating from the end of the first century A.D., clearly shows a metal sheet covering the front of the machine (Baatz, "Ein Katapult der *Legio IV Macedonica* aus Cremona,"*Römische Mitteilungen* 87 (1980), 283–99; Marsden, *Historical Development*, p. 185, pl. 1; and n. 20 below), and similar metal sheets cover the fronts of wooden-frame bolt-projecting catapults depicted on the Flavian relief pillars now in the Galleria degli Uffizi in Florence (Schramm, *Antiken Geschütze*, pp. 37–39, figs. 12–13).

[19] Nicolae Gudea and Dietwulf Baatz, "Teile Spätrömischer Ballisten aus Gornea und Orşova (Rumänien)," *Saalburg Jahrbuch* 31 (1974), 50–72; Dietwulf Baatz, "Recent Finds of Ancient Artillery," *Britannia* 9 (1978), pp. 2, 9–17, pls. 2, 5; and Dietwulf Baatz and Michel Feugère, "Éléments d'une catapulte romaine trouvée à Lyon," *Gallia* 39 (1981), 201–09.

[20] Baatz, "Recent Finds," pp. 1–9, pls. 1–4; his "The Hatra Ballista," *Sumer* 33.1 (1977), 141–51; and "Das Torsionsgeschütz von Hatra," *Antike Welt* 9.4 (1978), 50–57. The Hatra

During the fourth century classical artillery underwent a change in terminology. The word *ballista*, which in the Republican period had referred to a two-armed torsion stone-projector, came to signify a bolt-projector in the fourth century. New compound forms of the term *ballista* appear – *arcuballista, manuballista*, and *carroballista* – and these, too, signified bolt-projectors. Many of the changes reflected in this new terminology were underway by the second half of the first century when Rome introduced its most advanced artillery. The term *ballista* was probably applied to the new metal-framed, bolt-projecting catapult, since it was constructed in the palintone form, just like the palintone stone-projecting catapult. Marsden speculates that the term *ballista* may have been used interchangeably for both the new bolt-projector and the two-armed torsion catapult during the period that both machines were in use.[21] By the fourth century the old two-armed, wooden-framed stone-projector was replaced by the one-armed, torsion-driven sling machine known as the *onager*, or "wild ass," so named because "wild asses, when hunted in the chase, throw up stones so high behind their backs by kicking that they penetrate the chests of the their pursuers or actually break their bones and smash their skulls."[22] This machine consisted of a horizontal torsion-spring housed in a heavy wooden frame with a massive arm inserted through the middle of the spring. A sling, containing a stone missile, was attached to the extremity of the arm, and a windlass was used to draw down the arm to the frame of the machine. Once released, the arm shot upward, the sling opened, and the missile flew towards its target. A cushion, mounted on a subsidiary framework above the main frame of the machine, absorbed some of the kinetic energy of the arm and halted its motion.

Why did the simpler, cruder, more cumbersome *onager* replace the more advanced and complex two-armed torsion catapult as Rome's sole stone-projecting ordnance? Landels suggests that it was due to the decline in technical know-how in the Roman Empire.

> [The *onager*] was probably a good deal easier and simpler to make than the two-spring stone-thrower, and it did not require so much maintenance or adjustments such as the balancing of the springs, or accurate alignment of the slider and trough. So long as the available technical skills were adequate for this, the two-spring machine had the obvious advantage of better performance, but in later days, when craftsmanship declined, the simpler and cruder machine became preferable.[23]

---

ballista, a two-armed torsion catapult, was initially thought to be an *onager* (see Salāḥ Ḥusayn, "Manjanīq min al-Ḥaḍr," *Sumer* 32.1–2 (1976), 121–34).

[21] Marsden, *Historical Development*, p. 189.

[22] Ammianus, *Res gestae*, 23.4.7; Marsden, *Technical Treatises*, pp. 250–51. For a discussion of the *onager*, see Erwin Schramm, "Μονάγκων und Onager," *Nachrichten von der Gesellschaft der Wissenschaften zu Göttingen, Philologisch-historische Klasse* 2 (1918), 259–71, and his *Antiken Geschütze*, pp. 70–74, pl. 10; Ralph Payne-Gallwey, *The Crossbow, Medieval and Modern, Military and Sporting: Its Construction, History and Management with a Treatise on the Ballista and Catapult of the Ancients and an Appendix on the Catapult, Ballista and the Turkish Bow*, 2nd ed. (London: Holland Press, 1958), App., pp. 10–18; Marsden, *Technical Treatises*, pp. 249–65; Landels, pp. 130–32.

[23] Landels, p. 132.

If we accept Landels' thesis for the demise of the two-armed torsion stone-projector and the appearance of the *onager*, how can the alleged survival of the two-armed torsion catapult, now used solely as a bolt-projector, be explained? If technical skills did, indeed, decline, one would expect this highly sophisticated machine to have been phased out as well. And this appears to be what happened. The fifth century most likely saw the disappearance of the two-armed torsion catapult and its replacement by the tension catapult. Marsden has argued that all bolt-projectors of late antiquity, save for Vegetius' *arcuballista*, were torsion-powered machines.[24] Bert S. Hall has gone further and suggested that even the *arcuballista* was a torsion machine.[25] An examination of the descriptions of artillery found in texts dating from the fourth to the sixth century will help to clarify the matter.

III. Bolt-Projecting Artillery of Late Antiquity

A. Bolt-projecting artillery of Vegetius

Vegetius mentions artillery but has little to say about its construction and operation. He identifies five different types of artillery: a one-armed torsion stone-projector known as the *onager* and four bolt-projecting machines. These bolt-projectors are identified under the terms *ballista*,[26] *carroballista* (carriage-mounted *ballista*),[27] *manuballista* (hand-*ballista*) or *scorpio* (scorpion),[28] and *arcuballista* (bow-*ballista*).[29] Vegetius provides his most detailed account of artillery in Chapter 22 of Book 4 of *Epitoma rei militaris*, in which he mentions all of the pieces of artillery except the *carroballista*. Marsden drew attention to a portion of this chapter to bolster his claim that the standard catapult of the fourth century A.D. was a torsion machine. An examination of the full chapter will indicate that other interpretations are possible.

Epitoma rei militaris, 4.22

De ballistis, onagris, scorpionibus, arcuballistis, fustibalis, fundis per quae tormenta defenditur murus[30]

Adversum haec obsessos defendere consueverunt ballistae, onageri, scorpiones, arcuballistae, fustibali, sagittarii fundae. Ballista funibus nervinis tenditur, quae, quanto prolixiora brachiola habuerit, hoc est quanto maior fuerit,

---

24 Marsden, *Historical Development*, pp. 2, 188–98, and *Technical Treatises*, pp. 234–48.

25 Bert S. Hall, "Crossbows and Crosswords," rev. of *Greek and Roman Artillery: Historical Development* and *Greek and Roman Artillery: Technical Treatises* by E. W. Marsden, *Isis* 64 (1973), 527–33.

26 Vegetius, 2.10 (*ballistae*), 3.3 (*ballistisque*), 4.9 (*ballistae, ballistas*), 4.10 (*ballistas*), 4.18 (*ballistas, ballistae*), 4.22 (*ballistae, ballista*), 4.29 (*ballistae*), 4.44 (*ballistis, ballistas*).

27 Vegetius, 2.25 (*carroballistas, carroballistae*), 3.14 (*carroballistae*), 3.24 (*carroballistas*).

28 Vegetius, 2.15 (*manuballistas*), 3.14 (*manuballistarii*), 4.21 (*manuballistarii*), 4.22 (*manuballistas, scorpiones*), 4.44 (*scorpionibus*).

29 Vegetius, 2.15 (*arcuballistas*), 4.21 (*arcuballistarii*), 4.22 (*arcuballistae, arcuballistas*).

30 Vegetius, 4.22.

tanto spicula longius mittit; quae si juxta artem mechanicam temperetur et ab exercitatis hominibus, qui mensuram eius ante collegerint, dirigatur, penetrat quodcumque percusserit. Onager autem dirigit lapides, sed pro nervorum crassitudine et magnitudine saxorum pondera iaculatur; nam quanto amplior fuerit, tanto maiora saxa fulminis more contorquet. His duobus generibus nulla tormentorum species vehementior invenitur. Scorpiones dicebant, quas nunc manuballistas vocant; ideo sic nuncupati, quod parvis subtilibusque spiculis inferant mortem. Fustibalos, arcuballistas et fundas describere superfluum puto, quae praesens usus agnoscit. Saxis tamen gravioribus per onagrum destinatis non solum equi eliduntur et homines sed etiam hostium machinamenta franguntur.

Concerning *ballistae*, *onagers*, scorpions, bow-*ballistae*, staff-slings, and slings: Missile-launching devices by which the wall is defended

Against these machines[31] the *ballistae*, *onagers*, scorpions, bow-*ballistae*, staff-slings, arrows, and slings were usually used to defend the besieged. The *ballista* is strung with sinew-ropes.[32] The longer the arms it has – that is, the larger it is – the further it shoots its bolts. If it is tuned[33] according to mechanical rules and if it is aimed by trained men who have assembled data on its range,[34] it penetrates whatever it hits. The *onager*, however, throws stones of different weights according to the thickness and extent of its sinew-bundle; for the larger it is, the bigger the stones it can hurl, in the manner of a thunderbolt. One can find no piece of artillery which is more powerful than these two types [the *ballista* and *onager*]. Hand-*ballistae*, which used to be called "scorpions," were so designated because they kill by means of small and slender bolts. It is superfluous to describe staff-slings, bow-*ballistae*, and slings, since they are so well-known by present-day use. The stones thrown by the *onager* are of such great weight that they not only crush to death horses and men, but they even shatter the siege machines of the enemy.

Marsden concluded from the description of the *ballista* in this chapter that the standard bolt-projector of the fourth century was a torsion machine. However, Vegetius does not employ *ballista* as a generic term for all bolt-projectors, but for a specific type of large bolt-projecting engine, which is quite obviously a base-mounted, two-armed torsion catapult. According to him, this machine was used in the defense of cities[35] and aboard ships in naval warfare.[36] Aside from its

---

[31] These machines are the ones mentioned in *Epitoma*, 4.21: the scaling-ladder (*scala*), a mechanized scaling-ladder called a *sambuca*, the boarding plank of a mobile siege tower (*exostra*), and a rotating-beam device for hoisting men onto walls (*tolleno*).

[32] Marsden has translated this passage as, "the *ballista* is powered by sinew-ropes" (*Technical Treatises*, p. 237).

[33] On the translation of *temperare* as "to tune," see Marsden, *Technical Treatises*, p. 237, n. 3, and Vitruvius, *De architectura*, ed. and trans. Frank Granger, Vol. 2, The Loeb Classical Library (Cambridge: Harvard University Press, 1934), 10.11.9, 10.12.1–2.

[34] On the translation of *mensuram* as "range," see Marsden, *Technical Treatises*, p. 237, n. 4. Marsden has observed that Vegetius seems to indicate here that there are experts who know how to build and tune a *ballista* and those who are trained in shooting the machine. Additional evidence presented by Campbell corroborates this conclusion (Duncan B. Campbell, "Auxiliary Artillery Revisited," *Bonner Jahrbücher* 186 [1986], 118).

[35] Vegetius, 3.3, 4.9, 4.10, 4.18, 4.22, 4.29.

[36] Vegetius, 4.44.

use in naval engagements, the *ballista* was strictly used in siege operations, employed by besieger and besieged alike. It is cited along with other siege engines (battering-rams, *onagers*, and other missile-launching devices) as part of the equipment of an expeditionary force.[37] Vegetius does mention *ballistarii* (literally, *ballista*-men) in the context of field warfare, and it is clear that he intends the term to refer to *manuballistarii* or *arcuballistarii*, not to the crew that operated the *ballista* or to the artisans who manufactured it.[38] A number of *ballistae* are shown on Trajan's Column, built in A.D. 113. One is depicted being hauled up a mountain track on a mule-drawn transport-wagon.[39] Two others are displayed on the battlements of a Roman fort,[40] another is positioned in front of this fort in an advanced emplacement described as an artillery "pill-box,"[41] and Dacian defenders are shown operating their own *ballista* behind a wooden palisade.[42] These *ballistae* are all of a standard type: a two-armed, metal-framed torsion catapult mounted on a base-tripod. The sinew-bundles are protected by cone-topped metal cylinders and the upper metal strut holding the tension-frames in place are clearly shown with a distinctive arch in the center (figs. 2–5).

Following his remarks on the *ballista* and *onager* in the above passage, Vegetius goes on to mention two other pieces of artillery: the *manuballista* (hand-*ballista*), or "scorpion," and the *arcuballista* (bow-*ballista*). The only information provided on the *manuballista* is that it shoots small and slender bolts, which suggests that it was a small machine.[43] Its name suggests that it was

---

[37] Vegetius, 2.10.

[38] Vegetius, 2.2; cf. 2.15, 3.14. Vegetius (3.24) also mentions *ballista*-bolts (*sagittis ballistariis*) being shot by *carroballistae*.

[39] Conrad Cichorius, *Trajan's Column: A New Edition of the Cichorius Plates*, eds. Frank Lepper and Sheppard Frere (Gloucester: Alan Sutton, 1988), pp. 106–07, pl. 46 (lxvi/163–64); I. A. Richmond, "Trajan's Army on Trajan's Column," *Papers of the British School at Rome* 13 (1935), 14, and his "Roman Artillery," *Durham University Journal* 7 (March 1946), 62; Schramm, *Antiken Geschütze*, p. 32, fig. 8, p. 60, fig. 26; Marsden, *Historical Development*, pl. 10, and *Technical Treatises*, pl. 10.

[40] Cichorius, pp. 106–07, pl. 47 (lxvi/165); Marsden, *Historical Development*, pl. 11, and *Technical Treatises*, pl. 11.

[41] Cichorius, pp. 106–07, pl. 47 (lxvi/166); Marsden, *Historical Development*, pl. 12, and *Technical Treatises*, pl. 12.

[42] Cichorius, pp. 106–08, pl. 48 (lxvi/169); Marsden, *Historical Development*, pl. 13, and *Technical Treatises*, p. 13.

[43] Vernard L. Foley has suggested to me that Vegetius' reference to the bolts of the *manuballista* being small and slender indicates that these projectiles could not have been the heavy conical bolts which were discharged by larger static catapults. On these conical bolts, see Harald von Petrikovits, "Eine Pilumspitze von der Grotenburg bei Detmold," *Germania* 29(1951), 206–08; Dietwulf Baatz, "Zur Geschützbewaffnung römischer Auxiliartruppenin in der frühen und mittleren Kaiserzeit," *Bonner Jahrbücher* 166 (1966), 203–07, and "Hellenistische Katapulte aus Ephyra (Epirus)," 239–32, and "Eine Katapult-Spannbuchse aus Pityus, Georgien (UDSSR)," 63–64; Baatz and Feugère, p. 208; Vernard Foley, George Palmer, and Werner Soedel, "The Crossbow," *Scientific American* 252 (January 1985), 107–10; L. H. Barfield, "Ein Burgus in Froitzheim, Kreis Düren," in *Beiträge zur Archäologie des römischen Rheinlands*, ed. L. H. Barfield et al., Vol. 1 (Düsseldorf: Rheinland-Verlag, 1968), pp. 8–11, 13–14, fig. 46; Raymond Brulet, *La fortification de Hauterecenne à Furfooz* (Louvain-la-Neuve: Institut Supérieur d' Archéologie et d'Histoire de l'Art, 1978), pp. 13–14, fig. 77; Jean-Pierre Lemant,

a hand-held weapon, and a description of its Greek counterpart, designated by the Greek equivalent of *manuballista* (*chieroballistra* = hand-*ballista*), indicates that it was a hand-held weapon (see below). No details are provided for the *arcuballista*, but since it is mentioned in the context of other light weapons (the sling and staff-sling), it, too, must have been a small bolt-projector.

Marsden has interpreted the statement by Vegetius concerning the collection of sinew for artillery to imply that the conventional bolt-projectors of Vegetius' day had torsion springs. Vegetius states:

> It is also essential that a supply of sinews be collected with the utmost zeal, because *onagers* or *ballistae*, and other artillery are useless unless strung with sinew-ropes.[44]

Marsden translated "other artillery" (*ceteraque tormenta*) as "other torsion engines" and suggested that this phrase referred to the *carroballista* and *manuballista*. While *tormentum* originally referred to artillery with torsion springs, it came to be used as a general term for any missile-projecting device. By the fourth century, the term *tormentum* was not used exclusively to refer to torsion artillery. Vegetius categorizes *ballistae*, *onagers*, scorpions, and bow-*ballistae*, as well as staff-slings and slings, as *tormenta*.[45] The verb "to string" (*intenta*) may refer to the bracing of a hand-bow or the stringing of a tension or torsion catapult. If the machine had torsion springs, this verb would indicate the action of wrapping and stretching the sinew-ropes on the tension-frames of the catapult. If it were tension-powered, this verb would refer to the bracing of the machine as it was fitted with a bowstring. The sinews which Vegetius says should be collected for the artillery may have been used either for the bowstring of a tension catapult or the sinew-bundle of a torsion machine (*onager* or *ballista*). Following the statement regarding the collection of sinews, Vegetius devotes nearly the entire remaining portion of the chapter to the *ballista* and speaks of the use of horsehair and human hair in the torsion springs of this machine. Since Vegetius does not use the term *ballista* in a generic sense to indicate all bolt-projecting catapults, his remarks here on the *ballista* do not imply that his statement on sinews refers only to their use in torsion machines.

It cannot be assumed that the various compound forms of *ballista* (*carroballista*, *manuballista*, and *arcuballista*) necessarily refer to torsion engines. These machines were light and mobile enough to be used in field warfare. The *manu-*

Le cimetière et la fortification du Bas-Empire de Vireux-Molhain, dép. Ardennes (Mainz: Verlag des Römisch-Germanischen Zentralmuseums, 1985), pp. 63–69, fig. 67; W. J. H. Willems, "An Officer or a Gentleman? A Late-Roman Weapon-Grave from a Villa at Voerendaal (NL)," in *Roman Military Equipment: The Sources of Evidence, Proceedings of the Fifth Roman Military Equipment Conference*, ed. C. van Driel-Murray (Oxford: B. A. R., 1989), pp. 149–51. These conical bolts are too heavy for hand-held bolt-projectors, so the reference to small and slender bolts indicates that the *manuballista* was a hand-held bolt-projector.

[44] Vegetius, 4.9: "Nervorum quoque copiam summo studio expedit colligi quia onagri vel ballistae ceteraque tormenta nisi funibus nervinis intenta nihil prosunt."

[45] Vegetius, 4.22.

ballista and *arcuballista* were used on mobile siege-towers to drive defenders from the wall, which indicates that they were capable of a rapid sequence of discharge and, hence, must have been rather small antipersonnel weapons.[46] Their relative size can be determined by where they were placed on the field of battle. According to Vegetius, the army formed up in six parallel lines. Just behind the first line *tragularii* were stationed armed with *manuballistae* and *arcuballistae*.[47] *Carroballistae* and *manuballistae* were sometimes placed in the fifth battle line,[48] and in the rear, the larger *carroballistae*, having the greatest range, were positioned.[49] The location of the *carroballista*, or carriage-mounted *ballista*, in the formation of battle indicates that it was the largest piece of artillery used in field warfare. According to Vegetius, it was mounted on small carts drawn by two horses or mules and was serviced by an artillery crew of eleven men.[50] Two *carroballistae* are shown on Trajan's Column (fig. 6), which indicates that these catapults were in service in the early part of the second century and used in Trajan's Dacian campaigns.[51] Once the Romans had developed metal tension-frames for catapults and weatherproofed the new artillery pieces by enclosing the sinew-bundles in cylindrical metal cases, truly mobile field artillery became possible. Since the new Roman catapult design was probably introduced during the second half of the first century, the *carroballista* can be dated to this same period. When the *carroballista* first appeared, it was a two-armed torsion catapult, but it need not have remained a torsion machine. Anonymus describes a carriage-mounted *ballista* which is most probably a tension catapult (see below), indicating that by the fourth century the *carroballista* may have been a tension, not a torsion, machine. If the *carroballista* started out as a torsion engine, it may have eventually evolved into a tension machine.

Marsden stated that the *arcuballista*, from which the French term *arbalest* and other cognates are derived, was the ancestor of the medieval crossbow.[52] Hall has challenged this opinion, contending that the *arcuballista* was a two-armed torsion catapult.[53] Two Gallo-Roman stone reliefs of hunting scenes, which date

---

[46] Vegetius, 4.21.

[47] Vegetius, 2.15.

[48] Vegetius, 3.14.

[49] Vegetius, 2.25, 3.24.

[50] Vegetius, 2.25, 3.24.

[51] Cichorius, pp. 88, 106, 107, 268, pl. 31 (xl/104–05); Richmond, "Trajan's Army," pp. 13–14, and "Roman Artillery," p. 62; Schramm, *Antiken Geschütze*, p. 31, fig. 7; Marsden, *Historical Development*, pl. 9, and *Technical Treatises*, pl. 9. I. A. Richmond has suggested, *contra* Schramm and Marsden, that the carriage for the *carroballista* was not an ordinary cart for the transport of an artillery piece to some emplacement, as shown on Trajan's Column (Cichorius, pp. 106–07, pl. 46 [lxvi/163–64]). Rather, it was "a very stoutly built two-wheeled carriage of special design . . . built so low and so strong at the back as to suggest that it served as gun-carriage and ammunition-cart at one and the same time, with a rearward hopper for ammunition" (Richmond, "Roman Artillery," p. 62; Schramm, *Antiken Geschütze*, pp. 30–32; Marsden, *Historical Development*, pp. 180, 192, 196).

[52] Marsden, *Historical Development*, p. 2.

[53] Hall argues that the "bow" of the "bow-*ballista*" (*arcuballista*) referred to the inverted U-bend in the middle of the upper strut which held the tension-frames of a two-armed torsion

from the second or third century, clearly depict crossbows.[54] The thickness and design of the bows suggest that they were of composite construction. Neither weapon is provided with a mechanical pull-back system or a crescent-shaped rest at the rear of the stock for spanning the bow, indicating that they were either spanned by hand or by using a belt and claw spanning device. The mechanism used to retain the drawn bowstring is shown in one of the relief carvings (that found at Polignac) to be a nut revolving within the stock. Since no trigger mechanism is depicted on top of the stock, similar to the lever-hinged trigger mechanism of the *gastraphetes*, the trigger must have been inserted in the body of the stock and operated from below. The employment of such a trigger mechanism gives clear indication that the Roman crossbow was the ancestor of the medieval crossbow.

These reliefs also provide unambiguous evidence for the use of the crossbow during the Roman period for hunting purposes. It would seem natural for the Romans to devise a military use for the weapon, even if it were only utilized on a limited basis. Arrian (*c.* A.D. 96–180), a Greek historian who held command in the Roman army, describes a cavalry exercise in his military treatise in which a bolt-projecting machine is discharged from horseback: "there are performed shootings of various kinds, with light darts or bolts, these being shot not from a bow, but from a 'machine' (μηχανή)."[55] Howard L. Blackmore has concluded that this passage implies the use of "some form of hand crossbow."[56] Duncan B. Campbell, who has analyzed the same passage, provides a useful discussion of the many and varied meanings of μηχανή (*mēchaneâ*) – which include artillery of

---

catapult in place. He maintains this position even though he admits that, "the word – 'bow-*ballista*' – certainly sounds like a crossbow's name; certainly it gave rise to the later French *arbalest*, meaning crossbow; and certainly medieval vernacular versions of the *Epitoma rei militaris* translated it as crossbow" (Hall, p. 532). Hall's view has not gone unchallenged (Campbell, p. 131, n. 96).

[54] These stone reliefs, originally from Polignac and Saint-Marcel, are now in the Musée Crozatier in Le Puy in the Haute Loire region of south central France. For a brief description and illustration of both reliefs, see Émile Espérandieu, *Recueil général des bas-reliefs de Gaule romaine*, Collection de documents inédits sur l'histoire de France, série VI/9, Vol. 2 (Paris: Imprimerie Nationale, 1908), p. 442 (no. 1679), pp. 443–44 (no. 1683). The most important analysis of these reliefs for the information they provide on the construction of the Roman crossbow has been made by Dietwulf Baatz,"Die Römische Jagdarmbrust," *Archäologisches Korrespondenzblatt* 21 (1991), 283–90; see also Schramm, *Antiken Geschütze*, pp. 18–19, fig. 4; Howard L. Blackmore, *Hunting Weapons* (New York: Walker & Co., 1971), p. 174; Egon Harmuth, *Die Armbrust* (Graz: Akademische Druck- u. Verlagsanstalt, 1975), pp. 18–19; Arthur MacGregor, "Two Antler Crossbow Nuts and Some Notes on the Early Development of the Crossbow," *Proceedings of the Society of Antiquaries of Scotland* 107 (1975–76), 319; T. G. Kolias, *Byzantinische Waffen: Ein Beitrag zur Byzantinischen Waffenkunde von den Anfängen bis zur Lateinischen Eroberung*, Byzantina Vindobonensia, Vol. 17 (Vienna: Verlag der Osterreichischer Akademie der Wissenschaften, 1988), pp. 240–41. Eric McGeer kindly alerted me to this last publication.

[55] Arrian, *Tactica*, in *Flavii Arriani quae exstant omnia*, Vol. 2 of *Scripta minora et fragmenta*, ed. A. G. Roos, re-ed. G. Wirth (Leipzig: B. G. Teubner, 1968), p. 175 (43.1). I have used Blackmore's translation of this passage (p. 174).

[56] Blackmore, p. 174.

all types, cranes, scaling ladders, battering rams, mobile siege towers, flame-throwers, and mantlets – but he is reluctant to conclude that Arrian's "machine" is a crossbow, although he suggests that it may have been.[57] While it is possible that Arrian's "machine" may be a bow equipped with an arrow-guide, the evidence for the existence of the crossbow in Roman times suggests that this "machine" was, in fact, a crossbow.[58] Campbell has suggested that the "*ballista-men*" (*ballistarii*) which formed part of a mounted rapid deployment force organized by Julian to conduct a quick strike against the Alemanni in A.D. 356 were armed not with conventional torsion *ballistae*, which would have been impossible to transport on horseback, but with hand-held weapons. He con-cludes that these weapons were "related to those shown on the Gallo-Roman reliefs."[59] It is most likely, therefore, that Julian's *ballistarii* were armed with

---

[57] Campbell's study is not focused on the crossbow but on the use of artillery by auxiliary troops in the Roman army, for which he does not find evidence, except in some extraordinary cases. His interest in Arrian's "machine" is not to prove that it was a crossbow but to disprove that it was a piece of artillery. Hence, he goes no further than to indicate that his "machine" was some kind of hand-held mechanical weapon, which he states was obviously some form of *ballista*, perhaps even an *arcuballista*. Unfortunately, he does not define what an *arcuballista* was, but merely suggests that it may be identical with the crossbows depicted in the Gallo-Roman reliefs from Polignac and Saint-Marcel (Campbell, pp. 126–32).

[58] The arrow-guide is a tubular piece of wood used with a hand-bow to shoot small bolts. It has no mechanical pull-back system or locking mechanism. For Islamic arrow-guides, see Nabih A. Faris and Robert P. Elmer, *Arab Archery: An Arabic Manuscript of about 1500 "A Book on the Excellence of the Bow and Arrow" and the Description thereof* (Princeton: Princeton University Press, 1945), pp. 126–27, 130, 175–76; Cahen, pp. 110–11, 132–33, 153–54; J. D. Latham and W. F. Paterson, *Saracen Archery: An English Version and Exposition of a Mameluke Work on Archery (ca. A.D. 1368)* (London: Holland Press, 1970), pp. 106–07, 145–51; E. McEwen, "Persian Archery Texts: Chapter Eleven of Fakhr-i Mudabbir's *Adāb al-Harb* (Early Thirteenth Century)," *Islamic Quarterly* 18 (1974), 91; Ahmad b. Yahyá al-Balādhurī, *Futūh al-buldān*, ed. Michael Jan De Goeje (Leiden: E. J. Brill, 1866), p. 260; Muhammad b. Jarīr al-Tabarī, *Ta'rīkh al-rusūl wa-al-mulūk (Annales)*, ed. M. J. de Goeje et al., Series 3, Vols. 12–13 (1879–1901; Leiden: E. J. Brill, 1964), pp. 1579, 1626, 1982, 2003, 2004, 2054. For Byzantine arrow-guides, see David Nishimura, "Crossbows, Arrow-Guides, and the *Solenarion*," *Byzantion* 58 (1988), 422–35. For the arrow-guides of India, see G. N. Pant, *Studies in Indian Weapons and Warfare* (New Delhi: Army Educational Stores, 1970), p. 48, *Indian Arms and Armour*, Vol. 1 (New Delhi: Army Educational Stores, 1978), p. 107, pls. 74, 77, 78, and *Indian Archery* (New Delhi: Agam Kala Prakashan, 1978), pp. 197–98. For Korean arrow-guides, see Walter Hough, "Korean Crossbow and Arrow-tube," *American Anthropologist*, n.s. 1 (January 1899), 200; D. Elmy, "Korean Archery Accessories," *Journal of the Society of Archer-Antiquaries* 22 (1979), 9–10, and "Korean Mounted Archery," *Journal of the Society of Archer-Antiquaries* 27 (1984), 48.

[59] Campbell, pp. 131–32; Ammianus Marcellinus, 16.2.5. P. de Jonge also concludes that the *ballistarii* were mounted, like the armored horsemen (*catafractatii*) on the expedition, and were armed with *manuballistae* or *arcuballistae* (P. de Jonge, *Philological and Historical Commen-tary on Ammianus Marcellinus XVI* [Groningen: Bouma's Boekhuis n. v. Publishers, 1972], pp. 15–16). The *ballistarii* probably served as crossbow-armed mounted infantry, rather than mounted crossbowmen, since Roman troops would not have been able to reload a crossbow while mounted without the support provided by stirrups, which were unknown to the Romans. While it might be argued that both the *manuballista* and the *arcuballista* could have been carried by mounted infantry, the *ballistarii* were probably armed with the *arcuballista* or crossbow, since it was by far the less cumbersome of the two (see below) and the easiest to carry on

crossbows. Since the term *ballistarii* is used here to refer to crossbowmen, not artillerymen, the sense of the term has clearly changed from its earlier classical meaning.[60] The new meaning which it has taken on here is the meaning that it will have throughout the Middle Ages in many of the vernacular languages of Europe.

The crossbow was invented by the Chinese sometime during the fifth century B.C. Unlike the *gastraphetes*, the Chinese crossbow employed a trigger mechanism which operated from the underside of the stock. By the time of the Han dynasty (206 B.C.–A.D. 220), it had become a standard military weapon in the Chinese army and featured an intricate trigger-mechanism made of cast bronze. This device, consisting of a triple compound lever, was inserted in the body of the stock and was operated from below.[61] The crossbow was probably introduced into the Roman Empire during the first century of our era. This would put it in the Mediterranean region just prior to Arrian's account of it and before the two stone reliefs which depict it were erected. Archeological finds in Western Europe of crossbow components and surviving depictions of crossbows dating from late antiquity and the early Middle Ages suggest that the crossbow enjoyed continuous use in the Latin West from Roman times.[62] In the realms of Islam the crossbow is first mentioned as being used in 881 during the course of the Zanj revolt in southern Mesopotamia. It is identified as a *qaws al-rijl* (foot-bow), indicating that it was spanned by the archer placing his feet on either side of the stock while pulling the bowstring back by hand or by using a belt and claw

---

horseback. J. C. Coulston also concludes that the *ballistarii* were armed with crossbows ("Roman Archery Equipment," in *The Production and Distribution of Roman Military Equipment*, Proceedings of the Second Roman Military Equipment Research Seminar, ed. M. C. Bishop [Oxford: B. A. R., 1985], p. 261).

[60] For other examples of terminology not keeping pace with technological changes, see H. W. L. Hime, *Gunpowder and Ammunition: Their Origin and Progress* (London: Longmans, Green, & Co., 1904), pp. 8–9; David Ayalon, *Gunpowder and Firearms in the Mamluk Kingdom: A Challenge to a Medieval Society* (London: Frank Cass, 1956), pp. 9–44; G. Hollister-Short, "The Vocabulary of Technology," *History of Technology* 2 (1977), 125–55; Joseph Needham, *Science and Civilisation in China*, Vol. 5, Part 7: *Military Technology: The Gunpowder Epic* (Cambridge: Cambridge University Press, 1989), pp. 11–12, 21–22, 131, 276–84.

[61] On the Chinese crossbow, see Blackmore, pp. 172–73; Needham, p. 465; Robin D. S. Yates, "Siege Engines and Late Zhou Military Technology," in *Explorations in the History of Science and Technology in China*, ed. Li Guohao, Zhang Mehgwen, and Cao Tianqin (Shanghai: Shanghai Chinese Classics Publishing House, 1982), pp. 432–43; Robert Roth, *Histoire de l'archerie: Arc et arbalète* (Montpellier: Max Chaleil, 1992), pp. 181–83; Sun Tzu, *The Art of War*, trans. Samuel B. Griffith (Oxford: Clarendon Press, 1963), pp. 9, 36–38, 74, 92.

[62] Blackmore, p. 178; A. G. Credland, "Crossbow Remains," *Journal of the Society of Archer-Antiquaries* 23 (1980), 12–19, pl. I, and "The Crossbow in Europe: An Historical Introduction," in W. F. Paterson, *A Guide to the Crossbow* (N.p: n.p., 1990; distributed by the Society of Archer-Antiquaries, Bridlington, England), pp. 13–18; John M. Gilbert, "Crossbows on Pictish Stones," *Proceedings of the Society of Antiquaries of Scotland* 107 (1975–76), 316–17; MacGregor, pp. 317–20. Campbell concludes that, "it seems probable that hand-held mechanical arms were used continuously from the third century B.C. through to the Byzantine period" (p. 132). Needham has suggested that the crossbow was probably introduced twice to Western Europe, before the fifth century and again during the tenth century (Needham, p. 465).

spanning device.[63] Although Arabic sources do not refer to the crossbow as being employed earlier than the ninth century, this does not preclude it being used prior to this date or indicate the discontinuance of the crossbow in the early Islamic period. Because of its relatively long reloading time, the crossbow was best suited for the attack and defense of strongpoints or aboard ships in battles at sea. Chroniclers of the early Islamic period rarely provide information on the small arms used in such encounters, so it is entirely possible that the crossbow continued in use in the Islamic world and that the *qaws al-rijl* became the prototype of more powerful crossbows developed later in the Middle East (e.g., the *zanbūrak* and *ziyār*). Historical references to the use of the crossbow in the Latin West are not found again until the tenth century when it is recorded being used at the siege of Senlis in 949 and at the siege of Verdun in 984.[64] More references to the crossbow are found in the eleventh century, and during the twelfth century, the crossbow appears to have developed into a truly formidable weapon, receiving both a papal condemnation and a famous description by Anna Comnena.[65] The notoriety that the crossbow attained at this time does not indicate, according to Blackmore, the appearance of a new weapon, but rather the improved performance of an old one, which he believes to be related to an advance in the construction of the composite bow or the development of an easier release mechanism.[66] According to Lynn White, Jr., the essential improvement which propelled the crossbow into widespread use was most probably a firmer locking and trigger system.[67] The cylindrical bone nut was almost universally used after the eleventh century for the catch of the crossbow. This development was tied, according to A. G. Credland, to the spread of the pole lathe at this time, which made it possible to produce precision crossbow nuts from bone.[68] This new manufacturing technique may have been the key technological breakthrough which led to the production of a more effective crossbow, but the increased use of this weapon, particularly in field warfare, is linked to tactical developments in the Latin West related to the use of the heavily-armored knight in mounted shock combat.

Until recently the crossbow was thought to have survived in the realms of

---

[63] Tabarī, p. 204; Cahen, pp. 110, 132, 152, n. 12; Latham and Paterson, pp. 18–19; Paterson, pp. 35, 39.

[64] Richer, *Historia Francorum*, ed. and trans. Robert Latouche, in *Histoire de France 888–995*, 2 vols. (Paris: H. Champion, 1930–37), Vol. 1, p. 282 (*arcobalistis*), Vol. 2, p. 134 (*arcoballistae*).

[65] Blackmore, pp. 175–77; Harmuth, pp. 19–25; Anna Comnena, *Alexade: Règne de l'empereur Alexis I Comnène (1081–1118)*, ed. and trans. Bernard Leib, Collection byzantine publiée sous le patronage de l'Association Guillaume Budé, Vol. 2 (Paris: Société d'Édition "Les Belles Lettres," 1943), pp. 217–18 (10.8).

[66] Blackmore, p. 177.

[67] Lynn White, Jr., *Medieval Religion and Technology: Collected Essays* (Berkeley: University of California Press, 1978), pp. 266, 282. For a discussion and bibliography of the crossbow, see his *Medieval Technology and Social Change* (Oxford: Oxford University Press, 1962), pp. 35, 111, 128, 151, 152, 164, 166, 167.

[68] Credland, "The Crossbow in Europe," p. 18.

Byzantium, referred to during the early and middle Byzantine periods as the σωληνάριον (sōlēnarion).[69] Nishimura has reinterpreted the term sōlēnarion as an arrow-guide but, in doing so, has rejected the possibility that another Greek term may have referred to a crossbow or to a similar type of hand-held bolt-projector.[70] He rejects the notion that the Greek prefix cheiro- (hand), when applied to bolt-projectors, indicates a hand-held weapon. He further contends that the Greek suffix -bolístra "was consistently and exclusively reserved for artillery." The studies which he cites to support this interpretation, rather than advocating his view, are clearly opposed to it.[71] The Greek term χειροβαλλισ-τρα (cheiroballistra), or "bow-ballista," refers to a hand-held bolt-projector (see below), but the only text of the middle Byzantine period to employ this word is the treatise De administrando imperio, written and compiled by the Emperor Constantine VII Porphyrogenitos between the years 948 and 952. Constantine VII uses the term in his account of Byzantine relations with the Chersonites during the reigns of Diocletian (284–305) and Constantine (307–37) and mentions that these machines were placed in and used from military wagons.[72] Because these machines were operated from wagons, Huuri has suggested that cheiroballistra is an incorrect transcription of the Latin term carroballista.[73] This appears to be the case and rules out the possibility that the term cheiroballistra was used during the middle Byzantine period to refer to a crossbow. The term τοξοβολιστρα or τοξοβαλιστρα (toxobolistra or toxobalistra), meaning "bow-ballista," may also be dismissed as being equated with the crossbow, because it is mentioned exclusively as being used on fixed defenses or on

---

[69] J. F. Haldon, "ΣΩΛΗΝΑΡΙΟΝ: The Byzantine Crossbow?" University of Birmingham Historical Journal 12 (1970), 155–57; G. T. Dennis, "Flies, Mice, and the Byzantine Crossbow," Byzantine and Modern Greek Studies 7 (1981), 1–5; Kolias, pp. 239–53.

[70] Nishimura.

[71] Nishimura states that, "the prefix cheiro- (hand) denoted a weapon operable by one man but heavy enough to require two men to carry and a rigid support to shoot, "and that the cheiroballistra (bow-ballista) "was still too large to be truly portable" (Nishimura, pp. 431–32). Both Baatz and Drachmann, who are cited by Nishimura with approval, consider the cheiroballistra to have been a portable weapon, requiring no rigid support or stand, and which was operated by a single man who both spanned and discharged the weapon in a way similar to Heron's gastraphetes (A. G. Drachmann, rev. of Greek and Roman Artillery: Technical Treatises by E. W. Marsden in Technology and Culture 13 [July 1972], 493; Baatz, "Recent Finds," p. 14). Landels also identifies the cheiroballistra as a "hand-catapult" and "a compact, portable arrow-shooter" (Landels, p. 130). The suffix -bolístra was not consistently and exclusively reserved for artillery. When it was used in conjunction with cheiro- (hand), it referred to a hand-held bolt-projector. The Greek term cheiroballistra, as Baatz has pointed out, is a translation of the Latin term manuballista (Baatz, "Recent Finds," p. 14). If the Latin West was influencing Greek terminology for weaponry, there can be no truth to Nishimura's assertion that Byzantium saw the crossbow as a type of bow, whereas the Latin West saw it as a portable ballista (Nishimura, p. 432, n. 31).

[72] Constantine VII Porphyrogenitos, Constantine Porphyrogenitus, De administrando imperio, ed. Gy. Moravcsik, Engl. trans. R. J. H. Jenkins, rev. ed. (Washington DC: Dumbarton Oaks Center for Byzantine Studies, 1967), pp. 258 (53.30), 260 (53.34, 53.37), 264 (53.133).

[73] Huuri, p. 75, n. 3.

warships, indicating that it was most probably mounted on a stand.[74] The military equipment amassed for the unsuccessful expedition against Crete in 949 included both large and small *toxobolistrae*. These small machines may not have been crossbows, however, but rather small tension catapults mounted on stands.[75] Other weapons listed as being collected for this expedition include χειϱοτοξοβολιστϱων (*cheirotoxobolistrōn*) or "hand bow-*ballistae*."[76] These weapons are most likely crossbows. The prefix *cheiro-* indicates that they are hand-held, while *-toxobolistrōn* suggests that they are similar to tension catapults.

Anna Comnena's famous description of the crossbow as "a barbarian bow absolutely unknown to the Greeks" has led scholars to believe that the crossbow was introduced to Byzantium from the Latin West. The most plausible derivations of the two Byzantine terms for crossbow, τζάγγϱα (tzangra) and τζάϱχ (tzarch), which appear for the first time in the eleventh century, are from two Persian terms for crossbow, *zanbūrak* (little wasp) and *charkh* (pulley wheel), respectively. The former was a heavy military crossbow used in the defense and attack of strongpoints or employed aboard ships in naval warfare, which shot large bolts; while the latter was a light military crossbow, identical to the *qaws al-rijl* (foot-bow) and spanned by a cord and pulley spanning device attached to the archer's belt, from which it derived its name. If the Byzantine terms for crossbow come from Persian, there can be no question that the prototypes of medieval Byzantine crossbows are Islamic, rather than European, in origin. Although the Latin West did not introduce the crossbow to the East, it did make greater uses of it in battle, specifically in field warfare. Neither Byzantium nor the Islamic East emulated Europe in its extensive use of the crossbow, but in the Islamic West the crossbow was widely employed, imitating European military traditions.[77]

---

[74] In his account of the measures taken by Anastasius II in preparation for the Arab siege of Constantinople in 717–18, Theophanes states that the Emperor restored the land and sea walls, and installed bolt-projecting tension catapults (τοξοβολιστϱας), trestle-frame traction trebuchets (τετϱαϱεας), and pole-frame traction trebuchets (μαγγανικα) on the gates (Theophanes, *Theophanis Chronographia*, ed. C. de Boor, Vol. 1 [Leipzig: B. G. Teubner, 1883], p. 384 [A.D. 706]). Harry Turtledove has translated the terms used for the three machines cited by Theophanes above as "arrow-shooting engines, stone-throwing engines, and catapults" (Harry Turtledove, trans., *The Chronicle of Theophanes* [Philadelphia: University of Pennsylvania Press, 1982], p. 80). For other references to the use of the *toxobalistra* in the middle Byzantine period, see Theophanes continuatus, *De Basilio Macedone*, ed. Immanuel Bekker, Corpus Scriptorvm Historiae Byzantinae (Bonn: Weber, 1838), p. 298 (5.59); Leo VI, *Leonis imperatoris tactica*, in *Patrologiae cursus completus, series graeca*, ed. J.-P. Migne, Vol. 107 (Paris, 1863), col. 1008 (19.52); Constantine VII, *De ceremoniis*, ed. J. J. Reiske, Corpus Scriptorum Historiae Byzantinae (Bonn: Weber, 1829), pp. 670–71, 673, 676 (2.45); Polyaenus, *Parecbolae*, in *Strategemata*, ed. J.-A. de Foucault (Paris: Société d'Édition "Les Belles Lettres," 1949), p. 112 (44.16); Huuri, pp. 72–75; 77, n. 4; 78, n. 3; 80, n. 2; 85–86; 88, n. 1.

[75] Constantine VII, pp. 670–71, 673. Dennis, p. 3.

[76] Constantine VII, pp. 669–70.

[77] Anna Comnena's identification of the crossbow as "a barbarian bow" (p. 217 [10.8.6]) has recently been reinterpreted by Nishimura as indicating an Islamic, rather than a western, origin for the weapon. He discredits the commonly accepted etymology of τζάγγϱα (*tzangra*) as being

The military technology and weaponry of other peoples greatly influenced Byzantine arms, and this fact makes it likely that the crossbow was used during the early and middle Byzantine periods by forces of the Byzantine Empire. Haldon has stressed that, "Byzantine arms and armour did not exist in a vacuum, but were related in every way to types prevalent outside the empire."[78] If the crossbow was used continuously in the Latin West from Roman times, as well as in the realms of Islam, it seems likely that the same was the case in the Byzantine Empire, even though its use may not have been widespread.

The *manuballista*, or "hand-bow," was considered by Marsden to be very similar to the machine having the equivalent title in Greek – the χειροβαλλισ-τρα (*cheiroballistra*) or "hand-bow" – described by Heron.[79] Baatz has pointed out that the term *cheiroballistra* is clearly a translation of *manuballista*, which indicates that the two terms refer to the same machine.[80] Marsden reconstructed

derived from the medieval French term *cancre* or *chancre* (crab), since there is no evidence that crossbows were ever referred to by this word. In support of his argument, Nishimura cites Cahen's proposed derivation of *tzangra* and *tzarch* from the Persian term *charkh* (Arabic: *jarkh*). While there can be little doubt that *tzarch* was derived from *charkh*, the difference between *tzangra* and *charkh* is too great to suggest that they are related. It appears more likely that *tzangra* is a corruption of the Persian term *zanbūrak*. Joseph T. Reinaud, "De l'art militaire chez les Arabes au Moyen Âge," *Journal Asiatique*, 6th ser. 12 (September 1948), 211–13, was the first scholar to propose a correlation between *zanbūrak* and *tzangra*. For a discussion of the etymology of *tzangra* and *tzarch*, see Claude Cahen, "Les changements techniques militaires dans le Proche Orient médiéval et leur importance historique," in *War, Technology and Society in the Middle East*, ed. V. J. Parry and M. E. Yapp (London: Oxford University Press, 1975), pp. 118, 123, 124; Huuri, pp. 71–79; Nishimura, pp. 433–34; Kolias, pp. 245–53. The *zanbūrak* was used by the crusaders in Saladin's siege of Tyre in 583/1187 ('Abd al-Rahmān b. Ismā'īl Abū Shāmah, *Kitāb al rawdatayn fī akhbār al-dawlatayn*, Vol. 2 [Cairo: Matba'at Wādī al-Nīl, 1287–88/1871–72], p. 119; Jamāl al-Dīn Muhammad ibn Wāsil, *Mufarrij al-kurūb fī akhbār Banī Ayyūb*, ed. Jamāl al-Dīn al-Shayyāl, Vol. 2 [Cairo: Wizārat al-Thaqāfah wa-al-Irshād al-Qawmī, 1957], p. 244). A detailed description of the *zanbūrak* is found in the *History of the Patriarchs of the Egyptian Church* in its account of Saladin's siege of Acre in 585/1189 (Sawīrus b. al-Muqaffa', *History of the Patriarchs of the Egyptian Church*, ed. and trans. Antoine Khater and O. H. E. Khs-Burmester, Vol. 3, part 2 [Cairo: Publications de la Société de'archéologie Copte, 1970], pp. 85–86 [Arabic text], 145). Reinaud's view that Muslim armies did not employ the *zanbūrak* until the middle of the thirteenth century is unsupported; Arabic sources indicate that crusader and Muslim armies both utilized this weapon during the late twelfth century. On this question, see especially Ibn al-Athīr's account of Saladin's siege of Sahyūn (584/1188) in which he mentions the full array of Muslim bow weapons used in siege operations of this time: the hand-bow, the *jarkh*, the *zanbūrak*, and the *ziyār*, a base-mounted tension catapult ('Izz al-Din 'Alī ibn al-Athīr, *al-Kāmil fī al-ta'rīkh*, ed. C. J. Tornberg, Vol. 12 [Beirut: Dār Sādir and Dār Bayrūt, 1966], p. 11). Regarding the *qaws al-rijl* and the *charkh/jarkh*, these crossbows are essentially the same, but differ in the way that they are spanned. Al-Rammāh states that the *qaws al-rijl* corresponds to the *jarkh* (Najm al-Dīn Ayyūb al-Ahdab al-Rammāh, *Kitāb al-furūsīyah bi-rasm al-jihād*, MS 2825, fonds arabe, Bibliothèque Nationale, Paris, fol. 84v), and al-Tarsūsī notes that the *jarkh* is spanned by a pulley device (*lawlab latīf*), while the *qaws al-rijl* is spanned by a belt and claw spanning device (Cahen, pp. 110, 132). On these spanning systems, see Paterson, pp. 40–44.

[78] J. F. Haldon, "Some Aspects of Byzantine Military Technology from the Sixth to the Tenth Centuries," *Byzantine and Modern Greek Studies* 1 (1975), 45.

[79] Marsden, *Historical Development*, p. 197. For Heron's description of the *cheiroballistra*, see Wescher, pp. 123–34; Marsden, *Technical Treatises*, pp. 212–17.

[80] Baatz, "Recent Finds," p. 14.

it as a two-armed, metal-framed torsion catapult having a winch mechanism and a stand.[81] A. G. Drachmann and Dietwulf Baatz have challenged Marsden's interpretation of Heron's *Cheiroballistra* on a number of grounds. First, Marsden's dating and attribution of Heron's *Cheiroballistra* have been called into question. Marsden attributed this work to Heron of Alexandria who wrote the *Belopoeica* probably during the second half of the first century A.D. On the basis of Schneider's research on the text, which demonstrated that different technical terms were used in the *Cheiroballistra* to refer to the same components mentioned in the *Belopoeica*, Drachmann has concluded that the text was not written by Heron, and Baatz has supported Schneider's earlier finding that the work is of late Roman or Byzantine date.[82] Second, Drachmann and Baatz have questioned some of the measurements Marsden has given for components of the machine and have reconstructed the *cheiroballistra* as a smaller and less power-ful weapon than Marsden had made it, one capable of being hand-held, as its name indicates, and drawn without a windlass. Marsden rejected the measure-ment of 1⅓ dactyls (2.46 cm.) given in the text for the diameter of the hole for the sinew bundle and increased the diameter to 2⅓ dactyls (4.31 cm.). Drachmann has accepted the original measurement. Marsden rejected the meas-urement of 10½ dactyls (19.4 cm.) given in the earliest manuscript of *Cheiro-ballistra* for the tension-frames of the machine, considering this dimension to be a corruption of 20 dactyls (37 cm.). Earlier studies of this treatise by C. Wescher and Rudolf Schneider have accepted the reading of 10½ dactyls. Baatz agrees with this reading and offers archeological evidence indicating that low but wide tension-frames were used on Roman bolt-projecting catapults produced during the Imperial period. One tension-frame excavated in a late Roman fort at Gornea in Romania measures 14.4 cm. in height.[83] Lastly, Drachmann and Baatz have pointed out that the *Cheiroballistra* describes a "crescent-shaped piece" fitted to the butt of the stock where the winch mechanism or windlass is mounted on larger catapults. The presence of this device indicates that the machine had no mechanical device at the end of the stock for pulling the bowstring back. Both Drachmann and Baatz have identified the "crescent-shaped piece" with the καταγωγις (*katagōgis*) of Heron's *gastraphetes*, utilized for the manual span-ning of the weapon.

The *cheiroballistra* or *manuballista* was a sort of "torsion-crossbow," accord-ing to Drachmann and Baatz, operated as its name indicates, by only one man.[84] It was a hand-held weapon, as its name suggests, but unlike the medieval crossbow, it could not be reloaded on horseback due to its spanning system. Its manual pull-back system required the archer to fit the crescent-shaped rest at the

[81] Marsden, *Historical Development*, pp. 191, 197, and *Technical Treatises*, pp. 206–33. Hall, like Marsden, rejects the notion that the *manuballista* was a hand-held weapon (Hall, p. 531).

[82] Drachmann, pp. 492–93; Baatz, "Recent Finds," p. 14; Rudolf Schneider, "Heron's *Cheiroballistra*," *Römische Mitteilungen* 21(1906), 167–68.

[83] Drachmann, p. 493; Baatz, "Recent Finds," p. 15; Schneider, "Heron's *Cheiroballistra*" p. 154, n. 2; Wescher, p. 128.

[84] Drachmann, p. 493; Baatz, "Recent Finds," pp. 14–16.

rear of the stock to his stomach, and, by pushing against a stationary object, the slider, holding the bowstring in its claw-and-trigger device, was driven back to the rear of the stock and held in place by a linear ratchet. The *manuballista* shares many features with the *gastraphetes* (belly-bow), the earliest Greek catapult, but it could not have been introduced before the second half of the first century when the Romans first developed wide and low-set metal tension-frames for catapults. Vegetius and Anonymus are the only Roman authors to mention the *manuballista*.[85] Campbell has concluded that, "it seems probable that hand-held mechanical arms were used continuously from the third century B.C. through to the Byzantine period."[86] This is a reasonable deduction, but it is impossible to determine with certainty exactly what form these hand-held mechanical arms took. Since terminology can be quite fluid, a term which at one time referred to a hand-held, two-armed torsion bolt-projector may at a later period refer to a hand-held, tension-powered bolt- projector. With this in mind, it is not unreasonable to suggest that the *manuballista* mentioned by Anonymus may have been a tension-powered, rather than a torsion-powered, weapon. The two catapults described by Anonymus are tension-powered (see below), and so his *manuballista* may have been as well.

Vegetius is a difficult source to interpret. While most probably writing in the late fourth century, he utilized earlier sources, reflecting realities of the middle Republican or early imperial period, but he added information to suit the circumstances of his own day. Hence, his statements may contain information pertaining to any time period from the era of the middle Republic to the late Empire. Vegetius, for instance, mentions the *onager* – a piece of artillery which was not widely employed until the fourth century – as being used by the *antiqua legio* in defense of a camp. Baatz and Campbell contend that Vegetius, in this instance, has simply substituted "onager" – the only stone-projecting artillery piece of his day – for "ballista," utilized by his third-century source to refer to a two-armed, stone-projecting catapult.[87] Campbell is suspicious of artillery being used in Vegetius' day to defend a camp and concludes that "he is probably referring to the situation in the third (or even fourth) century."[88] Marsden noted that the ordinary legions in the fourth century possessed no artillery whatsoever.[89] If such conflation of the text occurs, it becomes very difficult to interpret Vegetius' description of artillery. Is his account of torsion artillery reflective of the middle Republican, Imperial, or late-Roman periods? Can his account of artillery be used as evidence to indicate the continued use of torsion artillery during the last century of the western empire? Given the conflated nature of the text and the existence of anachronistic information, Vegetius

[85] Vegetius, 2.15, 3.14, 4.21, 4.22. Thompson, pp. 102, 119 (16.5); *De rebus bellicis*, Part 2, pp. 15, 33 (16.5).

[86] Campbell, p. 132.

[87] Baatz, "Geschützbewaffnung," p. 195; D. B. Campbell, "*Ballistaria* in the First to Mid-Third Century Britain: A Reappraisal," *Britannia* 15 (1984), 83.

[88] Campbell, "*Ballistaria*," p. 81.

[89] Marsden, *Historical Development*, p. 195.

cannot be used exclusively as conclusive proof for the continued use of torsion artillery in late antiquity. What can be clarified is the terminology Vegetius uses to refer to artillery. The *onager* is his sole stone-projector, a one-armed sling machine with a massive torsion-spring mounted horizontally on a heavy base. Of the four bolt-projectors, the *ballista* is a large base-mounted, two-armed, metal-framed torsion catapult. The *carroballista* is a catapult mounted on a specially designed cart pulled by a team of horses or mules; it was clearly a two-armed, metal-framed torsion machine when it first appeared. The *manuballista* or "scorpion" is a hand-held bolt-projector used only by infantry; it was clearly a two-armed, metal-framed torsion machine when it was introduced. The *arcuballista* is a hand-held crossbow which could be utilized by mounted infantry and foot soldiers alike.

B.   The *Ballista* of Ammianus Marcellinus
Res gestae, 23.4.1–3

(1) . . . et ballistae figura docebitur prima. (2) ferrum inter axiculos duo firmum compaginatur et uastum, in modum regulae maioris extentum, cuius ex uolumine tereti, quod in medio pars polita componit, quadratus eminet stilus extentius, recto canalis angusti meatu cauatus, et hac multiplici chorda neruorum tortilium illigatus. eique cochleae duo ligneae coniunguntur aptissime, quarum prope unam assistit artifex contemplabilis, et subtiliter apponit in temonis cauamine, sagittam ligneam spiculo maiore conglutinatam, hocque facto, hinc inde ualidi iuuenes uersant agiliter rotabilem flexum. (3) cum ad extremitatem neruorum acumen uenerit summum, percita interno pulsu a ballista ex oculis auolat, interdum nimio ardore scintillans, et euenit saepius, ut, antequam telum cernatur, dolor letale uulnus agnoscat.

(1) . . . the design of the *ballista* will be explained first. (2) The iron strut is fastened firmly between two cases [enclosing the sinew-bundles].[90] It is long and extends like a large ruler.[91] From the cylindrical case, which is polished in the middle,[92] a squared arm [*stilus*] projects outward, notched vertically with a

---

[90] The "iron strut" (*ferrum*), as Marsden has correctly noted, is the bottom member of two parallel struts which hold the sinew-bundles of the two torsion-springs in place. The *axiculi* (literally, "two small axles") most probably refer to the cylindrical metal cases which enclose the tension-frames of the machine, as Marsden has suggested (*Technical Treatises*, p. 238). Brok has identified *ferrum* as the case of the stock of the machine (M. F. A. Brok, "Bombast oder Kunstfertigkeit," *Rheinisches Museum für Philologie* 120 [1977], 340). The basic component of the catapult was the stock made up of a compound plank, consisting of a case which had a dovetail groove along its top which held a slider. This slider could move freely back and forth in the case, and, along the length of its upper surface, was a semi-circular groove in which the bolt was placed prior to being discharged.

[91] Marsden observed that the length of the bottom strut of this machine indicated that the tension-frames were set much further apart than they were in earlier catapults (*Technical Treatises*, p. 238).

[92] The phrase, *cuius ex uolumine tereti*, must refer to the metal cases which enclosed the tension-frames of the machine. These cylindrical metal cases protected the sinew-bundles from the weather, as well as from enemy counter-battery. Marsden has translated this phrase as, "from a well-finished joint in this, which a smoothed portion in the middle forms." He believed that this phrase referred to the four clamps which secured the stock to the bottom strut of the

narrow groove,[93] and here [at the nock of the arm] is tied a [bow]string of plaited sinews under tension.[94] To this two wooden pulley wheels are very tightly joined, and near one of them stands an artilleryman who aims the shot.[95] He carefully places on the groove of the slider a wooden bolt with a larger head firmly joined to it.[96] When this is done, strong young men on either side

machine (*Technical Treatises*, pp. 238–39). Brok believes that this phrase refers to the dovetail groove of the case in which the slider is placed (p. 341).

[93] The "squared arm" (*quadratus stilus*) is the arm inserted in each sinew-bundle of the machine. This arm projects outward from the cylindrical metal cases enclosing the tension-springs. In his description of the *onager*, Ammianus also uses the term *stilus* to refer to the arm thrust into the middle of the sinew-bundle of the machine (23.4.5–6). The end of the arm is "notched vertically with a narrow groove" so that the loop of the bowstring will fit onto it. Marsden suggested that *quadratus stilus* referred to the case of the stock, and that the nock for the bowstring (*recto canalis angusti meatu cavatus*) indicated the female dovetail of the stock (*Technical Treatises*, p. 239). Brok identifies the *stilus* as the slider of the machine (pp. 339–40, 345).

[94] Marsden translated *hac multiplici chorda neruorum tortilium illigatus* as, "bound in the complex cordage of twisted sinews" and suggested that this passage erroneously indicated that the stock of the machine was in direct contact with the sinew-bundles. Marsden also suggested that at this point in his description of the *ballista*, Ammianus may have confused his account of the machine with that of the *onager* which follows it (23.4.4–6), or that Ammianus did not write the phrase, *et hac . . . illigatus*, which may have been added to the text "as a result of a marginal note by a copyist struggling to clarify a most unhelpful description" (*Technical Treatises*, p. 239). The *multiplici chorda neruorum* does not refer to the sinew-bundles of the machine but to the bowstring which is composed of plaited sinews. Heron describes the plaiting of sinew bowstrings in his *Belopoeica* (Wescher, p. 110; Marsden, *Technical Treatises*, pp. 38–39). The bowstring is directly affixed to the end of each of the machine's arms. Brok correctly equates *et hac . . . illigatus* with the machine's bowstring (pp. 340, 345).

[95] Marsden translated *cochleae duo ligneae* as "two wooden rollers" and believed that they referred to the "two bushes, one at each end of a single winch, in which the handspikes fit" (*Technical Treatises*, p. 239, n. 6). This interpretation, however, does not correspond to the text. Ammianus states that the "two wooden pulley wheels" are tightly joined to the bowstring and that an artilleryman is positioned near one of the pulley wheels to load the missile. Since the pull-back system of this catapult consists of "two wooden pulley wheels" which are tightly joined to the bowstring, this system must have been a windlass mechanism consisting of a winding drum and a pair of pulley wheels mounted on the rear of the stock which were connected by a system of cords to another pair of pulley wheels attached to a two-pronged claw-frame hooked over the bowstring. By turning the handspikes on the winding drum, the bowstring was pulled to the rear until it was gripped by the locking/trigger mechanism. A similar type of pulley system, using two opposing cranks with handles, was used on medieval crossbows (Payne-Gallwey, pp. 120–25; Harmuth, pp. 108–10). Vitruvius describes several mechanical means that were used to pull back the bowstring of a *ballista*, including a *polyspaston* or compound pulley (10.11.1), indicating that such devices were used. For another type of compound pulley pull-back system described in Heron's *Belopoeica*, see Wescher, pp. 84–85 and Marsden, *Technical Treatises*, pp. 25; 49, nn. 19 and 20; and 50, fig. 9.

[96] Ammianus does not intend to indicate that the artilleryman aims the catapult from the side of the machine, as one might possibly infer from the text. The operator of the machine, of course, must stand behind the catapult in order to aim it, as indicated in Heron's *Belopoeica* (Wescher, p. 86; Marsden, *Technical Treatises*, pp. 26–27). Ammianus simply locates the "artilleryman who aims the shot" at the time he is loading the missile. This operation is done from the side of the machine after the bowstring has been gripped by the locking/trigger mechanism. Once the bolt has been placed on the groove of the slider, the operator pulls the trigger and the missile is discharged. Marsden correctly pointed out that the procedure for shooting described by Ammianus contradicts what Heron says on this subject, but he gave the sequence of actions

energetically wind back the windlass [*rotabilem*]. (3) When its point [i.e., the head of the bolt] has reached the end [of the path] of the bowstring, the bolt flies away out of sight driven by internal thrust, sometimes emitting sparks because of the excessive heat. And it often happens that before the missile is seen, the pain of a lethal wound is felt.

The two-armed, metal-framed torsion catapult described by Ammianus can be identified with an improved catapult design developed by the Romans during the second half of the first century. Machines of this type had wide, low tension-frames enclosed in cylindrical metal cases which protected the sinew-bundles from moisture and counter-battery fire from the enemy. Ammianus' description of this type of machine indicates that this form of advanced artillery was still being produced and utilized by Rome during the second half of the fourth century. This is confirmed by archeological evidence consisting of components from bolt-projecting torsion catapults, attributed to this same period, which have been found at three late Roman forts.[97] Marsden has described such bolt-projectors as "the finest pieces of arrow-shooting artillery ever produced by ancient catapult designers."[98]

C. Artillery of Anonymus
De rebus bellicis, ch. 7

Espositio ballistae quadrirotis[99]

Exemplum ballistae cuius fabricam ante oculos positam subtilis pictura testatur. Subiecta namque rotarum quattuor facilitas, duobus subiunctis et armatis equis, ad usus hanc bellicos trahit, cuius tanta est utilitas pro artis industria ut omni latere in hostem sagittas impellat, sagittarii liberatem et manus imitata. Habet foramina per quattuor partes, quibus pro commoditate rerum circumducta et flexa, facillime ad omnes impetus parata consistat. Quae quidem a fronte cochleae machina et deponitur celerius et erigitur subleuata. Sed huius temo, in quamuis partem necessitas uocet, cita et facili conuersione deflexus erigitur. Sciendum est autem quod hoc ballistae genus duorum opera uirorum sagittas ex se, non ut aliae funibus, sed radiis intorta iaculatur.

specified by Heron in the wrong order. According to Marsden, Heron states that the procedure for shooting is as follows: "pulling back the slider (and, consequently, the bowstring and arms); loading the missile; aiming; pulling the trigger." Heron, however, adheres to the following order: pulling back the slider, aiming at the target, loading the missile, pulling the trigger (Wescher, pp. 89–90; Marsden, *Technical Treatises*, pp. 26–27, 239–340, n. 7).

   97 Gudea and Baatz, pp. 50–72; Baatz, "Recent Finds," pp. 2, 9–17, pls. 2, 5, and "Eine Katapult-Spannbuchse aus Pityus," pp. 59–64.

   98 Marsden, *Technical Treatises*, p. 231.

   99 See Thompson, pp. 61–65 (commentary), 97–98 (text), 114 (translation), and fig. III (manuscript illustration); *De rebus bellicis*. Part 1: *Aspects of the "De re bellicis"*; *De rebus bellicis*, Part 1, *Aspects of the "De rebus bellicis"*, p. 84 (analysis); *De rebus bellicis*, Part 2, pp. 8–9 (text), 29 (translation), 102–03 (textual criticism), pls. V–VI (Manuscript illustrations); and Marsden, *Technical Treatises*, pp. 240–43.

Description of the Four-Wheeled *Ballista*

An unadorned picture gives evidence of an example of a *ballista*, the construction of which is placed before your eyes. An easily moving four-wheeled
chassis, with two horses harnessed and armored, pulls it into battle. Its utility is
such, due to its skillful design, that it is able to discharge bolts against the
enemy on every side, imitating the free movement of an archer's hands. It has
sockets in its four sides, and, as it is turned round, it can be pivoted by means of
these as circumstances require, and so with great ease it is ready to meet all
attacks.[100] By a universal-joint at the front it is quickly lowered and raised.[101]
Thus, its stock can be turned round by a rapid and smooth revolution to face
whatever direction is required and can then be elevated. It must be understood
that this type of *ballista*, operated by two men, shoots bolts after [its bow] is
spanned, not by ropes, as others are, but by a [spanning] lever.[102]

[100] Neither Thompson nor Marsden understood the meaning or function of "sockets" (*foramina*). Thompson correctly referred to the *foramina* as "slots," but stated that their function and
placement were difficult to decide. Marsden, quick to interpret these as components of a torsion
machine, suggested that they referred to "the holes for the springs" of a torsion catapult, and
misrepresented the text to suit his opinion by stating that: "Anonymus specifically mentions four
foramina" (Thompson, pp. 63, 98, 114; Marsden, *Technical Treatises*, pp. 241–42). Anonymus
here refers to the pyramidal stand of the machine which has sockets on its four sides for the
placement of an elevation device. This device, attached to the underbelly of the case, acts as a
stabilizer for the stock when it is positioned at different angles. The reconstructions of the
ballista quadrirotis by both Oliver and Hassall assume that the manuscript illustrations of the
machine are to be interpreted literally (Revilo P. Oliver, "A Note on the *De rebus bellicis*,"
Classical Philology 50 [1955], 113–18; M. W. C. Hassall, "The Inventions," in *De rebus bellicis*,
Part 1: *Aspects of the "De re bellicis*," p. 84). Any reconstructions based on these Heath
Robinson-style illustrations are ludicrous and are not supported by any textual, pictorial, or
archeological evidence.
[101] Thompson translates "universal-joint" (*cochleae machina*) as "screw," and Ireland ren-
ders it as a "screw-thread device." Marsden, however, identified it as the universal-joint of the
machine, which allowed the catapult to be pointed in any direction (Thompson, pp. 62, 114; *De
rebus bellicis*, Part 2, p. 29; Marsden, *Technical Treatises*, pp. 241–42). An elevating screw
would not have allowed the turning of this machine to be achieved in both the horizontal and
vertical planes as the text clearly indicates was possible.
[102] Unlike most bolt-projecting catapults which use a winch mechanism to bend the bow in
order to bring it under sufficient tension for shooting, this *ballista* uses a spanning lever fixed to
the stock to achieve the same result. This device may have been similar to the lever used on the
Chinese repeating crossbow (Payne-Gallwey, pp. 237–42; Harmuth, pp. 149–52). A lever such as
this would not have been as powerful as a windlass for bending the bow, but it would still have
been quite strong and with two men operating it, by pulling on a transverse bar surmounting the
two lateral arms of the lever, it would have enabled the machine to achieve a very rapid sequence
of discharge. The plural of *radius* is used here to designate the spanning lever because this
device had two arms which were hinged to the sides of the stock by a cross-pin. Another
cross-pin intersected the two arms of the lever above its point of rotation and held a claw-frame.
This device swung loosely on the cross-pin and hooked the bowstring at its center-point with its
two lateral claws. As the two lever arms were rotated back, the bowstring was pulled to the rear
until it was gripped by the locking/trigger mechanism, where it was held until the bolt was
discharged. Vitruvius indicates in his account of artillery that several mechanical means were
used to pull back the bowstring of a *ballista*: a lever (*vectis*), a windlass (*sucula*), a compound
pulley (*polyspaston*), a capstan (*ergata*), and a system of drums (*tympani*) (Vitruvius, 10.11.1).
Thompson translated the last sentence of the description of this *ballista* as: "It must further be
recognized that this type of *ballista* is serviced by two men and fires arrows propelled, not by
torsion, as in the case of other *ballistae*, but by a windlass" (Thompson, pp. 62–63, 114). Hassall
has also suggested that *funes* refers to the torsion springs of the machine, while he identifies the

De rebus bellicis, ch. 18

Expositio ballistae fulminalis[103]

(1) Huiusmodi ballistae genus murali defensioni necessarium supra ceteras impetu et viribus praevalere usu compertum est; arcu etenim ferreo supra canalem, quo sagitta exprimitur, erecto, validus nervi funis ferreo unco tractus eandem sagittam magnis viribus in hostem dimissus impellit. (2) Hunc tamen funem non manibus necque viribus militum trahi fabricae ipsius magnitudo permittit, sed retro duabus rotis viri singuli radiorum nisibus adnitentes funem retrorsum tendunt, pro difficultate rei viribus machinis adquisitis. (3) Ballistam tamen ipsam ad dirigenda seu altius seu humilius tela cochleae machina, prout vocet utilitas, nunc erigit nunc deponit. (4) Hoc tamen mirae virtutis argumentum, tot rerum diversitate connexum, unius tantum otiosi, ut ita dicam, hominis ad offerendam tantummodo impulsioni sagittam opera gubernat; videlicet ne si hominum turba huius ministerio inserviret, minueretur artis inventio. (5) Ex hac igitur ballista, tot et tantis ingenii artibus communita, expressum telum in tantum longius vadit, ut etiam Danubii, famosi pro magnitudine fluminis, latitudinem valeat penetrare; fulminalis etiam nuncupata appellatione sua virium testatur effectum.

---

radii as "re-curve bow arms" (Hassall, p. 84). Oliver has pointed out that Thompson's translation of this passage is absurd, for no windlass or similar device can shoot a projectile (Oliver, pp. 113–14). Thompson's translation of *radii* as "windlass" and *funes* as "torsion" cannot be justified on lexicographical grounds. The word *radius* can refer to "a spoke" in a wheel, "a radial spike," "the radius of a circle," or "a rotating radial arm" (P. G. W. Glare, *Oxford Latin Dictionary* [Oxford: Clarendon Press, 1982], p. 1571). Ireland's translation of this passage modifies Thompson's interpretation somewhat: "It must also be pointed out that this type of *ballista* fires its arrows on being wound up not by ropes, as others are, but by a windlass, which is worked by two men" (*De rebus bellicis*, Part 2, p. 29). Oliver has concluded that the text of Anonymus suffers from numerous lacunae and inserts several words in the passage which he believes were omitted by error: *hoc ballistae genus duorum opera uirorum sagittas ex se, non ut aliae funibus [nervinis], sed [ferrei arcus] radiis intorta iaculatur* (Oliver, p. 117). In this text *radii* most likely refers to the two arms of a spanning lever, and *funes* to the ropes for pulling back the slider of catapults having a conventional winch pull-back system or a pull-back apparatus using a compound pulley (*polyspaston*). Always eager to find evidence for torsion machines, Marsden translated this passage as: "It must be realized that, by the efforts of two men, this kind of *ballista* hurls its bolts, after being wound up not by ropes as other machines are, but by rods" (*Technical Treatises*, p. 241). He noted that the proper interpretation of this sentence hinged on the word *intorta*, which is translated as "being wound up" by both he and Ireland, and by Thompson as "propelled." The verb *intorqueo* can convey several types of action: 1) to bend back or bend around in a circle; 2) to turn or spin round; 3) to twist in a spiral; to make ropes by twisting; to wind round; 4) to twist round; to wrench; or 5) to hurl or launch a missile (*Oxford Latin Dictionary*, pp. 952–53). Since its primary meaning is to bend something back, *intorta* is used in this case to refer to the spanning or bending of the tension-bow as the lever draws the bowstring back to the catch to ready the machine for discharge. Marsden suggested that "lever" (*radiis*) referred to toothed iron bars attached to the rear of the slider which pulled the slider back by means of a cog-wheel fitted on a winch (Marsden, *Technical Treatises*, p. 243). Marsden's ingenuity is admirable, but his interpretation exceeds the information provided in the text.

[103] See Thompson, pp. 61–65 (commentary), 102–03 (text), 120 (translation), and fig. XII (manuscript illustration); *De rebus bellicis*, Part 1: *Aspects of the "De rebus bellicis,"*, pp. 80–84 (analysis); *De rebus bellicis*, Part 2, pp. 17 (text), 34–35 (translation), pls. XII–XIII (manuscript illustrations); and Marsden, *Technical Treatises*, pp. 244–46.

Description of the "Thunderbolt" *Ballista*

(1) This type of *ballista*, essential for the defence of walls, has been found by experience to be superior to all others in range and power. When a steel bow has been placed in position above the groove from which the bolt is discharged,[104] a strong sinew-rope [i.e., the bowstring] is pulled back by an iron drawing-claw, and, when released, it shoots the bolt with great force at the enemy.[105] (2) The size of the machine does not allow this bowstring to be drawn back by the manual efforts of soldiers [alone]; instead, two men pull the bowstring back by pressing backwards on the handspikes of the two wheels [of the winch], mechanized force having been acquired by the machine commensurate with the difficulty of the operation. (3) A universal-joint alternately raises and lowers the *ballista* itself, so that it may discharge its missiles higher or lower, as needed.[106] (4) Proof of its amazing capability is evidenced by the fact that, although it is constructed of so many component parts, it is operated – so far as the shooting of the bolt is concerned – by one man, at his leisure, so to speak. For the ingenuity of the invention would be diminished if a throng of men were to operate it. A missile shot from this *ballista*, which has so many extraordinary features, can travel so much farther [than that shot from any other machine] that

[104] Marsden advanced the view that the "steel bow" (*arcus ferreus*) does not refer to a bow, but was equivalent to the *kamarion* (καμαριον) or "little arch" of Heron's *cheiroballistra*. To keep the cylindrical frames containing the cord-bundles of a two-armed torsion machine in place, two horizontal iron struts were required: a lower strut fixed to the stock of the machine and a upper strut (*kamarion*) which had a small arch in the middle to assist the operator in seeing his target and aiming the machine (Wescher, p. 130; Marsden, *Technical Treatises*, pp. 207, 214, 215, 223–26, 236, 245–47). This interpretation of "steel bow" is suspect. This non-technical description of a bolt-projector employs the term "bow" in the context of describing the drawing of the bowstring and the shooting of the bolt. Heron's "little arch" has nothing to do with these actions. Although the catapults on Trajan's Column prominently depict the *kamarion*, showing it larger than it actually is, this does not indicate that the *kamarion* is a preeminent component of the catapult, merely that it is an important feature of the iconography of the catapult. The *kamarion* is not one of the most conspicuous or important components of a catapult. The most significant parts of a torsion machine are its stock and sinew-bundles, while the stock and bow are the most important parts of a tension-powered machine. Hence, in descriptions of catapults, particularly non-technical descriptions which concentrate on major components of the machine, one would not expect the *kamarion* to receive much attention, and certainly not major attention, as it would if the *arcus ferreus* is interpreted here as the *kamarion*. Marsden suggested that "the groove" (*canalis*) is used here to refer to the whole stock. It seems more probable that it indicates the groove for the missile running the length of the upper surface of the slider (Marsden, *Technical Treatises*, p. 245). The reconstructions of the "Thunderbolt" *ballista* by Oliver and Hassall are not to be followed since they uncritically accept the manuscript illustrations of the machine which make no mechanical sense whatsoever (Oliver, pp. 113–18; Hassall, pp. 80–84). Ireland has the "steel bow" mounted "vertically above the channel along which the arrow is propelled," indicating that he, too, is interpreting the text according to the manuscript illustrations (*De rebus bellicis*, Part 2, p. 34).

[105] Marsden correctly identified the "strong sinew-rope" (*validus nervi funis*) as the bowstring of the machine. The "drawing-claw" *ferreus uncus*), or literally, "an ironhook" or "clamp," is interpreted by Marsden to refer to "a simple hook connecting the end of the winch-rope to the rear of the slider or a vague description of the trigger-mechanism" (*Technical Treatises*, p. 245). Since the text indicates that this device pulls the bowstring back, it must be a drawing-claw, not a hook at the end of the winch-rope or a trigger-mechanism.

[106] As Marsden has pointed out, *cochleae machina* can best be interpreted as a universal joint, not a "screw" or "screw-thread device," as Thompson and Ireland have translated the term respectively (Marsden, *Technical Treatises*, p. 245; Thompson, p. 120; *De rebus bellicis*, Part 2, p. 34).

it can even fly across the width of the Danube, a river famous for its size. Called the "Thunderbolt" *ballista*, it is so designated for the effectiveness of its power.

Virtually all attempts to reconstruct these two catapults have relied to a greater or lesser extent on the manuscript illustrations of the machines, the earliest of which date from the fifteenth century.[107] These illustrations cannot be used as evidence for reconstructing these machines because they are mechanically preposterous and are not corroborated by any other descriptions of catapults or extant artistic representations of ancient artillery (figs. 9–10).[108] Marsden was correct to reconstruct the artillery of Anonymus as conventional bolt- projecting catapults, but wrong to consider them two-armed torsion machines. He is alone in this interpretation. Oliver's analysis of the machines, while misguided on many points, makes a reasonable deduction regarding the similar construction and operating features of both pieces of artillery. He states that, "it is quite clear that both machines operate on the same principle, and differ only to the extent made necessary by the desire to attain maximum mobility in the one, and maximum destructive energy in the other."[109] The tension-power of a steel bow provides the propulsive force for the "Thunderbolt" *ballista*, as the text

[107] In addition to the studies cited above on *De rebus bellicis*, see Rudolf Schneider, *Anonymi de rebus bellicis liber* (Berlin: Weidmannische Buchhandlung, 1908), "Vom Büchlein *De rebus bellicis*," *Neue Jahrbücher für das klassische Altertum* 25 (1910), 327–42; Salomon Reinach, "Un homme d'ideés au Bas-Empire," *Revue archéologique*, sér. v, 16 (1922), 205–65. Schneider believed *De rebus bellicis* to be a fifteenth-century forgery, since he could not accept the possibility that a Roman author would have advocated using a tension-bow, rather than torsion springs, on a catapult. Schramm had no difficulty with this idea and suggested that the "Thunderbolt" *ballista* took the form of his *Übergangsgeschütz* which had a steel bow (Schramm, *Antiken Geschütze*, pp. 49–50). Thompson, while making a honest effort at translation, makes no serious attempt to reconstruct the catapults described by Anonymus, stating that, "all attempts to explain these machines should start from the assumption that in practice they would not have worked at all" (Thompson, p. 64). On the illustrations of *De rebus bellicis*, see J. J. G. Alexander, "The Illustrations of the Anonymus, *De rebus bellicis*," in *De rebus-bellicis*, Part 1: *Aspects of the "De re bellicis,"* pp. 11–15.

[108] According to the latest study of these illustrations, they were all transmitted via a single Carolingian intermediary (the *codex Spirensis*), dating from the late ninth or early tenth century, of which only a single, unillustrated, bifolium remains (Alexander, pp. 11–15). Since neither the original fourth-century illustrations of Anonymus are extant, nor the illustrations from the Carolingian copy, there is no way of telling whether or not the Renaissance illustrations of the catapults of Anonymus are based on the original Roman ones. Hence, there are two possible overlays of interpretation – Carolingian and Renaissance – with no assurance that either interpretation follows the Roman original. These illustrations are not only corrupt, they bear no resemblance to any classical depiction or medieval copy of a Greek or Roman illustration of a catapult. The Greeks, Romans, and Byzantines certainly knew how to depict machines that looked like catapults and so did the artists of the Renaissance. So why do the catapults of Anonymus not look like catapults? The Carolingian monk who produced the illustrations may either have (a) made them without the benefit of the Roman originals, or (b) chose not to follow the Roman originals. Surviving illustrations of ancient catapults appear very confusing to the untrained eye. If the Carolingian monk had the original Roman illustrations, he may have found them bewildering, and, rather than attempting to reproduce what he believed to be unintelligible illustrations, he decided to create ones which he thought made better sense of the text than the Roman illustrations.

[109] Oliver, p. 113.

clearly indicates. The description of the "Four-Wheeled" *ballista* does not explicitly indicate the manner of propulsive force utilized, but the past participle *intorta* (bent back) suggests that a tension-bow, rather than torsion springs, provides the motive power for the machine.[110] If the two machines were powered differently, Anonymus would most likely have indicated this essential fact in his accounts of these bolt-projectors. The "Four-Wheeled" *ballista* was probably fitted with a composite, rather than a steel, bow to enhance its mobility as a piece of field artillery.

Marsden rejected the conclusion that the "Thunderbolt" *ballista* obtained its propulsive force from a steel bow, because he believed that the ancients could not manufacture resilient steel in sufficient quantity to produce steel tension-bows for catapults.[111] If the Romans could produce high grade steel for swords and cutting tools, they possessed the technological expertise to manufacture high quality steel for the tension-bows for catapults. The fact that many surviving metal objects of Roman origin have thin steel layers or thin steel sheets welded on to them does not indicate that objects made entirely of steel were not produced, merely that steel was very expensive to make. Steel bows may never appear in the archeological record because (a) they represent a transient technology and were not produced in large quantity, and because (b) any surviving steel object would have been reused, made into objects having thin steel layers or thin steel sheets welded on to them.[112] Steel bows would have been expensive and heavy, but perfect for use on fixed defenses where space was limited, just as it is recommended for use here. Payne-Gallwey has described a heavy crossbow with a steel bow which was made in Geneva during the fifteenth-century. According to him, this weapon, weighing 18 lbs., was a "formidable siege crossbow . . . which was only employed in the attack or defence of a fortress, though it could be supported and aimed by a man of very strong physique, [and] was usually discharged either as it rested on a parapet, or when pivoted on a small tripod."[113] The steel bow of this crossbow measured 3 ft. 2 in. in length, and at its center it was 2½ in. wide and 1 in. thick. To draw the bowstring a distance of 7 in. to the catch of the lock required a drawing force of 1,200 lb. This was accomplished by the aid of a small portable fifteenth-century windlass, which, Payne-Gallwey observed, accomplished its task with ease by using the fingers of only one hand to draw it. The immense force required to draw the

---

[110] Marsden translated *intorta* both as "wound up" and "twisted up" and expanded his translation of the passage, *hoc ballistae genus duorum opera uirorum sagittas ex se, non ut aliae funibus, sed radiis intorta iaculatur*, to read: "this kind of *ballista* hurls its arrows from itself after it has had its springs twisted up not by ropes as other machines are, but by rods." This interpretation leads Marsden to conclude that the "Four-Wheeled" *ballista* "is plainly subjected to some sort of torsion and is definitely, therefore, a torsion engine" (*Technical Treatises*, pp. 241, 243).

[111] Marsden, *Technical Treatises*, p. 235, n. 4.

[112] On the production of high quality steel in the Roman Empire, see, K. D. White, *Greek and Roman Technology* (Ithaca: Cornell University Press, 1984), pp. 10, 126, 136, 250.

[113] Payne-Gallwey, pp. 14–15. I would like to thank Vernard L. Foley for alerting me to this description.

bowstring meant that the bowstring had to be strong, just as Anonymus recommends in his text. Like Anonymus, Payne-Gallwey could not resist the challenge of shooting bolts from this crossbow across a body of water to test the range of the machine. He shot several bolts across the Menai Straits, and the Ordnance Survey recorded the distance reached by the bolts to be between 440 and 450 yards (402.3–411.5 m.).

Marsden has remarked that during the fourth century "there seems to have been a special category of artillery designed particularly for the defence of walls and termed generally *tomenta muralia*."[114] If so, the account of the "Thunderbolt" *ballista* by Anonymus is the only description there is of Roman artillery specifically designed for the defense of fortified structures. Although the description of this catapult indicates that it has been tested in practice and "has been found by experience to be superior to all others in range and power," it cannot be determined whether this piece of artillery ever came into general use.[115] The tower-mounted *ballistae* described by Procopius most likely utilized a composite bow, which suggests that even if steel-bow tension catapults were employed on more than a limited scale in fortified structures of the Roman Empire, they were soon replaced by more cost effective composite-bow bolt-projectors.

D. Procopius' *Ballista*
De Bello Gothico, 1.21.14–18

(14) βελισάριος δὲ μηχανὰς μὲν ἐς τοὺς πύργους ἐτίθετο, ἃς καλοῦσι βαλλίστρας. τόξου δὲ σχῆμα ἔχουσιν αἱ μηχαναὶ αὗται ἔνερθέν τε αὐτοῦ κοίλη τις ξυλίνη κεραία προὔχει, αὐτὴ μὲν χαλαρὰ ἠρτημένη, σιδηρᾷ δὲ εὐθείᾳ τινὶ ἐπικειμένη. (15) ἐπειδὰν οὖν τοὺς πολεμίους ἐνθένδε βάλλειν ἐθέλουσιν ἄνθρωποι, βρόχου βραχέος ἐνέρσει τὰ ξύλα ἐς ἄλληλα νεύειν ποιοῦσιν, ἃ δὴ τοῦ τόξου ἄκρα ξυμβαίνει εἶναι, τόν τε ἄτρακτον ἐν τῇ κοίλῃ κεραίᾳ τίθενται, τῶν ἄλλων βελῶν, ἅπερ ἐκ τῶν τόξων ἀφιᾶσι, μῆκος μὲν ἔχοντα ἥμισυ μάλιστα, εὖρος δὲ κατὰ τετραπλάσιον. (16) πτεροῖς μέντοι οὐ τοῖς εἰωθόσιν ἐνέχεται, ἀλλὰ ξύλα λεπτὰ ἐς τῶν πτερῶν τὴν χώραν ἐνείροντες ὅλον ἀπομιμοῦνται τοῦ βέλους τὸ σχῆμα, μεγάλην αὐτῷ λίαν καὶ τοῦ πάχους κατὰ λόγον τὴν ἀκίδα ἐμβάλλοντες. (17) σφίγγουσί τε <σθένει> πολλῷ οἱ ἀμφοτέρωθεν μηχαναῖς τισι, καὶ τότε ἡ κοίλη κεραία προϊοῦσα {ἐκπίπτει} μὲν, ξὺν ῥύμῃ δὲ τοσαύτῃ ἐκπίπτει τὸ βέλος ὥστε ἐξικνεῖται μὲν οὐχ ἧσσον ἢ κατὰ δύο τῆς τοξείας βολάς, δένδρου δὲ ἢ λίθου ἐπιτυχὸν τέμνει ῥᾳδίως. (18) τοιαύτη μὲν ἡ μηχανή ἐστιν ἐπὶ τοῦ ὀνόματος τούτου, ὅτι δὴ βάλλει ὡς μάλιστα, ἐπικληθεῖσα.

---

[114] Marsden, *Historical Development*, p. 197, and *Technical Treatises*, p. 245, n. 1; Ammianus, 17.1.12, 18.9.1. Campbell adds that, "the new strategy of actively defending fortifications is a phenomenon of the later third century; the thickening of fort walls and the elaboration of outer defences indicate a trend toward resisting direct attack, instead of the garrison issuing out to meet the attacker" (Campbell, "Ballistaria," pp. 81–82). Thus, one should expect to find the widespread deployment of artillery in Roman fortifications only after the third century.

[115] Thompson discredits the claim of Anonymus that the "Thunderbolt" *ballista* was ever built or tested, stating that, "it is exceeding difficult to believe that this ballista had ever in fact been made and used, and still more difficult to believe that it had been found efficient" (p. 77).

(14) Belisarius placed on the towers siege machines which they call *ballistae*. These siege machines take the shape of a bow;[116] but underneath it a grooved wooden slider projects; this is so fitted that it can move freely and it rests in a straight iron-[plated] case.[117] (15) Whenever men want to shoot at the enemy with this, they make the two wooden ears[118] which form the extremities of the bow bend toward each other by means of the loop [of the bowstring] fastened to them, and they place the bolt in the grooved slider;[119] the bolt is about half the length of ordinary missiles which they shoot from hand-bows, but about four times as thick. (16) However, it does not have the usual fletching, but by inserting thin strips of wood in place of the fletching, they give it the general form of an ordinary arrow; they make the bolt-head very large in proportion to its thickness (fig. 8). (17) Men who stand on either side wind it up tight by means of certain devices,[120] and then the grooved slider discharging shoots[121] the bolt

---

[116] Marsden translates this passage as, "these machines have a component in the shape of a bow." He argued that "the shape of a bow" (τόξου δὲ σχῆμα) corresponds to the "little arch" (καμάριον) of the *cheiroballistra* described by Heron (Wescher, p. 130; Marsden, *Technical Treatises*, p. 247, n. 1). Procopius does not indicate that the *ballistae* have "a component in the shape of a bow," but rather that the main structural feature of these machines is a bow, clearly indicating that they are tension catapults. It is unlikely that the "bow" indicates the upper horizontal strut of the machine, and it is quite improbable that Procopius would begin his description of these siege engines by focusing on this minor detail of the machines.

[117] Marsden translated "grooved wooden slider" (κοίλῃ κεραίᾳ) as "hollow wooden beam" and suggested that this term referred to the stock of the machine. According to him, "Procopius would appear not to have had a very clear idea of [the stock] himself, but probably meant these words to give a brief general impression of all a stock's components which are fully described by Heron." Marsden failed to see that Procopius provides a rather detailed description of the stock. He describes both the slider and the case and indicates that the slider was grooved for the placement of the missile and that the case was iron, or rather, plated with sheet iron, rather than being made of solid iron. Having a sheet metal running course for the slider would reduce the friction coefficient between the case and the slider. Thinking that "the grooved wooden slider" refers to the entire stock, Marsden interpreted the text to indicate that the stock "could move freely [because it was] connected to the universal-joint which Procopius does not specifically mention." Marsden translated "a straight iron-[plated] case (σιδηρᾷ δὲ εὐθείᾳ) as the "straight iron beam"and suggested that it referred to the horizontal metal beam which kept the cylindrical frames containing the cord-bundles of this two-armed torsion machine in place, rather than to the case of the stock (*Technical Treatises*, pp. 246–47).

[118] The "two wooden ears" (τὰ ξύλα) literally refer to "two wooden parts" which form the extremities of the bow. Since these parts are distinct enough to be identified as separate from the rest of the bow, Vernard L. Foley has suggested to me that they may be the "ears" of the bow, which in archery nomenclature refer to the curved-like tips of a Oriental bow containing the nock. Believing that the machine was a torsion engine, Marsden translated the "two wooden ears" at the ends of the bow as "wooden beams," which he thought referred to the two arms of a torsion catapult. Unable to explain why the τὰ ξύλα were clearly indicated as being at the ends of the bow, Marsden concluded that, "Procopius seems here to be doing his best to explain that the arms of his torsion engine operate in a manner similar to the ends of an ordinary hand-bow" (*Technical Treatises*, p. 247). The most plausible explanation for this is that Procopius is, indeed, trying to indicate that this machine operates in a manner similar to an ordinary hand-bow because, as a tension catapult, it is similar to an ordinary hand-bow.

[119] The "loop" of the bowstring (βρόχου βραχέος) was translated by Marsden as "short noose" which, according to him, referred to the bowstring of the machine.

[120] Marsden correctly suggested that "certain devices" must refer to a winch-mechanism (*Technical Treatises*, pp. 247–48). In this case the device used was probably a circular ratchet placed at the rear of the stock.

[121] This passage twice employs the verb ἐκπίπτει. Since Procopius is not likely to have done

with such force that it reaches a distance of not less than two bow-shots;[122] and when it hits a tree or a stone, it pierces it easily. (18) Such is the siege machine which bears this name, so designated because it shoots with great force.

Marsden's claim that Procopius' catapult is a two-armed torsion bolt-projector is not supported by the evidence provided in the description of this machine. This piece of artillery appears to be a base-mounted tension catapult having a composite bow of Oriental design. Procopius singles out two components of the bow which he identifies as τὰ ξύλα (*ta xyla*), or "wooden parts," forming the ends of the bow. Since these parts must be distinct enough from the rest of the bow to be identified separately, this bow is not likely to be an ordinary self bow, but rather a reflexed Oriental composite bow fitted with rigid curved end-pieces made of wood. These end-pieces are known as "ears" and can be seen on a number of illustrations of ancient Greek catapults.[123] The catapult described by Procopius is most probably identical to the base-mounted, bolt-projecting

this, the double ἐκπίπτει may be assumed to have been inscribed by error. Editorial efforts to amend this passage have considered the first ἐκπίπτει to be a incorrect transcription of some other verb. Dewing suggested that the first ἐκπίπτει be read as ἐκλείπει, which he translates as "stops." Hence, his rendition of the passage reads: "and then the grooved shaft shoots forward and stops, but the missile is discharged from the shaft" (Procopius, *Works*, pp. 204–05). This implies that some part of the stock, presumably the slider, moves forward upon the release of the bowstring and then stops, but the missile continues on its course being discharged from the slider. Marsden followed Dewing's suggested reading in his translation of this passage but offered an alternative reading of ἐκπαύεται for ἐκπίπτει (Marsden, *Technical Treatises*, p. 248, n. 10). Eric McGeer has suggested to me an alternative amendment that does not require the substitution of another verb for ἐκπίπτει. The sentence may be read with only one ἐκπίπτει and still make perfect sense. The main verb of this sentence is ἐκπίπτει and is used with the active participle προϊοῦσα to describe the action of the slider as it simultaneously discharges the missile down its grooved channel – just as a gun discharges a bullet through its barrel – and ejects or expels the bolt out of this channel. Ἐκπίπτει is a transitive verb in the present tense, having βέλος as its direct object. This solution to the double ἐκπίπτει requires less textual amendment than the substitution of one verb for another, and I am indebted to Dr. McGeer for kindly suggesting this elegant solution.

122 Marsden considered the text to be corrupt at this point because he believed that, "Procopius thought that some part of the stock travelled forward when the trigger was released, and then stopped, allowing the missile to continue on its course." Marsden was right to indicate that neither the slider, nor any other portion of the stock, moves when the trigger is pulled, but wrong to suggest that the text indicates that the slider is driven forward by the bowstring upon release of the trigger. Procopius merely indicates that the slider serves to discharge the missile and eject it towards its target. Marsden's assessment that "Procopius' erroneous conception of the *ballista*'s action inevitably reduces our confidence in the rest of his account" is not substantiated (*Technical Treatises*, p. 248, n. 10).

123 Wescher, p. 48, figs. 13–14, p. 51, fig. 15, p. 52, fig. 16, p. 64, fig. 20, p. 67, fig. 21, p. 80, figs. 22–23, p. 90, fig. 26; Aage G. Drachmann, "Biton and the Development of the Catapult," *Prismata, Naturwissenschaftsgeschichtliche Studien, Festschrift für Willy Hartner*, ed. Y. Maeyama and W. G. Saltzer (Wiesbaden: Steiner, 1977), pp. 119–31, figs. 1–4, 6. Such ears are also visible on the arms of the two-armed, bolt-projecting torsion catapult depicted on a stone relief executed at Pergamum in the reign of Eumenes II (197–160/59 B.C.). The sculptor, however, has incorrectly represented the straight arms of a torsion catapult as being similar to the bow of a tension catapult. Marsden has interpreted this relief as evidence for the use of curved arms on torsion catapults, similar to those described by Vitruvius on his bolt-projecting catapult (*Technical Treatises*, pp. 7, 188–89, 230, 270, pl. 3, diagram 10).

tension catapult referred to in texts of the middle Byzantine period as the τοξοβολιστρα (*toxobolistra*) or "bow-*ballista*."[124]

IV. Conclusion

Textual accounts (Vegetius and Ammianus) and archeological finds of catapults indicate that Rome continued to use the two-armed torsion catapult through the second half of the fourth century. It is also clear from Anonymus' description of artillery that tension catapults were being put to wider use in the fourth century. The employment of the *onager* in this same century as Rome's sole stone-projecting ordnance suggests that simple, less sophisticated machines were viewed as preferable to advanced, yet complex, ones. Special mathematical and technical skills were required to construct and maintain a two-armed torsion catapult, and these skills appear to have been in decline in both the eastern and western portions of the Roman Empire from the fourth century onward. The two-armed torsion catapult demanded frequent attention to keep the springs in balance, and its sinew-ropes were subject to breakage, rotting, and changes in tension due to moisture and stretching. The tension catapult, while requiring skill to make, was less costly and far easier to operate and maintain. It was less powerful than the torsion catapult, but more reliable. Once the two-armed torsion catapult was retired as a stone-projector and used only as a bolt-projector, the advantages of having such a sophisticated machine to launch missiles of relatively light weight were soon outweighed by the machine's obvious disadvantages: its high production costs, complexity of operation, and frequent maintenance. The tension catapult, while unable to match the high performance of the two-armed torsion catapult, more than made up for this deficit by its lower cost of production, ease of operation, and reliability. The combination of these factors with the economic and political decline of the Roman Empire in late antiquity resulted in the abandonment of the two-armed torsion catapult and its replacement by the tension catapult.

Although there is little likelihood that the two-armed torsion catapult survived in the western Empire beyond the collapse of the western Roman army during the fifth century, scholarly opinion is divided on whether it survived in the eastern Empire, where the Roman army remained intact. Baatz concludes his discussion of recent finds of ancient artillery by stating that the new type of catapults developed by the Romans, having low but wide tension-frames, instead of the narrow and high tension-frames of Greek torsion artillery, "lasted for centuries into the Byzantine period."[125] There is no direct evidence for this. The fact that Heron's treatise on artillery, with the section on the *cheiroballistra* added to it, continued to be copied throughout the middle Byzantine period may simply indicate a conservative archaistic literary tradition, rather than evidence

---

[124] See n. 74 above and text.
[125] Baatz, "Recent Finds," p. 16.

for the continued use of torsion artillery. In the sixth century the only bolt-projector identified by Procopius is the tension catapult, which suggests that the two-armed torsion catapult was most likely phased out before this. His designation of this machine by the Greek form of the Latin word *ballista*, rather than by one of the classical Greek words for a torsion catapult which were familiar to him, indicates a change in Greek nomenclature for artillery which reflects a change in the form of artillery used: the tension, rather than the torsion, catapult.[126] The *Strategikon* of Maurice, dating from the early seventh century, also exhibits this change in nomenclature for the catapult, indicating that Procopius' use of the term *ballistra* does not reflect an individual or regional idiosyncrasy, but a genuine transition in terminology which mirrors a change in the form of artillery.[127] In Byzantine sources dating from the eighth to the eleventh century, the term τοξοβολιστρα (*toxobolistra*), or "bow-*ballista*," is used, giving clear indication of the transition from the torsion to the tension catapult. The absence of any term in post-Procopian Byzantine sources that refers to torsion artillery suggests that the production of the two-armed torsion catapult came to an end sometime prior to the siege of Rome by the Goths in 537–38, most likely during the fifth century.[128] The *onager*, the one-armed torsion machine of late antiquity, did survive into the sixth century, as we know from Procopius' mention of it at the siege of Rome by the Goths,[129] but its days were numbered. By the end of the sixth century a new stone-projector, the traction trebuchet, had appeared in the Mediterranean. This machine was not only far simpler to construct, operate, and maintain than the artillery of classical antiquity, it was considerably more powerful. The triumph of this new machine and the final end of torsion artillery must be left to another study.[130]

---

[126] The Greek term for the two-armed bolt-projecting torsion catapult was καταπέλτης ὀξυ βελής or either of these words used alone. The earliest term used for this type of artillery, however, was καταπάλτης ὀξυβόλος (Marsden, *Historical Development*, p. 1, n. 1).

[127] See βαλλίστρα and its compounds in George T. Dennis and Ernst Gamillscheg, eds. *Das Strategikon des Maurikios*, Corpus Fontium Historiae Byzantinae, 17 (Vienna: Verlag der Österreichischen Akademie der Wissenschaften, 1981), 12.B.6.9, p. 422; 12.B.18.9, p. 456; 12.B.21.13, p. 468; 12.B.21.43, p. 470. Since Maurice mentions that the βαλλίστρα was mounted on wagons (12.B.6.9, 12.B.18.9) – like the *carroballista* – there is little doubt that it was a bolt-projector.

[128] This statement requires substantiation far beyond what can be provided in a note. See my forthcoming article "The Terminology of Medieval Artillery," which deals with this subject.

[129] Procopius, *De Bello Gothico*, 1.21.19.

[130] My thanks are due to Donald J. Kagay and Theresa M. Vann for assisting me with the translation of the Latin texts presented in this paper and to Eric McGeer for his aid with the Greek text of Procopius. Vernard L. Foley provided me with many helpful suggestions pertaining to technical matters which are graciously acknowledged. I am grateful to Dietwulf Baatz, George T. Dennis, S. J., and Lawrence A. Tritle, who read an earlier draft of this paper, for their discussion and criticism. Full responsibility for the content and conclusion drawn here rests with the author alone.

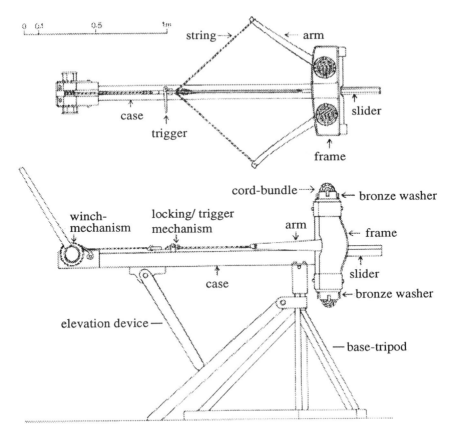

Figure 1. Two-armed, wooden-frame, bolt-projecting catapult of Vitruvius (reconstruction after E. Schramm).

Figure 2. Roman two-armed, metal-frame, bolt-projecting torsion catapult being hauled up a mountain track on a mule-drawn transport-wagon. Trajan's column, A.D. 113. Deutsches Archäeologisches Institut – Rom.

Figure 3. Two catapults mounted on the battlements of a Roman fort. Trajan's column,
A.D. 113. Both machines represent the new bolt-projecting torsion catapult introduced
by the Romans during the second half of the first century, having wide, low
tension-frames made of iron which were enclosed in cone-topped cylindrical metal
cases to protect the sinew-bundles from moisture and counter-battery from the enemy.
Trajan's column, A.D. 113. Deutsches Archäeologisches Institut – Rom.

Figure 4. Roman two-armed, metal-frame, bolt-projecting torsion catapult positioned in an artillery "pill box" constructed in front of a Roman fort. Trajan's column, A.D. 113. Deutsches Archäeologisches Institut – Rom.

Figure 5. Dacian artillerists operating a two-armed, metal-frame, bolt-projecting torsion catapult behind a wooden palisade. Trajan's column, A.D. 113. Deutsches Archäeologisches Institut – Rom.

Figure 6. Two Roman *carroballistae* depicted on Trajan's column, A.D. 113. The *carroballista* was the first truly mobile piece of field artillery. It consisted of a two-arm, metal-frame, bolt-projecting torsion catapult mounted on a specially designed two-wheeled cart drawn by two horses or mules.
Deutsches Archäologisches Institut – Rom.

Figure 7. An iron tension-frame (*kambestrion*) from a Roman two-armed, bolt-projecting, torsion catapult found at Lyon, France (length, 0.325 m.; dia., 0.22 m.; weight, 4.85 kg.). Lyon, Musée de la civilisation Gallo-Romaine. The arched strut at the rear of the tension-frame serves to accomodate the movement of the catapult arm as it is pulled back by the bowstring. The bottom pair of rings (R.) welded onto the two vertical struts holds the bottom transom, known as the *klimakion* (little ladder), while the upper pair of rings (L.) holds the upper transom, known as the *kamarion* (little arch).

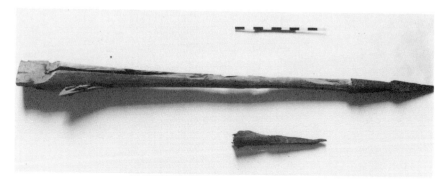

Figure 8. Complete Roman catapult bolt (above) and the head of a catapult bolt (below) dating from the middle of the third century A.D. from Dura-Europos. The shaft, made of ash, has a sharp four-sided iron head and three triangular wooden vanes made of maple (length, 0.375 m.; dia. tapering from 0.014 m. to 0.033 m.). Yale University Art Gallery, Dura-Europos Collection.

Figure 9. The four-wheeled *Ballista* (*ballista quadrirotis*) in *De rebus bellicis,* made
at Basel in 1436 for Pietro Donato, bishop of Padua, from a lost Carolingian
manuscript in the Cathedral of Speyer.
Bodleian Library, MS. Canon. Misc. 378, fol. 71v.

Figure 10. The "Thunderbolt" *Ballista* (*ballista fulminalis*) in *De rebus bellicis*, Bodleian Library, MS. Canon. Misc. 378, fol. 76r.

Siege as Metaphor and Literary Event

Siege Warfare in Medieval Hispanic Epic and Romance

Michael Harney
University of Texas at Austin

The emergence of the romance has been discussed in terms of literary trans-formations and socio-evolutionary transitions. Addressing the related but some-what broader question of the epic's relationship to the novel, Bakhtin defines the former genre as "completed in its development," and thus "already antiquated." Along with tragedy, epic is, therefore, one of the historically "fixed pre-existing forms." The novel, by contrast, is still a "developing genre," still fighting for "its own hegemony in literature."[1]

Accepting Bakhtin's model of the generic open-endedness of the novel, we may hazard that the medieval romances represent an early phase in the matura-tion of this eclectic genre. Proposing a developmental model of a different sort, R. W. Southern supposes a progression from the communal and religious (epic) world to the individualist and secular (romance) world. The solitary quest that was so much a part of medieval romance is contrasted, in his account, to the collective hostility which characterizes epic (e.g., *Song of Roland*, prefigured by the *Iliad*).[2] Comradeship, however, as Eugène Vinaver points out, is as much a part of Arthurian romance as it is of those earlier epics said to be circumscribed by the reciprocities of vassalage. Emphasizing linguistic and literary factors in the transition, he demonstrates that the medieval epic, exemplified by the *Roland*, is paratactic and repetitive, lacking in digression or thematic explana-tion to support its headlong narrative. For Vinaver, the feature of romance that distinguishes it from epic is not any specific theme, nor even any particular stylistic trait, but rather a predisposition to digression, explanation, and

---

[1] M. M. Bakhtin, "Epic and Novel," in his *The Dialogic Imagination. Four Essays*, trans. Michael Holquist (Austin: University of Texas Press, 1981), pp. 3, 4.

[2] R. W. Southern, *The Making of the Middle Ages* (New Haven: Yale University Press, 1953), in his chapter "From Epic to Romance" (pp. 219–57), quoted by Eugène Vinaver, *The Rise of Romance* (Oxford: Clarendon Press, 1971), p. 2. Southern (p. 227) sees the literary transition as a reflection of the passage from a society based on "the element of corporateness" (epitomized by St. Benedict and his rule) to one founded on individualism (represented by St. Anselm).

reflection. This exegetical component, bound up with the growth of schools, the spread of lay literacy and the expansion of the literate reading public, reveals a stylistic bias in authors who sought to convert pre-existing materials (folkloric or classical) into romances.[3]

Vinaver's approach has the virtue of being closely tied to an observable difference of style and tone in the two genres. Epics are, indeed, concerned with action – depiction without elucidation seems to be their rule. While not downplaying action, the romances do, indeed, show an obsession with explicating the meaning of action. As Vinaver demonstrates, rhetoric is the refashioning, elaborative instrument that, applied to pre-existing narratives, makes of the adaptor a creative author. This union "of narrative and commentary" is intimately connected with the romance's proclivity for interior monologue, for contrasting meaning and matter, for organizing the plot around courtly issues such as love and honor, and for personifying meanings and themes in the form of characters and situations.[4] It has likewise been suggested that the digressive, exegetical bias of romance is the direct consequence of a vernacular reading public whose appearance, notes J. N. H. Lawrance, bespeaks a "discovery of the self" and a self-conscious delectation in rhetorical expression and contemplative style. These factors, in turn, derive from the synergetic diffusion of money, libraries, and the leisure to read – all of them diagnostic of the bourgeois sensibility and way of life.[5]

The contrast established by Vinaver with reference to French epic and romance holds as well for analogous Peninsular works. This resemblance may or may not be due, in the case of either of the two genres, to Hispanic borrowing from French models. In the case of the epic, such borrowing has not been conclusively demonstrated. The problem of epic origins is exacerbated by the fact that the only more or less complete Spanish epic known to us is the *Poem of the Cid*. The school of thought represented by Ramón Menéndez Pidal, still perhaps predominant, has always maintained that this epic was but one of many, composed on a variety of themes within an indigenous popular epic tradition. However, Colin Smith has presented a very detailed counter-theory, emphasizing the poem's uniqueness as a *sui generis* adaptation of French epic stylistic models.[6]

While the genesis of Spanish epic remains uncertain, the origin of medieval

---

3   Vinaver, pp. 2–3, 5–8, 16–22.

4   Vinaver, pp. 22–31.

5   J. N. H. Lawrance, "The Spread of Lay Literacy in Late Medieval Castile," *Bulletin of Hispanic Studies* 62 (1985), 79, 87–90.

6   Smith presents his views on authorship by a Gallophile poet in his *The Making of the "Poema de Mio Cid"* (Cambridge: Cambridge University Press, 1983), p. 157. See also, on the subject of Peninsular epic cycles, Ramón Menéndez Pidal, *La Chanson de Roland et la tradition épique des Francs*, trans. Irenée-Marcel Cluzel, rev. ed. (Paris: A. et J. Picard, 1960), and his *Los godos y la epopeya española. "Chansons de geste" y baladas nórdicas* (Madrid: Espasa-Calpe, 1969), pp. 9–57. Louis Chalon provides an updated and comprehensive appraisal of epic cycles in the Hispanic tradition in *L'Histoire et l'épopée castillane du Moyen Âge: le Cycle du Cid, le cycle des comtes de Castille*, Nouvelle Bibliothèque du Moyen Âge, 5 (Paris: Champion, 1976).

Peninsular romances in translations or adaptations of French originals has been clearly demonstrated. Making a unique contribution to chivalric literature through a peculiar amalgam of forms and themes, Iberia produced some of the first best-sellers in the early years of printing. In particular, the late-fifteenth-century *Amadís of Gaul*, a work based on earlier versions dating back to the first decades of the fourteenth century, initiated a long series of sequels whose popularity gave rise to a host of imitations. This was the genre destined to vex the mind and ruin the personal economy of Don Quijote.[7]

A common denominator allowing us to compare the two types of narrative is also a focal point of generic divergence. Both epic and chivalric romance are preoccupied with sieges. However, while in the former genre the protagonist is the besieger, in the romance the hero sides with the besieged. Although I believe that this pattern may well hold true for other contexts, such as that of Homeric epic and Greek romances, or French epic and Arthurian romance, I will limit my analysis to the medieval Spanish tradition.

In Spanish epic, we have as besieging protagonists the Cid of the poem named for him, and Sancho II of the fragmentary *Cantar de Sancho II* ("Song of Sancho II"), also known as the *El cerco de Zamora* ("The Siege of Zamora").[8] The life of the Cid, both in history and epic, presents one of the most famous cases of siege warfare and its social impact. In besieging and conquering the Arabic city of Valencia, Rodrigo Díaz de Vivar, the Cid, successfully established an independent domain and exalted family, clan, and vassals. The Castilian hero thus provided a standard for social and military success whose influence was to linger for centuries in the Peninsular psyche.[9]

At first glance the epic and the chivalric romance seem to depict the same

---

[7] When I speak of medieval Hispanic romance in the present essay, I refer above all to the prose tradition. I thus exclude verse adaptations of late classical texts, such as the thirteenth-century *Libro de Alixandre* and the *Libro de Apolonio*, masterpieces of the so-called *mester de clerecía*. On Peninsular translations and adaptation of French romances, see A. D. Deyermond, *Historia de la literatura española*, Vol. 1: *Edad Media* (Barcelona: Ariel, 1985), pp. 279–81. As the "father of the Spanish romances of chivalry" and as a work greatly influenced by the thirteenth-century French prose *Lancelot*, the *Amadís* engenders a "monstrous progeny" of sequels and imitators. See Harry Sieber, "The Romance of Chivalry in Spain. From Rodríguez de Montalvo to Cervantes," in *Romance: Generic Transformation from Chrétien de Troyes to Cervantes*, eds. Kevin Brownlee and Marina Scordilis Brownlee (Hanover and London: University Press of New England, 1985), pp. 203–19 (esp. pp. 204–06). The extraordinary popularity of the chivalric romance is confirmed, suggests Keith Whinnom, by the large numbers of editions. See his "The Problem of the 'Best-Seller' in Spanish Golden Age Literature," *Bulletin of Hispanic Studies* 67 (1980), 189–98 (esp. pp. 192–93, 195). The chivalric romances referred to in the present study are: *Amadís de Gaula*, ed. Edwin B. Place, 4 vols. (Madrid: Consejo Superior de Investigaciones Científicas, 1959–65); *Tirant lo Blanc i altres escrits de Joanot Martorell*, ed. Martín de Riquer (Barcelona: Ariel, 1969); *El Libro del cauallero Zifar (El libro del cauallero de Dios)*, ed. Charles Philip Wagner (Ann Arbor: University of Michigan Press, 1929).

[8] Editions cited: *Poema de mio Cid*, ed. Ian Michael, 2nd ed. (Madrid: Castalia, 1984); *El cantar de Sancho II y cerco de Zamora*, ed. Carola Reig, *Revista de Filología Española*, Anejo 37 (Madrid: Consejo Superior de Investigaciones Científicas, 1947).

[9] The siege of Valencia is depicted in ll. 1098–220. For a summary of the social impact of

socio-political conditions and subscribe to the same notions of predatory economy that encourage and permit siege warfare. Economic and military opportunism was for many centuries the principal avenue of circumstantial mobility in Spain and throughout Europe. For example, the semi-nomadic Normans of the eleventh and twelfth centuries were organized, as Eleanor Searle has demonstrated, along the lines of a "predatory community" of war leaders whose success was based on a "segmental family fighting force." This group was recruited by "incorporation into the family" and derived its power from kinship, both consanguineal and fictive. The *Poem of the Cid* reveals a similar segmentary expansion in its depiction of the recruitment of warriors through ties of pseudo-kinship (expressed in a type of feudal vocabulary) and in its depictions of institutionalized redistribution of plunder. Joseph J. Duggan demonstrates that the *Poema*, "saturated with the theme of wealth," is obsessed with reciprocal economic mentalities ("interested gift-giving") that are shown to facilitate the Cid's foundation of an independent kingdom based in Valencia.[10]

The chivalric romances perpetuate the myth of pillage and redistribution as standard elements of military leadership and honorable advancement. In the late-fifteenth-century *Tirant lo blanc*, we see the hero, commander-in-chief of Constantinople's defenders, promulgating guarantees of money and honorific promotion as inducements to participate in the efforts to lift the siege:

> ordenà que tot home qui sostingués cavall e tingués armes fos dit gentilhom, e qui tendria dos rossins fos gentilhom e home de paratge, e qui tendria tres rossins fos dit gentilhom e home generós e cavaller, e la casa d'aquests tals no pagassen nengun dret al Rei, e cascun d'aquests que tendrien llocs, masos o alqueries, tots fossen haguts per francs e lliberts. (p. 917)[11]

Law codes support the romances in this retention of predatory economic mentalities dating from the centuries of the Reconquest. Legal statutes and romances assume that, in an environment of institutionalized economic predation (e.g.,

---

the Cid's legend, see Richard Fletcher, *The Quest for El Cid* (New York: Knopf, 1990), pp. 166–205.

[10] Eleanor Searle, *Predatory Kinship and the Creation of Norman Power. 840–1066* (Berkeley: University of California Press, 1988), p. 240; Michael Harney, "Class Conflict and Primitive Rebellion," *Olifant* 12 (1987), 185–88, 206–16; Joseph J. Duggan, *The "Cantar de Mio Cid." Poetic Creation in its Economic and Social Contexts*, Cambridge Studies in Medieval Literature, 5 (Cambridge: Cambridge University Press, 1989), pp. 5, 33. In chs. 2 and 4 (on "Amity" and "Polity") of my *Kinship and Polity in the "Poema de Mio Cid,"* Purdue Studies in Romance Literatures, 2 (West Lafayette IN: Purdue University Press, 1993), I discuss the various mechanisms of recruitment into the itinerant predatory band that is the nucleus of the Cid's fighting force.

[11] ". . . ordered that any man who maintained a horse and carried arms should be deemed a gentleman, and whoever possessed two horses should be a gentleman and a lord, and whoever possessed three horses should be called gentleman and nobleman and knight, and the estates of such should have no assessment whatever levied on them by the King, and all those who owned manors, residences or granges should be considered free and unencumbered."

Partidas, II.xxvi.1–34), men more willingly participate in campaigns contrived expressly with plunder in mind (*Partidas*, II.xxvii.1–10).[12]

The transformation in attitudes toward the siege, as reflected in the contrasting foci of sympathy in epic and chivalric romance, reflects a metamorphosis in the terminology and mentality of knighthood in its various meanings. To understand this development, we must examine the origins of knighthood itself. Every step in the development of the lexicon based on warlike horsemanship reveals changes in the relations of economic autonomy and dependency. These relations are the basis both of social inequality and siege warfare, which is its indirect manifestation. From the late tenth century, the word *miles* becomes, as Georges Duby demonstrates, "the specific qualifier applied to a dominant category of lay society." The diffusion of feudal concessions appears to coincide with increasing desire for social classification. There is a growing tendency to oppose *milites* to members of other social categories (variously designated as *rustici*, *populus*, *civis*, *suburbani*). Such distinctions reveal, argues Duby, both a "transformation of juridical institutions and a basic division between feudatory dependents and the general population." The *milites* serve a leader, are attached to the fortress commanded by him, and, in exchange for a share in the profits, assist him in the exploitation of the surrounding countryside. Thus correlation exists not only between chivalry and feudalism, but also between the former and the institution of seignorial exactions, from which knights were exempted. *Miles* and *caballarius* become, Duby notes, ever more the distinctive token of a specific social status, as if the functional military discrimination between *milites* and *pedites* were applied to all of society. While the *pedites*, or footmen, are reduced to the role of auxiliary force, the horsemen, distinguished by their very capacity as mounted soldiery, are perceived as the elite of true warriors.[13]

---

[12] *Siete Partidas del rey don Alfonso el Sabio*, ed. Real Academia de la Historia, nueva ed., 5 vols. (Paris: Librería de Rosa y Bouret, 1861; Rept. of 1807 ed., 3 vols. [Madrid: Imprenta Real]). See also Hilda Grassotti, "Para la historia del botín y las parias en León y Castilla," *Cuadernos de Historia de España* 39–40 (1964), 43–132 (esp. pp. 61, 64–81); James F. Powers, *A Society Organized for War. The Iberian Municipal Militias in the Central Middle Ages. 1000–1284* (Berkeley: University of California Press, 1988), pp. 162–87; Manuel González Jiménez, "Frontier and Settlement in the Kingdom of Castile (1085–1350)," in *Medieval Frontier Societies*, eds. Robert Bartlett and Angus MacKay (Oxford: Clarendon Press, 1989), pp. 49–74 (esp. pp. 52–59, 67–71).

[13] Georges Duby, "La diffusion du titre chevalresque sur le versant méditerranéen de la Chrétienté latine," in *La Noblesse au Moyen Âge. XIe–XVe siècles. Essais à la mémoire de Robert Boutruche*, ed. Philippe Contamine (Paris: Presses Universitaire de France, 1976), pp. 39–70, quotations from pp. 41, 45–47, and 49–52, respectively. See also Johanna Maria van Winter, "Die mittelalterliche Ritterschaft als 'Classe Sociale,' " in *Das Rittertum im Mittelalter*, ed. Arno Borst, Wege der Forschung, 340 (Darmstadt: Wissenschaftliche Buchgesellschaft, 1976), pp. 370–91 (esp. pp. 377–78, 390–91). She verifies the common lifestyle and sense of shared membership exhibited by a late medieval society that styled itself "chivalric." While these factors point to emergent class sensibility, and are accentuated by prohibitions against tilling one's own land or working for profit, Winter suggests that before the late thirteenth century the lack of strictly defined lower or competing strata (e.g., peasantry, bourgeoisie) impedes in this chivalric elite the development of class structure – i.e., in the strict Marxian sense, that of interest groups in self-aware confrontation.

The insertion of military terminology into the vocabulary of social classification reflects a growing awareness, argues Duby, of a breach in the middle stratum of the *populus*. Until as late as the early eleventh century, the peasant way of life in no way precluded participation in military expeditions, on one's own horse and with one's own arms. Over time, the vocabulary of chivalry and feudalism places one segment of the peasantry on the side of the *plebs*, while incorporating the other segment into the aristocracy, thus saving it from poverty "par l'association aux profits de la guerre et du pouvoir et par des alliances familiales qui mêlèrent à celui des nobles le sang de certains *boni homines* plus chanceux."[14] Military vocabulary thus marked off the lower boundary of a class defined by specific privileges and exemptions. The notion of society as somehow symbolized by the *exercitus militum* or the *cavalcata militum* was easily grafted onto the tripartite model of estates theory, a thinly disguised functionalist rationale for social inequality. Thus arises the dark side of chivalry: that of the knight as the henchman and enforcer of the robber baron, as the extortionate oppressor of peasant and burgher (pp. 59–61).

The patterns summarized by Duby are similarly encountered during the period of frontier expansion in the Peninsula, when the counts of Castile recruited men to defend their lands against the Leonese and the Muslims, as well as against their own nobles. During this expansionist phase, many peasant freeholders were transformed into *caballeros villanos*, a group characterized by an ideology of hardy self-reliance and materialist ambition. The social transformation in question is perhaps hinted at in the *Poem of the Cid's* version of the *milites/pedites* opposition. In that epic, battlefield promotions are portrayed in terms of straightforward opportunity and functional contribution: "Les que fueron de pie cavalleros se fazen" (l. 1213).[15]

Such situations are rare in the chivalric romances, which portray knights as finished products, confirmed in their social and ethical importance by their vital contribution to civil defense and their protection of the helpless, especially widows and damsels in distress. Here again a significant difference between the two genres may be discerned. In both epic and romance, the disinheritance of a

---

14 Duby, p. 52. Translation: "By its participation in the revenue derived from war and the exercise of power, and by familial alliances that blended with the blood of nobles that of certain of the luckier *boni homines*."

15 "Those who were on foot become horsemen." On knighthood in its emergent phase in Spain, see Claudio Sànchez-Albornoz, *España: un enigma histórico*, Vol. 2 (Buenos Aires: Editorial Sudamerica, 1956), p. 77. The definitive study of the Spanish commoner-knights is that of Carmela Pescador, "La caballería popular en León y Castilla." *Cuadernos de Historia de España* 33–34 (1961), 101–238; 35–36 (1962), 156–201; 37–38 (1963), 88–198; 39–40 (1964), 169–260. For social implications as they relate to such factors as kinship, social mobility and class formation, see Thomas Glick, *Islamic and Christian Spain in the Early Middle Ages* (Princeton: Princeton University Press, 1979), pp. 154–60; also Angus MacKay's introductory discussion in "The Lesser Nobility in the Kingdom of Castile," in *Gentry and Lesser Nobility in Late Medieval Europe*, ed. Michael Jones (Gloucester: Alan Sutton; New York: St. Martin's, 1986), pp. 159–62. See, with regard to the predatory aspect of chivalry, Salustiano Moreta, *Malhechores-Feudales* (Madrid: Cátedra, 1978), esp. pp. 44–81.

woman often figures prominently in stories of sieges. In the *Zamora* epic, for example, the imperiled heiress, Urraca, the sister of Sancho, defends the city and surrounding territory bequeathed to her by her father, Fernando I, against the depredation of her elder brother.[16] But what in epic is an occasional theme, in the chivalric romances becomes an obsession. Thus, in the early-fourteenth-century *Book of the Knight Zifar*, we have the siege of Galapia (Book I, pp. 40–84), and, later in the same book, a protracted siege of the capital of the kingdom of Mentón (Book II, pp. 136–59). Galapia, where the protagonist and his family linger just long enough for the hero's prowess to win the admiration and gratitude of the entire kingdom, constitutes a preview of the second, more important episode centering on the refugee Zifar's rescue of his new homeland. In the first episode a widow is the beneficiary of the hero's intervention; in the second, a princess. Both cases dramatize the plight of the female successors in terms of an imperilled estate. Similarly, towns and kingdoms in *Amadís* are generally the precariously held domain of widows and orphaned damsels. In one episode, King Lisuarte of Great Britain, the father of the hero's beloved and a renowned protector of damsels and widows, becomes himself the assailant. Madasima, the daughter and heiress of the dead giant Famongomedán, Lord of the Castle of the Boiling Lake, becomes the victim of siege warfare when Lisuarte seeks to appropriate her birthright in order to provide an inheritance for his younger daughter. Lisuarte threatening to execute hostages, including Madasima, the latter's mother declares – speaking for a number of similarly afflicted personages in these narratives – that she would sooner die than surrender (Book II, pp. 565, ll. 797–802). The long siege of Constantinople by the Turks, depicted in the latter half of the Catalan romance *Tirant lo blanc*, is portrayed in terms of despoiling a princess-heiress of her rightful inheritance. The quaintness of this view of polity as a familial domain does not impede a realistic portrayal of actual siege warfare. Thus the *Tirant* presents vivid scenes of attack and counter-attack, the pandemonium of trumpets and battle cries, the thunder of artillery, the clash of arms, the slaughter of prisoners (e.g., ch. 418). Nor can ideology be discounted, given that the work is pervasively anti-Saracen, and its mission frequently expressed in terms of "terrorizing infidels" (e.g., ch. 427). Nonetheless, the hero's mission is chiefly characterized as a personal crusade. Tirant is recruited by the imperial family to be the husband and protector of the Princess-heiress Carmesina – through his leadership of her besieged subjects to save first her lineage and her inheritance, and only secondarily the Empire which pertains to them (chs. 452–53).

As revealed in a multitude of scenes in *Amadís*, knights are the indispensable organizers and leaders of resistance to besieging forces and the salvation of the heirs and inhabitants of embattled cities. The morale of the besieged improves by the mere presence of knights: "todos los del lugar fueron mucho esforçados con su venida quando supieron quién eran" (*Amadís*, Book IV, p. 1204, ll.

---

[16] *El cantar de Sancho II*, pp. 238–51.

146–49).[17] Their leadership is revealed in the orders of the knights of Insula Firme who organize the young princes and their subjects. They convene "los más principales hombres de los suyos" in order to determine "que gente tenían por ver si auría copia para salir a pelear con los contrarios," and to see to it that all the young princes' subjects are armed and mustered "en vna gran plaça" (Book IV, p. 1204, ll. 178–87).[18] They soon lead an attack (Book IV, p. 1205) on the besieging duke's forces, a scene typical of all the romances. When the young knight Bruneo arrives with one of the young princes to an outlying city of the kingdom, the inhabitants declare: "no sabemos qué remedio tomar, pues no ay entre nos caudillo ni mayor que mandarnos sepa" (Book IV, p. 1209, ll. 513–15).[19] When Bruneo demands to know why they have not already come to the aid of the two young princes, besieged by the traitorous Duke of Sweden, a gentleman, one of "los mis honrrados de la villa," replies: "vos dezís gran verdad; mas como no tengamos quién nos guíe y nos mande, y seamos todos gentes que más por las haziendas que por las armas beuimos, no nos sabemos dar el recaudo que a nuestra lealtad conuiene" (Book IV, p. 1209, ll. 513–15, 529–36).[20]

The purpose of siege warfare as a collective project varies according to the social and economic perspective of the protagonists. The psycho-economic attitudes that characterize, on the one hand, the *Poem of the Cid*, and, on the other, the chivalric romances, give rise to distinct styles of itineration in the lives of the protagonists. Thus, while wandering is an important element in the life style of both the Cid and Amadís, the former hero's exploits support a community of followers, while the latter's adventures facilitate individual ambitions. The *Poem of the Cid* portrays the siege as a necessarily collective enterprise, the occupation of dauntless opportunists. There is a hint that siege warfare might be sporadic, migratory – the work of farmers and pastoralists who supplement their livelihood by raiding and pillage. Like those tribal practitioners of economic predation, the Bedouins, the majority of the Cid's followers appear, in other words, to be engaged in seasonal banditry. The latter practice promotes a movement of money and goods from a more prosperous zone to a less prosperous one, with the war-leader/bandit chieftain a vector of this redistributed wealth. It is, in other words, more than likely that many of those who respond to the Cid's numerous calls to arms look to a triumphant return to homeland, rather than an outright emigration in search of a new life. We may deduce this from references

17 "All those of that place were much heartened with their arrival, when they found out who they were."

18 "The most prominent men among them . . . how many people they had available to see if there would be enough to sally forth and do battle with the enemy . . . in a central square."

19 "We do not know which way to turn, since there is among us no captain or leader capable of commanding us."

20 "the most prominent of the town . . . what you say is very true; but since we have no one who might lead or command us, and we are all people who make our living more from landholding than from warfare, we are unable to give such an account of ourselves as our fealty demands."

to the greetings received from loved ones back home; from the harsh penalties (hanging, confiscation of booty) prescribed for those who abandon the campaign without permission.[21]

No such sanctions would be instituted were there no significant risk of desertion, as there is in all contexts of chronic cyclical raiding, whether the *razzia* of North Africa and the Near East, or the array of medieval Spanish practices discussed by James F. Powers, in his study of the medieval Iberian militias, under such names as *fonsado* (pp. 31–33), *arrobda* (pp. 135, 143), *rebatos* (pp. 136, 143, 149), *faciendas* (p. 146), *almofalla* (p. 158), *corredura* (pp. 158–59). The expeditionary activities covered by these terms, ranging from impromptu reconnaissance to full-scale incursion, constituted, in their aggregate, a kind of military and pseudo-military transhumance, part of the give-and-take of reciprocal and largely seasonal raiding warfare between Peninsular Christians and Muslims and an important conduit of goods and money flowing back and forth between Al-Andalus and the Christian north. For example, the *fonsado* – also known, less commonly, as *exercitus* or *expeditio* – comprised "offensive service . . . initiated by the king or his representative to go forth on campaign" (p. 15). While sieges were not the exclusive business of the *fonsado* or of the other operations, they were certainly not avoided if deemed necessary or feasible. Indeed, the municipal *militias*, which are the chief focus of Powers' study, were particularly important in siege warfare. Important incentives were provided in various charters and codes to encourage knights and infantrymen in the investments of castles and towns, and especially the latter.[22]

Chronic siege warfare is to be expected in an age before the nation state, with its consolidation of police power and elimination of private or local armies. In such conditions, the city, as Philippe Contamine has observed, is of far greater significance than the fortified castle or fortress. The latter structures, while often impregnable by virtue of geographic isolation or structural integrity, were significant chiefly in military – i.e., tactical – terms. By contrast, the strategic

---

[21] For the scene of greetings from kith and kin, see ll. 928–29. Sanctions against unauthorized departure are depicted in ll. 1249–61b. Here it should be noted that traditional societies, characterized by fierce egalitarianism, do not typically exhibit this sort of authoritarianism. In this the Cid of the poem, while in most ways a traditionalist, engages in the impromptu austerity, the pragmatic discipline, of the bandit chief who, for the purposes of the project at hand, cannot permit defection.

[22] Powers, pp. 15, 156–57. The Cid epic employs some of the terms cited by Powers, although with slightly different meanings from the codified definitions cited in the latter scholar's study. In the poem, for example, *fonsado* means simply "band," "army," "host," with, apparently, no necessary reference to the size of the group (ll. 764, 926). *Arrobda* (ll. 658, 660, 694) appears to signify "vanguard," "(group) of scouts," "patrol," perhaps even something like "reconnaissance mission." Forms related to *rebato* are *rrebata* (l. 468), *arrebata* (l. 562). They denote "assault," "sudden attack." The term *almofalla* (l. 660, 694, 1124, 1839), meaning "horde," "host," apparently refers exclusively to Moorish forces (and thus, as in l. 1124, with the derogatory connotation "rabble," "mob"). In the *Poem of the Cid*, the verb *correr*, "to run," the underlying verb of the noun *corredura*, often means "to effect an armed incursion," "to overrun," "to attack" (ll. 445, 464b, 477, 952, 958); the poem's noun form derived from this verb is *corrida* (l. 953), meaning "raid," 'foray."

importance of towns and cities is revealed by the frequency with which they are besieged. "It was absolutely vital," notes Contamine, "to control such centres of economic, administrative and human resources." The urban centers, then, with their "material and moral resources," were both more difficult to conquer than castles and more tempting for conquest: they were, affirms Contamine, "the true masters of space."[23] This pattern is particularly evident in the *Amadís*, where there are numerous sieges of cities, including London, the capital of the heroine's home kingdom, and the fortress-city of princess Madasima (Book I, pp. 295–98; Book III, pp. 673–77).[24]

The Peninsular Christian agrarian society which perfected the culture of cattle ranching, which elaborated the sheep-pasturing system of the Meseta, also supported marauding campaigns such as those depicted in the *Poema de Mio Cid*. It was this economic environment that provided the pool of manpower for sieges, and which backgrounds the enterprises of the epic hero, who, though perhaps exiled or outlawed, engages in a purposeful expedition rather than a random trajectory. In contrast to this temporary and expedient wandering of the Cid, whose earlier roaming and raiding subsidize his ultimate objective – the attack on Valencia – the wandering of Amadís and other chivalric heroes is habitual. It is the chronic itineration of the man who bides his time, who roams at random on the circuit of castles and tournaments until something happens. Itineration – derived from the Latin *iter*, "road," "journey," "way" – implies a movement continual and repetitive: always the same characteristic activity in each place, always the same set of places. Itineration, strictly speaking, is thus individualist, vocational, the mobility of those whose occupation requires touring on circuits: judges, country doctors, preachers. This sort of wandering results, therefore, not from the collective life style of clan or community, but rather from the idiosyncratic choice of participating individuals. In the *Poem of the Cid*, wandering is a temporary way of life; in the romances, it is an occupational hazard.

The typical knights of earlier European history, and the fictional knights of the Peninsular genre, engage in a quest at times intense and purposeful, at times desultory or momentarily abandoned. It is the life-course of the knight, and not any episodic interlude, however successful momentarily, that betrays his fundamentally dependent nature. The typical knight is an unmarried male. What he ultimately searches for is the means of founding an independent household, which is to say, an autonomous lineage defined by a patrilocal name, usually marked by the so-called noble particle (thus Amadís *de Gaula*, and the multitude

---

[23] Philippe Contamine, *War in the Middle Ages*, trans. Michael Jones (Oxford: Basil Blackwell, 1984), p. 101.

[24] The defense of Madasima's Castle of the Boiling Lake, the capital of her Isle of Mongaza, is actually an offense, since it involves the retaking of the fortress which has already been invested by Lisuarte's men. Amadís' men, seeking to restore Madasima to her throne, are shown carrying out an amphibious landing, involving makeshift bridges for the landing of horses (Book III, p. 673); a pitched battle, in which spears, arrows, and rocks effect severe casualties on both sides (Book III, p. 674); and an uprising among hostages and townsfolk, who assist in the overthrow of the invaders (Book III, pp. 675–76).

of names, real or fictional, linking kinship with toponymy in this well-known European naming practice).[25]

The career of the knight, as Duby has conclusively demonstrated, may be characterized, in terms of its central preoccupation, as an "heiress hunt." For it was the heiress (or widow), controlling an inheritance in the form of landed property, who offered the only practical possibility of attaining the knight's essentially domestic objective. This reflects, on the one hand, the demographic impact of agnatic practices, especially primogeniture, on medieval noble families. Younger sons, disinherited, sought fame and fortune on the circuit of wars and tournaments. Marriage to a suitable heiress, however, was the most assured means of securing, in Duby's phrase, a "bel établissement" (a nice situation). The travels of real-life knights, reflected in the wanderings and loves of their fictional embodiments, focused, therefore, on the "chasse à la fille riche" (the hunt for a rich girl).[26]

Among the knights in the romances, besiegers and defenders want the same thing: control of the city and its economic resources. By the fourteenth century, which begins the heyday of the chivalric romance, outright territorial conquest had long since ceased to be a viable alternative. We may, therefore, take this depiction of the heiress-hunting knight errant as a sublimated, allegorized expression of the unattached male's search for aggrandizement in the establishment of an agnatic lineage of his own.

It is in light of this demographic background that we may better understand the confrontation of nomadism and itineration on the one hand, and the sedentarism of the city as fortress and economic hub on the other. City, citizen, citizenship, civility, civilization – all these terms derive from and reflect an origin akin to that of the complex "bourg", "borough", "burgess", "bourgeois", "bourgeoisie." The first series tinkers itself together into a modernizing political idiom; the second has been cobbled into the Marxian jargon of socioeconomic barriers between have's and have-not's. Both continue to echo the primordial discontinuity between the social womb inside the walls, and the countryside, the wasteland, the forest, all of them the zone of operations of the epic warrior and the knight errant. Both types are outsiders who want in. The distinction between them resides in the intended use of the bourgeois *locus amoenus*. The Cid and his men want to take towns by storm, to conquer for reasons of plunder and tribute. Their intent is appropriation. The knight of the chivalric romance, by contrast, wants to be absorbed by the amniotic, intramural

---

[25] Karl Ferdinand Werner, "Liens de parenté et noms de personne," in *Famille et parenté dans l'occident médiéval*, eds. Georges Duby and Jacques Le Goff (Rome: École Française de Rome, 1977), pp. 25–34 (esp. pp. 25–29, 32). See also Karl Schmid, "The Structure of the Nobility in the Earlier Middle Ages," in *The Medieval Nobility*, ed. Timothy Reuter (Amsterdam: North-Holland Publishing Company, 1978), pp. 37–59.

[26] Georges Duby, "Dans la France du Nord-Ouest au XIIe siècle: les 'Jeunes' dans la société aristocratique," in his *Hommes et structures du Moyen Âge* (Paris: Mouton, 1973), pp. 213–25 (esp. pp. 221–22).

polity, even as he dreams of being its savior and its master. His objective, in other words, is assimilation rather than acquisition.

The respective attitudes are reflected in diametrically opposed perspectives on money and markets. To understand this point of contrast requires some deciphering of the texts' superficial idiom. The *Poem of the Cid*, as Miguel Garci-Gómez has pointed out, "is replete with commercial language and trading activities." Wealth is "an obsession." Both the hero and his principal adversaries, the Infantes de Carrión, are consumed by the search for "haberes monedados" (i.e., cash money), as well as the pursuit of estates, property, and goods (p. 229).[27] Duggan explains the role of property and commodities, and their distribution in the economy of the *Poem of the Cid*, in terms of Spanish feudalism. While the landed fief was the basis of classic feudalism north of the Pyrenees, the Peninsula, throughout the period of the Reconquest (roughly ninth through mid-thirteenth centuries) tended to emphasize the "conferral of movable goods" (p. 19). Duggan points out the extreme variety and detail with which the booty taken in the poem is depicted and the meticulous portrayal of procedures for weighing, counting, reckoning, and divvying up. Gold, silver, coin, weaponry, tents, clothing, slaves, camels and horses – all these and more figure in the poet's depiction of property acquired and redistributed through siege and battle (pp. 20–22).

The Cid does not hesitate to "dirty his hands" in the pursuit of cash to finance his expedition into exile. A famous scene shows him bilking the two moneylenders, Rachel and Vidas, of six hundred marks. Pawning a chest filled with sand which his lieutenant, Martín Antolínez, has declared to be filled with treasure, the Cid, a brazen, though reluctant, con man (ll. 84, 95), assures them that so long as they live, the moneylenders will never regret the agreement they have made (ll. 100–158). Later, the usurers, so eager to accept the deal for the expected interests, discover the hoax to their dismay (ll. 1431–38).

Garci-Gómez suggests that because of the commercial importance of Burgos – the city most conspicuously connected with the historical and poetic Cid – and because of the early prominence of that emporium's bourgeoisie, a mercantile life-style emerged that was imbued with "commercial interest and the love of money" (p. 229). This twelfth-century environment, Garci-Gómez affirms, greatly influenced the composition of the poem as we know it. He contends that this "is indeed a very special type of song with a special type of epic hero: the epic song and the epic hero of the bourgeoisie" (p. 229). Because the Cid seeks at all times to increase his earnings, like the merchant defined in the *Partidas* (V.vii.1–2) as the man motivated by the desire to garner wealth, we may speak of this poem, then, as one which conveys the message: "go forth and become rich" (p. 229).

While it is true that the bourgeois and the merchant may identify with epic warriors – one thinks of those Japanese business manuals based on samurai

---

[27] Miguel Garci-Gómez, "The Economy of the Cid," in *Romance Epic*, ed. Hans-Eric Keller (Kalamazoo MI: The Medieval Institute, 1987), pp. 228–29.

codes of conduct – it is by no means certain that the epic warrior, no matter how materialist, identifies with the merchant. Colin Smith has noted that the Cid, as seen in his dealings with the Jewish moneylenders, may hardly be considered the upstanding bourgeois, paying off his bills in respectable fashion.[28] The Cid's acceptance of "street-level" money-making, haggling, and even the expeditious swindle, precisely opposes the knight errant's studious avoidance of questions monetary. The paradox of economic attitudes in epic and romance is that the genre which denies economy is the more bourgeois of the two. The knight errant ignores money and property sought or obtained for their own sake, thus incarnating, among other things, the ethical criterion imposed by the *Partidas*: that those most worthy of reward are precisely those who perform great deeds "non por miedo de pena nin por cobdicia de gualardon que esperen haber, mas por facer lo mejor por bondat que ha en sí naturalmente" (II.xxvii.2).[29] Maurice Keen, referring to this aspect of the chivalric mentality, observes that it was considered a characteristic of poor knights to attend tournaments with a specific eye toward booty, horses, and ransomable captives. More praiseworthy, however, were those who competed in tournaments or made war solely to enhance their honor and to gain renown for themselves and their lineage, or who performed valiant feats of arms for love (*par amours*) of their mistress.[30]

The knight's adventures, which seem to have to do with everything but economic reality, are in point of fact a direct result of his ultimate objective, which, as it centers on marriage, family, and property, is entirely economic in nature. Knight errantry is an itineration which achieves its consummation in marriage defined as a social, political and economic arrival. The centerpiece of the chivalric dream, the household, is a complex residential formation. Headed by a patriarch presiding over a nuclear family, and marked by a tendency to extend family membership through adoption and fosterage, the household enhanced its prestige by increasing its size and complexity. The ambitious noble youth of history, as well as many social climbing commoners aspiring to a noble status confirmed by possession of landed property, often grew up in extended households of this very type. The residential pattern, in any event, was regarded as a principal element in the status profile of the successful man.[31]

---

[28] Colin Smith, "Did the Cid Pay the Jews?," *Romania* 86 (1965), 520–38 (esp. p. 537).

[29] "Not by reason of fear of punishment nor desire for reward which they might wish to obtain, but rather in order to do the proper thing by reason of that goodness which they naturally have in themselves."

[30] Maurice Keen, *Chivalry* (New Haven: Yale University Press, 1984), p. 13. We may also point out the overt penalties prescribed for those nobles or knights who worked for money. The *Partidas*, for example (II.xxi.12), assert that the title of knight has traditionally been denied or revoked for whomever "por su persona anduuiesse faziendo mercaduría." (personally goes about engaging in commerce). The law further states that "ninguno non recibiesse honrra de caualleria, por precio de auer, nin de otra cosa que diesse por ella, que fuesse como en manera de conpra" ("no one should receive the honor and title of chivalry, in exchange for payment of money, nor anything else that might be by way of purchase").

[31] David Herlihy, *Medieval Households* (Cambridge: Harvard University Press, 1985), pp. 82–83; Duby, "Dans la France du Nord-Ouest au XIIe siècle," pp. 213–25 (esp. p. 220).

Far from being the "knight of sovereign prowess" described by Maurice Keen, the knight of the Peninsular chivalric romances is, in fact, a remarkably insecure, dependent creature. His valor, martial proficiency, and all-around machismo are only meaningful – or even functional – in terms of service to a specific king or lord, or, more significantly, a specific lady who is the daughter or sister of this authority figure. But the knight's servitude is not the love-service of the Provençal poets, which was more often than not adulterous, showing sexual rivalry between hero and husband. The amorous servitude of Amadís and his brethren, focusing on the hope of eventual matrimony and foundation of an autonomous household, defines the hero's chief adversaries as those very rivals who dispute the castle, estate, or town that is the object of the siege and, ultimately, of the marital suit, which is usually the basis of the contention.

Here, again, the two genres might seem at first to coincide. But the dissimilarity of their genealogical perspectives points to an underlying discontiunity. Bakhtin speaks of the epic and its world as one of the "national heroic past," a dimension of "fathers and founders of families" (p. 13). At the same time, it is of course not the past which is represented. The epic is characterized, rather, by a "transferral of a represented world into the past, and the degree to which this world participates in the past" (p. 13). The author of epic speaks "about a past that is to him inaccessible, the reverent point of view of a descendant" (p. 13). Adapting Bakhtin's terms, we may say that the Cid's orientation with regard to siege warfare shows his affinity to the heroes and monarchs of the *Iliad*. The Cid, depicted as the founder of his line (cf. ll. 3724–25, the poet's reference to present-day kings now related to the Cid), represents what the anthropologists call the apical ancestor of his lineage. For him, the successful siege facilitates a dynastic project which we may characterize, to paraphrase R. Howard Bloch's analysis of genealogical mentalities, as a "biopolitical" enterprise.[32]

The dilemma of the knight errant, by contrast, parallels that of the parasitical suitors of the *Odyssey*, that most romance-like of epics. Rivals for the attention of a woman in control of landed property, the suitors, like the rival knights of the romances, show little sense of that comradeship said to be the hallmark of the epic. The Cid and his men, like the heroes of the *Iliad* at their most purposeful, are teammates in siege warfare practiced as collective aggression. Where dissension or insubordination occur, they are portrayed as side issues, as distractions – as deviations from warrior's business, which is the taking of strongholds and the sharing-out of pillage. For the knight of romances, the besieged place represents less a heroic opportunity than a desirable concentration of resources – the means of maintaining a household which in turn supports a style of life defined as chivalric.

---

[32] R. Howard Bloch, *Medieval French Literature and Law* (Berkeley: University of California Press, 1977), p. 162.

The Slings and Arrows of Outrageous Love in the *Roman de la rose*

Heather Arden
University of Cincinnati

What can be said for certain about the *Roman de la rose*? It is a 22,000-line allegorical dream-vision in two parts, the first written by Guillaume de Lorris (*c.* 1225), the second by Jean de Meun (*c.* 1270), both from the province of Orléans. While nothing certain is known about the author of the first 4,000 lines except what the second one states in the poem itself,[1] Guillaume appears to have been of noble birth and to have received some education.[2] There is much more information about Jean de Meun, who lived in Paris and had apparently studied at the Sorbonne in the second half of the thirteenth century, a time of great intellectual turmoil and change. In addition to composing his 18,000-line continuation of the *Rose*, Jean translated five Latin works, including Vegetius' military treatise *Epitoma rei militari*, Boethius' *De consolatione Philosophiae*, and appropriately enough for the poet who will later write on all kinds of love, the letters of Abelard and Heloise.[3] Another aspect of the literary history of the *Rose* is also beyond dispute – its literary importance. It has been called

---

[1] See ll. 10496–648 of Felix Lecoy's edition, *Le roman de la rose*, 3 vols. (Paris: Honoré Champion, 1965–75). Subsequent references to the *Rose* will be to this edition.

[2] Questions about the historical reality of Guillaume de Lorris have been raised by David F. Hult, *Self-Fulfilling Prophecies: Readership and Authority in the First "Roman de la rose"* (Cambridge: Cambridge University Press, 1986), and by Roger Dragonetti in *Le mirage des sources: l'art du faux dans le roman médiéval* (Paris: Éds. du Seuil, 1987) and in "Pygmalion ou les pièges de la fiction dans le *Roman de la rose*" in his *La musique et les lettres: études de littérature médiévale* (Geneva: Droz, 1986), pp. 381–97.

[3] Leena Löfstedt, ed., *Li abregemenz noble honme Vegesce Flave René des establissemenz apartenanz a chevalerie, traduction par Jean de Meun* (Helsinki: Suomalainen Tiedeakatemia, 1977); V. L. Dedeck-Héry, ed., "Boethius' *De Consolatione* by Jean de Meun," *Mediaeval Studies* 14 (1952), 165–275; Eric Hicks, ed., *La vie et les epistres Pierres Abaelart et Heloys sa fame: traduction du XIIIe siècle attribuée à Jean de Meun*, 2 vols. [1 vol. to date] (Geneva: Slatkine; Paris: Champion, 1991). The intriguing hypothesis that Jean de Meun may have written as well as translated the letters is outlined by Hubert Silvestre in "L'idylle d'Abélard et Héloïse: la part du roman," *Bulletin de la classe des lettres et des sciences morales et politiques de l'Acaémie royale de Belgique*, 5th series 70 (1985), 157–200.

"historically and perhaps esthetically the most important single work of literature produced during the medieval period," "the undisputed French masterpiece of erotic allegory," and "medieval France's greatest poem, a work without which Dante's *Comedy* would have been inconceivable."[4] What cannot be agreed on is what the *Rose* is about.[5]

While scholars have been disputing the question of the meaning of the *Roman de la rose*, Jean de Meun appears to reveal its subject in the dedication to his translation of Boethius' *De consolatione*, where he introduces himself to his patron, Philippe le Bel, as "je Jean de Meun, qui jadis, ou Rommant de la Rose, puis que Jalousie ot mis en prison Bel Acueil, enseignai la maniere du chastel prendre et de la rose cueillir" (I, Jean de Meun, who formerly, in the *Roman de la rose*, when Jealousy had imprisoned Warm Welcome, taught the way to take the castle and to pluck the rose).[6] Although the castle is clearly one of the central ideas of the romance, as well as one of the most widespread erotic images in medieval literature,[7] scholars have given it little attention. There is only one article on the hand-to-hand combat that takes place outside the castle, and no extended study of the metaphor of the castle itself.[8] It is worth following up Jean's observation on the castle for a number of reasons, especially for what it can reveal about the castle as part of what I would like to call "the military-erotic complex" of the poem. This complex includes not only the castle but the siege and other aggressive elements such as the arrows of the God of Love. Ultimately I believe the function of this military-erotic complex can better be understood as an expression of male-female relations in medieval literature.

Angus Fletcher, in *Allegory: The Theory of a Symbolic Mode*, observes that: "The tendency is for allegories to resolve themselves into either of two basic forms. . . . The two may be labeled *battle* and *progress*."[9] One indication of the allegorical complexity of the *Rose* is that it does both. The dream begins as a

---

4 William Calin, *A Muse for Heroes: Nine Centuries of the Epic in France* (Toronto: University of Toronto Press, 1983), p. 125; Aldo S. Bernardo, "Sex and Salvation in the Middle Ages: From the *Romance of the Rose* to the *Divine Comedy*," *Italica* 67 (1990), 305–18 (esp. p. 311); Karl D. Uitti, "The Myth of Poetry in Twelfth- and Thirteenth-Century France," in *The Binding of Proteus: Perspectives on Myth and the Literary Process*, eds. Majorie W. McCune, Tucker Orbison, and Philip M. Withim (Lewisburg: Bucknell University Press; London: Associated University Presses, 1980), pp. 142–56 (esp. p. 150).

5 See Charles Lenient, *La Satire en France au Moyen Âge* (Paris: Hachette, 1883), p. 116: "Si l'on en excepte l'Apocalypse, nous ne croyons pas qu'aucun livre ait subi autant d'explications." (With the exception of the Apocalypse, we do not believe that any book has undergone so many interpretations.)

6 Dedeck-Héry, ed., p. 168 (all translations are mine).

7 Calin (p. 123) has pointed out that "assault on a fortress is a fundamental image of love-conquest."

8 Thérèse Bouché, "Burlesque et renouvellement des formes: l'attaque du château dan le *Roman de la rose* de Jean de Meun," in *Hommage à Jean-Charles Payen: farai chansoneta novele: essais sur la liberté créatrice au Moyen Âge* (Caen: Centre de Publications de l'Université de Caen, 1989), pp. 87–98.

9 Angus Fletcher, *Allegory: The Theory of a Symbolic Mode* (Ithaca: Cornell University Press, 1964), p. 151.

progress, as the Dreamer moves through a springtime landscape and finds and enters the Garden of Deduit (Amorous Diversion). He observes the ugly people portrayed on the outer wall and the beautiful people inside the garden in Love's dance, and he wanders about the garden, past the Fountain of Narcissus to some rosebushes, where he spots the most beautiful bud of all. At this point, the God of Love shoots the hero with his arrows, simultaneously transforming the Dreamer into the Lover and the allegorical progress into a battle between the forces that support or oppose passionate love. The unity of the *Rose* is, therefore, more a function of the conflictual mode of the allegory, rather than of the theme of the lover's progress, as scholars have suggested.[10] That is, rather than approaching such crucial elements as the speeches of the personifications (Reason, Nature, and the others) as part of the Dreamer's progress in love, they are better understood as another tactic in the war to take the castle.

This War of the Rose, so to speak, is made up of both aggressive and defensive elements. The castle constitutes the major defensive element, which also includes the wall around the garden. The siege of the castle and the erotic weapons of the God of Love and Venus are major aggressive elements. While many of these elements are found in earlier works, such as Ovid's poetry and many courtly romances, I believe that the *Rose* is the first work to offer a full arsenal of castle, siege, and aggressive gods of love: it is the work in which the military-erotic complex is found at its most developed. I would like to look briefly at the aggressive aspects of the conflict before discussing the castle itself.

Cupid's arrows have become such an erotic cliché that it is difficult to believe the image may have been invented by one writer, but according to Edmond Faral, it was Ovid "à qui on est d'accord pour en attribuer l'invention; car elle ne se rencontre nulle part ailleurs avant lui" (it is Ovid to whom people agree to attribute the invention, for it is found nowhere before him).[11] Faral cites the passage in the *Metamorphoses* where Cupid antagonizes Phoebus by drawing his bow: "You naughty boy, [says Phoebus] what have you to do with a warrior's arms?"[12] Furthermore, already in this early passage Cupid's erotic armory is divided into categories of darts with different properties, as they are in the *Rose*: "The one puts love to flight, the other kindles it. That which kindles love is golden, and shining, sharp-tipped; but that which puts it to flight is blunt, its shaft tipped with lead."[13] This image of Cupid, the omnipotent archer, became popular with other Latin writers such as Catullus and, in the twelfth century,

---

[10] In particular, Alan M. F. Gunn, *The Mirror of Love: A Reinterpretation of the "Romance of the Rose"* (Lubbock: Texas Tech Press, 1952).

[11] Edmond Faral, *Recherches sur les sources latines des contes et romans courtois du Moyen Âge* (Paris: Honoré Champion, 1967), p. 144.

[12] Ovid, *The Metamorphoses*, trans. Mary M. Innes (Hammondsworth, Middlesex: Penguin Books, 1955), p. 41.

[13] Ovid, p. 41.

with French romance writers, in great part due to the use of the image in the *Roman d'Eneas*.[14]

The imagery of Cupid's shafts is expanded in the first part of the *Rose*, where Guillaume de Lorris names the five arrows with which the God of Love shoots the Dreamer – Beauté, Simpleice, Courtoisie, Compaignie, and Biau Samblant (Beauty, Simplicity, Courtesy, Company, and Fair Appearance; see ll. 1679–879) – and describes in detail the sweet suffering they cause. While these themes of love-inspiring qualities and the delicious pain of love are commonplaces by the time of Guillaume de Lorris, one finds in his account a significant innovation in the image of the arrows of love. After the Dreamer has chosen the most beautiful rosebud, the God of Love lets fly with the first arrow:

> et tret a moi par tel devise
> que par mi l'ueil m'a ou cuer mise
> sa saiete par grant roidor . . . (ll. 1691–93)
>
> [and shoots at me in such a way that he put the arrow firmly into
> my heart through my eye]

This scene combines, for the first time, two widespread but distinct themes: that of Cupid the archer and the darts of love sent by one person's eye to enter the eye of the viewer and to lodge in the heart. Thus, in earlier versions it was the eyes of the (future) beloved that sent the arrow into the (future) lover's heart, while the God of Love simply shot his victims either in the eye or the body. Guillaume's new version effectively removes the beloved as the source of love's arrows that affect the heart through the eye and substitutes for her the male deity (see Figure 1).

This first overt conflict in the *Rose* – between the God of Love and the Dreamer – becomes a military alliance when the Dreamer-now-Lover agrees to be Cupid's vassal, thereby feudalizing Ovid's warrior imagery. This tendency to feudalize love's conflicts may be linked with the surge in popularity of the aggressive image of love in twelfth-century France. Thus the amorous feelings that the Dreamer has begun to experience for a woman have been translated into an armed conflict, in which the protagonist feels himself to be the victim of an embattled attack by a male deity, who wounds and captures him. This imagery relating to the God of Love has of course many connotations, both psychological and mystical, and is certainly in part a projection of an aspect of the Lover's self.[15] It is significant that in courtly romance it is most commonly the male

[14] Faral, pp. 143–46. See also Ruth Cline's detailed study of arrow imagery relating to love in "Heart and Eyes," *Romance Philology* 25 (1972), 263–97. Eugene Vance has discussed the "dialectique de l'érotique," the conjoining of love and conflict in lyric poetry and in the romances of Chrétien de Troyes, in "Le combat érotique chez Chrétien de Troyes: de la figure à la forme," *Poétique* 12 (1972), 544–71. However, he sees the aggressive expression of love as normal and necessary, while I argue that it is largely a cultural construct.

[15] According to Winthrop Wetherbee: "The castle that immures the Rose is a projection of this sense of inner bondage, an image of the Lover's despair that constitutes the antithesis to the rose garden that had focused his initial innocent desire" ("The *Romance of the Rose* and

lover who is shot by Cupid's arrows, who is given the military expression of the love experience. For the purposes of this discussion it is on the specifically warlike aspect of the male love experience that I want to focus our attention.

These aggressive elements lead in the *Rose* to a related military image, that of the prison of love, for as a logical consequence of his defeat, the Lover becomes the God of Love's delighted prisoner. Prison imagery recurs in the *Rose* when the personification, Bel Accueil (Warm Welcome), and the rosebushes are imprisoned in the castle by Jalousie, but here the basis of the imprisonment seems to be the opposite of the Lover's: the male lover is a prisoner when he loves, the female beloved when she resists or is prevented from loving. Thus while the prison is a positive image for the lover, translating his feelings of being overwhelmed by the force of love and of remaining loyal come what may, for the woman it is a negative image, suggesting the barriers she or her society have thrown up to defend or protect her from "love" (castle as contraceptive, so to speak).

The other warlike deity in the *Rose* is Venus, Cupid's mother, who intervenes twice. In the first part she uses her torch to warm up Warm Welcome, who is cool to the idea of the lover kissing the rose. In the second she shoots her torch, which has become a fiery arrow, into the castle, setting it aflame and causing the enemies of love to flee. Much could be and has been said about the significance of Venus in the *Rose*; what interests me here is her weapon. According to a study by Carlos Alvar, in works such as Ovid's *Ars amatoria*, *Remedia amoris*, and *Amores*, the torch was an attribute of Cupid, not Venus. Alvar argues that Guillaume de Lorris created "un attribut tout à fait nouveau'[16] (a completely new attribute) in handing the torch to Venus – an understandable new attribute, if Venus suggests the fire of physical desire that can overcome a woman's resistance to love. But Jean de Meun changes Venus' torch into the more masculine arrow in order to overcome Jalousie's anti-amorous forces. The significance of this change will be apparent when one looks at the taking of the castle.

The last aggressive element is the combat between mental states, or psychomachia, that occurs in front of the castle. This is of course a traditional element of allegory going back to late Latin writers and before. C. S. Lewis, in *The Allegory of Love*, argues that the appeal of the psychomachia in late Antiquity and early Christianity is a function both of the decline of classical mythology and the increased importance of the idea of internal moral conflict, the *bellum intestinum*, as a conception of the human mind. In Seneca, for example, there are metaphors for moral experience "borrowed from the battle-field and the arena."[17] In late Latin literature, the emphasis on moral conflict led to an

Medieval Allegory," in *European Writers: The Middle Ages and the Renaissance*, ed. W. T. H. Jackson, Vol. 1 [New York: Scribners, 1983], pp. 309–35; esp. p. 327).

[16] Carlos Alvar, "Oiseuse, Venus, Luxure: trois dames et un miroir," *Romania* 106 (1985), 108–17; esp. p. 114.

[17] C. S. Lewis, *The Allegory of Love: A Study in Medieval Tradition* (London: Oxford University Press, 1936), p. 63.

exploration of the inner world, which is "already on the verge of allegory."[18] This agonistic moral view, taken up by early Christianity, was expressed in Prudentius' fourth-century work, *Psychomachia*, as a hand-to-hand combat between such personified virtues and vices as Patientia, Sobrietas, Libido, and Luxuria (Patience, Sobriety, Desire, Lust). Prudentius eloquently summarizes the concept at the end of the *Psychomachia*: "Savage war rages hotly, rages within our bones, and man's two-sided nature is in an uproar of rebellion."[19] The allegory of moral conflict was reworked many times before the *Rose*, in such works as Alan of Lille's *Anticlaudianus* and Huon de Méri's *Torneiment Anticrist*.[20]

It is noteworthy that the psychomachic conflict of the *Rose* is entirely an erotic one – a logical development, since the *Roman de la rose* sees love as an inherently conflictual experience. The character Raison, for example, describes love in a famous series of oxymorons (based on Alan of Lille's *De planctu Naturae*):[21] it is loving hate, loyal disloyalty, confident fear, desperate hope (and so on, for 42 lines; see *Rose*, ll. 4263–304). Above all it is the "douz mal" (sweet suffering; l. 4283) and "leesce dolente" (sad gladness; l. 4590). These oppositions suggest a psychomachic image of love in brief, which the narrative structure of the romance plays out. But in the *Rose*, amorous conflict is not simply experienced on the psychological level, that is, in the mind of one or both of the lovers – it is also exists on two other levels, between the lovers themselves as well as between them and their society. The goal of the conflict is not simply a moral victory, or bliss in the Hereafter, as in the religious psychomachiae, but an actual physical prize – sexual possession of the woman. For these reasons the erotic conflict in the *Rose* is particularly complex.

Already in the first part Guillaume de Lorris suggests a psychomachic structure through the implied opposition between the images of the uncourtly "vices" frozen forever on the wall of the garden (Villainie, Tristesse, Vieillesse, Pauvreté, Envie [Vilainy, Sadness, Old Age, Poverty, Envy] and their sisters) and the beautiful noble "virtues" eternally dancing and loving in the Garden (Courtoisie, Beauté, Jeunesse [Courtliness, Beauty, Youth], etc.). Although there is witnessed no direct confrontation, the courtly virtues can be seen to have won an implied victory. Secondly, Guillaume de Lorris creates a series of skirmishes in the mind of the beloved between erotic feelings, such as Bel Accueil, Franchise, Pitié, and Courtoisie (Warm Welcome, Openness, Pity, Courtliness), and anti-erotic feelings and forces, including Dangier, Peur, Honte, and Male Bouche (Resistance, Fear, Shame, and Slander). The narrator says that the God of Love

---

[18] Lewis, p. 60.

[19] Prudentius, *Psychomachia*, in *Prudentius*, trans. H. J. Thomson, Vol. 1 (Cambridge: Harvard University Press; London: William Heinemann, 1949), pp. 274–343 (esp. p. 343).

[20] Alan of Lille, *Anticlaudianus*, trans. James J. Sheridan (Toronto: Pontifical Institute of Mediaeval Studies, 1973); Huon de Méri, *"Le torneiment Anticrist": A Critical Edition*, ed. Margaret O. Bender (University, Miss. Romance Monographs, 1976).

[21] Alan of Lille, *The Plaint of Nature*, trans. James J. Sheridan (Toronto: Pontifical Institute of Mediaeval Studies, 1980), pp. 149–50.

will eventually take the castle that Jalousie built to defend the roses (ll. 3485–86), but the apparently unfinished state of the first part prevents the readers from knowing how this conflict would have developed.[22]

Amorous conflict in the first part of the *Rose* is, therefore, limited to threats, blandishments, deception, and the immuring of the rose. It is in the second part that war erupts and the castle is taken. In addition to the subtler confrontational methods of the first part, Jean de Meun develops the overt military elements when the God of Love assembles his barons and attacks the castle, an assault which takes place in two parts. First the forces of Love and the roses' jailers fight to a draw before the castle; then Venus arrives and burns it down. The description of the psychomachic combat between the two armies plays with traditional literary elements, such as allegorical weapons, epic insults, and more or less appropriate battle behavior. In her study of these elements, Thérèse Bouché argues that Jean de Meun burlesqued traditional literary descriptions of internal conflict in order to show the chaotic nature of amorous feelings.[23] But one also needs to look at the conflict of the *Rose* in terms of the military-erotic subtext: what does such military imagery say about psychological conflict concerning love's ambivalences, about conflict between lovers (that is, seduction and resistance), and finally about conflict between the lovers and society?

The give-and-take of the combat during the siege of the castle can be summarized briefly. Noble Franchise approaches the peasant Dangier, but is no match for his crude violence and misogyny. She has been reduced to begging for mercy when her friend Pitié arrives to save her, which she does by weeping so profusely on Dangier that she not only softens him up but almost drowns him. Another guardian of the rose, Honte, exhorts her companion Dangier by describing, in horticultural terms, the possible impregnation of the rose if they lose the battle; then she uses her sword, made of "soussi d'aperçoivement" (anxiety about being observed), to render Pitié speechless. Deliz (Pleasure) rushes to her defense, accompanied by a young knight called Bien Celer (Skillful Concealment), and they manage to beat back Shame. The third and final guardian of the rose, Shame's cousin, Peur, jumps in and attempts to hack Bien Celer to pieces. He calls in Hardement (Boldness), a tournament champion, and finally Seurtez (Security), who attacks Peur, and a general mêlée follows. Yet despite the fact that the God of Love's forces outnumber the defenders two to one, they are losing, and the God of Love calls a truce.

C. S. Lewis and others have maintained that this passage is a psychological description of what goes on in a young lady's mind when she is being courted.[24] But can these allegorical characters be seen simply as personifying aspects of

---

[22] For speculations on how Guillaume might have ended the *Rose*, see Douglas Kelly, " 'Li chastiaus . . . Qu'Amors prist puis par ses esforz': The Conclusion of Guillaume de Lorris' *Rose*," in *A Medieval French Miscellany*, ed. Norris J. Lacy (Lawrence: University of Kansas Press, 1972), pp. 61–78. In *Self-Fulfilling Prophecies*, David Hult argues that the first part may be complete as is (see my review of his argument in *Speculum* 66.1 [1991], 170–73).

[23] Bouché, pp. 87–98.

[24] Lewis, pp. 131, 135–36.

her mind? It is possible that Franchise, who suggests openness and friendliness (and was one of the arrows that cause love), and Dangier, who is usually interpreted to mean the lady's proud resistance to love, are personifications of a conflict in the lady's mind when she is confronted with her suitor's desires. Honte and Peur suggest that her anxiety is about the social consequences of giving in, rather than a direct concern with virtue; and these feelings of anxiety may be stronger than her natural feeling of pity for the poor suffering lover, despite the reassurances that the personifications Delit, Hardement, and Seurtez give her.

But it is also clear that many of these feelings do not reflect spontaneous psychological movements in the woman's mind but responses to the lover and to other people in her surroundings. Pleasure certainly suggests feelings that result from the lover's words or behavior; feelings of boldness and security or assurance may describe his words or actions. In fact there is a progressive masculinization of the barons of love. Three new male personifications are introduced in the conflict, and this turns the psychomachia away from an inner conflict in a woman's mind and toward a struggle between the desiring, importunate lover and the fearful, defensive lady. And behind them lurk the social forces that inspire fear and shame, suggested by Jalousie and Chasteté (Chastity), who owns the roses.

One also discovers in this supposed socio-psychological allegory an increasingly burlesque realism in the detailed descriptions of the warriors and their armaments. Described in comic detail are their lances and daggers, shields and bucklers, as well as the blows and parries of the mêlée. Franchise, for example, brandishes her lance and throws it against Dangier, and though his shield splits, it is strong enough to protect his belly from being cut open. The conflict ends in a hyperbolic free-for-all: "Never," exclaims the narrator, "have you seen such a combat, never in any tourney have such blows rained down" (ll. 15582–96). Clearly there is more going on, in a literary sense, than an internal conflict between desire and repugnance. Jean has appropriated for satiric purposes the venerable psychomachic battle as he will appropriate the castle image for satiric reversal of courtly erotic imagery.

The detailed description of the major defensive element in the *Rose*, the castle, is surprising in a courtly allegory of love and seduction. In the first part, Guillaume tells how Jalousie, desiring to protect the roses from dangerous liaisons by immuring them along with the too-friendly Bel Accueil, summons all the masons and earth-workers in the country and spends great sums to build not a simple enclosure but a full-fledged fortress (described ll. 3779–919), with moat and four-sided outer wall of hewn stone built on solid rock and thicker at the bottom than the top, each side being 100 "toises" (fathoms) long. The square curtain wall has four main towers at the corners and small towers along the walls; there are four fortified gates with portcullises, one in each wall, that are impervious to catapults. In the center is a great, high, round tower, also resistant to artillery because it is built of natural rock – judged to be very strong – and mortar mixed with vinegar and quick lime. The rose bushes have been planted between this inner wall and the tower for greatest protection. The fortress's weaponry includes the medieval versions of Scud missiles – mangonels and other siege weapons, such as "arbelestes a tor" (l. 3840), and it is manned by Jalousie's four lieutenants, Dangier, Honte, Peur, and Male Bouche, who in turn command troops of Norman mercenaries.[25] All of this simply to defend the roses from seducers and preserve their chastity?

This detailed description of a castle led the nineteenth-century architect Viollet-le-Duc to argue that it is a representation of a real castle – the Louvre of Philippe-Auguste (see Figure 2).[26] He calls Guillaume de Lorris' description of a castle "[l]'une des plus anciennes, des plus complètes et plus curieuses" (122) in medieval literature and observes the mixture of historically accurate and inaccurate details. The fact that the *Rose* castle's walls are twice as long as the Louvre's he attributes to poetic exaggeration, but the rest of the description is generally realistic. It was unusual for a castle at that time to have four gates and a tower in the center, but the Louvre had these features, in part because it was built near Paris and thus was used to "maintenir la population dans le respect."[27] The round dungeon of the Louvre was also a treasury, as is the tower in the romance, which guards the woman's "treasure," her chastity. The detail of mortar mixed with vinegar and quick lime puzzled Viollet-le-Duc, as these substances do not seem to have been used in mortar in the Middle Ages, but Guillaume's statement that the artillery could be seen over the curtain wall is exact, according to Viollet-le-Duc, who argues that curtain walls were built low in that period. The architect further points to the precision of Guillaume's description of the garrison, with each tower defended by an independent troop of men under their captain, a defensive system which he believed reflected the "morcellement féodal" of the time.[28] It can be added to Viollet-le-Duc's observations that the lower level of this thirteenth-century castle, which can be seen in the present-day Louvre museum, does resemble the castle in the *Rose*, with towers at the four corners, four doors, and the round, as opposed to square, tower in the center.

Clearly Guillaume de Lorris enjoyed creating this elaborate fortress, over and beyond the needs of his allegorical love story. One can speculate on what this passage reveals of Guillaume's literary history – was he hoping to amuse and please a royal patron? Had he lived in the Louvre or did he simply think of it as the quintessential castle? But as useful as the answers to these questions would be, it is the fortress' allegorical significance that most concerns this study.

Castles appear frequently in medieval allegorical literature, both religious and

[25] See René G. B. Mongeau's "Thirteenth-Century Siege Weapons and Machines in *L'art de chevalerie*," *Allegorica* 7 (1987), 123–43; for a discussion of Jean de Meun's use of terms for siege weapons, see his translation of Vegetius' *Epitoma rei militari* (n. 3 above).

[26] Eugène-Emmanuel Viollet-le-Duc, *Dictionnaire raisoné de l'architecture française du XIe au XVIe siècle*, Vol. 3 (Paris: B. Bance, 1857), pp. 122–28.

[27] Viollet-le-Duc, p. 123, n. 3.

[28] Viollet-le-Duc, p. 126, n. 2.

secular.[29] The castle is often an allegory of the Church, the human body, or the Virgin Mary, as in Robert Grosseteste's *Château d'amour*.[30] It also appears in medieval love poetry. In a *chanson courtoise* by the twelfth-century troubadour, Giraut de Borneil, the poet describes himself as though he were in a castle besieged by grim barons ("fortz senhors"), the towers of which are attacked by catapults and mangonels, while a fierce onslaught rages on every side and those within cry out in great anguish for mercy, just as the poet is humbly crying for mercy from his "bona domna, pros e valens," his good lady, noble and worthy.[31] A similar image of the lover is found in the narrative work, the *Roman de la poire*, probably written shortly after the first part of the *Rose*: the lover-narrator claims that Amor assaults him every day in his "tor orgueilleuse et haute." Amor in the *Roman de la poire* is supported by hundreds and thousands of sergeants and knights, commanded by Beauté, Courtoisie, Noblesse, and Franchise. As with the image of the prison of love, in these works it is the poor lover who imagines himself besieged by Love and his lady, it is the lover who has chosen a military image to translate his erotic feelings of helplessness and suffering.

The castle in the *Rose* serves, of course, the realistic purpose of defending the woman's chastity, as observed above, but, in addition, the imagery associated with the castle in the final assault suggests a complex metaphor for women's sexuality. The castle is a liminal structure, on the boundary of two worlds, of two psyches, and, as such, it both protects and repels: the castle both keeps people in (the roses/women) and out (the seducers). In this sense, it is easy to understand the castle as a metaphor for the fears and resistance of the woman and her society in the face of male erotic aggression. Although a character imagined by Ami (Friend), the Jealous Husband believes that any woman can be seduced, just as any tower can be taken if assaulted from all sides (ll. 8565–66), the tower in the *Rose* serves as a defensive structure, for so long as the woman is seen as an individual imprisoned in the castle, the lover cannot get to her. When the castle is finally taken, when Venus is able to shoot her firebrand, it is because the woman has become the castle. As the poem says, Venus

> ... avise, con bone archiere,
> par une petitete archiere
> qu'ele vit en la tour reposte,
> par devant, non pas par ancoste,

---

29 See studies by Roberta D. Cornelius, *The Figurative Castle: A Study in the Mediaeval Allegory of the Edifice with especial Reference to Religious Writings* (Bryn Mawr: Bryn Mawr College, 1930), and C. L. Powell, "The Castle of the Body," *Studies in Philology* 16 (1919), 197–305. It is likely that Jean was familiar with allegorical works portraying the Virgin Mary as a castle, which makes his transformation of this image for the most virginal, spiritual of women into a metaphor for the most physical aspect of women extremely audacious.

30 Robert Grosseteste, *Le château d'amour*, ed. J. Murray (Paris: Honoré Champion, 1918).

31 Giraut de Borneil, "Can lo glatz e.l frechs e la neus," in *Anthology of Troubadour Lyric Poetry*, ed. and trans. Alan R. Press (Austin: University of Texas Press, 1971), pp. 134–37.

> que Nature ot par grant mestrise
> antre .ii. pilerez assise. (ll. 20761–66)

[Venus, like a good archer, aims at a little arrow-slit that she saw hidden in the tower – in front, not on the side – which Nature, with great skill, had situated between two pillars.]

Clearly this arrow-slit, described as placed between two silver pillars and topped by the statue of a beautiful woman, suggests female genitalia (see Figures 3 and 4).[32] The woman has become solidified, architecturalized, into a part of the wall containing a "petitete archiere," a little opening through which the flaming arrow can enter.[33] And it is significant that at the moment when Venus takes aim at the opening, Jean de Meun stops the action to tell the story of Pygmalion, who also loved a stony woman made sexually receptive by Venus. Although the woman at the end of the *Rose* goes through an amazing number of metamorphoses – from arrow-slit to statue to sanctuary to moat to road and back to sanctuary – the dominant image is that of the woman turned to stone who is set aflame by a man's physical desire. Jean de Meun thus suggests that so long as the woman is seen as a complex individual who feels conflict over love, the lover and his "army" have little chance, but when the lover sees her as reified into a stony object, like the castle, he can set her on fire by passion.

The readers thus see a clear shift in point of view concerning the military-erotic complex from the courtly first part of the allegory to the satiric second part. Guillaume treats the rose and the castle with respect and admiration, and his feudalization of love is accomplished by means of discrete, elegant metaphors that appear to valorize the woman as object of desire. Love, as war, is taken seriously. In the decidedly realistic, even burlesque second part, Jean de Meun manipulates the courtly metaphors for amorous conflict by materializing, and thus debunking, them. Thus Guillaume's subtle suggestion of internal conflict in a young woman's breast becomes a comic free-for-all of stabbed bellies and outrageous insults, while Guillaume's imposing royal fortress becomes a woman's sexual organs. It is worth considering that this radical shift in the conception of amorous conflict may express differences in the authors' views of armed conflict itself: that is, that Jean de Meun, an urban intellectual living at the end of the reign of Saint Louis, reflects down-to-earth bourgeois ridicule of the outward show of chivalry celebrated by the noble Guillaume de Lorris at the beginning of the reign.[34] Thus Jean de Meun undoes the courtly admiration for both war and women through the revelation of its falsity.

---

[32] See also the illustration at the end of John V. Fleming, *The "Roman de la rose": A Study in Allegory and Iconography* (Princeton: Princeton University Press, 1969).

[33] Aldo Bernardo sees the tower as "nothing but a glorified vagina" (p. 311).

[34] William Calin has analyzed perceptively the connection between medieval misogyny and the opposition of certain writers to courtly love in "Contre la *fin'amor*? Contre la femme? Une relecture de textes du Moyen Âge," in *Courtly Literature: Culture and Context; Selected Papers of the 5th Triennial Congress of the ICLS, Dalfsen, The Netherlands, 9–16 August 1986,* eds. Keith Busby and Erik Kooper (Amsterdam: John Benjamins, 1990), pp. 11–21.

This overview of the militaristic images of erotic desire in the *Rose* has raised questions that need to be explored further, but I hope it has begun to show how the *Rose* uniquely combines the intense, conflicting elements of love and war that pervade medieval thinking and still underlie many modern erotic images and behaviors.

Figure 1. Bodleian Library, Oxford, MS Douce 195, fol. 13v.

Figure 2. Bodleian Library, Oxford, MS Douce 195, fol. 28r.

Figure 3. Bodleian Library, Oxford, MS Douce 195, fol. 148v.

Figure 4. Paris, Bibliothèque Nationale, MS FR 380, fol. 135r.

Chivalry under Siege in Ricardian Romance

Winthrop Wetherbee
Cornell University

The purpose of this study is to assess the implications of the questioning of chivalry that is a consistent element in the English courtly poetry of the late fourteenth century. Detecting references to contemporary social realities in medieval poetry is, of course, a tricky business, still more so in the case of high courtly romance, sustained as it is by aristocratic patronage, and committed almost by its nature to presenting an optimistic view of courtly culture and the code and practice of chivalry. But in the poetry of Chaucer and the Gawain-poet there is a steady ironic focus on the contradictions and blind spots inherent in the chivalric outlook. In the major works of all three poets there recur moments when this critical attitude becomes crystallized in elaborate formal constructs that enable reflection on the contradictions that the noble facade of chivalric culture denies or conceals. At such moments chivalry is effectively caught off-guard, and its limited ideological purview is opened to a scrutiny which translates the *ambages* of the romance narrative into social and political terms, lending a new urgency to the traditional romance metaphorics of warfare, siege and amorous heroism.

These themes are virtually built into medieval romance from the beginning. Romance originates as the imitation of classical epic, the matter of epic is war, and the motif of siege provides a focus for martial action. The city under siege is necessarily the setting for much of the action of the twelfth-century romances of *Eneas* and *Thebes*, the French vernacular versions of Vergil's *Aeneid* and the *Thebaid* of Statius, though in the romance narratives its function is essentially symbolic. One purpose of these works is to test and affirm the values of an emergent courtly-chivalric culture, and the framing of the action within a state of siege functions as a largely repressed reminder of this culture's precarious status. The action centers on the feats of individual heroes, and

My friend Jim Rhodes gave an earlier version of this essay a careful reading, and I am grateful for his comments. For advice on specific points I would like to thank Karen Cherewatuk, Alice Colby-Hall, and Paul Hyams.

especially their adventures in love. The capacity of love to discipline and legitimize martial energy is a central issue, and the continuity this imposes on the complex action of a poem like the *Aeneid* is a way of affirming the legitimacy of the ascendant nobility for whom such poems were produced.[1]

This basic pattern, in which *prouesse* is subjected to the discipline of *court-oisie,* is inherited by later writers of romance, and appears in an artfully distorted form in the culminating episode of the most popular of all romance narratives, the *Roman de la rose,* where heroic *aventure* is wholly subsumed to the pursuit of love, yet manages to inform that pursuit with its potential for violence. In both the truncated narrative of Guillaume de Lorris and Jean de Meun's vast sequel, the action finally comes to center on a fortress, the castle of Jealousy. The climactic episode, briefly foretold by Guillaume and vastly elaborated by Jean, is the successful besieging of this castle by the barons of *Amors*. The decisive stratagem is Venus' launching of an arrow which penetrates a loophole of the castle, awakening anarchic desire and thereby enabling both the overthrow of the fortress and the final conquest of the Rose-maiden. The episode and its motifs are carefully chosen: they recall, and in a sense reciprocate, the moment in the *Eneas* when Lavine, newly smitten with love for Eneas, binds a love-letter to an arrow and bids an archer shoot it toward the Trojan host.[2]

In the *Eneas* the act is a dangerous one, for it is liable to be viewed as a violation of the precarious truce between the Trojan and Italian armies, but in the event it proves a tour de force of *courtoisie*: Eneas reads its message correctly, and its net effect is to portend the union whereby Eneas will succeed to the rule of Italy. In the *Rose,* by contrast, it is just such attempts to govern affairs by means of courtly decorum that are the real target of Venus' arrow. The violence which the *Eneas* had suppressed resurfaces in a sexual form in the bizarre act of defloration that concludes Jean de Meun's poem, and the effect is to underscore the limited efficacy of *courtoisie* as a means of tempering a social energy which expresses itself far more readily in aggression.

Both the courtly and the anti-courtly versions of the siege of love are import-ant to the reworking of traditional romance undertaken by the great English poets of the late fourteenth century. In their work, as already in the *Rose,* the influence of chivalric romance combines with that of a long-established tradition of psychological allegory,[3] for which the motif of the assault of vice on the

---

[1] On the implications of the revision of Vergil in the *Eneas,* see Daniel Poirion, "De l'*Enéide* à *Eneas*: mythologie et moralisation," *Cahiers de civilization médiévale* 19 (1976), 213–29; Lee Patterson, *Negotiating the Past* (Madison: University of Wisconsin Press, 1987), pp. 173–83.

[2] *Eneas,* ed. J.-J. Salverda de Grave, 2 vols. (Paris: Champion, 1925–29), ll. 8776–44; *Roman de la Rose,* ed. Felix Lecoy, 3 vols. (Paris: Champion, 1965–70), ll. 20755–80, 21221–36.

[3] On this tradition, see especially H. R. Jauss, "La transformation de la forme allégorique entre 1180 et 1240 d'Alain de Lille à Guillaume de Lorris," in *L'Humanisme médiéval dans les littératures romanes du XIIe au XIIIe siècle,* ed. Anthime Fourrier (Paris: Klincksieck, 1964), pp. 107–46; Marc-Réné Jung, *Études sur le poème allégorique en France au Moyen Âge,* Romanica Helvetica 82 (Bern: Francke, 1971), pp. 227–89.

stronghold of virtue is so much an archetype as to be taken virtually for granted. Both traditions are at work in the thirteenth-century guide for religious women known as the *Ancrene Wysse*, in which Christ is represented as a knight-lover who sends his retainers to defend the castle where his beloved Lady, the human soul, is besieged, and the defenders are enjoined to drive back the marauding vices by pouring down the scalding tears of their contrition from the ramparts.[4] Here, as in the *Château d'amour* of Robert Grosseteste, the warlike motifs are obviously drawn from the romance tradition, but in the *Livre de Seyntz Medicines*, a work of private devotion by the fourteenth-century soldier Henry of Grosmont, Duke of Lancaster, the elaborate description of how the virtues, who guard the castle of his body, defend the heart's *donjon* against the engines and stratagems of vice clearly draws on the experience of an old campaigner in France, Scotland, and the Holy Land.[5] One of the most interesting features of this unique and fascinating book is the way in which the author gets caught up in the particulars of his military allegory. As the enemy approaches through the "faubourgs," the vehicle of his allegory comes to dominate its tenor, and he speaks as one concerned less for his sinful nature than for his duty as a commanding officer.[6]

The rather incongruous effect of these realistic touches in Henry's *Livre* suggests the extent to which war was a preoccupation for the aristocracy of his day. It is largely by rendering the fabric of romance, where knighthood is largely a confection of attitudes and ideals, permeable to similar intrusions of practical reality that a coherent critique of chivalry and its social impact emerges in the poetry of Chaucer and the Gawain-poet. But unlike Henry, or the anonymous author of the alliterative *Morte Arthure*, who seems to have deliberately incorporated the realities of fourteenth-century warfare into his poem,[7] these poets can seem, at first glance, to have deliberately distanced themselves from the

4   *Ancrene Wysse*, Parts 4 (the defense of the castle) and 7 (Christ as knight). On the latter motif, see Rosemary Woolf, "The Theme of Christ the Lover-Knight in Medieval English Literature," in her *Art and Doctrine. Essays in Medieval Literature* (London: Hambledon Press, 1986), pp. 99–117.

5   On Henry and his book, see Kenneth Fowler, *The King's Lieutenant: Henry of Grosmont, First Duke of Lancaster, 1310–1361* (London: Paul Elek, 1969), pp. 187–96; John Barnie, *War in Medieval English Society: Social Values in the Hundred Years War 1337–99* (Ithaca: Cornell University Press, 1974), pp. 58–65.

6   As Henry remarks, "nul forteresce est si forte, qi garder ne la siet ne ne voelt, perdre la lui estut, sicom il est bien sovent apparant en ces guerres" (no fortress is so strong [but that] he who cannot or will not defend it will lose it, as is very often to be seen in the wars); *Le Livre de Seyntz Medicines*, ed. E. J. Arnould, Anglo-Norman Texts II (Oxford: Basil Blackwell, 1940), pp. 81–82.

7   On the debated question of the attitude expressed in the alliterative *Morte Arthure* toward the campaigns of Edward III, see Richard W. Kaeuper, *War, Justice, and Public Order: England and France in the Later Middle Ages* (Oxford: Oxford University Press, 1988), pp. 336–38; also Barnie, pp. 147–50; George R. Keiser, "Edward III and the Alliterative *Morte Arthure*," *Speculum* 48 (1973), 37–51; Karl Heinz Göller, "Reality versus Romance: A Reassessment of the *Alliterative Morte Arthure*," in *The Alliterative Morte Arthure: A Reassessment of the Poem*, ed. Karl Heinz Göller (Cambridge: D. S. Brewer, 1981), pp. 15–29.

traditional romance themes of war and siege.[8] *Sir Gawain and the Green Knight* combines the broad cultural program of twelfth-century romance with the psychological intricacy of the *Rose* and the homiletic tradition, but though the poem offers vivid scenes of heroic challenge and the slaying of wild beasts, it is wholly devoid of human combat: the siege that constitutes its central action consists in a clever lady's penetration of Gawain's elaborate edifice of Christian-chivalric virtues and social graces, and even her success does not lead to erotic aggression on either side. The action of *Troilus and Criseyde*, Geoffrey Chaucer's great exercise in the tradition of the *roman d'antiquité*, adapts a love-story which Chaucer's source, Giovanni Boccaccio, had deliberately excerpted from the martial context of the *Roman de Troie* of Benoît de Sainte-Maure. The hero is a Trojan prince and a great warrior, but his love runs its course, from the initial pangs of love to the height of bliss, then down again through the pain of betrayal to loss and death, in a sort of charmed space that seems, until the moment of the hero's death at the hands of Achilles, virtually unaffected by the ongoing siege of Troy. It is only in Chaucer's *Knight's Tale* that warfare intrudes in a recognizable form, as the Knight's painful, flawed attempt to affirm chivalric values exposes, in spite of itself, the gap between aristocratic vision and the facts of life. But even here the Knight's commitment to chivalry proves stronger than his will to understand it; he never acknowledges that the recurring violence that finally defeats Theseus is inherent in chivalry itself, and his tale ends with a marriage designed to perpetuate the dominance of the very chivalric values its complex narrative has largely undermined.

Given that England was at war throughout the half-century within which all of these works were produced, their largely non-violent character is worth pondering, but so, too, is the question of why even the least warlike nevertheless contain vivid references to siege – medieval warfare in perhaps its most violent form. The action of *Sir Gawain* is framed at beginning and end by lines which recall the overthrow of Troy, the inaugural event in the historical chain which has led to the "building of Britain" and the establishment of Arthur's Round Table, the paradigmatic chivalric institution. The story of Chaucer's Troilus, too, is framed by the grim prophecy of Calchas, priest of Apollo, whose Delphic inspiration has led him to abandon Troy in the certain knowledge that the city will be overrun and brought to ruin. And the consequences of siege are not merely evoked but vividly defined. Chaucer's Troy will be "beten down to grownde," ravaged by fire until it turns "to asshen dede" (*Troilus* 4.76–77, 118–19).[9] The first lines of *Sir Gawain* refer tersely to "the siege and the assault" which left Troy "brittened and brent to brondez and askez." Much of the point of these references is in the character of the saga of Troy itself. As

---

[8] On the unwarlike character of the major English poetry of the period, see J. A. Burrow, *Ricardian Poetry: Chaucer, Gower, Langland and the Gawain Poet* (New Haven: Yale University Press, 1971), pp. 93–102.

[9] All references to Chaucer's poetry are to text of the *Riverside Chaucer*, ed. Larry D. Benson, 3rd ed. (Boston: Houghton Mifflin, 1987).

Malcolm Andrew remarks in discussing the function of the references to the destruction of Troy in these two poems, the causes of the city's downfall form an intricate pattern involving "the public and the private, love and conflict, nobility and treachery – 'bliss and blunder.' "[10] The same oppositions provide the focus of the two poets' critique of a chivalry in which a vast, often unscrupulous desire for self-aggrandizement and a frank love of violence coexist with self-idealization and the mystique of warfare as a more or less sacred vocation.

In late fourteenth-century England, where the promotion of knighthood assumed lavish forms, and the nobility of warfare was strenuously asserted by a monarchy anxious to ensure the solidarity of the English aristocracy with its designs against France,[11] it was probably inevitable that the cult of chivalry should generate a reaction to itself in the form of a tendency to question chivalric values and prerogatives and the chivalric view of life. This is not just a matter of increasing disillusionment with the French war in the long aftermath of the great victories of the mid-century; indeed there is good evidence that the failures of the later years of Edward III tended to be imputed as much to a waning of an earlier generation's chivalric spirit as to any defect of chivalry itself.[12] But it is clear that for many a significant source of difficulty was the character of the knightly ideal itself. The criticism of chivalry that emerges in many kinds of writing at virtually all social levels during this period centers on the contradiction between the lofty standards of personal honor and duty that the chivalric code enjoins and the collaboration of English knighthood in a state of affairs in which war and its demoralizing effects exerted virtually a constant pressure on the economy and social order of England.[13]

The problems posed by chivalric practice were serious ones. On the one hand, it was the unifying element in aristocratic education, imbuing the knight-in-training with a combination of manners, skills and ideals centered on the twin values of *prouesse* and *courtoisie*.[14] Warfare was the vocation of chivalry, and loyalty and personal honor combined, in principle and in practice, to make warfare in the service of the realm and Christendom a matter of *noblesse oblige*. But chivalry, by its very nature, was a catalyst to violence. Honor thrived on military achievement, and the violence stirred up by the provocation to defend honor and fulfill the obligations of loyalty was intensified by the promise of preferment and wealth that demonstrated prowess and military success could

---

[10] Malcolm Andrew, "The Fall of Troy in *Sir Gawain and the Green Knight* and *Troilus and Criseyde*," in *The European Tragedy of Troilus*, ed. Piero Boitani (Oxford: Clarendon Press, 1989), p. 93.

[11] On this subject, see Barnie, pp. 66–67, and especially Juliet Vale, *Edward III and Chivalry: Chivalric Society and Its Context, 1270–1350* (Woodbridge, Suffolk: Boydell Press, 1982).

[12] See Barnie, pp. 75–76, 117, 120–23.

[13] See Barnie, pp. 117–38; Kaeuper, pp. 336–78.

[14] See Chris Given-Wilson, *The English Nobility in the Late Middle Ages: The Fourteenth-Century Political Community* (London: Routledge & Kegan Paul, 1987), pp. 2–19; Nicholas Orme, *From Childhood to Chivalry* (London: Methuen, 1984).

offer.[15] A distinction between the obligations of chivalry on the one hand and the pursuits of the professional soldier on the other was maintained in principle through most of this period, but the line between them became steadily harder to draw in the later years of the century, and there can be no doubt that the aristocracy was deeply involved in the careerism and self-aggrandizement that did so much to prolong the war with France.[16] The economic impact of sustained warfare on England itself has been matter for debate among modern scholars,[17] but the social effect was probably in many ways as demoralizing as that of English marauding on the French. The serious threat of a French invasion was a source of widespread anxiety throughout the period, and the money and man-power needed to preserve adequate defenses, together with the pressure of taxation and conscription in the interest of pursuing the war, not only bred widespread hardship but constituted a source of popular unrest sufficiently powerful to be considered by some modern historians as the principal cause of the Peasants' Revolt.[18]

Stated in simple terms and at a historical remove, the problems created by the inherent contradictions of chivalry seem obvious enough, and many of them were noted by astute contemporary writers on the state of the realm and the duties of the three estates.[19] What is harder to discover is direct criticism of chivalric values as such. As M. H. Keen observes, the religious and ideological bases of chivalry made it difficult for contemporary observers to recognize its abuses for what they were.[20] The chivalric code was taken seriously not only by noble and pious soldiers like Henry of Grosmont and Geoffrey de Charny, but also by the real-life counterparts of the fictive "popular" audience of *Piers Plowman* and the *Canterbury Tales* and by the authors of these poems. More-over, the literary representation of war itself is deeply conditioned by these

[15] See Barnie, p. 95; Keith Haines, "Attitudes an Impediments of Pacifism in Medieval Europe," *Journal of Medieval History* 7 (1981), 381–83; M. H. Keen, "Chivalry, Nobility, and the Man at Arms," In *War, Literature, and Politics in the Late Middle Ages*, ed. C. T. Allmand (Liverpool: Liverpool University Press, 1976), pp. 44–45; John Gillingham, "War and Chivalry in the *History of William the Marshal*," in *Thirteenth Century England II: Proceedings of the Newcastle upon Tyne Conference, 1987*, eds. P. R. Coss and S. D. Lloyd (Woodbridge, Suffolk: Boydell Press, 1988), pp. 12–13.

[16] See Haines, p. 383; Barnie, pp. 34–35.

[17] See M. M. Postan, "Some Social Consequences of the Hundred Years' War," *Economic History Review* 12 (1942), 1–12; K. B. McFarlane, "England and the Hundred Years War," *Past and Present* 22 (1967), 3–18; Kaeuper, pp. 292–93.

[18] On the threat of invasion, see Barnie, pp. 23, 28; H. J. Hewitt, *The Organization of War under Edward III* (Manchester: Manchester University Press, 1966), pp. 3–21, 164–68; Kaeuper, pp. 355–58. On the social consequences of this threat, see Eleanor Searle and Robert Burghart, "The Defense of England and the Peasants' Revolt," *Viator* 3 (1972), 365–88; Kaeuper, pp. 348–55; R. B. Dobson, "The Risings in York, Beverly and Scarborough, 1380–81," in *The English Rising of 1381*, eds. R. H. Hilton and T. H. Aston (Cambridge: Cambridge University Press, 1984), pp. 132–33.

[19] See especially Barnie, pp. 117–38; also C. T. Allmand, "The War and the Non-Combatant," in *The Hundred Years War*, ed. Kenneth Fowler (London: St. Martin's Press, 1971), pp. 171–81.

[20] Keen, pp. 44–45.

values. Chroniclers and other writers on war habitually deal selectively and in an idealizing way with knightly behavior, and one would be hard put to realize from their accounts the relative rarity of pitched battle and hand-to-hand combat as compared to the long, slow processes of attrition and devastation in which so much of the warfare of the period consisted.[21] Froissart, whose world view as historian is tailored to the interests of a "warrior caste,"[22] is frankly admiring of war as spectacle, and a great part of his purpose in writing is to preserve the memory of exemplary feats of arms and displays of honor.[23] And such writing is not merely honorific or servile in motive, for it had the serious function of promoting and exemplifying the "law of arms."[24] Though his method is more pragmatic and at times self-contradictory than that of treatises like the *Tree of Battles*, which attempt to define and regulate violence in terms drawn from canon law, Froissart is everywhere concerned to show that the chivalry embodied in his heroes has a coherent purpose, and he is sensitive to the symptoms of its corruption or decline.[25]

For the same reasons, as well as for more delicate ones involving position and patronage, the critique of chivalry that emerges in the courtly poetry of the late fourteenth century is for the most part tentative and oblique, and at times almost fatalistic. Whatever excesses the chivalric spirit may have provoked, it is an established, perhaps a necessary, evil, and the poets who address its adherents on their own terms are in a position much closer to that of Froissart than to that of contemporary preachers and satirists. But a perceptible hardening of attitude takes place under Richard, and though the relative dates of the major works of the three poets I am concerned with remain uncertain, it would be tempting to suppose that my sequence of texts forms a chronological sequence as well. There is an attractiveness in identifying *Sir Gawain and the Green Knight*, attentive as it is to niceties of knightly conduct and perhaps linked to the Order of the Garter,[26] with the heyday of chivalric renewal under Edward III, as the more somber elements in Gower and Chaucer seem clearly to express the

---

[21] See especially Hewitt, pp. 99–118, 131–36; also, for a broader view, John Gillingham, "Richard I and the Science of War in the Middle Ages," in *War and Government in the Middle Ages*, ed. John Gillingham and J. C. Holt (Woodbridge, Suffolk: Boydell Press, 1984), pp. 78–91.

[22] Peter F. Ainsworth, *Jean Froissart and the Fabric of History: Truth, Myth and Fiction in the "Chroniques"* (Oxford: Oxford University Press, 1990), p. 74.

[23] See Ainsworth, pp. 70–85; John Bell Henneman, "The Age of Charles V," in *Froissart: Historian*, ed. J. J. N. Palmer (Woodbridge, Suffolk: Boydell Press, 1981), pp. 46–49; Philippe Contamine, "Froissart: Art militaire, pratique et conception de la guerre," in *Froissart: Historian*, pp. 132–44.

[24] Ainsworth, pp. 78–85.

[25] On the subject generally, see M. H. Keen, *The Laws of War in the Late Middle Ages* (London: Routledge & Kegan Paul, 1965); on Honoré Bonet, see G. W. Coopland's introduction to his translation of *The Tree of Battles* (Cambridge MA: Harvard University Press, 1949), p. 15–69, and Keen, *The Laws of War*, pp. 7–22.

[26] See Michael J. Bennett, *Community, Class and Careerism: Cheshire and Lancashire Society in the Age of "Sir Gawain and the Green Knight"* (Cambridge: Cambridge University Press, 1983), pp. 234–35.

growing dissatisfaction with the effects of the war in the Ricardian period.[27] In fact *Sir Gawain* seems at least as likely to be a product of the royal household of the 1390s, when, as M. J. Bennett has argued, its northwest Midlands dialect and preoccupation with provincial court life would have had a special appeal for the Cheshire soldiery who upheld royal authority in Richard's final years.[28] If Bennett is right about the poem's provenance, it is no doubt this special intimacy with the world of active chivalry, as much as the deliberately archaizing features of the poem's theme and style, give it the air of belonging to an earlier time. In any case, as I will try to show, its shrewd assessment of the chivalric mentality is at one with the attitude of Chaucer, though less obviously conditioned by a half-century of warfare and its pervasive social effects.

The long painful denouement of *Sir Gawain* includes the moment when Gawain, having stood unflinching under the Green Knight's axe, is released at last from the anxious burden he has borne for a year. His "covenant" with the Green Knight has been fulfilled, the perfidious green girdle remains hidden, and his sense of relation to chivalry is still inviolate. In this brief interval Gawain makes his one self-assertive gesture, instantly leaping into a posture of readiness to withstand any further menace from the Green Knight:

> He sprit forth spenne-fote more then a spere lenthe,
> Hent heterly his helme and on his hed cast,
> Schot with his schulderez his fayre schelde vnder,
> Braydez out a bryght sworde and bremely he spekez –
> Neuer syn that he watz barne borne of his moder
> Watz he neuer in this worlde wyghe half so blythe[29]

A moment later Gawain's elation will be dashed by the Green Knight's exposure of his deception, but in this instant we behold him fixed in the act of reconstructing an identity which, like the lengthy account of his arming earlier in the poem, leaves him literally encased in the trappings of chivalry, hemmed in by it as if by the battlements of a fortress.

---

[27] On this subject, see R. F. Yeager, "*Pax Poetica*: On the Pacifism of Chaucer and Gower," *Studies in the Age of Chaucer* 9 (1987), 97–121; Bruce Kent Cowgill, "The *Knight's Tale* and the Hundred Year's War," *Philolgical Quarterly* 54 (1975), 670–79; Paul A. Olson, "Chaucer's Epic Statement and the Political Milieu of the Late Fourteenth Century," *Medievalia* 5 (1979), 61–87; Alcuin Blamires, "Chaucer's Revaluation of Chivalric Honor," *Medievalia* 5 (1979), 245–69.

[28] Bennett, p. 235, finds it "likely" that the poem assumed its final form in or after 1399. Evidence for an earlier dating is discussed by Elizabeth Salter, "The Alliterative Revival," in her *English and International: Studies in the Literature, Art and Patronage of Medieval England*, eds. Derek Pearsall and Nicolette Zeeman (Cambridge: Cambridge University Press, 1988), pp. 106–10 (originally published in *Modern Philology* 64 [1966], 233–37).

[29] *Sir Gawain and the Green Knight*, ll. 2316–21, in *The Poems of the Pearl Manuscript*, eds. Malcolm Andrew and Ronald Waldron (Berkeley: University of California Press, 1978). I have replaced the Middle English characters "thorn" (þ) and "yogh" (ȝ) with "th" and "gh." The passage may be translated as follows: "He leapt forth more than a spear's length with his feet together, quickly siezed his helmet and clapped it on his head, with his shoulders shook down his fair shield, draws out a bright sword and grimly speaks. Never since he was a babe new born of his mother has he ever in this world been half so happy."

The aggressive posture so abruptly taken up in this moment is an aspect of Gawain's chivalry that the poem thus far has largely suppressed, but it clarifies and underscores what has been the hero's situation throughout a narrative in which the authority and integrity of chivalry code have been a major concern. We move from the static, idealized innocence of Arthur's court, where chivalric perfection is the stuff of legend, through the courtly intrigue of Gawain's testing by the household of Bertilak, to the final crisis which leaves him convinced that his claim to uphold the standard of chivalry has been utterly discredited. The importance of chivalry to Gawain's identity is made clear not only by his behavior in the passage quoted above, but by the abruptness with which, a split-second later, his aggression turns upon himself. Once his acceptance of the supposedly life-protecting green girdle at the hands of his hostess has been exposed, he can see himself only as cowardly, covetous, and untrue. He can no longer claim a place in the Arthurian pantheon on the basis of the impossible synthesis of values expressed in the pentangle on his shield; henceforth his link to Arthur's court will be the equivocal, if more realistic, assertion of solidarity implicit in their adoption of his dearly purchased green girdle as a badge. But whatever affirmation the court's gesture may imply, for Gawain himself the trappings of chivalry and *courtoisie* – the heraldic tour de force of the pentangle emblazoned on his shield and the concealed love-token which implicitly mocks its claims – have become the emblems of his failure. He resumes the life of *aventure*, but when he returns to Arthur's court, the groans and "tene" which punctuate his account of his comeuppance (ll. 2501–02) show him still at the mercy of the unconscious pride which had played so large a role in his commitment to chivalry. To have once been bound by the chivalric code, it seems, is to lose the power to view one's situation in less than absolute terms. Christian humility is one facet of the chivalric perfection Gawain has sought to embody, but it has no real hold on him except as a necessary component of his idealized chivalry. He is chronically incapable of accepting his situation as an ordinary sinful human being, or recognizing that his failure in the face of a superhuman challenge is a function of his having presumed to embody a more than human perfection.

The poet's attitude toward his hero includes humor and deep sympathy, and both would surely have had a strong appeal for the knightly audience to whom *Sir Gawain* is likely to have been first presented.[30] Harder to know is how

---

[30] The fullest argument on the poem's likely audience is that of Bennett, pp. 225–35, who sees it as having been produced for the shared delectation of Richard II and the Cheshire soldiery who were his henchmen in the 1390s; see also his "The Court of Richard II and the Promotion of Literature," in *Chaucer's England: Literature in Historical Context,* ed. Barbara Hanawalt (Minneapolis: University of Minnesota Press, 1992), pp. 3–20. Lee Patterson has questioned Bennett's views, noting ways in which the poem sets a provincial courtly milieu in implicit opposition to the royal court, and the political differences between Richard and the men of Cheshire: "Court politics and the Invention of Literature: The Case of Sir John Clanvowe," in *Culture and History 1350–1600: Essays on English Communities, Identities and Writing,* ed. David Aers (London: Harvester, 1992), pp. 19–20.

readily such an audience would have recognized the ways in which the poem quietly calls chivalry itself into question. Gawain's failure is in large measure a failure of self-knowledge, an inability to see himself apart from the role imposed on him by Arthur's court, whose values characteristically express themselves in such wholly external forms as heraldry, social ritual, and feats of arms, while preserving a wall of privilege around their private existence. For all his charm, beauty, and goodness, there is a sense in which Gawain lives in a state of chronic alienation from the world at large, where nature, women, and virtually all forms of social intercourse are potential threats, tests of the validity of his claim to embody the many-faceted chivalric ideal. Within the world of chivalry, class solidarity and the presumption of shared values render the Arthurian court and its champions immune to scrutiny, but in the larger world the ideals of even a civilized and ingratiating figure like Gawain can be so beset as to appear unwieldy, self-contradictory, and finally unreal.

Chaucer's *Troilus and Criseyde* opens the private world of chivalry to public scrutiny. The limited and self-affirming vision of courtly-chivalric culture is treated on its own terms, as in *Sir Gawain*, but simultaneously set in an intricate and complex relation to the realities of war and politics, which exposes it as insulated chiefly from self-awareness and consequently incapable of acknowledging the complicity of its upholders in political and military disaster. From beginning to end the stage of action is set within the walls of a city under siege and surrounded by intelligible signs of the intrigue and division that are helping to undermine this city from within. Chaucer's Troy exhibits remarkably little of the ideal centrality and rich cultural symbolism with which romance poets commonly endow their fictive cities.[31] Indeed, it is largely by emphasizing the ordinariness, even the banality, of the life of his un-Homeric heroes and heroines that Chaucer creates his poem's unique effect, managing to do his own kind of justice to the tradition of the city's fall while preserving around his noble Trojans an atmosphere of relaxed and almost cozy domesticity.[32]

This emphasis is established by the remarkable moment with which the action of the *Troilus* can be said to begin. Criseyde, left behind in the remove of her father, the priest-prophet Calchas, to the camp of the Greeks, goes to seek the protection of Hector (1.92–133). She is, Chaucer writes, at her wits' end, for she is a widow, apparently friendless, and understandably anxious about the likely reaction to her father's defection. Hector, moved by her plight and beauty as she kneels before him, promises her protection. In one sense the primary importance

---

[31] See Eugene Vance, "Signs of the City: Medieval Poetry as Detour," *New Literary History* 4 (1972–73), 557–60, on the "dogged consistency" with which medieval poets carry forward the theme of the city as a version of "cosmic plenitude"; this can be seen to be parodied in the opening scene of the *Troilus*, where the Palladium is reduced to a version of the love-garden of Guillaume de Lorris. By contrast, even John Gower, whose Troy is plainly an image of recklessness and disorder, finds space to commemorate the potency of Priam and hints at an archetypal significance in the city's fall; see *Confessio amantis* 1.1187–89, 5.7305–19.

[32] Mark Lambert, "*Troilus*, Books I–III: A Criseydan Reading," in *Essays on "Troilus and Criseyde,"* ed. Mary Salu (Cambridge: D. S. Brewer, 1979), pp. 105–25.

of this scene is emblematic. In it can be seen history, and the premonition of the Trojan tragedy, signaled by Calchas' defection, is displaced on the story's stage by the the abandoned widow's pathetic appeal. Epic heroism, in the person of Hector, is drawn away from the outward vision proper to a guardian of the city and reduced to the lesser role of the chivalric hero whose public self responds to nothing more readily than the spectacle of beauty in distress.

But the scene involves something more, or other, than the well-attested medieval substitution of romance for epic, for it does not end when Criseyde (after many expressions of humble gratitude) takes her leave. Instead, in a manner proper to neither epic nor romance, the readers pass behind the scenes and follow Criseyde home. There they learn that her situation is not in fact as desperate as it had seemed. She lives like any Trojan lady of her station, the evidently affluent condition appropriate to one whose father is a prominent member of the Trojan priesthood. Far from being friendless and alone, she presides over an extensive household, a "meignee," and is well thought of by Trojans young and old (1.127–31). Once at home, she "holds her still" (1.126), apparently awaiting future developments.

In thus extending the reach of his narrative, Chaucer prepares the readers for the fuller articulation of the urban setting of his story, which is one of its most telling features. Unlike the typically self-contained court world of traditional romance, Troy is a place where people promenade, discuss the latest news and gossip, and participate in civic festivals, where political factions compete and money changes hands. These facts of life inevitably impinge on the lives of Chaucer's pseudo-Homeric nobility, but Chaucer carefully allows his nobles to maintain a sense of transcendent separateness, while suggesting at the same time the limitation implicit in that separateness. When Hector's magnanimity is set in perspective by our discovery of the larger awareness of Criseyde, and Chaucer implicitly invites the readers to share that awareness, there is a breach of the decorum of romance, which defines the limits of his chivalric world or his chivalric ability to see the world. The world view of the Trojan aristocracy, as Chaucer presents them, is very much conditioned by their view of themselves, and the gestures by which they affirm their nobility are shown to be, like the code and armor of Gawain, at once constitutive of authority and an index to the limits of that authority. Their generosity and bravery are the best Troy has to offer, but these qualities are infinitely manipulable in the hands of characters like Pandarus and Criseyde, less chivalrous than they, and to that extent smarter. Again and again the readers see the noble Trojans acting on what they take to be their own chivalrous initiative, while in fact being manipulated by others to ends of which they are wholly unaware.

The scene which most strikingly defines the relation between Chaucer's treatment of the Trojan aristocracy and the larger political context of the *Troilus* is a dinner-party at the home of the Trojan prince Deiphobus. Organized by Pandarus, it is billed as an occasion for enlisting high-level support for Criseyde in her allegedly precarious political situation, but it will also provide the occasion for a first interview between Criseyde and the love-sick Troilus, who, on

Pandarus' instruction, will pretend to be taken ill before she arrives and await her in an inner chamber of his brother's house. Much of the significance of the episode is conveyed by Pandarus' elaborate preparations, which involve catching everybody, including Criseyde, to some extent off-guard. Having effortlessly enlisted Deiphobus, as Criseyde herself had enlisted Hector, by introducing into his mind the image of a fair lady in distress, Pandarus prepares Criseyde by falsely informing her that she is about to be sued by one Polyphete, apparently a priest and evidently a political rival of her father. From Criseyde's reaction the readers learn that she has been sued by Polyphete before, that she can well afford to buy him off, and that her only concern is to avoid falling foul of his two noble connections, Aeneas and Antenor (2.1464–78). The astuteness of Criseyde's analysis of this plausible situation is set off by the perfectly timed entry of the guileless Deiphobus, who comes, programmed by Pandarus and full of noble solicitude, to personally deliver his invitation to Criseyde. Hector, Deiphobus says, will surely be at the dinner, for he has often spoken well of Criseyde. Helen is Deiphobus' dear friend and will help with the preparations, and Deiphobus adds, a bit roguishly, that she can make Paris do what she will – meaning, as is eventually learned, that he will not be there (2.1447–54).

The effect is prescient of the world of "Dynasty," but an all-too-coherent plot lies just below the surface. As the readers and Pandarus await the encounter of Troilus and Criseyde, they watch the noble company indulge its feelings of concern and indignation on Criseyde's behalf in an atmosphere charged with intimations of future disaster of a more serious kind. The names of Antenor and Aeneas, whom Criseyde associates with the plot against herself (2.1473–75), will, of course, eventually be linked directly to the betrayal of the city. Hector leaves for Troilus' perusal a letter questioning whether a certain spy (Sinon?) should be put to death (2.1697–99), and this document provides an excuse for Deiphobus and Helen who, it is learned, are indeed good friends, to withdraw in order to discuss it together. This clears the scene for the meeting of Criseyde and Troilus, but not before the readers follow Deiphobus and Helen down a flight of steps into a secluded garden, where they pass the better part of an hour together (2.1702–08). Even in the coy hint that something is up between these two, there is an ominous foreshadowing. Deiphobus will in fact marry Helen after Paris' death, and his shade appears memorably in the Vergilian underworld (*Aeneid* 6.494–530), displaying the mutilations at the hands of the Greeks which mark him as an adulterer, to bemoan the folly and "false joys" of the final days of Troy.

The point of the dinner-party scene, then, as of Chaucer's treatment of the Trojan aristocracy in general, is largely in the extent to which, when political reality has been palpably acknowledged, their abiding preoccupations reduce it to an occasion for private pursuits. We are, so to speak, at home with the Trojan nobility, whose vision has turned wholly inward to focus, in an orgy of noble good will, on the situation of Criseyde. In this and the many similar scenes, the narrator – with all good will in the world – speaks of things of which romance would keep us ignorant, creating an effect like that which Walter Benjamin

ascribes to the moving camera.[33] Like the movie actor, and unlike a stage actor
or the hero of a traditional romance, Chaucer's Hector cannot control the scene
in which he appears. We see him from more angles, and thus know far more
about his situation than he can possibly be aware of, let alone deliberately reveal.
He has lost the "aura" that traditionally pertains to his status as an aristocrat and
cultural symbol and, by implication, has forfeited the social authority traditionally associated with that status. We can believe all the more readily in his
commitment to chivalry for having been shown the innocence that sustains it,
but we can hardly accept it on its own terms or avoid seeing its sustaining
innocence as willful and culpable, an abrogation of responsibility.

The blindness of the Trojans to the significance of their situation, as well as to
the role of chivalry in upholding it, is suggested in other ways, and by nothing
more plainly than the chivalric aura that surrounds the Trojan heroes' deaths. It
appears in the banal rhetoric of knightly piety with which the narrator laments
the fall of Hector, reducing Hector himself to virtual anonymity and wholly
obliterating the significance of his death for world history:

> For which me thynketh every manere wight
> That haunteth armes oughte to biwaille
> The deth of hym that was so noble a knyght . . .   (5.1555–57)

Troilus' death, too, though intimately linked to the fate of Troy,[34] is similarly
circumscribed by chivalric preoccupations. He grieves for the loss of Hector, but
all such feelings are quickly displaced in his mind by the sorrows of love and the
score he must settle with his rival Diomede. It is in these wholly private terms
that he forms the resolution to "seek his own death in arms" (5.1716–18),
sealing his fate with a vow which, despite its melancholy tone, is as true to
chivalry as the "die all, die merrily" of Shakespeare's Hotspur.

But for all their commitment to chivalry, the Trojan aristocracy have com-
promised themselves irreparably. The ravishing of Helen is emblematic of their
situation that draws an array of Homeric figures to collaborate, wittingly or
unwittingly, in Pandarus' domestic campaign, even as intrigues and espionage of
a more serious kind create a network around them. The preoccupation for their
plight is an index of the social and ideological blindness that seals their fate.[35]

---

33 "The Work as Art in the Age of Mechanical Reproduction," in Walter Benjamin's *Illumi-
nations*, ed. Hannah Arendt (New York: Schocken, 1968), pp. 221–28.

34 See Lee Patterson, *Chaucer and the Subject of History* (Madison: University of Wisconsin
Press, 1991), p. 111, who rightly notes the emblematic significance of *Aeneid* 1.474–78, describing the representation in Juno's temple at Carthage of Troilus' death at the hands of Achilles. On
this passage see also Winthrop Wetherbee, *Chaucer and the Poets. An Essay on "Troilus and
Criseyde"* (Ithaca: Cornell University Press, 1984), pp. 90–92.

35 On this aspect of the medieval Troy cycle, see Emmanuelle Baumgartner, "Benoît de
Sainte-Maure et le modèle troyen," in *Modernité au Moyen Âge: le défi du passé*, eds. Brigitte
Cazelles and Charles Méla (Geneva: Droz, 1990), pp. 101–11.

The siege of Criseyde complements and collaborates in the siege of Troy.[36] Lee Patterson has clearly stated the political implications of this aspect of the poem. It deals with issues important to the England of the 1380s – "a society under siege," "conspiratorial factionalism," "disastrous militarism" – but its socio-political argument is not specific or partisan: while doing justice to the heroic side of chivalry, "it also measures the cost of war upon the amorousness that is the other crucial element of the chivalric life-style, and it shows the noble life at odds with itself, fulfilling its deepest romantic needs in a context that dooms them to extinction."[37]

The *Troilus* shows the chivalric ideal suspended in a state of blind and seemingly helpless complicity in its own betrayal. In Chaucer's *Knight's Tale* the chivalric mentality is shown besieged by concrete manifestations of social realities that it has repressed, willfully ignored, or simply failed to recognize. The *Knight's Tale* constitutes Chaucer's statement of the case for chivalry as a basis for political order. Its hero, Theseus, is intended as the embodiment of an enlightened chivalry capable of harmonizing valor in war with political responsibility and courtly grace. The *Knight's Tale* offers a complex and ambiguous statement on the status and function of chivalry, and the problems it poses are anticipated in two lines of the famous portrait of the Knight in Chaucer's *General Prologue* (50, 67):

> And ever honoured for his worthynesse.
> And everemoore he had a sovereyn prys [high value]   (ll. 50, 67)

Similar and almost redundant, these lines serve to link two passages which, taken together, form an unambiguously ideal portrait, but in context the first is separated from the second by sixteen lines which provide a long list of campaigns in which the Knight has fought at various points on the Christian frontier and beyond. The sum of his campaigns is all the life the Knight is given; no social or political role in England is suggested. In the context of the General Prologue, where the state of contemporary English society is the central concern, this absence invites questioning the status of the Knight and his values in this place and time, and the question should remain in the readers' minds as they proceed to the tale.

The central action of the *Knight's Tale* pits the erotic visionary Palamon against the scrupulously chivalrous Arcite for possession of a woman. It is preceded by brief accounts of Theseus' successful besieging of "Feminye," the realm of the Amazons, and his overthrow of Creon, the last of the ruling house of Oedipean Thebes. These victories are intended to exemplify the way in which chivalry fulfills its civilizing mission, but both have consequences which return to bedevil Theseus and the Knight as they seek together to discipline and contain

---

[36] The complementarity of the two themes, as well as the elaborate imagery of the walled town under siege common to both, is well analyzed by Andrew Sprung, "The 'Townes Wal': A Frame for 'Fre Chois' in Chaucer's *Troilus and Criseyde," Medievalia* 14 (1988), 127–42.

[37] Patterson, *Chaucer and the Subject of History*, p. 162.

the poem's central conflict. The chivalric code is shown incapable of dealing with its own inherent violence or of assimilating the feminine as anything but an occasion for violence. The male characters' more or less hapless oscillation between the forces of love and war provides the basis for a powerful critique of chivalric culture, committed to pursuits that leave it at the mercy of its own inherent weaknesses, powerless to distance itself from self-idealization and so incapable of reading its own history in the traces of the heroic past.

The Knight's narration has a strongly existential character, as though he were side-by-side with Theseus, experiencing each new turn of the action for the first time, and growing steadily more puzzled and dogged in his commitment as the story becomes more than he can control.[38] What confounds him is ultimately the fundamentally flawed character of the code of values he seeks to affirm, its vulnerability to the random activity of forces inherent in itself which it cannot acknowledge. The tension between incipient awareness of these problems and the "official" purpose which obliges the Knight to suppress them is the source of an odd and powerful drama. But while the Knight never fully recognizes the nature of his difficulty, one remarkable scene provides an insight into his embattled vision.

Having decreed a tournament to resolve the enmity of Palamon and Arcite, Theseus creates an immense arena, with temples to Venus, Mars, and Diana set high on its outer wall. Ostensibly created to honor these patron deities, the decoration of the temples shows their influence at its most malign. In Venus' world a decadent *courtoisie* provides a veil for continual restless movement, intrigue, and violence. Mars' power effects not only the ruin of war but the treachery of the back streets, and it is latent in ordinary activities like cooking, keeping pigs, driving carts, the work of barber, butcher, and smith. Diana's activity consists almost entirely in harsh reprisals against such unwitting offenders as Acteon, Callisto, and Meleager, who offend her savage purity unawares.

The sheer unwieldy power of these gods suggests the Knight's lurking awareness of the complexity of a world with which his warrior's vocation has not prepared him to deal. But in the temple of Mars he is also made to confront war itself. Amid a nightmarish proliferation of instances of random violence (ll. 1995–2040), he sees "open war," drenched in blood, armed Complaint, a battlefield where a thousand men lie dead, violent pillage, and in a single stark line, the aftermath of siege:

> The toun destroyed; there was no thyng laft. (l. 2016)

As the horrors of the temple of Mars proliferate in his mind, moreover, the

---

[38] In stressing the Knight's imperfect awareness of the implications of his project, I am following an argument first put forth in my "Romance and Epic in Chaucer's *Knight's Tale*," *Exemplaria* 2.1 (1990), 303–28. For a different view, see H. M. Leicester, Jr., *The Disenchanted Self: Representing the Subject in the "Canterbury Tales"* (Berkeley: University of California Press, 1990), pp. 221–382, who offers a "disenchanted" Knight, well aware of the danger inherent in the fantasies of chivalry.

Knight begins to describe this ancient pagan shrine as something he has actually seen, intruding "I rekned" and "I saw" as if a kind of self-hypnosis allowed thoughts normally repressed to surface in his mind. He withstands his own "dark imaginings" sufficiently to end by affirming the temple's function as a monument "in redoutynge of Mars and of his glorie" (l. 2050), but for a moment the readers have been allowed to contemplate the tension between his conscious social vision, deeply conditioned by chivalry, and his lurking awareness of the hungry rapacity of the world around him, with its many violent symptoms of social unrest.

Warfare itself was changing throughout the late fourteenth century, and technological advances were undermining the authority of chivalry in a variety of wholly practical ways. Cannons were probably used as early as the battle of Crécy in 1346, and the development of artillery inevitably worked to further distance the realities of warfare from the image of it promoted by chivalry and chivalric literature.[39] Romance is by its nature anachronistic in dealing with such things, but the impact of practical shifts in the nature of warfare gradually intrude into its pages. The "grete gunnes" with which Malory's Mordred lays siege to Guinevere, though they are probably only siege engines of a traditional kind,[40] are nonetheless a striking breach of romance decorum and a symptom of the obsolescence of the chivalric order Malory wrote to commemorate. And when the pragmatic Sir Baldwin of the anonymous "Avowing of King Arthur" tells the King and Sir Gawain of a coward who lost his life during a siege when the cask in which he had hidden himself was struck by a "gunne," he evokes a world of war in which the pretensions of traditional chivalry are clearly beside the point.[41] No guns appear in the panorama of the temple of Mars, but the temple expresses Chaucer's awareness of these changes. Much of its traumatic power for the Knight is due to the fact that it expresses the side of warfare that chivalry and its self-representations normally transcend. The interspersal of individual acts of predatory violence with the broader panorama of siege is a reminder of the motley character of a medieval fighting force, which commonly included men convicted of violent crime, and the extent to which sheer

---

[39] See Malcolm Vale, "New Techniques and Old Ideals: The Impact of Artillery on War and Chivalry at the End of the Hundred Years War," in *War, Literature, and Politics in the Late Middle Ages*, pp. 57–60, 72; Philippe Contamine, *War in the Middle Ages*, trans. Michael Jones (Oxford: Basil Blackwell, 1984), pp. 193–202.

[40] See Malory, *Works*, eds. Eugène Vinaver and P. J. C. Field, Vol. 3 (Oxford: Clarendon Press, 1990), p. 1227, where Mordred, laying siege to the Tower of London, "threw engynnes unto them, and shotte grete gunnes." That these "guns" are siege engines rather than cannons is persuasively argued by Dhira B. Mahoney, "Malory's Great Guns," *Viator* 20 (1989), 291–310.

[41] *The Avowing of King Arthur*, ed. Roger Mahood (New York: Garland, 1984), ll. 1013–36. Here "gunne" seems to mean the missile rather than the instrument and, again, need not imply cannon in the modern sense. See David Johnson, "The Real and the Ideal: Attitudes to Love and Chivalry as seen in *The Avowing of King Arthur*," in *Companion to Middle English Romance*, eds. Henk Aertsen and Alasdair A. MacDonald (Amsterdam: VU University Press, 1990), pp. 189–208, who argues on the basis of this and other passages that the "Avowing" contrasts the chivalry of romance with a new, more realistic standard of knightly conduct.

devastation was the objective of such a force.[42] It is a moment of realism comparable in power and directness to that of contemporary poems depicting actual battles, and its power is all the more striking in the context of a poem committed to affirming the power of chivalry to contain and transcend violence.[43]

But Chaucer's resources are above all those of a great and innovative poet. Like the Gawain-poet he was acutely aware of the ideological power of literary convention and of how readily the romance mode lent itself to the promotion of the ideals and interests of chivalry. But in the *Troilus* and the *Knight's Tale* the readers can see him exploiting the very innocence of romance, its perfect fit as a vessel for ideology, with a finely calculated naïeveté that is in its own way more subversive than straightforward satire or complaint. Nothing could be further from the drawing-room comedy that plays so large a role in *Troilus and Criseyde* than the tense martial pageantry of the Knight, but in his narration, too, the innocence of romance is being put to new ends. By making the Knight affirm the ideals of chivalry with such conviction, and by allowing him to express his hearty delight in the clash of arms and the folly of lovers, Chaucer is setting his narrator up for disaster, as surely as Pandarus and Criseyde set up the princes of Troy. The surfacing of the dark imaginings of the temple of Mars is a unique moment in medieval poetry, a simultaneous failure of romance decorum and chivalric self-confidence from which the Knight's narrative enterprise never really recovers. Like the alienating burden of Gawain's armor, these distinctive fictional modes, turning as they do the energies of romance against itself, are the engines by which he lays siege to the chivalric mentality.

---

[42] See Hewitt, pp. 28–47, 100–05; Kaeuper, pp. 15–32.

[43] For these reasons I find it difficult to accept the view of Derek Pearsall, *The Life of Geoffrey Chaucer* (Oxford: Blackwell, 1992), pp. 42–46, for whom Chaucer is an enthusiastic and essentially uncritical proponent of chivalry and its martial activities.

Siege Warfare in Transition

The Impact of Gunpowder Weaponry on Siege Warfare in the Hundred Years War

Kelly DeVries
Loyola College in Maryland

Concerning the siege of Beauvais in June 1472, Philippe de Commynes writes: "My Lord of Cordes . . . had two cannons which were fired only twice through the gate and made a large hole in it. If he had more stones to continue firing he would have certainly taken the town. However, he had not come with the intention of performing such an exploit and was therefore not well provided."[1] Even at this late date, with gunpowder weaponry in use for more than 150 years, the Lord of Cordes clearly did not fully comprehend the use of his gunpowder artillery in siege warfare. For although he made the effort to transport his cannons to Beauvais, not an easy nor an inexpensive task, he evidently did not consider the necessity of transporting many cannon balls, nor does he seem to have had a mason along to make the balls on site.[2]

It is comments like these, made so long after the introduction of gunpowder weapons to western Europe, that have given rise to the modern historical opinion that these weapons added little to siege warfare during the Hundred Years War. Read, for example, the words of Sir Charles Oman, who for close to one hundred years has spoken the sentiments of military historians:

> While cannon, and ribaulds too, had been used in sieges from the very first time of their invention, they had been more useful for shooting at men, or at woodwork, than at stone walls . . . It is only at battering in doors, bringing down

---

[1] Philippe de Commynes, *Mémoires*, eds. J. Calmette and G. Durville, Vol. 1 (Paris: Libraire Ancienne Honoré Champion, 1924), p. 235, reads in the original:
> Monsr des Cordes assaillit d'un autre costé; mais ses eschelles estoient courtes et n'en avoit guères. Il avoit deux canons, qui tirèrent au travers de la porte deux coups seulement et y feirent ung grant trou; et, s'il eust eu pierres pour continuer, il y fust entré sans doubte; mais il n'estoit point venu fourny pour tel exploit, pour quoy estoit mal pourveü.

[2] The best description of these fifteenth-century artillery trains can be found in Joseph Garnier, *L'artillerie des duc de Bourgogne d'après les documents conservés aux archives de la Côte d'Or* (Paris: Honoré Champion, 1895).

brattices, ruining palisades and drawbridges, or smashing in roofs of towers, or of houses inside the besieged town, that we find them effective. . . . We may almost say that the triumph of artillery only commences in the middle years of the fifteenth century.[3]

Even historians of technology have not varied from this opinion, as Lynn White has written:

> The earliest cannon were crude, cumbersome, and inefficient. They were costly to make and costly to supply with their chemical fuel. They could not be aimed with any great exactness; they were slow to load and to fire; they could rarely hit the same spot on a fortification twice because of irregular composition and combustion of the powder. . . . Any rational technology assessment of the cannon in 1326 or for a hundred years later would have concluded: "Stick to the trebuchet."[4]

Finally, historians of military architecture, like Sir John Hale, John R. Kenyon, Judith Hook, Horst de la Croix, Simon Pepper and Nicholas Adams, have so emphasized the artillery fortifications of the sixteenth century that they have almost completely ignored changes in fortification construction made to check gunpowder artillery attacks before that time.[5] This has also been accepted without criticism by Geoffrey Parker in his recent book, *The Military Revolution*, as proof of widespread military changes brought about by the introduction of gunpowder weapons.[6]

But these are unfortunate underestimations of the capabilities of gunpowder weapons in late medieval warfare. Early gunpowder weapons did indeed have an impact on late medieval siege warfare. In particular, the use of guns altered the number of and the time required for these sieges. They also necessitated that

---

[3]   Charles Oman, *A History of the Art of War in the Middle Ages*, Vol. 2 (London: Methuen, 1924), pp. 225–26. For similar statements, see N. J. G. Pounds, *The Medieval Castle in England and Wales: A Social and Political History* (Cambridge: Cambridge University Press, 1990), p. 253; D. J. Cathcart King, *The Castle in England and Wales* (London: Croom Helm, 1988), p. 169; and Pierre Barbier, *La France féodale*, Vol. 1: *Châteaux-forts et églises fortifées* (Saint-Brieuc: Les Presses Bretonnes, 1968), p. 286.

[4]   Lynn White, Jr., "Technology Assessment from the Stance of a Medieval Historian," in his *Medieval Religion and Technology: Collected Essays* (Berkeley: University of California Press, 1978), pp. 268–69.

[5]   J. R. Hale, "The Early Development of the Bastion: An Italian Chronology," in *Europe in the Late Middle Ages*, eds. J. R. Hale, R. Highfield, and B. Smalley (Evanston: Northwestern University Press, 1965), pp. 466–94, and his *Renaissance Fortification: Art or Engineering?* (London: Thames and Hudson, 1977); John R. Kenyon, "Early Artillery Fortifications in England and Wales: A Preliminary Survey," *Archaeological Journal* 138 (1981), 205–40; Judith Hook, "Fortifications and the End of the Sienese State," *History* 62 (1977), 372–87; Horst de la Croix, "The Literature on Fortification in Renaissance Italy," *Technology and Culture* 4 (1963), 30–50; and Simon Pepper and Nicholas Adams, *Firearms and Fortifications: Military Architecture and Siege Warfare in Sixteenth-Century Siena* (Chicago: University of Chicago Press, 1986).

[6]   Geoffrey Parker, *The Military Revolution: Military Innovation and the Rise of the West, 1500–1800* (Cambridge: Cambridge University Press, 1988).

defensive changes be made in the fortifications which were to face these new siege weapons.

It can be judged by the fortification depicted as the target in the Walter de Milemete illumination, the earliest artistic impression of a gunpowder weapon, dating from *c.* 1326, that the first and most enduring impact of gunpowder weapons was on siege warfare. The earliest gunpowder artillery pieces were heavy cannons with large calibers which fired heavy projectiles.[7] Huge guns were ideal for this type of fighting as the walls of castles were easily damaged by the ballistic force of gunshot, and by the middle of the fourteenth century nearly every siege was accompanied by gunpowder artillery bombardment.

By the end of the century, cannons were even breaching fortification walls. The first of these victories came in 1374 when the French used them to bring down the town walls of Saint-Saveur-le-Vicomte.[8] This was followed in 1377, at the siege of Odruik, when Philip the Bold, Duke of Burgundy, used cannons which fired 91-kilogram balls to bring down the walls of the castle.[9] And, at the siege of Oudenaarde in 1382, it is recorded by Jean Froissart that the rebellious Philip van Artevelde:

> had made and operated a marvelously large bombard, which had a calibre of fifty-three inches and shot quarrels of marvelously great size and weight; and when this bombard discharged, one could hear it for five leagues away during the day and during the night ten, and there was such a noise at the discharge that it seemed as though all the devils of hell had been on the road.[10]

With this weapon, he captured the fortification.

In the siege warfare of the fifteenth century, gunpowder weaponry continued to be significant. By 1412 and the siege of Bourges, the Duke of Berry, who was defending the city, was forced to vacate his residence no fewer than seven times to avoid the persistent and accurate gunfire of the French and Burgundian cannons.[11] This is conveyed colorfully in the *Chronique des religieux de Saint-Denis*:

---

[7] *The Treatise of Walter de Milemete: De nobilitatibus, sapientiis et prudentiis regum*, ed. M. R. James (London: The Roxburgh Club, 1913), p. 140. See also Pounds, pp. 252–53; DeVries, *Medieval Military Technology* (Peterborough: broadview press, 1992), pp. 144–45; M. G. A. Vale, "New Techniques and Old Ideals: The Impact of Artillery on War and Chivalry at the End of the Hundred Years War," in *War, Literature and Politics in the Late Middle Ages: Essays in Honour of G. W. Coopland*, ed. C. T. Allmand (Liverpool: Liverpool University Press, 1975), p. 59.

[8] Edouard Perroy, *The Hundred Years War*, trans. W. B. Wells (London: Eyre & Spottiswoode, 1959), p. 166.

[9] Jean Froissart, *Chroniques*, eds. S. Luce et al., Vol. 8 (Paris: Libraire Renouard, 1888), pp. 248–50.

[10] Froissart, Vol. 10, p. 248:
> il firent faire et ouvrer une bombarde merveilleusement grande, laquelle avoit cinquante et trois pols de bée et jettoit quarreaux merveilleusement grans, gros et pesans; et, quant celle bombarde desclicquoit, on l'ooit par jour bien cinq lieues loing et par nuit de dix, et menoit si grant tempeste au desclicquer que il sambloit que tous les deables d'enfer feussent sur le chemin.

[The besiegers] . . . caused a cannon called Griette, which was bigger than the others, to be mounted opposite the main gate. It shot stones of enormous weight at the cost of large quantities of gunpowder and much hard and dangerous work on the part of its expert crew. Nearly twenty men were required to handle it. When it was fired the thunderous noise could be heard four miles away and terrorized the local inhabitants as if it were some reverberation from hell. On the first day, the foundations of one of the towers were partly demolished by a direct hit. On the next day this cannon fired twelve stones, two of which penetrated the tower, thus exposing many of the buildings and their inhabitants. At the same time, other batteries at the siege were also making breaches in other parts of the wall.[12]

Other examples are numerous. I will choose only a few. In 1406, the Florentines used gunpowder weapons against the Pisans with such vehemence that it was recorded that "almost every house had been smashed or riddled with gunshots . . . the place had been brought to well-nigh total ruin."[13] At the siege of Étampes in 1411, the duke of Guyenne used both mining and gunpowder artillery together to breach the walls of the fortress, but before the mines could be completed the town had been taken by bombardment.[14] At Harfleur, in 1415, Henry V had to rely on his guns to bring down the walls of the town when his mines were continually countermined. Eventually he moved his guns on clumsy platforms next to the walls of the town before the siege was effective.[15] At Melun, in 1420, a combined Burgundian and English army, heavily supplied with gunpowder weapons, fought an artillery duel with an equally well supplied French defensive force; eventually the allies' technological superiority in

---

[11] *Chronique du religieux de Saint-Denis*, ed. L. Bellaguet, Vol. 4 (Paris: Crapelet, 1842), pp. 686–88. See also Richard Vaughan, *John the Fearless: The Growth of Burgundian Power* (London: Longman, 1966), pp. 150–51.

[12] *Chronique du religieux de Saint-Denis*, p. 652:

> Sed videntes quod machine jam erecte muros modicum debilitabant, unam omnibus majorem, vocatam Griete, ante portam principalem erigi preceperunt, que non sine pulveribus nimium sumptuosis, expertorum quoque artificum et sibi famulancium sudore et periculoso labore, lapides ingentis ponderis emitteret. Quociens ministerio fere viginti hominum id fiebat, ad aures quatuor milibus distancium veniebat, et emissum tonitruum viciniores terrebat, ac si ex infernali furia processisset. Jactu quoque violento prima die turris in parte destruxit fundamenta. Sequenti iterum die lapides molares emisit duodecim, e quibus due turrim illam penetrantes multa edificia cum habitoribus exposuerunt ultimo discrimini. Reliqua iterum obsidionalia instrumenta murorum precinctam locis plurimis confregerunt.

[13] As quoted in James Hamilton Wylie, *The History of England under Henry IV*, Vol. 3 (London: Longmans, Green & Co., 1898), p. 372.

[14] See *Chronique du religieux de Saint-Denis*, p. 576 and Euguerran de Monstrelet, *Chronique*, ed. L. Douet-d'Arcq, Vol. 2 (Paris: Librairie Renouard, 1858), p. 223.

[15] See, for example, *Gesta Henrici quinti*, eds. and trans. F. Taylor and J. S. Roskell (Oxford: Clarendon, 1975), pp. 23–28. See also Alfred H. Burne, *The Agincourt War* (London: Eyre & Spottiswoode, 1956), pp. 42–46 and Jim Bradbury, *The Medieval Siege* (Woodbridge: The Boydell Press, 1992), pp. 163–64, 291. Henry had taken 65 guns and more than 10,000 gunstones with him to Harfleur.

gunpowder weapons prevailed and Melun fell.[16] Fortepice was flattened in 1433 by a single great bombard, the Bourgoigne,[17] with a similar incident occurring at the siege of Harcourt in 1449, when a single shot from a French gun pierced the wall of the castle and caused the English to surrender their fortress.[18] And the town of Bouvignes fell in 1466, when, as contemporary chronicler Philippe de Commynes states, "two bombards and other large pieces of artillery, [shattered] the houses of the town . . . and (forced) the poor people to take refuge in their cellars and to remain there."[19] Finally, in August 1466, the town of Dinant, which had resisted 17 sieges during the Middle Ages, fell to Charles the Bold, the Duke of Burgundy, after only a week of gunpowder artillery bombardment.[20]

Sometimes it was a long and heavy bombardment which was required to defeat a besieged fortification. For example, at the siege of Maastricht from November 24, 1407, to January 7, 1408, the town received 1514 large bombard balls, an average of 30 per day; at the siege of Lagny in 1431, 412 stone cannonballs were fired into the town in a single day; at Dinant in 1466, 502 large and 1200 smaller cannonballs were fired; and finally, at the siege of Rhodes in 1480 over 3500 balls were shot into the town.[21]

At other times, simply the presence of large gunpowder weapons among the besieging army intimidated the inhabitants of a town or castle. An example of this came at the siege of Bourg, in June 1451, which Charles VII captured in just six days after his heavy artillery was brought up to the walls of the castle, although they never fired a shot.[22] In 1405, Berwick-upon-Tweed fell to the English after a single shot was fired from a single bombard.[23] In 1412, a similar situation occurred when Charles VII was able to take the castle of Dun-le-roi using only one cannon.[24] At the siege of Ham in 1411, only three shots were fired from the bombard known as "Griette." The first passed over the town and fell into the Somme; the second destroyed a tower and two adjacent walls; and the third made a breach in the wall itself. Before a fourth shot could be fired, the

---

[16] See E. Viollet-le-Duc, *Dictionnaire raisonné de l'architecture française du XIe au XVIe siècle*, Vol. 8 (Paris: Ve. A. Morel and Cie., 1866), p. 422.

[17] Garnier, pp. 98–99. This is taken from an original document found in the Chambre des Comptes de Dijon B 11868.

[18] Berry, Heraut du Roy, *Le recouvrement de Normandie*, in *Narratives of the Expulsion of the English from Normandy, 1449–50*, ed. J. Stevenson (London: Longman, 1863), p. 274.

[19] Commynes, p. 95:

> et tiroient de deux bombardes et autres pièces de grosse artillerie con-
> tinuellement durant ce temps au travers des maisons de ladicte ville de
> Bouvynies et contraignoient les pouvres gens de eulx cacher en leurs caves et
> y demourer.

[20] See Richard Vaughan, *Philip the Good: The Apogee of Burgundy* (London: Longman, 1970), p. 397.

[21] See Philippe Contamine, *War in the Middle Ages*, trans. M. Jones (Oxford: Basil Blackwell, 1984), pp. 200–01.

[22] See M. G. A. Vale, *War and Chivalry: Warfare and Aristocratic Culture in England, France and Burgundy at the End of the Middle Ages* (London: Duckworth, 1981), p. 138.

[23] See Wylie, Vol. 2, pp. 264–73.

[24] *Chronique du religieux de Saint-Denis*, pp. 652–54 and Monstrelet, p. 272.

town capitulated.[25] And the rebellious Douglas castle at Abercorn, one of the strongest Scottish fortifications, fell to James II's guns in 1455 in less than a month. On this siege the *Auchinleck Chronicle* reports: "The king remanit at the sege and gart strek mony of the towris doun with the gret gun, the quhilk a Francheman schot right wele, and failyeit na shot within a faldom quhar it was chargit him to hit."[26]

Sometimes, it must be admitted, gunpowder siege artillery was unsuccessful, especially since many commanders, trained in the old tactics of siege warfare, did not recognize the capabilities of these new weapons and were thus unable to use them effectively. Certainly this was the case in the example mentioned above, when the Lord of Cordes unsuccessfully besieged Beauvais in 1472, at least according to the chronicler Philippe de Commynes, because he failed to bring along enough projectiles to take the town. On other occasions, the misuse of guns by inexperienced operators caused problems. Frequently these early gunpowder weapons exploded, and sometimes more bizarre accidents occurred. For example, at the battle of Gavere in July 1453 the Ghentenaars broke ranks and fled because one of their cannoneers inadvertently allowed a spark from his ignitor to fly into an open sack of gunpowder which burst into flames. All the nearby cannoneers panicked and ran; when the rest of the army saw this, it also took flight.[27] But these examples are few and should not be used to determine the overall impact of early gunpowder weapons in sieges.

Indeed, so effective were gunpowder weapon bombardments during sieges that an anonymous poet wrote the following lines after witnessing the siege of Calais by the Burgundians in 1435:

> Gonners began to show thaire art
> into the town in many a part
> Shot many a full grete stone.
> Thanked be god and marie mylde
> They hurt neither man woman ne childe,
> House, thouh, they did harme,
> "Seynt Barbara" then was the crie
> Whan the stones in the toun did flye,
> They cowde noon other charme.[28]

Naturally, the threat of attack by gunpowder weapons influenced those responsible for the construction or maintenance of fortifications. It was quickly

[25] *Le Livre des trahisons de France envers la maison de Bourgogne*, in *Chroniques relatives à l'histoire de la Belgique sous la domination des ducs de Bourgogne (textes français)*, ed. M. de Kervyn de Lettenhove (Brussels: F. Hayez, 1873), p. 96:

[26] As quoted in Geoffrey Stell, "Late Medieval Defences in Scotland," in *Scottish Weapons and Fortifications, 1100–1800*, ed. D. H. Caldwell (Edinburgh: J. Donald, 1981), p. 40.

[27] This incident is recorded in the *Kronyk van Vlaenderen van 580 tot 1467*, eds. P. Bloomaert and C. P. Serriere, Vol. 1 (Ghent: D. J. Vanderhaeghen Hulin, 1840), p. 194. See also Vaughan, *Philip the Good*, p. 34.

[28] See Ralph A. Klinefelter, ed., " 'The Siege of Calais': A New Text," *Publications of the Modern Language Association* 67 (1952), 888–95. The quote above is found on pp. 892–93.

realized that traditional medieval castles and town walls with their tall, flat surfaces were easy targets for guns, especially for the large calibre bombards so frequently used in sieges. The tall walls of medieval fortifications had been built to withstand weapons which could not inflict the continual barrage on a single area as could the new gunpowder weapons, and in fact the weight and relative thinness of the base of these walls invariably made it easier to penetrate these fortifications.[29]

It was both too expensive and time-consuming to rebuild all fortifications to meet the attacks of gunpowder weapons. Therefore, the initial move was to outfit these fortifications with guns as a defense against attacking gunpowder weapons. Gunpowder weapons began to be delivered to castles and town walls by the middle of the fourteenth century, but guns mounted on the tops of castle and town walls made little sense as they could not effectively defend the wall below them, an area which was most likely to be attacked.[30] This meant that the wall itself needed to be pierced with gunports so that defending fire could be more directly aimed at attacking artillery. This may have occurred as early as 1347 when the gate at the castle of Bioule was recorded as having been defended on its first floor by two men firing cannons,[31] but, if so, the idea did not become popular in England until at least 1365 and in France until after 1380. Germany, Italy and Spain may not have constructed gunports in their fortifications until even later than this.[32]

Once it did become popular in England and in France, however, the number of fortifications, both castles and town walls, which received gunports multiplied rapidly. In England, gunports were added to Quarr Abbey on the Isle of Wight in 1365–66 (perhaps their earliest English use), to Queensborough Castle in 1373, to Asseton's Tower at Porchester in 1379, to Carisbrooke Castle in 1379–80, to the Canterbury town wall in 1380, to Cooling Castle in 1381, to Southampton Castle and town wall in 1382–86, to Saltwood Castle in 1383, to Norwich town wall and probably Dover Castle in 1385, to Bodiam Castle in 1386 and to the Winchester town wall in 1390.[33] In France, gunports were added more slowly

---

[29] See Viollet-le-Duc, Vol. 1 (1854), p. 404 and Philippe Contamine, "France à la fin du Moyen Âge: aspects financiers et économiques," *Revue historique* 260 (1978), 25. Also, in the early fifteenth century, Christine de Pisan believed that alterations needed to be made to fortifications so that they could adapt to sieges with gunpowder weapons (Christine de Pisan, *The Book of Fayettes of Armes and of Chyvalrye*, trans. W. Caxton, ed. A. T. P. Byles, Early English Text Society 189 (London: Early English Text Society, 1932), pp. 39, 136–37).

[30] Viollet-le-Duc, Vol. 1 (1854), p. 410; B. H. St. J. O'Neil, *Castles and Cannon: A Study of Early Artillery Fortifications in England* (Oxford: Clarendon Press, 1960), pp. 4–5, 10–11, 22; and D. F. Renn, "The Earliest Gunports in Britain?" *Archaeological Journal* 125 (1968), 302–03.

[31] "Règlement pour la défense du château de Bioule, 18 mars 1347," *Bulletin archéologique* 4 (1846–47), 490–95. See also Contamine, *War*, p. 202.

[32] Nevertheless, several fifteenth-century Spanish and Italian castles were pierced by gunports. See King, p. 160.

[33] A general reference guide to English gunports is John R. Kenyon, "Early Gunports: A Gazateer," *Fort* 4 (1977), 4–6. On Quarr Abbey, see Renn, "Earliest," pp. 301–03; Kenyon, "Early Artillery Fortifications," p. 207; and Pounds, p. 255. On Queensborough Castle, see R. A.

and in fewer numbers. Besides those which may have existed at Bioule Castle, it is only the gunports in the town wall of Mont-Saint-Michel and at the castles of Blanquefort and Saint-Mâlo which can be confirmed to have been built before 1400.[34] Others were not built until after 1412, with the large towns of Paris and Rennes receiving their gunports in 1415 and 1418 respectively.[35] However, gunport construction in France does continue until 1480, while in England it declines drastically after 1420, with the placement of gunports primarily in fortified manor houses – i.e., Berry Pomeroy, Baconsthorpe, Kirby Muxloe, Cotehele and Oxburgh – and in monastic buildings – i.e., Titchfield and Tavistock Abbeys.[36]

Brown, H. M. Colvin and A. J. Taylor, *The History of the King's Works*, Vol. 2 (London: Her Majesty's Stationary Office, 1963), pp. 801–02. On Asseton's Tower, see O'Neil, p. 10, and Kenyon, "Early Artillery Fortifications," pp. 207, 209. On Carisbrooke Castle, see Brown, Colvin and Taylor, p. 594; O'Neil, p. 10; Kenyon, "Early Artillery Fortifications," pp. 207, 210; and Pounds, p. 255. On Canterbury town wall, see O'Neil, p. 17; Kenyon, "Early Artillery Fortifications," pp. 207–08; King, p. 170; Pounds, p. 255; M. J. Jones and C. J. Bond, "Urban Defences," in *Urban Archaeology in Britain*, eds. J. Schofield and R. Leech (London: The Council for British Archaeology, 1987), p. 112; and S. S. Frere and S. Stowe, *The Archaeology of Canterbury*, Vol. 2: *Excavations on the Roman and Medieval Defences of Canterbury* (Maidstone: Kent Archaeological Society, 1982), p. 23. On Cooling Castle, see O'Neil, p. 9; Kenyon, "Early Artillery Fortifications," p. 207; King, p. 155; and Pounds, p. 255. On Southampton Castle and town wall, see Brown, Colvin and Taylor, p. 844; O'Neil, pp. 10–11; Kenyon, "Early Artillery Fortifications," pp. 207, 210–11; King, p. 165; Pounds, p. 255; D. F. Renn, "The Southampton Arcade" *Medieval Archaeology* 8 (1964), 226–28; and John R. Kenyon, "Artillery and the Defences of Southampton circa 1360–1660," *Fort* 3 (1977), 9. On Saltwood Castle, see O'Neil, p. 20; Kenyon, "Early Artillery Fortifications," p. 207; and Pounds, p. 255. On Norwich town wall, see Kenyon, "Early Artillery Fortifications," pp. 211–12. On Dover Castle, see Kenyon, "Early Artillery Fortifications," p. 208 and Pounds, p. 255. On Bodiam Castle, see O'Neil, p. 17; Kenyon, "Early Artillery Fortifications," pp. 207, 209; and D. J. Turner, "Bodiam, Sussex: True Castle or Old Soldier's Dream House?," in *England in the Fourteenth Century: Proceedings of the 1985 Harlaxton Symposium*, ed. W. M. Ormond (Woodbridge: The Boydell Press, 1986), pp. 267–77. And on Winchester town wall, see O'Neil, pp. 17–18; Kenyon, "Early Artillery Fortifications," p. 207; and Jones and Bond, p. 112.

[34] On the gunports at Mont-Saint-Michel, see Contamine, *War*, p. 202. On those at St. Mâlo, see Michael Jones, "The Defence of Medieval Brittany: A Survey of the Establishment of Fortified Towns, Castles and Frontiers from the Gallo-Roman Period to the End of the Middle Ages," *Archaeological Journal* 138 (1981), 174. And on gunports at Blanquefort Castle, see M. G. A. Vale, "Seigneurial Fortification and Private War in Late Medieval Gascony," in *Gentry and Lesser Nobility in Late Medieval Europe*, ed. M. Jones (Gloucester: A. Sutton, 1986), p. 141. Christine de Pisan also understood the need for gunports (Christine de Pisan, pp. 136–37).

[35] On Paris, see *Choix de pièces inédites relatives au règne de Charles VI*, ed. L. Douet-d'Arcq, Vol. 2 (Paris: Libraire Renouard, 1863–64), pp. 32–33. And on Rennes, see Jones, p. 175.

[36] Contamine, *War*, pp. 202–03; Kenyon, "Early Artillery Fortifications," p. 232; and Vale "Seigneurial Fortification," pp. 141–42. Scotland, like the French, also continued to build gunports until the end of the fifteenth century. See Stell, pp. 44–45. On the post–1420 English gunports there is a general consensus that they were of poor quality with little utility. Colin Platt asserts that they showed no advancement in form to those in castles a century previously, despite the extensive evolution of guns since that date (Colin Platt, *The Castle in Medieval England and Wales* [New York: Charles Scribner's Sons, 1982], p. 164). While N. J. G. Pounds is even more critical in his assessment of their defensive worth:

> Many of the 'houses' equipped with gunports in the later fifteenth century were neither capable of withstanding a sustained attack, nor were they

In the late fourteenth century most gunports were shaped like inverted key-holes with circular openings for guns below long vertical slits. This may indicate then that they were initially nothing more than arrow-slits adapted for gunpowder weapons by adding a circular opening to the bottom, as fifteenth century gunports were usually built without the vertical slit; however, some architectural historians contend that the slits were there merely to facilitate the sighting of the weapon.[37] This certainly agrees with Lord Cobham's orders to his mason constructing the gunports at Cooling Castle: "[There are to be made] ten *arket* (haquebus) holes of three feet in length without cross-slits."[38] Other, rarer types of gunports include: the double-ended or dumbbell port, which were made for the use of guns mounted in pairs or to give handguns the most wide-ranging field of fire, the circular opening in the middle of a slit, the "letterbox" port (inside circular, outside horizontal), and the square port.[39]

Gunports were also quite small: the slits ranged in length between 381 and 813 millimeters and in width between 65 and 152 millimeters, while the circular openings ranged between 127 and 305 millimeters in diameter. They were also built near to the ground, generally no higher than one meter from the inside floor.[40] This may indicate a desire to attack not the opposing guns themselves, but their mounts. D. J. Cathcart King describes the placement and use of these gunports, using Kirby Muxloe Castle as an example:

> There is a rectangular gatehouse with turrets at each corner, and there were to have been seven square or rectangular towers [Kirby Muxloe was left incomplete at the beheading of its owner, William, Lord Hastings] . . . Both the gatehouse and the one surviving tower were amply provided for the use of guns, apparently of fairly heavy calibre; the gatehouse has six ports and the tower seven, all on the lowest floor. The ports have a fair amount of internal splay, and are in general well arranged. In the tower the inner arches of the ports were blocked by a thin skin of brickwork which excluded draughts, rats, etc. in

intended to do so, but one or two guns might give some advantage against local raids of lawless bands. (p. 255)

37 O'Neil, pp. 12–13; Kenyon, "Early Artillery Fortifications," p. 207; Pounds, pp. 254–55; Platt, pp. 166–67; King, pp. 166–67; Stell, pp. 40–41; Stewart Cruden, *The Scottish Castle* (Edinburgh: Nelson, 1960), pp. 215–18; and A. M. T. Maxwell-Irving, "Early Firearms and their Influence on the Military and Domestic Architecture of the Borders," *Proceedings of the Society of Antiquaries of Scotland* 103 (1970–71), 192–223. Circular ports alone appear first at Cooling Castle in 1381 (King, pp. 166–67).

38 As quoted by Pounds, p. 255: "x arket holes de iii peez longour en tout saunz croys."

39 On the circular in the middle of a slit, "letterbox," and square ports, see King, pp. 166–67. On the double-ended gunport, see Stell, pp. 40–41.

40 See O'Neil, pp. 7–11, 17–20, 29–30, 37; Kenyon, "Early Artillery Fortifications," pp. 207–08; Renn, "Earliest," p. 301; Frere and Stowe, p. 117; John R. Kenyon, "The Gunloops at Raglan Castle, Gwent," in *Castles in Wales and the Marches. Essays in Honour of D. J. Cathcart King*, eds. J. R. Kenyon and R. Avent (Cardiff: University of Wales Press, 1987), pp. 143–60; Jean-Pierre Leguay, *Un réseau urbain au Moyen Âge: les villes du duché de Bretagne aus XIVeme et XVeme siècles* (Paris: Maloine, 1988), p. 185. Caister Castle had gunports not only along the base of the fortification, but also higher, with six ports in the turret room at the top of the tower in a sort of "sniper's nest" which, in the words of D. J. Cathcart King, "can hardly have been of much use" (p. 162).

peacetime, but could have been knocked out in short order when war was at hand; the ports in the gatehouse seem to have been left open, as more likely to have been needed without warning.[41]

The number and distribution of gunports around the fortifications varied greatly. Sometimes there was only one or two gunports in a fortress, while other fortifications, especially those built in the fifteenth century contained a much larger number. For example, the West Gate at Canterbury, built 1375–81, had 19 gunports,[42] and Raglan Castle, built c. 1450, contained no fewer than 32 gunports.[43] Most also were located in the fortification's gates and towers. This allowed them to provide some flanking fire along the wall and causeways, although such flanking fire may have been of limited effect, as most gunports allowed less than a 45 degree angle of fire.[44] Guns are also recorded to have been fired from coastal fortification gunports at ships sailing past them.[45]

The small size of these gunports also meant that they did not allow for the use of large guns for defense of the fortification. This is seen also in the small size of the gunport embrasures on which these guns were mounted, most of which were less than 70 centimeters long. This allowed only the smallest of mounted gunpowder weapons, probably culverins, or hand-held guns to be fired from these gunports.[46] Some gunports, for example those at Winchester and the Dutch Castle of Doornenburg, have square sockets close to the opening of the port, meant to carry a timber or wood transom across the opening which may indicate the use of "hook-guns" (hakenbuchs) in those ports.[47]

Still, gunports alone could not supply sufficient defense against most gunpowder artillery bombardments. Although defensive guns provided some protection against enemy gunfire, the height of castles and town walls still afforded an ideal target to any force attacking with guns, especially as those guns by the

---

[41] King, pp. 161–62.

[42] King, p. 170.

[43] Kenyon, "Raglan Castle," p. 162, and Anthony Emery, "The Development of Raglan Castle and Keeps in Late Medieval England," *Archaeological Journal* 132 (1975), 169–70. Raglan Castle's restricted field of fire may have been supplanted by its numerous gunports. See Kenyon, "Raglan Castle," and Platt, p. 154.

[44] Kenyon, "Early Artillery Fortifications," p. 209; King, p. 162; Frere and Stowe, p. 117; and Renn, "Southampton," pp. 226–28.

[45] See, for example, Gutierre Díaz de Gámez' *Le victorial: chronique de Don Pedro Nino, comte de Buelna*, ed. and trans. Ramón Iglesia (Paris, 1867), p. 373, which reports that Don Pedro Niño received fire from Calaisien batteries of "very strong bombards" located in the Lancaster Tower when he sailed too close to the English-controlled town.

[46] Kenyon, "Early Artillery Fortifications," p. 207; Kenyon, "Raglan Castle," p. 165; Kenyon, "Southampton," p. 9; Renn, "Southampton," pp. 226–28; and Pierre P. F. M. Rocolle, *2000 ans de fortification française*, Vol. 1 (Limoges: Charles-Lavauzelle, 1973), p. 146. For example, the gunports at Threave Castle in Scotland show that only small guns and handguns could be used there (John R. Kenyon, *Medieval Fortifications* [New York: St. Martin's Press, 1990], pp. 75–76). See also Pounds (p. 255) who claims that the frequency of gunports for small weapons only indicates that most owners could own only handguns or smaller cannons.

[47] King, pp. 165–66.

early fifteenth century had evolved into more powerful and more accurate siege weapons. Other methods of improving defense were needed.

Some towns and castles tried to meet the threat of gunshot bombardment by thickening their walls with piles of earth behind them. While this did protect the walls from being easily breached in some instances, it was not always successful. The earthen rampart exerted a heavy pressure on the wall and frequently weakened the masonry instead of strengthening it. As Philip, Duke of Clèves, noted at the end of the fifteenth century, "whenever the guns batter the wall, the earth tumbles down with the masonry, which makes it all the easier for the enemy to climb into the breach."[48]

Other fortifications also tried to thicken their walls, although with more masonry instead of earth. Or they added a sloping *glacis* of masonry to the front of their walls to produce glancing gunshots rather than direct impact on the flat wall. Some even chose to replace older masonry walls or to build new walls from different building materials, such as blocks of granite – as at Fougères, Largoët, and Lassay Castles – red sandstone – as at Haut-Koenigsbourg Castle – or in brick – as at Rambures and Kirby Muxloe Castles.[49] However, all of these additions were very expensive and thus not generally obtainable for many towns or castle owners whose resources were usually quite limited.[50] Still others tried to increase the size of the ditches surrounding their fortifications, noting the relative security against bombardment of large moated fortresses, like Bodiam, Kenilworth or Caerphilly Castles, but this, too, was more expensive than most towns or castles were able to afford.[51]

Some fortification builders tried to increase the defense of castles and town walls by adding new fortifications to the existing defensive structures and then filling these new fortifications with defensive artillery. In essence, the theory behind these defensive additions was the same as that of gunports, facing guns with guns, except that as they were separate from the castles and town walls themselves, their defeat did not necessarily mean the collapse of a fortification. Generally, these were built in two styles. The first style was the low earthwork defense, known as a boulevard, which was generally placed before a vulnerable gate or wall. Its defense derived from a large number of guns (which increased the amount of defensive firepower), a low height (which made it easier to fire) and earth and timber walls (which more readily absorbed the impact of stone

---

[48] As quoted in Louis Napoléon Bonaparte and I. Fave, *Études sur le passé et l'avenir de l'artillerie*, Vol. 2 (Paris, 1851), p. 104. See also Pepper and Adams, pp. 17–18; Christopher Duffy, *Siege Warfare: The Fortress in the Early Modern World. 1494–1660* (London: Routledge & Kegan Paul, 1979), p. 2; and David Eltis, "Towns and Defence in Later Medieval Germany," *Nottingham Medieval Studies* 33 (1989), 94.

[49] Platt, p. 160, and J.–F. Finò, *Forteresses de la France médiévale* (Paris: Éditions A. & J. Picard, 1970), p. 292.

[50] Contamine, *War*, p. 204. For the cost of some fourteenth- and fifteenth-century rebuilding projects, see Contamine, "Fortifications," pp. 26–27.

[51] Finò, pp. 292, 297–300; Contamine, "Fortifications," pp. 27, 43–44; and D. J. Turner, p. 269. At Parthenay, three "pairs" of ditches and two "pairs" of walls were built as a deterrent to artillery attack. See Contamine, "Fortifications," p. 47.

and metal cannonballs). Although the English were known to have built boule-vards, particularly around their captured towns and fortifications during the Hundred Years War, as at Poitiers, Orléans, and Cadillac,[52] they seem to have been especially popular in mid-fifteenth-century France among fortresses which were more open to gunpowder artillery bombardment. There they could be found in the fortifications of Gisors, Arjony, Bonaguil, Brest, Avignon, Ham, Amiens, Dijon, Salces, Verteuil, Budos and Présilly.[53] It is also in the boulevard where ravelins, casements, hornworks, and perhaps even bastions have their origins, all important anti-artillery fortifications in the *trace italienne*.[54]

Certainly the most famous boulevard to withstand artillery attacks was that built outside the Tourelles gate across the bridge from Orléans. Built in June 1426 as one of many English boulevards constructed around the town at the time of their siege of Orléans – at least that is the date when gunpowder weapons were ordered to be delivered there – the boulevard of Tourelles, as it came to be known, became the focal point of the May 5–6, 1429 siege of Orléans by the French who were trying to recapture the town. Despite the French making "many marvelous assaults, during which many marvelous feats of arms were performed," according to the contemporary *Journal d'un siège d'Orléans*, the boulevard was able to hold off these sorties and repulse the attack with the result that "many Frenchmen were killed or wounded."[55]

---

[52] Contamine, "Fortifications," pp. 26–27, and Leo Drouyn, *La Guienne militaire: Histoire et description des villes fortifiées, forteresses et châteaux*, Vol. 2 (Paris: Didron, 1865), p. 258.

[53] Finò, pp. 295–96; Contamine, *War*, p. 204; Leguay, pp. 171–72, 185–86; Jones, p. 176; Rocolle, pp. 171–73; Viollet-le-Duc, Vol. 1 (1854), pp. 422–31; and Vale, *War*, p. 133.

[54] Rocolle, pp. 171–74, and Viollet-le-Duc, Vol. 1 (1854), pp. 425–31.

[55] *Journal du siège d'Orléans, 1428–1429*, eds. P. Charpentier and C. Cussard (Orléans: H. Herluison, 1896), pp. 84–85:

> Le jour d'après au plus matin, qui fut samedy, sixiesme jour de may, assaillir-ent les Françoys les Tournelles et les boulevars et taudis que les Angloys y avoyent faiz pour les fortiffier. Et y eut mout merveilleux assault, durant lequel y furent faitz plusieurs beaux faiz d'armes, tant en assaillant que en deffendant, parce que Angloys y estoient grant nombre fort combatans, et garnis habondanment de toutes choses deffensables. Et aussi le monstrèrent ilz bien, car nonobstant que les Franchois les eschelassent par divers lieux moult espessement, et assaillissent de fronc, au plus hault de leurs fortiffi-cacions de telle vaillance et hardiesse, qu'il sembloit à leur hardi maintien que ilz cuidas-sent estre immortelz: si les reboutèrent ilz par maintes fois et tresbuschèrent de hault en bas, tant par canons et autre traict, comme aux haches, lances, guisarmes, mailletz de plomb, et mesmes à leurs propres mains, tellement qu'ilz tuèrent que blecèrent plusieurs Françoys.

> Early in the morning on the day after, which was Saturday, the sixth day of May, the French attacked Les Tourelles and the boulevard while the English were attempting to fortify it. And there was a spectacular assault during which there were performed many great feats of arms, both in the attack and in the defense, because the English had a large number of strong soldiers and had strengthened skillfully all of the defensible places. And also they fought well, notwithstanding that the French scaled the different places adeptly and at-tacked the angles at the highest of the strong and sturdy fortifications so that they seemed by this to be immortal. But the English repulsed them from many places and attacked with artillery both high and low, both with cannons and

The second of these additional defensive fortifications was the artillery tower. This was a newly constructed tower, equipped with numerous gunports and filled with a large number of gunpowder weapons, which was added to the most exposed part of a fortress. Its purpose was nearly the same as the boulevard, both to increase the amount of defensive firepower and add flanking fire to a vulnerable wall or gate, but it was generally much thicker and taller, sometimes three or four stories high, and constructed in stone. Sometimes these towers were extremely large. For example, the tower built at Ham, after its easy capitulation in 1411 mentioned above, was 33 meters in diameter and 33 meters in height; the tower at Fougères was 20 meters in diameter and 20 meters in height.[56] The artillery tower was usually round in shape which provided no flat surfaces to enemy gunfire, although they can be found in L- and D-shape as well. The artillery tower was also the preferred artillery fortification added to English castles and town walls and would, in fact, continue to be built there into the sixteenth century.[57]

An example of the use of artillery towers in the fifteenth century can be found at Threave Castle in Scotland. There a fourteenth-century tower-house, built initially as a residence for the Douglas family, had three round three-story artillery towers, each with an internal diameter of 2.6–2.8 meters, added to a curtain wall in the 1440s. A rock-cut moat was also added at that time. Gunports were numerous in all three towers, as can be seen today in the one remaining tower, which were designed to use small calibre cannons or handguns. Furthermore, at the same time, two buildings in the outer enclosure were demolished so that flanking fire from these towers would not be impeded. Threave castle held out for three months in 1455 against James II's best gunpowder weapons, until the Douglases submitted to bribery; at least 34 examples of gunshot have come from excavations around the Threave fortifications.[58]

other weapons, such as axes, lances, pole-arms, lead hammers, and other personal arms, so that they killed and wounded many French.
See also Jacques Debal, "Les fortifications et le pont d'Orléans au temps de Jeanne d'Arc," *Dossiers de archéologie* 34 (May 1979), 88–92; Jacques Debal, "La topographie de l'enceinte fortifiée d'Orléans au temps de Jeanne d'Arc," in *Jeanne d'Arc: une époque, un rayonnement*, Colloque d'histoire médiévale, Orléans – Octobre 1979 (Paris: éditions du Centre National de la Recherche Scientifique, 1982), pp. 25–27; and Françoise Michaud-Fréjaville, "Une cité face aux crises: les remparts de la fidélité, de Louis d'Orléans à Charles VII, d'après les comptes de forteresse de la ville d'Orléans (1391–1427)," in *Jeanne d'Arc: une époque, une rayonnement*, p. 53. The boulevard stood as late as 1676. See Debal, "Topographie," p. 37.

[56] Finò, p. 291.

[57] On English artillery towers, see King, pp. 161–63; Brown, Colvin and Taylor, p. 606; Platt, p. 160; Kenyon, *Medieval Fortifications*, pp. 75–76; and Hilary L. Turner, *Town Defences in England and Wales* (London: John Barker, 1971), pp. 60, 165. On French artillery towers, see Finò, pp. 291–96; Vale, *War*, p. 133; Leguay, p. 187; Jones, pp. 175–76; Barbier, pp. 287–89; Viollet-le-Duc, Vol. 1 (1854), pp. 414–22; and Rocolle, pp. 174–76. On Italian artillery towers, see Contamine, *War*, p. 204, and Hale, "Bastion," p. 479. And on Scottish artillery towers, see Stell, p. 41.

[58] Kenyon, *Medieval Fortifications*, pp. 75–76, 172, and Christopher J. Tabraham and George L. Good, "The Artillery Fortification at Threave Castle, Gallowey," in *Scottish Weapons and Fortifications, 1100–1800*, ed. D. H. Caldwell (Edinburgh: J. Donald, 1981), pp. 55–72.

The artillery tower may have been the impetus behind the construction of larger round-shaped castles at Queensborough in England and at Rambures in France. However, only Rambures' dates (1421–70) allow for a construction possibly conscious of the power of gunpowder weaponry; Rambures Castle is also known to have stored cannons, although there are no apparent gunports in the castle walls.[59] Queensborough Castle, on the other hand, was constructed in the 1360s, which may have been before the time it was recognized that the round shape of castle walls was a viable defense against gunpowder artillery bombardment. Still, it is known that guns were an important early defense of the castle, together with non-gunpowder artillery, and that they were fired off in honor of a visit by Edward III in 1373. This may mean that the builders of this castle did, indeed, perceive the anti-bombardment defensive capabilities of this fortification style, although if they in fact did, it was not similarly recognized by other castle builders of the late fourteenth and fifteenth centuries, as its style was never copied.[60]

The problem was that none of these additions to existing fortifications provided a "complete" security against gunpowder artillery attack, and by the end of the fifteenth century it was recognized that traditional medieval fortifications, even with the addition of gunports, artillery towers, or boulevards, could not provide an adequate defense against a gunpowder weapon attack on their inhabitants. As well, the lack of castles similar to those at Queensborough and Rambures reveal that fortification builders either ascertained that these were too expensive to construct, or that they provided no secure defense against gunpowder weaponry once completed. A more elaborate system of fortifications was needed, a system with walls that could withstand the constant impact of stone or metal cannonballs while at the same time offering its own forceful gunshot bombardment against those besiegers.

Initially, the question seemed to be not one of defending the fortification against attacks made directly on gates or towers – gunports, artillery towers, boulevards, and even ditches could accomplish this – but of defense against attacks made against the so-called "dead zones" along the walls between the towers and gates. The dead zones could only be defended by flanking fire.[61]

There is no doubt that the necessity for flanking fire was an issue early in the

---

[59] Finò, pp. 421–23, and Rocolle, pp. 167–68.

[60] Brown, Colvin and Taylor, pp. 801–02, and M. W. Thompson, *The Decline of the Castle* (Cambridge: Cambridge University Press, 1987), p. 36. D. J. Cathcart King disputes the link between Queensborough Castle and gunpowder artillery:

> The Circular arrangement suggests some sort of kinship with Henry VIII's artillery-castles, and the plan has certainly an odd resemblance to that of Deal; but a gap of nearly two centuries separates the two, and from what we know of artillery and its use in the fourteenth century it is wildly unlikely that a castle would have been specially designed for its employment as early as 1361. (p. 154)

[61] See Hale, "Bastion," p. 475; Pepper and Adams, p. 3; Duffy, p. 2; Parker, p. 10; and Jean Richard, "Quelques idées de François de Surienne sur la défense des villes à propos de la fortification de Dijon (1461)," *Annales de Bourgogne* 16 (1944), 38–39.

fifteenth century, as many of the anti-gunpowder weaponry innovations added to fortifications at that time attempted to provide some defense against dead zones.[62] But invariably these proved inadequate for such a task. Gunports cut into fortification walls could not be numerous enough to adequately defend them against all attacks without weakening the actual structure of the wall itself. Gunports from artillery towers often pointed down the walls, but their flanking fire capabilities were hampered by their small size and by the limited ballistic force of the small calibre weapons firing from them. Boulevards, too, attempted some flanking fire, but built at a distance from the walls, they could not adequately cover their dead zones without doing damage to their own fortifications. Thus new anti-gunpowder weaponry fortifications needed to be designed and constructed.[63]

The answer was the development of the bastion. The bastion borrowed greatly from both the artillery tower and the boulevard for its design.[64] Like the artillery tower, it was constructed at the corner of and extending several meters beyond the fortification walls; and like the boulevard, it was built at a low height and filled with defensive gunpowder weapons which fired not from gunports but from platforms perched near the top of the wall.[65] But unlike artillery towers and boulevards, bastions were built in an angular style, jutting out as a triangle, their sides, mounted with large calibre cannons, facing down the walls they were meant to protect.[66]

Remains of early bastions demonstrate that the Italians held a particular fondness for the anti-gunpowder weaponry innovation in the last four decades of the fifteenth century.[67] Angular bastions were added to the fortifications of Cesena c. 1466, Volterra c. 1472, Senigallia c. 1480, Ostia Antica in 1482–86, Sarazana c. 1487, Poggio Imperiale c. 1487, Ferrara c. 1492, Sarazanello in 1493, and Castel Sant' Angelo in 1492–95.[68] Sometimes these were minor

[62] Christine de Pisan, for one, suggests that defensive artillery be placed on platforms projecting from fortress walls for flanking fire (Christine de Pisan, pp. 136–37). See also Croix, pp. 33–34.

[63] Hale, "Bastion," p. 479.

[64] Hale, "Bastion," p. 476. M. W. Thompson sees the artillery tower at Ham Castle as a definite point of origin for the bastioned fortress of the late fifteenth century (p. 41).

[65] Pepper and Adams, p. 6.

[66] Croix, p. 31, and Pepper and Adams, p. 3.

[67] Viollet-le-Duc contends, in fact, that bastions were a discovery made simultaneously by the Germans, French, and Italians: "Les Italiens prétendent être les inventeurs de ce genre de défense; mais nous ne voyons pas que les faits viennent appuyer cette prétention" (The Italians claim to be the inventors of this type of defense; but we do not see where the facts are able to support this claim) (Vol. 2 [1859], p. 177). However, the non-Italian bastions he cites, at Langres and Nuremburg, for example, are round and not angular (Vol. 2, pp. 177–79).

[68] On Cesena, see Hale, "Bastion," p. 479. On Volterra, see Duffy, p. 3; J. R. Hale, *Renaissance Fortification: Art or Engineering?* (London: Thames and Hudson, 1977), p. 30; and Michael Mallett, "Preparations for War in Florence and Venice in the Second Half of the Fifteenth Century," in *Florence and Venice: Comparisons and Relations*, Acts of Two Conference at Villa I Tatti in 1976–1977, Vol. 1: *Quattrocento* (Florence: La Nuova Italia Editrice, 1979), p. 158. On Senigallia, see Duffy, p. 3. On Ostia Antica, see Hale, "Bastion," pp. 481–82, and Rocolle, pp. 177–78. On Sarazana, see Hale, *Renaissance*, p. 30; Duffy, p. 3; and Mallett, p.

additions to existing fortifications, but others altered significantly the original fortress. For example, although Castel Sant' Angelo had added some gunpowder weapons for defensive purposes before the end of the fourteenth century, a century later Pope Alexander VI desired to reinforce the fortification, adapting it more completely to gunpowder weaponry defense. To do this, he hired Antonio da San Gallo, whose family had designed and constructed several fortifications throughout Italy.[69] San Gallo's reconstruction of this fortress was extensive: its central tower was enlarged; its foundation was covered by a large, square platform; finally, four angular bastions were added to the angles of the platform with a fifth constructed on the bridge over the Tiber in front of the castle. The transformation was completed with the addition of more than 200 gunpowder weapons in December 1494.[70]

As well, unlike earlier anti-gunpowder artillery innovations, angular bastions also appear frequently in engineering drawings and writings. As early as the 1440s Leon Battista Alberti's *De re aedificatoria* addressed the issue of flanking fire in defensive fortifications. His solution was to construct "buttresses with triangular bases . . . to be built at ten-cubit intervals along the line of the wall, with one angle pointing toward the enemy." These were to be "filled with a mixture of clay and straw, and packed down. Thus the softness of the clay will deaden the force and impact of the engines." Later, Alberti adds:

> The wall should be flanked by towers acting as buttresses every fifty cubits. These should be round, standing out from the wall, and somewhat taller, so that anyone venturing too close would expose his flank to missiles and be hit; thus the wall is protected by the towers and the towers by each other.

Although not identifying these structures as "bastions," it is clear that Alberti had the concept well in mind.[71]

Alberti may not have influenced later engineers – the *De re aedificatoria* was not popular until after its 1485 printing – but several later fortification architects do discuss what would later be considered the bastion. The Italian Antonio Francesco Averlino, called Filarete, who wrote *Trattato dell'architettura c.* 1461,

158. On Poggio Imperiale, see Hale, "Bastion," pp. 482–83; Hale, *Renaissance*, p. 12; Pepper and Adams, pp. 6–7; and Mallett, p. 158. On Ferrara, see Hale, *Renaissance*, p. 49. On Sarazanello, see Hale, "Bastion," p. 484. And on Castel Sant' Angelo, see Hale, "Bastion," pp. 483–84, and Rocolle, p. 178.

69 Antonio's brother, Giuliano, designed the bastioned fortifications at Poggio Imperiale. Antonio's son, also named Antonio, would later design the bastions at Florence in 1534 and at Rome in 1542.

70 Rocolle, p. 178. See also Hale, "Bastion," pp. 483–84.

71 Leon Battista Alberti, *On the Art of Building in Ten Books*, trans. J. Rykwert et al. (Cambridge: MIT Press), 1988. The quotations here are on pp. 104–05. There is also an apparent discrepancy on the space between Alberti's buttresses, once mentioning 10 cubits distance in between buttresses and later mentioning 50 cubits as this distance. No reason for this discrepancy is given. See also Hale, "Bastion," pp. 472, 477; Hale, *Renaissance*, p. 21; and Bertrand Gille, *Les ingénieurs de la Renaissance* (Paris: Herman, 1964), pp. 94–97. Croix seems to have missed these references to bastions, as he claims that, "aside from a few passing remarks on the cannon, Alberti makes no comments on the new weapon and its possible consequences" (p. 34).

was perhaps the first to follow Alberti's lead. He, too, struggled with the problem of flanking fire to protect the fortifications of the "ideal" city he was planning. Although also not proposing bastions by name, his solution was to design the circumference of the city as an eight-point star, the points of the star performing the same function as bastions.[72] (This, of course, will be the solution sought by Vauban to defend against gunpowder weaponry bombardment in the eighteenth century.) At the same time in Burgundy, François de Surienne, Duke Philip the Good's master of artillery, was redesigning the fortifications of Dijon. His design, written but never fully enacted, recommended countering gunpowder artillery attacks first by digging two ditches around the fortifications and constructing artillery towers. But then, also beset by the problem of flanking fire, he suggested making these towers no more than 2–4 feet taller than the walls so that the defensive gunpowder artillery "could fire in a line along the wall, from one tower to the other, between the walls and the ditches."[73]

These engineers were followed by Francesco di Giorgio Martini, whose treatise, *Trattati di architettura ingegneria e arte militare*, was written between 1482 and 1495. Giorgio Martini's work is extensively written and elaborately illustrated. Composed as it was after bastions began appearing on fortifications throughout Italy, the *Trattati di architettura ingegneria e arte militare* includes bastions on all fortification designs. They are low, angular, sloped, and provide effective flanking fire to protect against dead zone attacks along the walls of the fortifications. They are also not the only anti-gunpowder weaponry innovations used by Giorgio Martini on his fortification designs. Also included are wide ditches and artillery towers, more conventional gunpowder weaponry defenses for the fifteenth century. Giorgio Martini's architectural treatise was the culmination of late medieval military architectural thought, all of which was now directed entirely at the use of gunpowder weaponry, both offensively and defensively.[74] It was also extremely influential, being used by such early sixteenth-century engineering notables as Buonaccorso Ghiberti and Leonardo da Vinci.[75]

---

[72] Gille, pp. 98–99; Hale, "Bastion," pp. 477–78; Hale, *Renaissance*, p. 21; and Croix, p. 34.

[73] Richard, pp. 36–43. The quotation comes from a transcription of the original document on pp. 42–43:

> et que lesdictes tours soient assises là où les murs de ladicte ville font code tellement que la deffense et artillerie puisse tirer en droict ligne et à aultre, au long des murs et dudict fossé.
>
> These towers were set there where the walls of the town were angled such that the defense and artillery could fire in a straight line, from one tower to another, between the walls and the ditch.

[74] Francesco di Giorgio Martini, *Trattati di architettura ingegneria e arte militare*, 2 vols. (Milan: Edizioni il Polifoli, 1967). See also Gille, pp. 107–28; Hale, "Bastion," pp. 484–86; Hale, *Renaissance*, pp. 21–22, 43–44; Croix, pp. 36–37; Pepper and Adams, pp. 18–19, 22; and Rocolle, p. 177.

[75] For Ghiberti, see Gustina Scaglia, ed., "A Miscellany of Bronze Works and Texts in the *Zibaldone* of Buonaccorso Ghiberti," *Proceedings of the American Philosophical Association* 120 (1976), 485–513, and Croix, p. 37. For Leonardo, see *The Unknown Leonardo*, ed. L. Reti (New York: McGraw-Hill, 1974); Gille, pp. 153–75; Hale, "Bastion," pp. 486–88; Hale, *Renaissance*, p. 22; and Rocolle, p. 177. Croix sees Leonardo's *Codex Atlantico*, which contains his

The angle bastion was, in the words of Sir John Hale: "The most significant of all architectural forms [which] evolved during the Renaissance."[76] It easily solved the problem of defending against dead zones along fortification walls by providing flanking fire from larger, more powerful weapons aimed directly down the sides of these walls. Guns could be now mounted so that anyone attacking the fortification walls would have to pass through a cross fire from the two adjacent bastions. It also was the foundation on which the sixteenth-century *trace italienne* was built.[77]

Attempting to show that early gunpowder weapons were effective means of besieging fortifications in the fourteenth and fifteenth centuries is of course a problem of relativity. Certainly in comparison with later gunpowder weaponry used in sieges this artillery was not effective. But in comparison with earlier non-gunpowder-weapon siege attempts, by focusing not only on the number and length of sieges, but also on the attempts to thwart successful gunpowder bombardments by changes in fortification construction, the conclusion can only be that guns had, by the end of the Middle Ages, completely altered siege warfare.[78]

fortification drawings, predating Giorgio Martini's work, and thus not being influenced by, but possibly influencing, the latter work (p. 37). Most other historians, including the extremely reliable Bertrand Gille, disagree with this dating.

[76] Hale, "Bastion," p. 466.

[77] On the *trace italienne*, see Hale, "Bastion," pp. 466–67, and Parker, pp. 10–13.

[78] This paper builds on a thesis contained in my *Medieval Military Technology* (Peterborough: broadview press, 1992).

Siegecraft in Late Fifteenth-Century Italy

Michael Mallett
University of Warwick

The main concern in this study is with the early history of gunpowder weapons and their use and effectiveness in siege warfare. Two contrasting views about the role of guns in the fifteenth century have been prevalent. The traditional one tends to emphasise a significant turning point in 1494 when Charles VIII of France invaded Italy with an army equipped with a formidable artillery train. That train consisted of as many as 40 medium-sized, mobile, horse-drawn guns; guns with apparently unheard of destructiveness and efficiency, manned by trained professional gunners.[1] The novel sound and fury of these guns is said to have crucially affected the subsequent decades of the Italian Wars; fortresses and cities surrendered at the first whiff of gunpowder, military architects turned frantically to devise new defensive systems; even on the battlefield the guns began to command respect and fear. Guicciardini's *Storia d'Italia* was one of the main sources for this view of a whole new dimension to warfare, but the idea that there was little significant impact of gunpowder technology before 1500 has pervaded discussions of sixteenth- and seventeenth-century warfare.[2] Even the most recent work of Geoffrey Parker on the "Military Revolution" is not immune from such an interpretation.[3]

Fifteenth-century military historians have tended to present a somewhat different view. They suggest that dramatic changes in the effectiveness of guns took place in the first half of the century as a result of a significant improvement in the quality and preparation of gunpowder, probably developed in France. As a result, greater velocity and hitting power could be achieved with smaller, stronger cast guns rather than the monster bombards currently favoured; therefore, the guns could then be made more mobile. Thus the revolutionary changes,

---

[1]   Philippe Contamine, "L'artillerie royale française à la veille des guerres d'Italie," *Annales de Bretangne* 71 (1964), 221–61.

[2]   Francesco Guicciardini, *Storia d'Italia*, Collezione Salani, I Classici (Florence: Salani, 1932), Book I, ch. 11.

[3]   Geoffrey Parker, *The Military Revolution: Technological Innovation and the Rise of the West, 1500–1800.* (Cambridge: Cambridge University Press, 1988), pp. 9–10.

RENAISSANCE ITALY.

which culminated in the French and other artillery trains of the late fifteenth century, started much earlier in the century.[4] English guns played an effective role in Henry V's conquest of Normandy after Agincourt, and French artillery contributed substantially to the eviction of the English from Normandy and Gascony in the final decade of the Hundred Years War.[5] The Turkish guns were the main factors in the speedy fall of Constantinople in 1453. In Italy the fifteenth century was filled with guns; many of them cumbersome, unduly heavy and immobile, it is true, but nevertheless much prized and frequently used. The Milanese artillery train in the 1470s consisted of sixteen large guns,[6] and well before 1494 the Venetians were producing considerable numbers of medium-sized cast bronze guns in imitation of the French models. A Venetian senate minute of 16 June 1489 announced that "without these munitions and artillery one cannot preserve any state, nor defend it, nor attack the enemy."[7]

Some of the most telling evidence of these precocious developments lies in the nature of the fortifications built in some parts of Italy during the second half of the fifteenth century. From the 1450s a generation of military architects, working particularly in the Papal States and Tuscany, were designing and building fortresses which responded both to the new threat of guns and the new possibilities of defence provided by guns. The bastion, a low, solid gun emplacement, projecting from the walls to provide covering fire for the walls, was an increasingly common feature of these projects, and the word itself was much used by Italian architects and commentators of this period.[8]

The evidence of large numbers of guns, the costs of guns and the training of gunners, of new fortifications adapted to guns, of feverish debate about guns, is all abundant in fifteenth-century Italy. But what of the practical use of guns? What can we learn from a study of Italian sieges in the crucial decades before 1494? Is there evidence of artillery playing a major role? Were sieges significantly speeded up? Can one link siege experience to decisions to change fortification techniques? How effective were the guns? I want to look briefly at some of the sieges of the 1470s and 1480s to seek answers to these questions. I shall deal with the siege of Volterra by the Florentines in 1472 and of Colle di Val

[4] Philippe Contamine, *War in the Middle Ages*, trans. Michael Jones (Oxford: Basil Blackwell, 1984), pp. 196–207; Kelly DeVries, *Medieval Military Technology* (Peterborough: Broadview Press, 1992), pp. 143–68.

[5] Christopher Allmand, *The Hundred Years War: England and France at War, c. 1300–c. 1450* (Cambridge: Cambridge University Press, 1988), pp. 76–82; Malcolm Vale, *War and Chivalry: Warfare and Aristocratic Culture in England and Burgundy at the End of the Middle Ages* (London: Duckworth, 1981), pp. 129–46.

[6] Michael Mallett, *Mercenaries and their Masters: Warfare in Renaissance Italy* (London: The Bodley Head, 1974), p. 161.

[7] State Archives, Venice, Senato Terra, 10, fol. 148, 16 June 1489: "senza dicta munition et artigliarie non se puol conservar alcuno stado, ne defender quello over offender li inimici."

[8] J. R. Hale, "The Development of the Bastion: An Italian Chronology," in *Europe in the Late Middle Ages*, eds. in J. R. Hale, J. R. L. Highfield and B. Smalley (Evanston: Northwestern University Press, 1965), pp. 466–94; Giancarlo Severini, *Architetture militari di Giuliano da Sangallo* (Pisa: Grafiche Lischi, 1970).

d'Elsa by Neapolitan and papal troops in 1479; with Otranto, first taken by the Turks and then retaken by the Neapolitans in 1480–81; Ficarolo, besieged by the Venetians in 1482; and finally Pisa, intermittently under siege from the Florentines for 15 years between 1494 and 1509. They were all ultimately successful sieges; there were in fact few serious sieges that were not ultimately successful in this period. But is that the whole story?

Volterra was one of the Florentine subject cities which enjoyed a considerable degree of autonomy. Its citizens had a reputation for rebelliousness and obstinacy, and Florentine determination to break their spirit and destroy their independence went far beyond the immediate circumstances of 1472. The issue which provoked this crisis concerned contracts for the mining of alum in the hinterland of Volterra which had been given by the municipal council on very favourable terms to a consortium in which certain leading Florentines played a key role. The favourable contract provoked popular outrage in Volterra; the council was forced to revoke it and two of the contractors were lynched.[9] Florence, led by Lorenzo de'Medici who had a strong personal interest in the exploitation of alum deposits, treated the matter as a rebellion. With quite astonishing speed over a period of three weeks an army of 10,000 infantry and 2,000 cavalry was put together under the command of the most distinguished condottiere of the day, Federico da Montefeltro. Troops arrived from Milan and the Papal States; 100,000 florins were voted for the cost of the siege; and guns were wheeled out from the armouries in Florence and laboriously transported over the poor roads of southern Tuscany.[10] The Volterrans, despite desperate appeals to all the states of Italy, were effectively isolated; only a small contingent of Venetian infantry arrived to help them. 1500 miscellaneous mercenaries and the citizens themselves were all that faced the Florentine army.[11] But the citizens were very divided; a strong and influential faction, made up of some of the most prosperous families in the city, were reluctant to oppose the will of Florence. However, Volterra had exceptionally strong natural defences; its fortifications had not been modernised, but sited on a hill top with strong outer walls and a massive medieval fortress, it was no easy target.

By 28 May 1472, after less than a month of preparation and build-up, Federico da Montefeltro had the city in a vice-like grip and the bombardment began. It seems likely that the Volterrans had few guns with which to respond, and a stretch of the walls was soon brought down. However, their decision to seek to negotiate was more the result of internal dissensions and a generally hopeless situation than of these opening salvoes. An offer to surrender on terms was rejected by the Florentines who insisted on unconditional surrender. How-

---

9 Enrico Fiumi, *L'impresa di Lorenzo de'Medici contro Volterra (1472)* (Florence: L. S. Olschki, 1948), pp. 30–43. *Lettere di Lorenzo de'Medici*, ed. Riccardo Fubini, Vol. 1 (Florence: Giunti, 1977), pp. 547–53.

10 Fiumi, pp. 114–30; *Memorie di ser Giusto d'Anghiari*, Biblioteca Nazionale di Firenze, MS II.II.127, fol. 101r.

11 Fiumi, pp. 125, 129.

ever, Federico da Montefeltro, reluctant even at this stage to undertake a full-scale assault, did on 16 June promise to spare the lives and property of the inhabitants and forego any general retribution.[12] At this point the really memorable part of the story starts. It was notoriously difficult to organise the surrender of a city after siege in a way that ensured that the terms of the surrender were implemented. In this case, there was even doubt as to what the terms really were; talk of unconditional surrender had not only aroused the expectations of the besiegers but also the fears of the mercenaries in the defence. The Volterran leaders, fearful of the effects of a sudden opening of the gates, admitted a company of Montefeltro's own troops secretly to take over the castle and hopefully protect them. News of this alarmed the poorer sections of the populace, and they and the Venetian mercenaries called in the besieging Milanese companies through the breach in the walls and joined them in an impromptu sack. Confusion and licence took over; women crowded into the churches for protection. There were strong suspicions that the Florentines were not averse to Volterra being taught a lesson, and Federico took only limited steps to control his army.[13] Despite his promises, 76 families were subsequently exiled; the alum mines were formally taken over by Florence, and a great new fortress was built in two years, incorporating some of the latest defensive ideas. The Florentine military architect Francione was probably responsible for the work, which had a considerable influence on the better known Francesco di Giorgio Martini.[14]

But, of course, the main purpose of the new fortress was to hold the city in subjection, rather than protect it from external threat. The siege had not really revealed the weakness of the defences nor had they been damaged to the extent of needing a complete rebuilding. What the siege did reveal and highlight was the contrast between a very determined besieging force and a disunited defence. The speedy conclusion of this siege was the result of a combination of circumstances. The work of the guns had more effect on the subsequent sack, for which the breach in the walls was important, than on the siege itself.

The siege of nearby Colle di Val d'Elsa seven years later took place in very different circumstances. Colle was one of the key points on the frontier between Florence and Siena; both its population and its fortifications, which were modernised in the late 1460s, had been favoured and nurtured by Florence. During the war following the Pazzi conspiracy, Neapolitan and papal troops, supported by the Sienese, made considerable progress on this frontier, taking a number of

---

[12] Fiumi, pp. 129–37.

[13] The sack of Volterra was much discussed by the chroniclers of the time and the event did considerable damage to the reputations of Federico da Montefeltro and Lorenzo de'Medici. See Fiumi, pp. 137–42; A. Ivani, *Historia de Volterrana calamitate*, ed. F. L. Mannucci, in Antonio Lodovico Muratori, *Rerum Italicarum Scriptores*, Vol. 23, Part 4, 2nd ed. (Città di Castello: S. Lapi, 1913); L. Frati, *Il sacco di Volterra nel 1472* (Bologna, 1886) with publication of the contemporary account of Bartolomeo Lisci; A. Allegretti, "Diarii Senesi," *Rerum Italicarum Scriptores*, 1st ed., Vol. 23 (Milan, 1773), cols. 777–80.

[14] Fiumi, p. 154; M. Battistini, *Nel Maschio di Volterra* (Pescia, 1925), pp. 10–12; Severini, pp. 11–16.

Florentine towns. Colle di Val d'Elsa was regarded as the key to the defensive system; its fall would open the way to Florence itself. Federico da Montefeltro and Alfonso, Duke of Calabria, were the leaders of the combined army, and they set up their guns against Colle round 20 September 1479.[15] The town was garrisoned by a substantial force of professional infantry led by Andrea dal Borgo, the chief Florentine infantry constable, and Carlino di Novello, a veteran Venetian constable who had seen long service against the Turks. These men were part of an extending tradition of professional and faithful military service to particular states; they were not mercenaries in the strict sense of the word.[16]

The defence of Colle against the entire papal-Neapolitan army became a legend in its time. Colle was strong and well equipped with artillery, but over a period of nearly two months its walls were reduced to rubble. According to the Florentine diarist Luca Landucci, 1024 heavy balls were fired by the besieging force: i.e., about 30 shots a day over the seven weeks of the siege.[17] Four separate assaults were beaten back with heavy losses; a number of the besieging captains were wounded by the heavy fire from the light cannon and handguns of the defenders, and the hospitals of Siena were said to be filled with the wounded from the siege. At one stage the *borgo*, the lower town which was largely unfortified, was burnt in order to avoid it providing cover for the besiegers. A sortie from the defence succeeded in capturing and spiking two of the three main guns being used for the bombardment and killing the gunners. At a certain point the spirits of the defenders were lifted by a decree in Florence that full Florentine citizenship should be conferred on all the native inhabitants of Colle.[18] But in the end the pressure was too great; Florence was unable to relieve the siege; the main army could not be risked in a confrontation with the papal-Neapolitan army. Colle accepted terms on 12 November and on this occasion the surrender seems to have been successfully carried out. The garrison were allowed to march out with full military honours, although not with their cannon, which were taken in triumph to Siena, and Neapolitan troops took over without significant looting.[19] They garrisoned the town for 16 months before it was handed back to Florence and systematic rebuilding of the fortifications could begin. Colle was one of those Florentine towns on this frontier, along with

---

[15] *Lettere di Lorenzo de'Medici*, ed. Nicolai Rubinstein, Vol. 4 (Florence: Giunti, 1981), pp. 224, 238–39; Emanuele Repetti, *Dizionario geografico, fisico, storico della Toscana*, Vol. 1 (Florence, 1833), p. 753.

[16] For a discussion of the development of professional infantry in fifteenth-century Italy, see Mallett, pp. 153–59; Michael Mallett and John Hale, *The Military Organisation of a Renaissance State: Venice, c. 1400–1617* (Cambridge: Cambridge University Press, 1984), pp. 74–81.

[17] Luca Landucci, *Diario fiorentino del 1450 al 1516*, ed. Iodoco del Badia (Florence, 1883), p. 32.

[18] For details of the siege, see *Lettere di Lorenzo de'Medici*, Vol. 4, pp. 234, 243–48; A. Municchi, "Alcune lettere inedite relative alla difesa di Colle contro gli Aragonesi nel 1479," *Miscellanea storica della Valdelsa* 10 (1902), 49–55. Repetti, p. 753.

[19] Repetti, p. 753.

Brolio, Castellina and Poggio Imperiale, that became models of the new fortification systems of Francione and Giuliano di Sangallo.[20]

Colle could be described as a classic late medieval siege – hard-fought on both sides with a small number of heavy guns playing a prominent role, supported by large quantities of light firearms which were basically anti-personnel. However, the impact of the guns was not such as to make defence impossible; indeed, it is probable that even without them Colle would have fallen in about two months because of the general strategic situation. Its defence had served its purpose; the enemy advance had been held up for long enough to allow the army to reorganise; by November the campaigning season was over. The work of the guns served perhaps to animate the besiegers and tempt them into frequent assaults rather than the more traditional pattern of encirclement and gradual strangulation.

Only a year later a large Turkish army landed in Puglia, on the heel of Italy, and assaulted the small town of Otranto. Needless to say, the invasion was not completely unexpected, but there was relatively little that the King of Naples could do to prepare for it. His main army was still in Tuscany; the defences of the Adriatic ports were adequate against pirate raids but were not expected to withstand a full-scale invasion. Otranto had a castle and a deteriorating circuit of outer walls; it had a small garrison equipped with a large stock of miscellaneous gunpowder weapons; the citizens numbered about 6,000.[21] In late July 1480, about 12,000 Turks disembarked from a fleet of 150 ships, with seven large bombards. After quickly clearing the surrounding countryside of resistance, they concentrated on Otranto itself. Their methods were swift and decisive; only eleven days were needed for the siege; the guns were brought to bear at close range with their crews protected by great metal shields; mass assaults on the breaches by the janissaries were protected by the guns firing blank rounds up to the last moment to keep the heads of the defenders down. In the circumstances of a limited defensive capability, the method was direct and effective. Despite the fear of what was likely to happen to them, the inhabitants of Otranto and their handful of defenders had little chance of resisting for long. Help from Naples was impossible. As the Turks broke into the city, the archbishop was murdered in the cathedral, 800 men of the city were massacred, and the women and children shipped off to slavery. Just 300 of the population of 6,000 survived, and Otranto became a Turkish military base not a populated city. One citizen

---

[20] Severini, p. 17; Hale, p. 480.

[21] The literature on the events in Otranto in 1480–81 is enormous; as the one significant Turkish invasion of the mainland of Western Europe in the early modern period, it has attracted considerable attention. However, the description of the military events of the taking of Otranto and the subsequent siege by Neapolitan forces is largely subsumed in *Otranto 1480: Atti del congresso internazionale di studio promosso in occasione del V centenario della caduta di Otranto ad opera dei Turchi (Otranto, 19–23 maggio 1980)*, ed. C. D. Fonseca, 2 vols., Saggi e ricerche 21–22 (Galatina: Congedo, 1986).

was deliberately released to carry to the neighbouring towns the details of the fate of a Christian city which dared to resist the Turks.[22]

However, a full-scale Turkish invasion did not materialise. Whatever the Sultan's original plan may have been, there was no immediate follow-up. Distractions elsewhere and the death of the sultan Mohammed II in the next year, left the Otranto garrison isolated, a foothold on Christian shores perhaps to be exploited at a later date. The Duke of Calabria hurried south from Tuscany with the bulk of his army, and by mid-September the danger of a Turkish break out had passed as the blockading force built up to over 10,000 men. Throughout the winter the Turks were watched; their communications across the Adriatic and their control of a large stretch of country around Otranto remained uncontested. They occupied themselves with improving the fortifications of the captured city. It has been suggested that the Turkish fortifications at Otranto were the beginning of genuine gunpowder fortification in western Europe, but in fact there seemed to be little novelty here. Certainly the emphasis was on thicker, lower walls and defence in depth with advance earthworks out in front of the walls, but there is no evidence that the Italian engineers who confronted these fortifications in 1481 were struck by significant innovations.[23]

The chief figure responsible for the gradually tightening siege on Otranto in 1481 was Federico da Montefeltro's architect, Scirro Scirri, who was lent to the Duke of Calabria for this operation. Federico did not come himself; the Pope forbad it because he was needed to defend the Marches from possible further Turkish attack. But Scirri had been at Colle, and probably also at Volterra; he was an expert in placing of siege guns and, above all, in the preparation of emplacements, mines and siege trenches for the besiegers.[24] The siege of Otranto, which began in earnest in late April 1481 and lasted for four and a half months, was notable for its systematic and cautious character. The Duke of Calabria's army grew to 20,000 men, of which about three-quarters were infantry, including an Hungarian contingent which arrived during the summer. A tightening naval blockade and a gradual reduction of the Turkish garrison to 2,000 seasoned troops were the other ingredients of the situation. In fact the Turkish leadership probably miscalculated in reducing the garrison so far. What seemed an adequate force to defend the small circuit of walls in April was gradually eroded by casualties and sickness during the summer, and by then it was too late to send in reinforcements. Nevertheless, Turkish resistance was

---

[22] A. Rovighi, "L'Occidente cristiano di fronte all'offensiva del Turco in Italia nel 1480–81," in *Otranto 1480*, Vol. 1, pp. 95–99.

[23] A. Guglielmotti, *Storia della marina pontificia nel Medioevo del 728 al 1499*, Vol. 2 (Florence, 1894), p. 428; L. A. Maggiorotti, "Le origini della fortificazione bastionata e la guerra di Otranto," *Rivista della Artiglieria e del Genio* (1931), 93–110; Rovighi, pp. 108–09, 120–21.

[24] On Scirri, see *Lettere di Lorenzo de'Medici*, ed. Michael Mallett, Vol. 6 (Florence: Guinti Barbera, 1990), p. 81; for the correct identification of his name (not Ciri as often thought) see C. H. Clough, "Federico da Montefeltro and the Kings of Naples: A Study in Fifteenth-Century Survival," *Renaissance Studies* 6 (1992), 143.

fierce throughout; repeated sorties hindered the Neapolitan preparations; continuous engineering work countered the effect of the Neapolitan bombardment which was delivered by nine great bombards brought in by sea. When the Neapolitans were finally ready to assault in late August and sought to swarm through the breaches in the walls, they found that a great new ditch and defending ramparts had been created inside the breaches, and 2,000 stakes linked by chains prevented the cavalry from breaking into the city. In addition, heavy enfilading fire across the face of the breaches inside the walls turned these areas into carefully organised killing grounds. The Duke was forced to call off the assault with over 400 picked men dead. Some days later, however, the Turkish garrison, recognising its isolation and seriously short of supplies, agreed to surrender.[25]

Otranto was the prototype for many sixteenth-century sieges; both attack and defence were sophisticated and reasonably well directed; engineering played a major role alongside the guns. But stalemate seemed the likely outcome but for the wider situation of increasing hopelessness for the Turkish garrison. Unusually, in this case, there was little civilian involvement in the siege; Otranto was a fortress without a population, which had significant implications for its defence. The military had a completely free hand and need fear no fifth column element in their midst; but on the other hand the crucial support and numbers which a committed civilian population could give, was missing.

If the entry of the Turks on to the Italian scene undoubtedly gave a new and ferocious dimension to the fighting, the wars in Italy were already not lacking in these qualities. The War of Ferrara which involved all the Italian states between 1482 and 1484 produced another memorable siege – that of Ficarolo, which held out for over a month against the Venetian army of Roberto di Sanseverino. Ficarolo, a strongly fortified town on the north bank of the Po, was seen as the key point on the Venetian advance towards Ferrara. Roberto di Sanseverino had invaded the Ferrarese across the marshes from Padua and was intent on getting to Ferrara quickly. He was supported by a Venetian river fleet of over 400 vessels which forced its way up the Po and joined the army for what was seen as the last formality before the triumphant advance on Ferrara – the siege of Ficarolo.[26] Ficarolo was bombarded intensely both by Sanseverino's guns and the guns of the river fleet; at one stage canisters of supposedly poison gas were fired into the town.[27] Federico da Montefeltro commanded a relieving army which was camped on the south bank of the Po, but he could not risk crossing to confront Sanseverino's superior force because of the presence of the Venetian fleet. However, his guns on the south bank were able to inflict losses on that fleet, and even to counter-bombard Sanseverino's guns round Ficarolo. But the key

[25] Rovighi, pp. 109–21; V. Zacchino, "La guerra di Otranto del 1480–1: operazioni strategiche e militari," in *Otranto 1480*, Vol. 2, pp. 274–94.

[26] Edoardo Piva, *La guerra di Ferrara del 1482*, Vol. 1 (Padua, 1893), pp. 74–81; *Lettere di Lorenzo de'Medici*, ed. Michael Mallett, Vol. 7 (forthcoming), n. 477.

[27] Mallett and Hale, pp. 84–85.

moment of the siege came when Montefeltro sought to flood the besiegers'
camp by diverting the waters of the Mincio and Tartaro to the northwest. This
move was countered quickly by the Venetian engineers who created a breach in
the Po's flood barriers so as to drain the advancing waters into that river. The
failure of this scheme sealed the fate of Ficarolo; the defence began to weaken
despite Federico da Montefeltro sending in fresh troops across the river at night.
In the end there was probably also an element of treachery as some of the
defenders were persuaded to admit the besieging forces. On 29 June 1482,
Ficarolo fell, but the Venetian advance had lost its momentum, and the army had
been badly mauled.[28] Much was made at the time of the loyalty of the people of
Ficarolo to their lord, the Duke of Ferrara; but the main factors here were
primarily military, involving the organisation and discipline of troops and engineering, as much as new technology.

The episodes described all took place well before 1494. The final siege to be
examined briefly was the long-running, intermittent siege of Pisa, which
stemmed from the Pisan declaration of independence from Florence in 1494 and
lasted until the eventual surrender of the city to the Florentines in 1509. For
much of these fifteen years, the Florentine pressure was either inactive or held at
a distance from the walls of the city; so this was in no sense a continuous siege
situation. But a period of close siege occurred in most years after 1496, with the
Florentines employing large forces of mercenaries: French troops in 1500 and,
after 1506, the militia raised by Machiavelli. The Pisans, in turn, had substantial
help up to 1499, but the core of the defence was the Pisans themselves – about
10,000 strong, men and women – and large numbers of countryfolk who retreated into the city for security. The tenacious defence of the city against all that
the Florentines could throw at it aroused deep admiration and sympathy
throughout Italy. "Fare come Pisa" became a proverb for gallantry and determination, and the crux of this defence was the ability of the Pisans constantly to
create new fortifications inside those destroyed by artillery fire, just as the Turks
had done at Otranto. Parts of the Pisan fortifications had been modernised, but
other parts were extremely vulnerable to bombardment; each time the guns
destroyed stretches of the walls, the defenders went to work inside to nullify the
effects of the damage. In the end, Pisa had to be starved into submission as all
the work of the gunners and the engineers had been in vain.[29]

What conclusions can be drawn from these examples? As far as the guns

[28] Domenico Malipiero, "Annali veneti dell'anno 1477 al 1500," *Archivio storico italiano*,
Ser. 1, Vol. 7, Part 1 (1843), pp. 260–61; A. C. Arico', ed., *Marin Sanuto il Giovane: le vite dei
dogi (1474–1494)*, Vol. 1 (Padua: Antenore, 1989), pp. 250–69; Piva, pp. 78–80.

[29] The events of the Pisan War have been often alluded to but never fully described, except in
the copious but diffuse references of Francesco Giucciardini. P. Pieri, *Il Rinascimento e la crisi
militare italiana* (Turin: G. Einaudi, 1952) is the best account of the wars of this period, and see
particularly pp. 376–77 for a description of the Pisan resistance. M. Luzzati, *Una guerra di
popolo: lettere private del tempo dell'assedio di Pisa (1494–1509)*, Publicazioni dell'Istituto di
Storia, Facoltà di lettere dell'Università di Pisa 6 (Pisa: Pacini, 1973) gives many insights into
the events of the siege, and see particularly pp. 31–53.

themselves were concerned, it can be said that they were already effective agents of destruction well before 1494. Great reliance was placed upon them; they could, on occasions, be moved up with considerable speed and be handled with skill and precision. The big guns remained relatively few in number and tended to be of different calibre, which made it difficult to think of using batteries in the true sense of the word.[30] However, also of importance were the very large numbers of spingards and other smaller guns which were used against men rather than against walls. Above all, guns were as useful to the defence as to the attack, and this tended automatically to create a stalemate. The guns of the defenders could be better protected and more easily supplied than those of the besiegers.

Yet, the really important point is that neither guns nor the new fortifications, which were the reaction to them, changed the nature of siege warfare. The crux of successful siegecraft remained the spirit and commitment of the defenders and attackers and the extent to which the besieged city could be isolated from support, relief and supplies. Training, permanent service and professionalism were improving the quality of infantry by the late fifteenth century and, in the last resort, the availability of good infantry for storming the breaches was likely to be more important than the speed and effectiveness with which the breaches could be created. Guns gave the opportunity for storming, provided that good enough infantry were available to take that opportunity; but they could not guarantee success. But the question remained – what were the storming troops going to find on the other side of the breach? The way up to the breach in the walls of Otranto in August 1481 was described as being "like the steps leading up to St. Peters," but on the other side, as the Neapolitans and Hungarians stormed, it was an inferno.[31]

A final point: the fifteenth century saw increasingly sophisticated use of propaganda and news. Part of the development of siege warfare was the way in which fear and clemency could be exploited. The guns gave a new image of frightfulness; they seemed to offer limitless opportunities to besiegers. Properly utilised, their propaganda value was actually greater than their real effectiveness.

---

[30] For a discussion of the continuation of this problem in the sixteenth century, see Simon Pepper and Nicholas Adams, *Firearms and Fortifications: Military Architecture and Siege Warfare in Sixteenth-Century Siena* (Chicago: University of Chicago Press, 1986), pp. 131–37.

[31] Zacchino, p. 294.

The Changing Face of Siege Warfare: Technology and Tactics in Transition

Bert S. Hall
University of Toronto

> War is a science covered with darkness, in the obscurity of which one cannot move with assured steps; habit and prejudice make up its base, the natural result of ignorance.
>
> Maréchal M. de Saxe (1696–1750), *Mes rêveries*

Military historians do not, as a rule, devote too much attention to sieges. They are usually dismissed with only a few lines, or considered only insofar as they present colorful anecdotes to enliven the narrative. As one moves across that fine temporal boundary separating the later Middle Ages from the early modern period, scholarly understanding becomes only slightly clearer, but the importance attached to siege warfare has gone up dramatically in the last few years. This is because of the work of Geoffrey Parker and his attempts to breathe new life into an old thesis known as the "Military Revolution" argument. The thesis, that there was a dramatic change in sixteenth-century warfare amounting to a revolution in tactics, strategy, organization, scale, and overall impact, owes its genesis to Michael Roberts, who first articulated it in 1955.[1] Considering how short the lifespan of most grand historical theses has become these days, Roberts' idea has enjoyed remarkable longevity, but at the cost of being modified almost beyond recognition.

Parker is the most important exponent of a revised "revolution." His 1988 work *The Military Revolution: Military Innovation and the Rise of the West 1500–1800* was independently acclaimed best book of the year by both the Society for the History of Technology and the American Military Institute. It is also a work that has produced a strong critical response, more than is usually the case in the sometimes sleepy atmosphere of pre-modern military history.[2] I need

---

[1] Michael Roberts, *The Military Revolution 1560–1660* (Belfast: M. Boyd, 1956).
[2] Jeremy Black, *A Military Revolution? Military Change and European Society, 1550–1800* (Atlantic Highlands NJ: Humanities Press International, 1991). Bert S. Hall and Kelly DeVries, "The Military Revolution Revisited," *Technology and Culture* 31 (1990), 500–507. John Lynn,

to begin today by reviewing as briefly as possible some of Parker's claims and the response they have provoked. This should clear the way for a closer look at the transition from medieval to early modern warfare on an evolutionary, rather than a revolutionary, model.

The central historical phenomenon underlying the "military revolution" thesis is the fact that armies grew larger and larger throughout the early modern period. Living under a hostile army, or sustaining one's own version of these swollen Leviathans, had far-reaching effects and implications for the making of the nation-state, the growth of bureaucracies, the economic development of Europe, and even the genetic make-up of peoples. Insofar as the "military revolution" thesis points to the importance of military organizations in history, it seems unobjectionable. Accounting for the phenomenon of army growth, however, has been more difficult for the thesis. Most military historians are, at heart, believers in the power of technology to drive other events, and the "military revolution" has always treated the advent of firearms as a decisive turning point in the history of warfare. However, articulating the mechanism by which the adoption of firearms led to the enlargement of armies has proven problematic.

For Geoffrey Parker, the answer is clear. A certain historical dialectic of assault and defense in sieges resulted in the growth of armies. In the Middle Ages, Parker maintains, the defensive predominated. Castles and urban fortifications were strong and difficult to assault, while mechanical engines were weak and largely ineffectual. Medieval siege warfare changed little over the decades and was primarily "an affair of manoeuvres, skirmishes, and protracted sieges."[3] With the advent of gunpowder weaponry in the fourteenth century, little changed at first; then, towards the middle to end of the fifteenth century, technological progress in heavy artillery – pioneered by the French – led to a period in which offensive tactics overcame the defensive principles embedded (literally) in walled fortifications. Mehmet II could conquer Constantinople in 1453 with guns already obsolete, but more sophisticated siege trains made up of batteries of smaller guns were the way of the future. With such weapons the French reduced the English to their final toehold at Calais.[4]

When Charles VIII of France crossed the Alps in 1494, he brought with him a siege train of some forty guns, improved versions of the batteries that won the Hundred Years War. The Italians, the most technologically sophisticated people in Europe, were shocked at the speed with which the French could reduce cities thought almost invulnerable. In Guicciardini's words, the French "infused so

---

"The *trace italienne* and the Growth of Armies: The French Case," *Journal of Military History* 55 (1991), 297–330.

[3] Geoffrey Parker, *The Military Revolution: Military Innovation and the Rise of the West, 1500–1800* (Cambridge: Cambridge University Press, 1988), p. 7.

[4] Parker, p. 8. Parker also attributes the final Catholic triumph in the *reconquista*, the conquest of Granada, to Ferdinand and Isabella's use of a large siege train of more than 180 guns. On this campaign, see Weston F. Cook, Jr. "The Cannon Conquest of Nasrid Spain and the End of the Reconquista," *Journal of Military History* 57 (1993), 43–70.

much liveliness into our wars,"[5] that none of the old forms of the military arts could withstand them.

> The space between the shots was so little, and the balls flew so quick and were impelled with such force, that as much execution was done in a few hours as formerly, in Italy, in the like number of days.[6]

In warfare, any serious disequilibrium between attack and defense will almost certainly produce a reaction. Italy responded to the French threat – too late to save itself – with a new military architecture meant to provide better protection against assault by firearms. Low, thick sloping walls replaced the high curtain walls of medieval fortifications. Firearms were to be employed against firearms, and the new system provided ample grounds for mounting heavier and lighter pieces whose fire could keep attacking batteries at bay or render suicidal any attempt to storm the fortress. The most conspicuous feature of the new style was the bastion, an arrowhead-shaped projection designed to give defensive artillery the best possible field of fire. (See Figure 1 for a modern rendition of critical details.) The overall outline or ground plan of the developed form of this new style fortress is unmistakable, and this is usually called the *trace italienne* after its inventors and apostles. The actual placements of bastions had to take into account features of the local terrain, of course, and at times the shape of the bastion itself could be altered to accommodate difficulties of the site, as indicated in Figure 2, taken from a textbook by Jean Errard published in 1594. Whatever its precise form, the developed bastion-style fortification is immediately and obviously different from the medieval high walled forms with turrets that antedate it. Low polygonal forms in the *trace italienne* contrast with the high circular elements in plans of such developed old-style fortifications as Harlech Castle in Wales. (See Figure 3.) Complete with assorted moats, *glacis*, covered ways, hornworks and ravelins, the entire system of new fortifications could become very elaborate indeed, but the single underlying principles were fairly simple: try to cover all approaches with defensive fire and present the worst possible target to the besiegers. The latter meant sloping walls and as many oblique or acute angles in the plan as possible; it also meant reinforcing the masonry work with soft earthen back-fills to absorb the shock of a cannonball's impact.

The system as a whole was successful enough to spread from Italy as far as Canada and the Philippines. For Parker, the *trace italienne* is the key to the military revolution. As the new system spread it re-established the superiority of the defensive principles that the early triumph of gunpowder had temporarily

---

[5] "E introdussono nelle guerre tanta vivezza . . ." *Ricordi politici e civile*, n. 64, in *Opere inedite*, ed. Giuseppe Canestrini (Florence, 1857), p. 102. See Simon Pepper and Nicholas Adams, *Firearms and Fortifications: Military Architecture and Siege Warfare in Sixteenth-Century Siena* (Chicago: University of Chicago Press, 1986), p. 11.

[6] Francesco Guicciardini (1483–1540), *The History of Italy*, trans. Chevl. Austin Parke Goddard, Vol. 1 (London, Towers, 1753–56), p. 149. Quoted in Pepper and Adams, p. 11.

displaced. But in doing so, the *trace italienne* put upward pressures on the size of armies. As early as 1976, Parker articulated his vision of the bastion's real importance. "It soon became clear that a town protected by the *trace italienne* could not be captured by the traditional methods of battery and assault. It had to be encircled and starved into surrender."[7] This meant that warfare lost much of its earlier mobility and fluidity, becoming instead a "struggle for strongholds, a series of protracted sieges."[8] This new strategic reality "compelled an army to augment its numbers."[9] Parker in his 1976 article emphasizes the numbers of men needed to assault a fortress with bastions: military forces were increased in a manner "necessitated by the vast numbers of men required to starve out a town defended by the *trace italienne*."[10]

In his 1988 work, Parker's focus of attention shifted. No longer does he emphasize the size of besieging armies as the factor that "compelled" armies to grow. Rather, it is the need to garrison these new fortresses that propelled numbers ever upward. Parker now differentiates between those states where the *trace italienne* gained ready acceptance and those where it was resisted. The former, France, the Low Countries, Italy and Spain, became the "heartland of the military revolution."[11] These were also the localities where enlarged armies first appear. In those lands where the bastion was delayed, England, for example, or Eastern Europe, "wars of manoeuvre with smaller armies were still feasible."[12] The *trace italienne* is thus for Parker the "key variable."[13] Wherever it is present, the demand for troops to garrison these forts made certain that armies would have to be enlarged.

Parker has not completely abandoned his older notion that attacking armies had to grow in order to succeed in besieging a bastion. He cites the case of 'sHertogenbosch in 1629, where a *trace* 1,500 metres in circumference was surrounded by some forty kilometres of siegeworks manned by an army of some 25,000.[14] But the emphasis has clearly shifted to garrison troops. He cites the case of Gustavus Adolphus in the critical month of November, 1632. The King of Sweden was nominally in command of an army numbering some 183,000 soldiers. But 34,000 remained at home, in Sweden, Finland and the Baltics, while 62,000 were garrisoned permanently in northern Germany. Some 66,000 others were independently operating throughout the Holy Roman Empire,

---

[7] Geoffrey Parker, "The 'Military Revolution,' 1550–1660 – A Myth?" *Journal of Modern History* 48 (1976), 195–214. The quoted passage is on p. 204. For a history of early modern siegecraft, the standard work is Christopher Duffy, *Siege Warfare: The Fortress in the Early Modern World 1494–1660* (London: Routledge & Kegan Paul, 1979).

[8] Parker, "The 'Military Revolution,' " p. 204.

[9] Parker, "The 'Military Revolution,' " p. 208.

[10] Parker, "The 'Military Revolution,' " p. 208.

[11] Parker, *Military Revolution*, p. 24.

[12] Parker, *Military Revolution*, p. 24.

[13] Parker, *Military Revolution*, p. 24.

[14] Parker, *Military Revolution*, p. 13.

leaving Gustav with only about 20,000 men under his command when he died on the field at Lützen.[15]

Parker's theses have not gone unchallenged. The most coherent response has come from Parker's former colleague at Illinois, John Lynn, a specialist in French military history of the seventeenth and eighteenth centuries. Unlike Parker, whose argument is presented through anecdotes, selected cases and rhetorical claims, Lynn presents a sample of 135 sieges undertaken in France or by French armies between the years 1451 and 1714.[16] The data do not support Parker's claims, but instead reveal some surprisingly stable numbers. (See Table 1: French Sieges: 1500–1714.) The average number of besiegers actually declines between 1500 and about 1650, then rises, only to decline again. The overall range is from 20,000 to 40,000 men. The average size of a defending garrison does rise, but only from about 3,000 to around 5,000 or so, and the rise does not take place until late in the seventeenth century. The average length of siege also actually declines from 65 days to about 43 days on average. It is also clear that a few very atypical cases distort the results rather seriously; when one manipulates numbers so as to reduce the effects of the extremes on the averages, numbers remain more stable over the long term. This is the case, for example, in the sixteenth century, where eliminating the single case of Metz (1552) reduces the average number of defenders by almost 16 percent. Likewise in the "Length of Siege" column, where there is a strong difference between that average and the median figures, one can see the distortion that a few variant cases cause. Note also, in regard to length, that in every category the average is longer than the median, meaning a few very long sieges throw the average greatly upward.

Moreover, these figures are only for urban areas actively under siege, when the garrisons would presumably have been reinforced as much as circumstances permitted. The average garrison in an untroubled fortification was likely much lower. Return for a moment to Gustavus Adolphus in the last month of his life, November, 1632. Those 62,000 Swedish troops garrisoned permanently in northern Germany were scattered through 98 permanent garrisons, yielding an average of only 633 men per garrison. Looking at anecdotal evidence, the mid-seventeenth-century military intellectual Raimundo Montecuccoli gives a range of 100–500 men as the best garrison size, indicating that these can be raised to several thousand for cities in danger.[17] Likewise, Maurice of Nassau in his autobiographical *Triumphs of Nassau* repeatedly mentions garrisons of only several hundred men who defended Dutch towns and fortresses.[18] Late in the seventeenth century, a still unpublished survey memoir by Vauban indicates an average garrison size of 751 men, while another, dated November, 1705,

---

[15] Parker, *Military Revolution*, p. 40.

[16] Lynn, "The *trace italienne*."

[17] See Hans Delbrück, *History of the Art of War Within the Framework of Political History*, trans. Walter J. Renfroe, Jr., Vol. 4 (Westport CT: Greenwood, 1975–85), p. 317, n. 18.

[18] Maurice of Nassau, Prince of Orange, *The Triumphs of Nassau*, trans. W. Shute (London, 1613).

indicates this had fallen to 582.[19] Vauban's published treatises included recommendations to the effect that a fortress should hold larger garrisons, about
500–600 men per bastion, together with ancillary cavalry (perferably dragoons);
his ideal example, predicated on a six-bastion fortress, comprised exactly 3600
infantry and 360 cavalry defenders, for a total of 3960 men.[20] Thus, the figures
presented for the sieges indicated above seem to represent reasonable values for
wartime, while in times of peace, the average garrison was doubtless in the
range of half a thousand men. When threatened, important sites expanded their
forces nearly ten-fold.

These are not figures that lend much support to Parker's claims. They indicate
that force levels rose slowly and rather inconsistently, at least in France, and that
neither the size of field armies, nor the size of defensive garrisons, nor the
length of sieges can be made to serve as an explanation for the growth of early
modern armies. One could perhaps argue that the French represent a less typical
nation than, say Spain, but Parker himself included France on the list of nations
that comprise the "heart of the military revolution." One can see that some
sieges in this period were extraordinarily long and very, very bloody. One thinks,
for example, of the siege of Ostende, which lasted from July, 1601 to September,
1604, and cost the lives of perhaps 40,000 or more men.[21] Looking at Parker's
argument, it becomes obvious that spectacular examples like Ostende misled
him into assuming something is typical when it is really still quite unusual.

What is apparent from Lynn's figures and also from the work of other scholars critical of Parker, is that the way fortifications contributed to the general
increase in army size is through the multiplication of fortifications themselves.
That is, the number of fortified cities and sites needing some personnel to
garrison them does seem to increase after the middle of the sixteenth century. At
this point it seems necessary to bring in one other technical point. The fact that
medieval curtain walls could be made serviceable against cannon fire by the
simple expedient of reinforcing them with earthen ramparts or berms, which
could, with some additional engineering, be made to support rude bastions. The
Dutch claim credit for this innovation, dating it from the 1570s, when the threat
of Spanish conquest was very real.[22] As a system, these earthen reinforcements
were inferior to a fully articulated *trace italienne*. Earth slopes at what an
engineer calls the "angle of repose," which is often less than ideal for taking

[19] Cited in Lynn, "The *trace italienne*," pp. 315–16.

[20] Sebastian LePrestre de Vauban, *A Manual of Siegecraft and Fortification* (Amsterdam,
1740), trans. George Rothrock (Ann Arbor: University of Michigan Press, 1968), pp. 141–42.
Note that although Vauban's work was first published in the 1740s, it was composed in manuscript long before he fell from grace with Louis XIV and died in 1707. It reflects Vauban's
experiences as a master of siege warfare in the second half of the seventeenth century.

[21] Christopher Duffy, *Siege Warfare: The Fortress in the Early Modern World 1494–1660*
(London: Routledge & Kegan Paul, 1979), pp. 85–89.

[22] J. P. C. M. van Hoof, "Fortifications in the Netherlands (c. 1500–1940)," *Revue Inter-
nationale d'Histoire Militaire* 58 (1984), 97–126; the earlier earthen fortifications are discussed
on pp. 99–101.

cannon shots, or for preserving the sight lines needed for returning fire. Still, this "old Netherlands system" was very cheap, and if the threat were imminent, could be erected in a matter of weeks. The French still practiced this system late into the seventeenth century.[23] Although largely ignored by historians, this "poor man's *trace italienne*" may turn out to have been at least as influential as the genuine article. I want to return to this point after a review of the medieval side of sieges.

Looking back over the information presented so far, the historian familiar with medieval military practices may have noticed some comfortingly familiar elements. A wall some 1,500 meters in circumference is not very different from several medieval sites, and as for lengthy sieges, Harlech Castle witnessed the longest siege ever to take place in the British Isles, lasting for seven years and ending only in 1468. A garrison size of approximately six hundred men, for example, is exactly what Christine de Pizan takes as her model in her 1408 paraphrase of Vegetius' *Epitoma rei militaris*. And she uses this figure as the basis for a detailed list of munitions, provisions and supplies that extends for many chapters and stipulates in very exact terms what is needed.[24] I have argued elsewhere that Christine's work is well-informed in respect to siegecraft, prob- ably from a source close to John the Fearless, and that it should be taken seriously as a military handbook.[25] I cannot produce a table showing that all medieval garrisons averaged 600 fighting men, but the number has a plausible, as well as a familiar, ring.

Take the case of a field army in the range of 20,000–30,000 men, Gustavus Adolphus' 20,000 men at Lützen, for example, or the 28,000 Dutch troops who besieged 'sHertogenbosch in the spring of 1629. These are probably larger than most medieval armies that took the field. William the Conqueror subdued England, for example, with an army estimated at 10,000–14,000 men.[26] On the other hand, in 1298 Edward I's army in England consisted of a reliably estimated 29,000 men.[27] And a half century later, Edward III's army at Crécy in 1346 probably had a paper strength of some 32,000 troops, of whom about 15,000

[23] Lynn, "The *trace italienne*," pp. 308–09.

[24] See A. T. P. Byles, ed., *The Book of Fayttes of Armes and of Chyualrye*, Early English Text Society, 189, 2nd ed. (London: Early English Text Society, 1937), Book 2, ch. 16 ff.

[25] See Bert S. Hall " 'So Notable Ordynaunce': Christine de Pizan, Firearms and Siegecraft in a Time of Transition," in *Culturhistorisch Kaleidoskoop: Een Huldealbum aangeboden aan Prof. Dr. W. L. Braekman*, ed. C. De Backer (Brussels: Stichting Mens en Kultuur, 1992), pp. 219–40.

[26] The figure is from Bernard Bachrach, "William the Conqueror's Horse Transports," *Technology and Culture* 26 (1985), 505–31, n. 3 (where differing estimates and the associated issues are reviewed). The earlier consensus of opinion held that William employed only about 7,000 men in the Conquest, but this lower figure reflects only the effectives at the Battle of Hastings, not the size of William's army of invasion. See R. Allen Brown, *The Normans and the Conquest* (London: Constable, 1968), p. 150, for this older view.

[27] Philippe Contamine, *War in the Middle Ages*, trans. Michael Jones (Oxford: Basil Black- well, 1984), pp. 116–18.

[27] For Edward's army see Alfred H. Burne, *The Crecy War: A Military History of the Hundred Years War from 1337 to the Peace of Bretigny, 1360* (London: Eyre & Spottiswoode, 1955),

were effectives.[28] The French size at Agincourt in October, 1415 seems to have numbered about 24,000,[29] while the Spanish completed the conquest of Granada in the 1480s and '90s with a swollen army estimated to have varied between 36,000 and 56,000 men.[30] Charles the Rash of Burgundy invaded Switzerland in the late winter of 1476 with an estimated 25,000 professional soldiers.[31] Figures like these could probably be produced for many other conflicts as well. The point is that medieval armies grew over time to levels quite comparable to those of the sixteenth century, but without any help from the *trace italienne*.

The common impression that medieval field armies were miniscule is the result of two things. First, medieval crowd estimates of any sort have been held in low repute since the beginnings of scientific medieval historiography in the nineteenth century. Army sizes have been customarily downgraded from the figures given in the chronicles to levels that historians have felt more reasonable. It would be a foolish historian who would challenge such deep-rooted professional opinions, but it is worth pointing out that army sizes for all medieval conflicts are only artifacts of modern scholarship. The second reason for the common opinion that medieval states fielded small armies is that historians frequently cite as examples battles fought after the demographic disaster caused by bubonic plague. The Black Prince at Poitiers in 1356, for example, fought with only about 6,000–8,000 men, roughly one-half to one-sixth the size of his father's army at Crécy a mere ten years earlier.[32] And as every Shakespeare fan

---

pp. 166–68. Burne estimates the French at Crécy only as "markedly superior in numbers to the English" (p. 186).

[29] Alfred H. Burne, *The Agincourt War: A Military History of the Latter Part of the Hundred Years War from 1369 to 1453* (London: Eyre & Spottiswoode, 1956), pp. 90–94. The French army's size is more difficult to estimate than the English. Contemporary chronicle sources vary widely, but Burne accepts a general four-to-one superiority of French over English troop strength, yielding an estimate of some 24,000 men.

[30] Contamine, p. 135, quotes troop strengths from M. A. Ladero Quesada, *Castilla y la conquista del reino de Granada* (Valladolid: Universidad de Valladolid, 1967) as follows:

Footmen (*Peones*)	Light Cavalry (*Jinetes*)	Total	Expedition Year
25,000	11,000	36,000	1485
40,000	12,000	52,000	1486
45,000	11,000	56,000	1487
40,000	13,000	53,000	1489

[31] (Col.) Charles Brusten, "Les Compagnies d'ordonnance dans l'armée Bourguignonne," in *Grandson–1476: Essai d'approche pluridisciplinaire d'une action militaire du XVe siècle*, ed. Daniel Reichel (Lausanne: Centre d'Histoire, 1976), p. 158.

[32] Burne, *Crécy War*, p. 298. Burne estimates the French strength at Poitiers at approximately 20,000, but he admits this number is inflated by including late-arriving feudal levies, little more than militia troops, who did not fight in the battle. Eyewitness accounts are uncharacteristically modest, giving French strength at only around 11,000 effectives. See Burne, *Crécy War*, pp. 312–26. Herbert J. Hewitt, *The Black Prince's Expedition of 1355–1357* (Manchester: Manchester University Press, 1958), p. 114, summarizes the consensus of historical opinion, estimating the Anglo-Gascon forces at 6,000–8,000 and the French at 10,000 regulars plus irregular troops sufficient to bring about a total of 15,000–16,000.

must remember, Henry V met the French at Agincourt in 1415 with a mere 6,000 men.[33] But these were small armies even by medieval standards.

There were also field armies, that is to say, a fraction of a monarch's total military capacity. Trying to estimate an army's actual size is more difficult than it seems at first glance. Does one count only combatants, or the larger number of auxiliaries lumped under the French term "effectives," or does one look to the sum total of sworn soldiers on the muster-rolls, the so-called "paper strength."[34] The latter is a splendid standard in a society that has become bureaucratized to the point that it can keep paper muster-rolls that conveniently enumerate (and often name) just those men who had sworn an oath to their king. Medievalists lack such documents and focus their attentions on something they can estimate within reasonable limits, namely how many men (and women) actually moved when an army took to the countryside. Medievalists and early modernists are frequently comparing apples and oranges when they deal with army size; medievalists follow restrictive definitions and tend to minimize numbers, while early modernists do the opposite.

The point of rummaging about for statistical comparisons before and after 1500 A.D. is to suggest that the growth of armies is not a unique phenomenon to the sixteenth century, and thus something whose etiology has to be related to phenomena unique to the sixteenth century. Quite the opposite! Armies grow as large as they reasonably can, and the standard of reason has more to do with the economic and demographic state of society than with technological changes. Moreover, there are limits to the size of any army that can be fielded under pre-modern conditions, loose limits to be sure, but limits that can be transcended only at rapidly increasing costs. Several historians[35] have noted that Western European field armies do not increase beyond the 20,000–35,000 range until the late eighteenth century, and this rough limit tends to be persistent for quite cogent logistical reasons.

An army numbering more than 20,000 individuals was equivalent to a medium-sized city in the late Middle Ages or the sixteenth century, and like any city, it had to supply its needs and remove its wastes. On the march, the latter

---

[33] Estimates for troops on both sides at Agincourt are criticized and adjusted by Burne, *Agincourt War*, pp. 90–94. Henry V's expeditionary force as it embarked was enumerated at 10,000 effectives; diseases, as well as garrisoning the captured port of Harfleur, reduced Henry's army to the figure given above.

[34] John A. Lynn, "The Growth of the French Army During the Seventeenth Century," *Armed Forces and Society* 6.4 (Summer, 1980), 568–87, presents the methodological issues in detail and opts for the "paper strength" standard as the only historiographically defensible procedure. This, of course, is nearly impossible for a medievalist to follow, in that the comparable medieval situation involves large numbers of men with military obligations that are owed to the crown in some ultimate sense, but whose proximate loyalties are "feudal" in character and therefore local.

[35] Simon Adams, "Tactics or Politics? 'The Military Revolution' and the Hapsburg Hegemony, 1525–1648," in *Tools of War: Instruments, Ideas, and Institutions of Warfare, 1445–1871*, ed. John A. Lynn (Urbana: University of Illinois Press, 1990), pp. 28–52; David A. Parrott, "Strategy and Tactics in the Thirty Years War: The 'Military Revolution,' " *Militärgeschichtliche Mitteilungen* 38.2 (1985), 7–25.

could be left behind (as it were), but under siege conditions, the problem would not go away. The problem does not centre on human beings, but on the beasts of burden needed to serve their needs. Even relatively small pack horses – say 12 hands high weighing about 500 kg. – consume far more per day than humans can. Horses require grain as well as grass or hay, and they would quickly exhaust any pasturage available at the beginning of a siege. If one assumes that an army of 25,000 soldiers would have one-tenth as many horses (a very conservative assumption, by the way), then each of the 2,500 beasts would require approximately 12 kg. of food per day, half of which must be grain (barley, spelt or oats). The remainder could be hay or grass, but if grass is supplied, then the amount needed grows to about 18 kg. per horse per day. In addition, horses require, at a minimum, approximately 30 litres of fresh, cool water per day (depending on weather conditions). Thus to supply the beasts alone, an army of 25,000 encamped for a siege would have to transport over 40,000 litres of water and 30,000 kg. of fodder per day.

It must be remembered as well that immobile armies not only need their supplies brought to them, but their wastes removed, including the animal wastes. Equines, as a rule, retain far less of their intake than do humans. Fed as I indicated a moment ago, most horses will produce, on average, about 20 kg. of manure per day, and also a volume of urine averaging about 20 litres. For the hypothetical army, this means some 50,000 kg. of solid horse waste and 50,000 litres of urine needing disposal daily. The human burden to this waste stream adds about 9,000–10,000 kg. of solid excrement and 30,000 litres of liquid. Humans can be instructed in where to deposit their wastes (although they often fail to heed), but horses must be looked after. Urine build-up in the soils of stalls will quickly decay into ammonia compounds, which in turn attack the keratinous tissue of horses' hooves and promote debilitating foot diseases. The accepted – and indeed the only practical – method of prevention is to line the stables with fresh straw daily, usually about 3 kg. worth. This adds another 7,500 kg. of rather bulky material that needs to be supplied and removed on a daily basis. If it is assumed an average siege lasts about 60 days, the attacking army must remove some 4,000,000 kg. of solid biological wastes and also deal with some 4,800,000 litres of human and animal urine, in addition to whatever detritus may remain from cooking or other daily activities. For the non-metric, those amounts convert to 8,800,000 pounds of manure and 1,273,210 US gallons of urine.[36]

Deplorable conditions in respect to sanitation will tell far more quickly than defects in matters of supply, since any buildup of liquid or fecal wastes quickly penetrates into the local water table, and tainted water becomes a vector for all

[36] Bernard Bachrach, "*Caballus et Caballarius* in Medieval Warfare," in *The Study of Chivalry: Resources and Approaches*, eds. Howell Chickering and Thomas H. Seiler (Kalamazoo MI: Medieval Institute Publications, 1988), pp. 173–211, provides average daily figures for horses. I have altered these only to reflect the greater number of smaller pack horses and mules, as opposed to large war horses, that we would expect to find in a besieging force.

manner of debilitating diseases. Armies working under siege conditions were well aware of the need for adequate sanitation, by the way, and they issued and enforced instructions designed to achieve that end. On the other side of the walls, the besieged offered prayers hoping for an outbreak of some particularly virulent gastrointestinal malady might break out among the besiegers. Armies could only grow larger by coming to terms with the increased logistical burden that growth implied.

It may be desirable to look at claims about early modern siege warfare in light of a case study that is indisputably "medieval," the siege of Berwick in 1333. Despite pressure from the south, the Scots proved unwilling to accept the hapless Edward Balliol as their king, and he was obliged to flee Scotland in the spring of 1333. Edward III, at this point, prepared a major invasion force for the campaigning season of that year. English strategy was determined to avoid the earlier frustrations they experienced in the Weardale in 1327, where the Scots led the English a merry chase without offering battle. The English would begin by laying siege to a fortified city the Scots could ill afford to lose, Berwick, guardian of the mouth of the Tweed.[37] Edward commissioned one Richard the Goldsmith at Cowick in Yorkshire to pre-fabricate two catapults for use at Berwick and granted him the use of 24 oxen to haul timbers for these machines. This clearly means that they were counterweight trebuchets. Richard also employed the labour of 37 stone masons and six quarrymen to fashion stones "*in pellotis*" as missiles. A third catapult, possibly a traction machine, was taken from York castle for the Berwick operations, and on 16–17 May 1333, three vessels laden with these machines left Hull for Berwick. The trebuchets destroyed or damaged several important structures within Berwick, including a church and the Maison Dieu. The English may also have used "gonnes" in the siege,[38] but clearly trebuchets were the major causes of damage within Berwick. Only trebuchets could be set to throw in a high trajectory, which allowed besiegers to attack structures behind defensive walls rather than just seeking to batter the walls themselves. Damage to town buildings was much more important to the inhabitants than corresponding amounts of devastation to outworks, and this served to bring pressures to bear on the local garrison to surrender. This emerged with unusual clarity at Berwick. In return for short term relief from bombardment by trebuchet, Berwick pledged itself to surrender if not relieved by dawn on 20 July 1333.

It was by no means clear whether the Scots would seek to relieve Berwick, given their long-standing preference for avoiding pitched battles, but in the end, Alexander Douglas, the Scottish commander, had little choice. The terms of the

---

[37] Ranald Nicholson, *Edward III and the Scots: The Formative Years of a Military Career, 1327–1335* (London: Oxford, 1965), p. 121.

[38] Friedrich W. D. Brie, ed., *The Brut or The Chronicles of England*, Early English Text Society, 131 and 136, Vol. 1 (London: Kegan Paul, 1906 and 1908), p. 281, mentions "gonnes" along with "othere engynes," but credits both weapons with destroying many houses and churches.

partial truce left Douglas with no time to maneuver or to seek any advantage whatsoever. Knowing relief could only come from the north, Edward positioned his forces near Halidon Hill and commanded all the northern routes into Berwick. There, on 19 July 1333, the long-awaited battle took place. Douglas was forced to attack uphill against English troops in prepared positions. Edward III had his men-at-arms dismount and take places, presumably with regular infantry, in a line where archers formed small wings beside each division. As the Scots attacked, arrows flew at them "as thik as motes on the sonne beme."[39] The Scots found themselves stalemated while under heavy fire from the archers, and the mounting casualties on their flanks caused the attackers to begin to break off. It is clear from the chronicles that the English losses were minimal and the Scottish losses terrible. Eventually, the Scots simply broke and dispersed.

The narrative contains many themes regarding medieval warfare that have been highlighted in modern work by many different scholars. Far from being undisciplined, the course of events was governed by strong strategic considerations, in this case the use of siege as a means to force an unwilling enemy away from his Fabian tactics. The use of trebuchets as the means to bring a town to the point of surrender corresponds to our understanding of the importance and effects of this under-studied machine.[40] It is particularly interesting here to note how the English anticipated the strategic bombing logic of World War II by concentrating on creating morale-damaging destruction to civilian targets. Once this end had been gained, the town was spared. Forces were redeployed to take advantage of the superiority in defense that the English enjoyed through their mastery of archery. The Scots were forced into combat on English terms and were destroyed with a precision the practical limitations of this study do not permit me to describe.

In addition to exemplifying much modern scholarship, does not the case of Berwick also suggest how fundamentally similar siege warfare remained between the fourteenth and the seventeenth century? Change the names and much of this pattern repeats itself in Turenne's siege of Dunkirk in 1658,[41] to take but one example. Even the time occupied by events, roughly sixty days, equals the average for those sixteenth-century French sieges Lynn tabulated. Seventeenth-century terminology would have called Douglas' force an "army of relief," and Turenne used mortars instead of Edward's trebuchets, and he had musketeers instead of Edward's archers, but clearly the patterns of actions would have been familiar if any participant in either action could have somehow magically witnessed the other. Perhaps one should have listened more closely to Professor Parker. He argues that, while medieval warfare was "an affair of manoeuvres,

---

[39] Nicholson, p. 135, quoting an unpublished contemporary account, British Library MS Harl. 4690, fol. 82v.

[40] Donald R. Hill, "Trebuchets," *Viator* 4 (1973), 99–116.

[41] The operations are discussed briefly by Jean Berenger, *Turenne* (Paris: Fayard, 1987), pp. 334 ff.

skirmishes and protracted sieges,"[42] under the influence of the *trace italienne* early modern warfare became a "struggle for strongholds, a series of protracted sieges."[43]

As noted above, military historians are convinced believers in the power of technological change to shape events, and they have wrapped the problem of growing armies in the mantle of the technology-driven "military revolution." Allowing for the possibility that firearms may not have transformed siege warfare beyond recognition, then the way early modern warfare differs from medieval warfare may be able to be explained. It is true that from the mid-fifteenth to the mid-sixteenth century, changes in artillery threatened to upset an old and stable element in European warfare, the ability to rely on fortified sites to delay an attacker. The advent of the *trace italienne* initiated a process of restoring the balance, and the "old Dutch" imitation of the expensive masonry work in cheap earthworks completed the change. Geoffrey Parker sees this as a dialectic process, where in good Hegelian fashion the synthesis is a considerable advance over the original thesis. I argue that the new fortifications actually represent a restoration of the *status quo ante* so far as siege warfare itself is concerned.

Yet not only siege warfare but also field warfare had been altered. The tactical patterns that Edward III pioneered with archers could become much more widespread once cheap and plentiful small arms flooded the battlefield. These matchlock arquebuses and muskets were not superior to archery in many respects, but they were less expensive and much easier to learn to use. Small arms put an end to the dominance of cavalry, and like the longbow before them, elevated defensive tactics to prominence. Firearms worked, however, only when they were massed in large numbers, and tactically firearms had to be protected by comparable numbers of pikemen. Sixteenth-century armies became slow moving masses of infantry even before they began to grow larger. Battles also became bloodier by far – another pattern adumbrated by the English use of archers – and much more difficult to win through any sort of skill. Sheer weight of numbers told more than any other factor.

In addition, economic changes in the sixteenth century drove peasant and working-class wages down while simultaneously elevating state revenues. Soldiers became cheaper and monarchies richer. Battles became more costly in lives, and armies maneuvered to avoid, rather than to offer, combat. In the midst of this complex of changing military factors, the Spanish decided to reassert Hapsburg control over the Low Countries, with the result we know as the Eighty Years War. The Dutch Wars of Independence came to hinge on large numbers of fortified places; there was in general very little of large-scale field warfare.[44] The Dutch Wars absorbed military manpower on an unprecedented scale to

---

[42] Parker, *Military Revolution*, p. 7.

[43] Parker, *Military Revolution*, p. 7.

[44] Charles Oman, *A History of the Art of War in the Sixteenth Century* (London: Methuen, 1937), pp. 541–46, comments on the peculiar features of the Netherlands' War of Independence and laments that they "are so barren in the matter of general actions in the field" (p. 546).

garrison innumerable Spanish strongholds. Spanish policy toward the Netherlands emphasized fortifications to control flows of men and materiel to the
rebels, and simultaneously to act as citadels watching over unreliable urban
populations. Dutch resistance, the Spanish felt, could be crushed only with
overwhelmingly superior force, and pitched battles were to be avoided if
possible.[45] It was a strategy for a war of attrition, and that is exactly what the
Eighty Years War became. It was also a strategy that called for a large, quasi-
permanent military establishment, and that, too, became Spain's burden to supply and support.

In the long run, it was these policy decisions, rather than the characteristics of
fortifications, that made the difference. What served as the sponge soaking up
military manpower was the need to garrison a great many fortresses, not the
needs of single fortresses. Field armies did not, indeed could not, expand, and
the size of garrisons did not grow larger until late in the seventeenth century. But
the strategic reliance on fortifications meant that there had to be many such loci
to be garrisoned, and this imperative applied to both sides of the conflict. Once
the pattern was established there was a strong tendency for cycles of growth to
reassert themselves. The continued deterioration of real wages meant flat or
declining curves for soldiers' pay and military equipment in the sixteenth century.[46] This in turn meant that each marginal addition to the force levels was in
real terms cheaper than its predecessors. Common men joined the colors out of
economic need, and once trained in the profession of arms, they possessed a
trade they could practice virtually as much as they cared to, and the willingness
of veterans to re-enlist made new force enlargement even easier as recruiters
simply paid for previously-trained manpower blocks. Governments who did
little to ameliorate the general decline of the rural poor and urban artisans
nevertheless quickly discovered how to manipulate their system of revenue
generation so as to command an increasing fraction of all the available resources. The combination of men who needed work and states who felt rich was
dangerous, for it allowed ambitious monarchs practically free reign to build up
their forces. But the flaw in this system was that soldiers had to be fed (or to feed

[45] Adams, "Tactics or Politics?," pp. 39–42; William S. Maltby, *Alba: A Biography of
Fernando Alvarez de Toledo, Third Duke of Alba (1507–1582)* (Berkeley: University of California Press, 1983), pp. 151–52, emphasizes the construction of citadels, especially that of
Antwerp, which Alba seems to have considered a monument to himself and as "the most
beautiful plaza in the world" (p. 152).

[46] The price of gunpowder in particular remained fixed for most of the later sixteenth
century, as did gunpowder's principal ingredient, saltpetre. See J. F. Guilmartin, *Gunpowder and
Galleys: Changing Technology and Mediterranean Warfare in the Sixteenth Century* (Cambridge: Cambridge University Press, 1974), p. 224 and A. R. Williams, "The Production of
Saltpetre in the Middle Ages," *Ambix* 22 (1975), 125. The latter argues this stability must derive
from improved processes to extract and refine saltpetre. Yet James E. Thorold Rogers, *A History
of Agriculture and Prices in England: From the Year After the Oxford Parliament (1259) to the
Commencement of the Continental War (1793)*, Vol. 3 (Oxford: Clarendon Press, 1882), pp.
552–81, presents data suggesting that prices of gunpowder were quite stable in England from the
1460s onward.

themselves) in an economy of steeply mounting food costs; this was what proved difficult almost beyond the ability of authority to cope. It was not difficult to recruit an army, or even to field one, but providing for it was practically impossible. By the early seventeenth century the generalization of a system of large armies began to break down of its own weight. The system began to career out of control. This led to the imposition of general conscription and the infamous system of "contributions" whereby occupied regions were forced to pay the bill for their occupation.[47] From its beginnings in Spain's desire to capitalize on its resource advantage by waging a war of attrition in the Low Countries, larger and larger armies in the end became a Leviathan, indeed a biblical Moloch, that demanded the treasure as well as the blood of its devotees.

[47] On the system of contributions, see Geoffrey Parker et al., *The Thirty Years War* (London: Routledge and Kegan Paul, 1984), pp. 198–99; also Geoffrey Parker, *The Army of Flanders and the Spanish Road, 1567–1659* (Cambridge: Cambridge University Press, 1972), pp. 142–43; also Fritz Redlich, "Contributions in the Thirty Years War," *Economic History Review* 12 (1959–60), 247–54.

TABLE 1:
FRENCH SIEGES: 1500–1714[1]

Average figures

Period	Besiegers	Length of Siege Average (Median)	Defending
16th Century – Combined Totals			
1500–1600	26,600	65 (61) Days	3,028
16th Century by Half-Century			
1500–1550	29,000		
1551–1600	25,000		
Adjusted:	[16,000][2]		[2,563][3]
Selected Intervals: 17th and 18th Century			
1635–1659	17,000	76 (34) Days	3,194
Adjusted:			[2,205][4]
1672–1684	41,000	32 (25) Days	4,667
1688–1697	42,200	36 (26) Days	6,443
Adjusted:			[4.929][5]
1702–1714	26,500	43 (37) Days	4,844
Adjusted:			[4,075][6]

[1] Adapted from: John Lynn, "The *trace italienne* and the Growth of Armies: The French Case," *Journal of Military History* 55 (1991), 297–330.

[2] Adjusted by eliminating effects of three anomalously large sieges: Metz (1552), Renty (1554), Saint-Quentin (1557).

[3] Adjusted by eliminating Metz (1552).

[4] Adjusted by eliminating Saint-Omer (1638).

[5] Adjusted by eliminating Namur (1695) and Barcelona (1697). Note that this is the smallest sample (N=10).

[6] Adjusted by eliminating the four anomalously large cases: Turin (1706), Lille (1708), Ghent (1708), Barcelona (1714). Note that this is the largest sample (N=59).

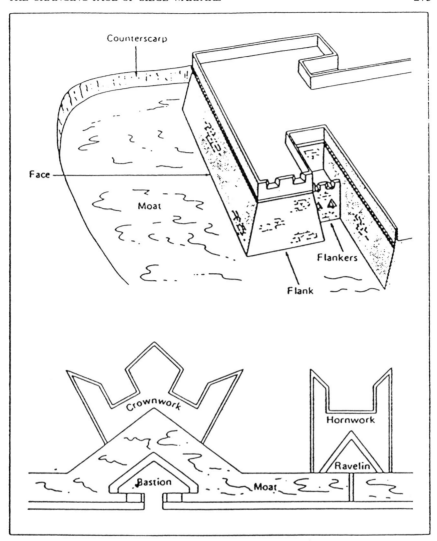

Figure 1. Bastions and associated works in the *trace italienne* system of fortifications. Source: Geoffrey Parker, *The Military Revolution*, p. 11. Reprinted with the permission of Cambridge University Press.

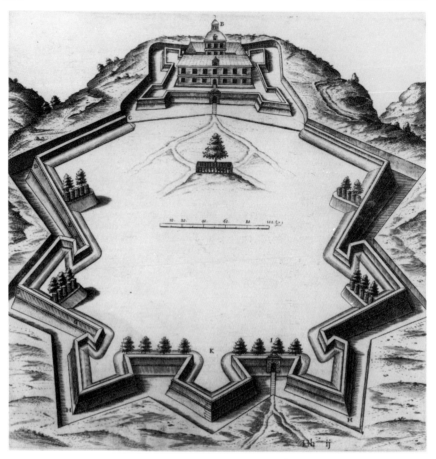

Figure 2. Idealized view of fortification with different variations on the bastion.
Source: Jean Errard (1554–1610), *La fortification démonstrée et réduite en art*, 2nd
ed. (Paris: 1604), p. 126. This photo is used with the permission of the Special
Collections Library, University of Michigan, Ann Arbor.

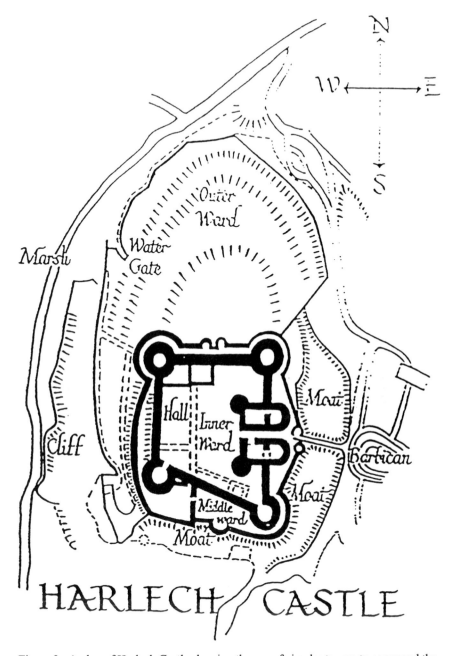

Figure 3. A plan of Harlech Castle showing the use of circular towers to command the corners and the approaches. Source: Philip Warner, *Sieges of the Middle Ages* (London: Bell, 1968), p. 200, Fig. 21. Reprinted with the permission of Harper Collins Publishers Ltd.

Index